The Man Without Talent

YOSHIHARU TSUGE

TRANSLATED AND WITH AN ESSAY BY
RYAN HOLMBERG

New York Review Comics • *New York*

第一話

Chapter 1

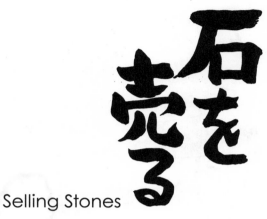

石を売る

Selling Stones

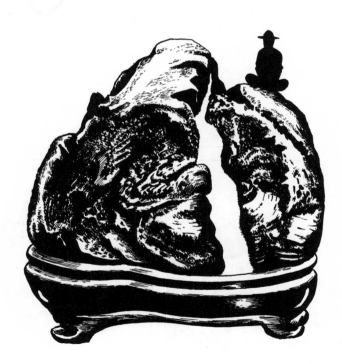

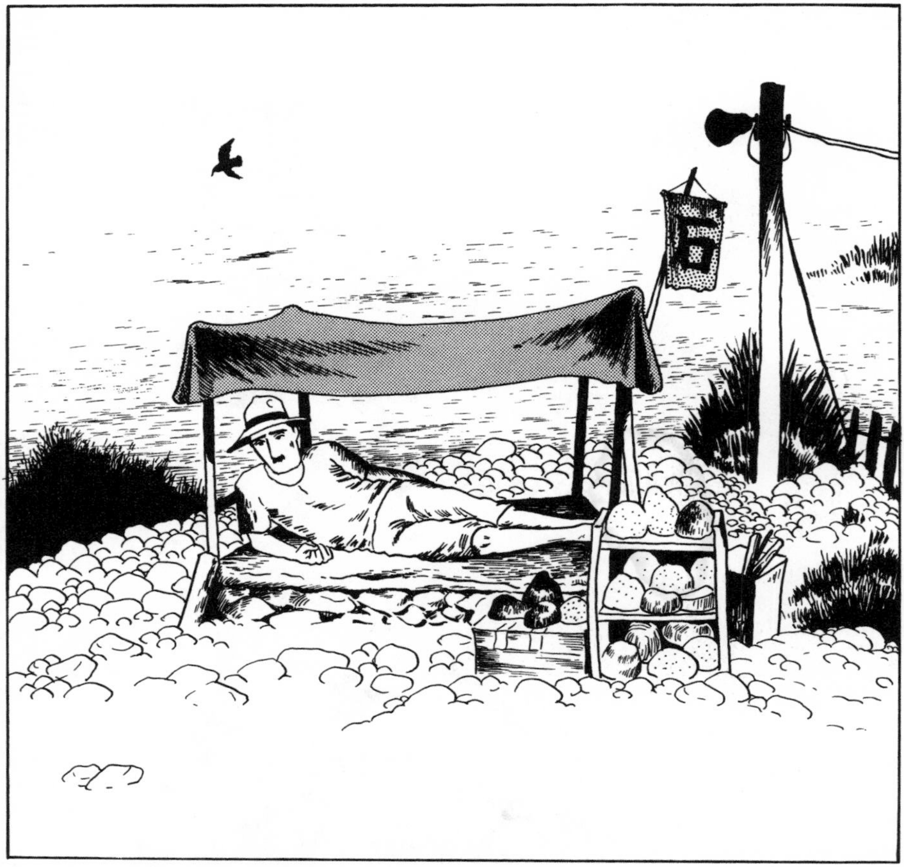
石

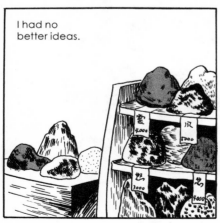

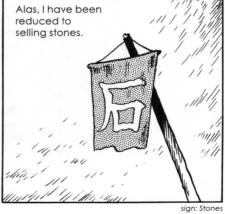

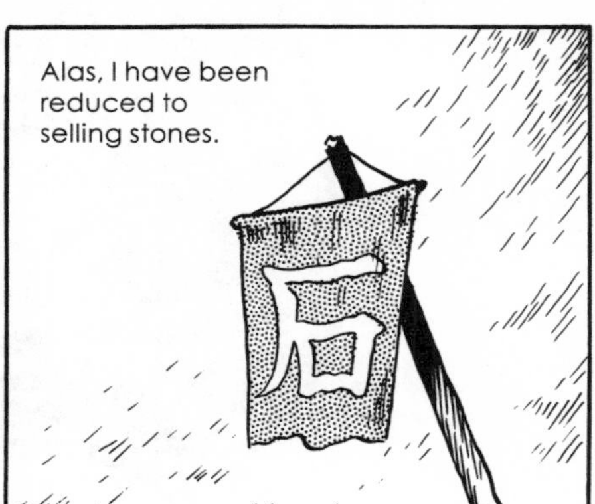
Alas, I have been reduced to selling stones.
石

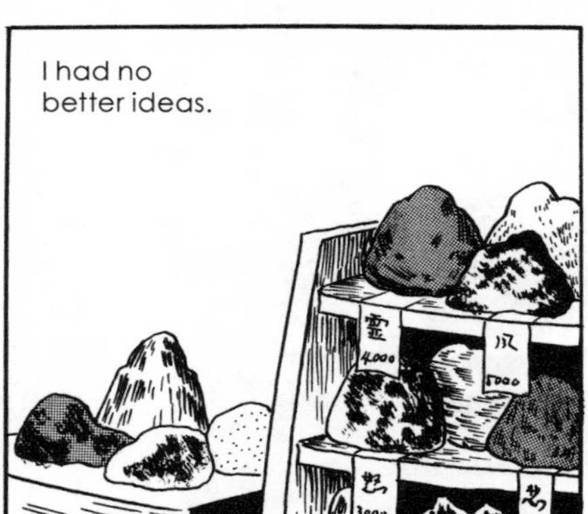
I had no better ideas.
5000
4000
4000
3000

sign: Stones

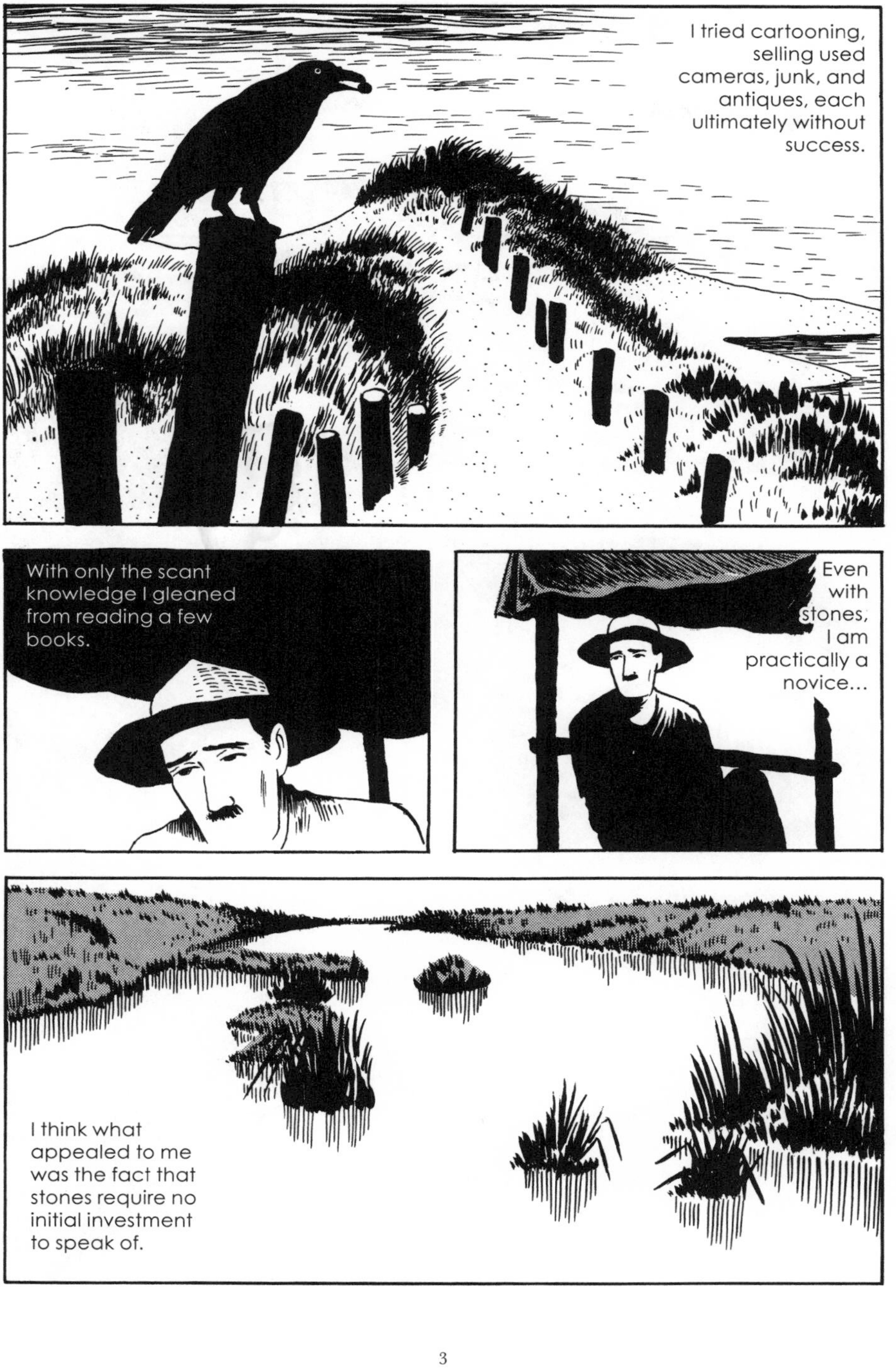
I tried cartooning, selling used cameras, junk, and antiques, each ultimately without success.
Even with stones, I am practically a novice...
With only the scant knowledge I gleaned from reading a few books.
I think what appealed to me was the fact that stones require no initial investment to speak of.

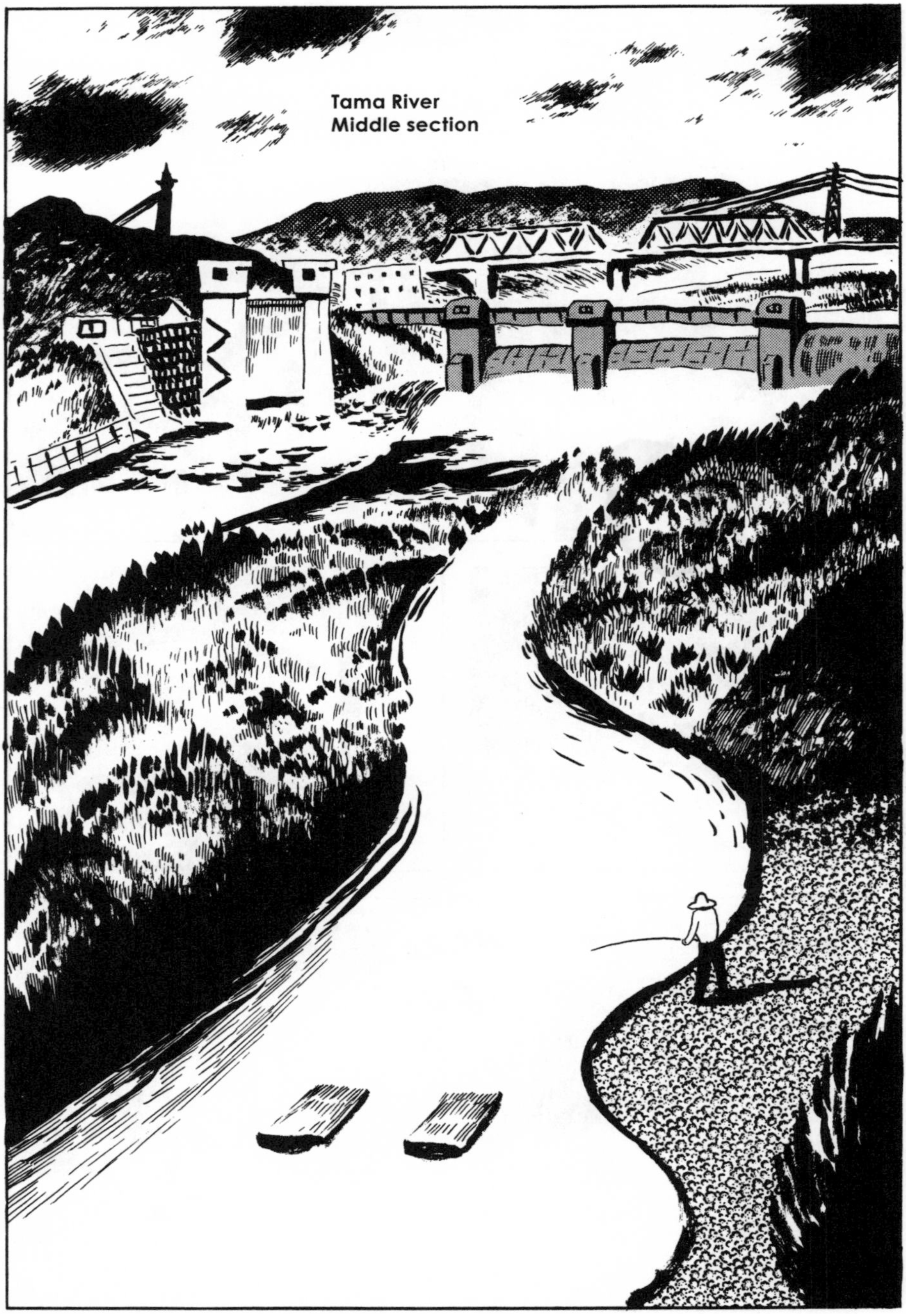
Tama River
Middle section

But don't go thinking I'm about to give up.

Yes, dreams...

We all have dreams.

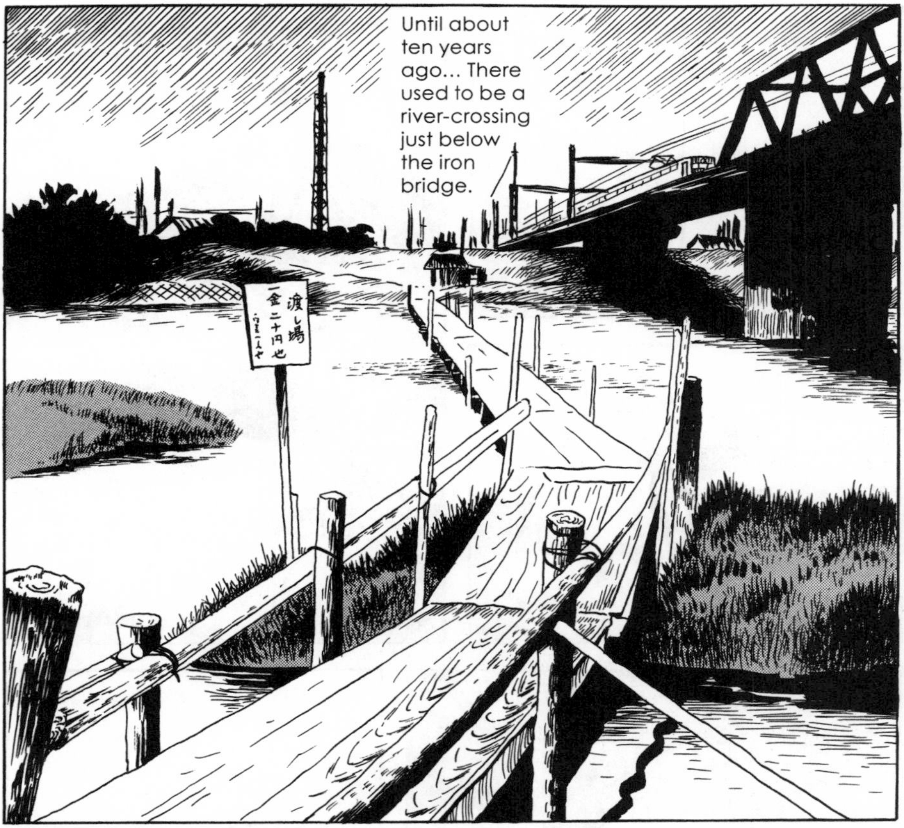
Until about ten years ago… There used to be a river-crossing just below the iron bridge.
渡し場
一金二十円也
sign: Crossing 20 yen

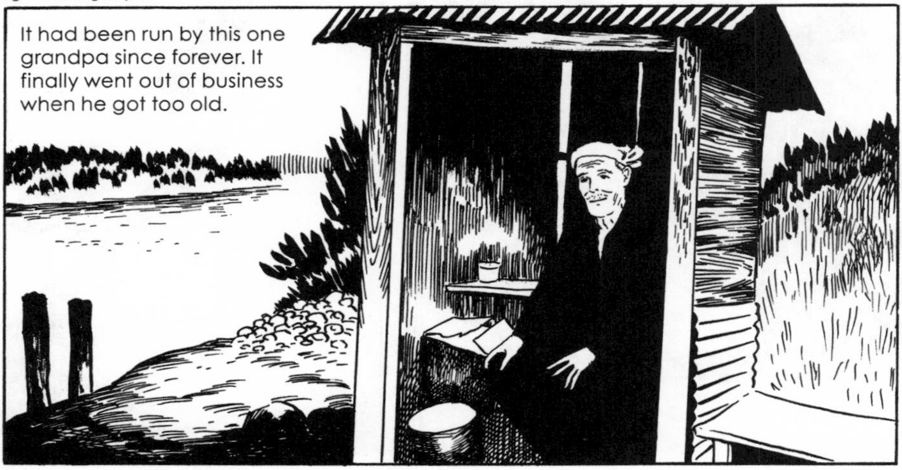
It had been run by this one grandpa since forever. It finally went out of business when he got too old.

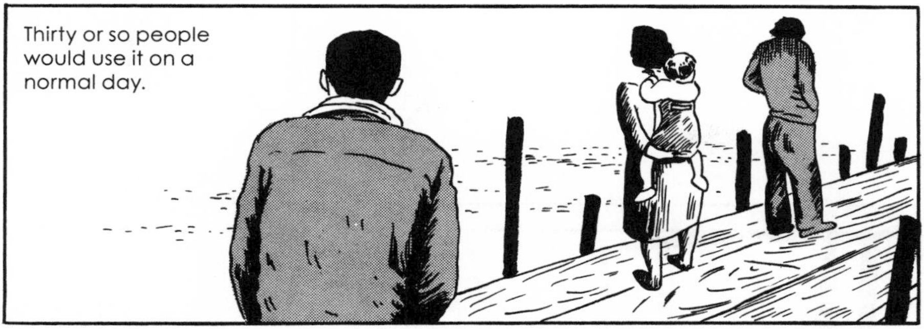
Thirty or so people would use it on a normal day.

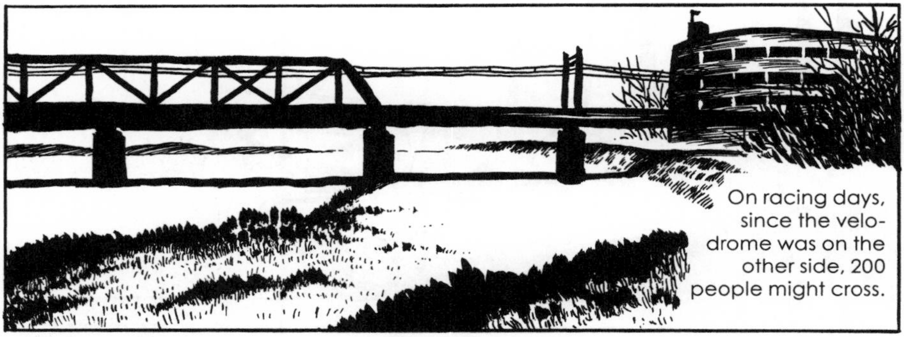
On racing days, since the velo-drome was on the other side, 200 people might cross.

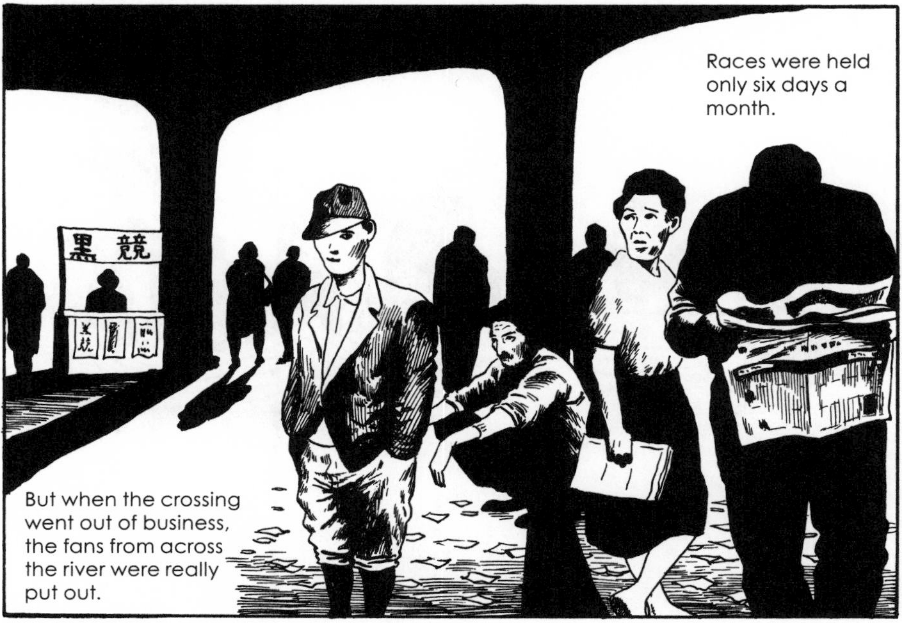
Races were held only six days a month.
黒競
But when the crossing went out of business, the fans from across the river were really put out.

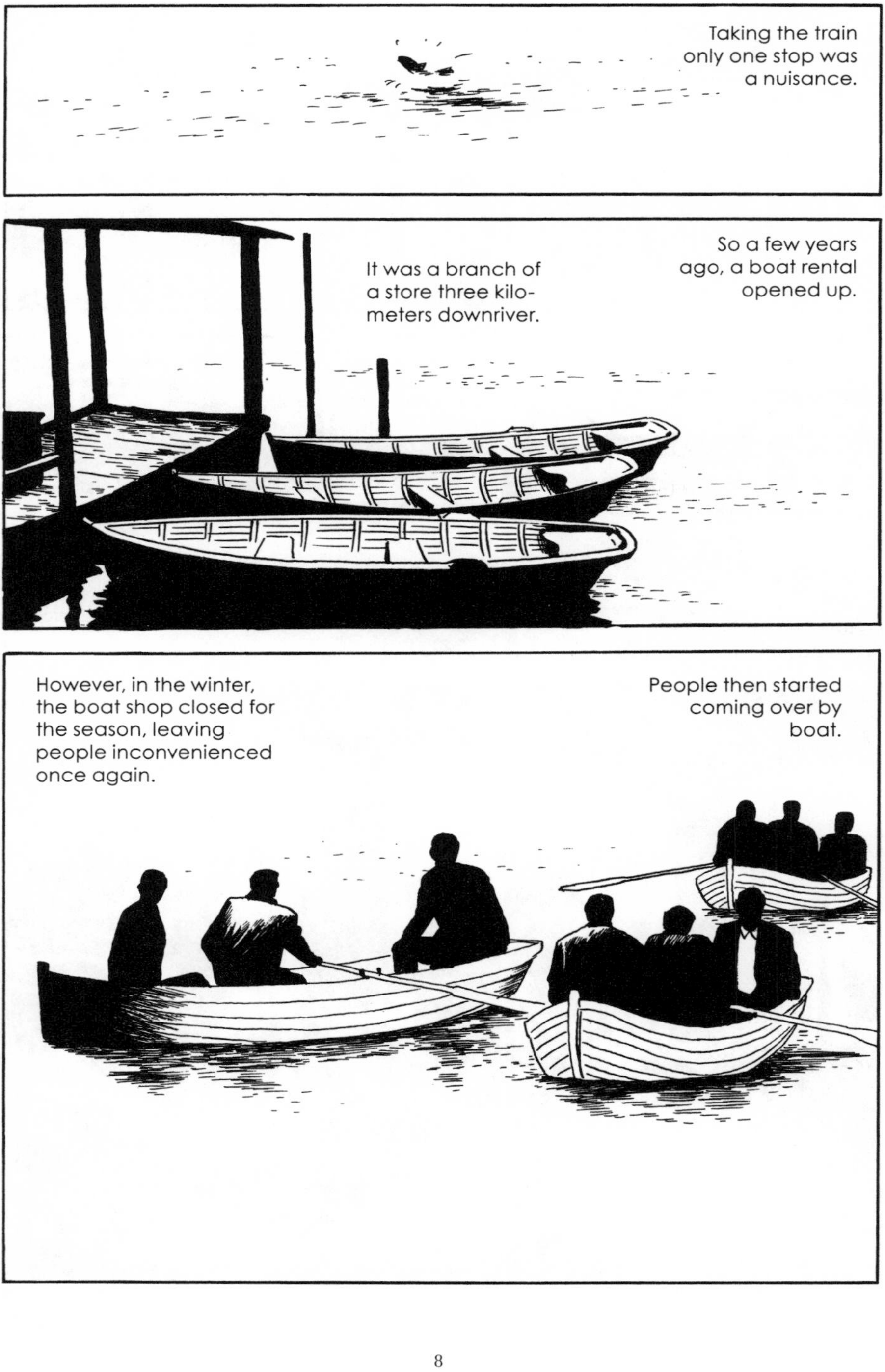
Taking the train only one stop was a nuisance.
So a few years ago, a boat rental opened up.
It was a branch of a store three kilometers downriver.
People then started coming over by boat.
However, in the winter, the boat shop closed for the season, leaving people inconvenienced once again.

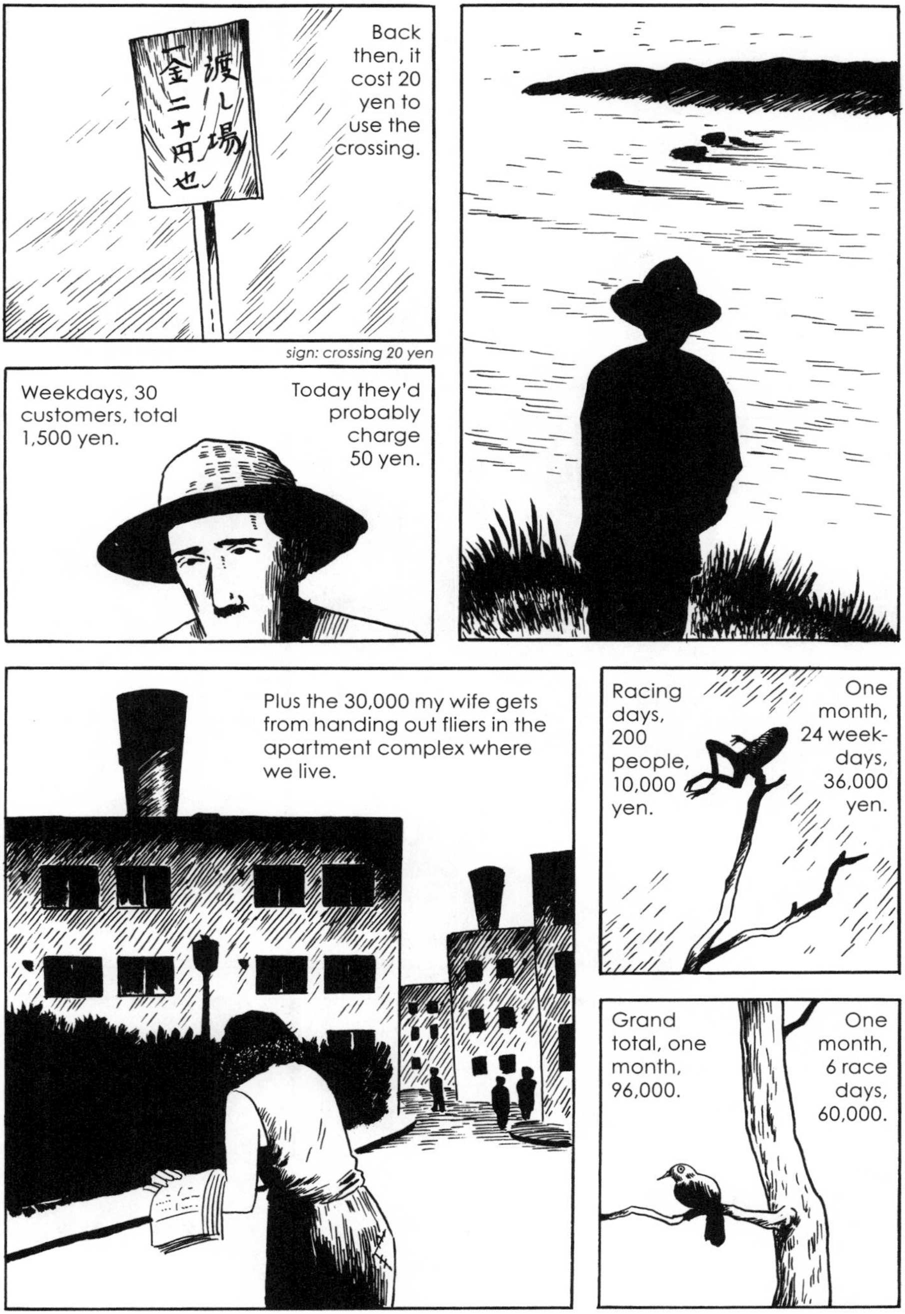
Back then, it cost 20 yen to use the crossing.
渡し場
一金二十円也
sign: crossing 20 yen
Today they'd probably charge 50 yen.
Weekdays, 30 customers, total 1,500 yen.
One month, 24 week-days, 36,000 yen.
Racing days, 200 people, 10,000 yen.
One month, 6 race days, 60,000.
Grand total, one month, 96,000.
Plus the 30,000 my wife gets from handing out fliers in the apartment complex where we live.

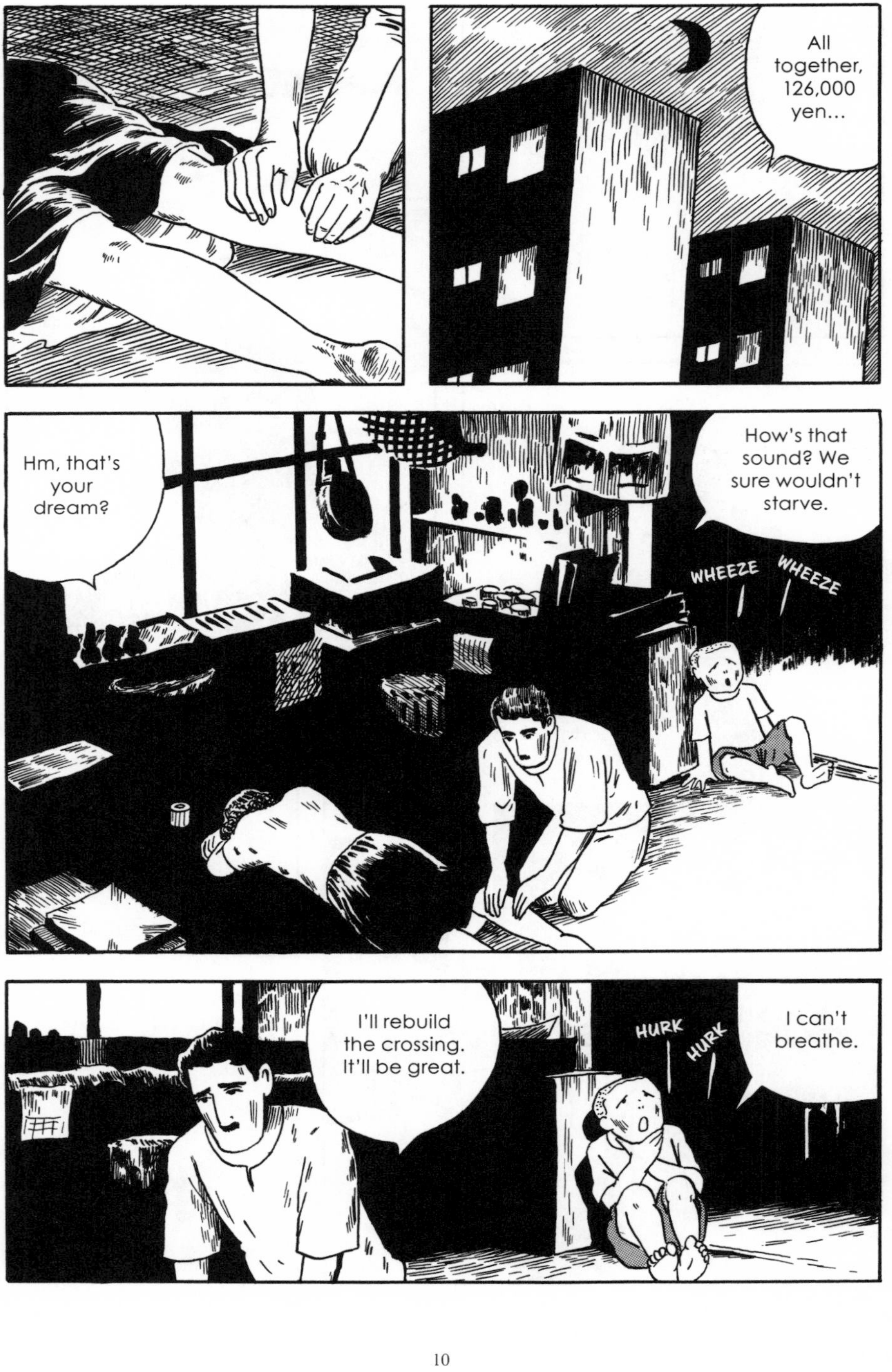
All together, 126,000 yen...
How's that sound? We sure wouldn't starve.
WHEEZE
WHEEZE
Hm, that's your dream?
I can't breathe.
HURK
HURK
I'll rebuild the crossing. It'll be great.

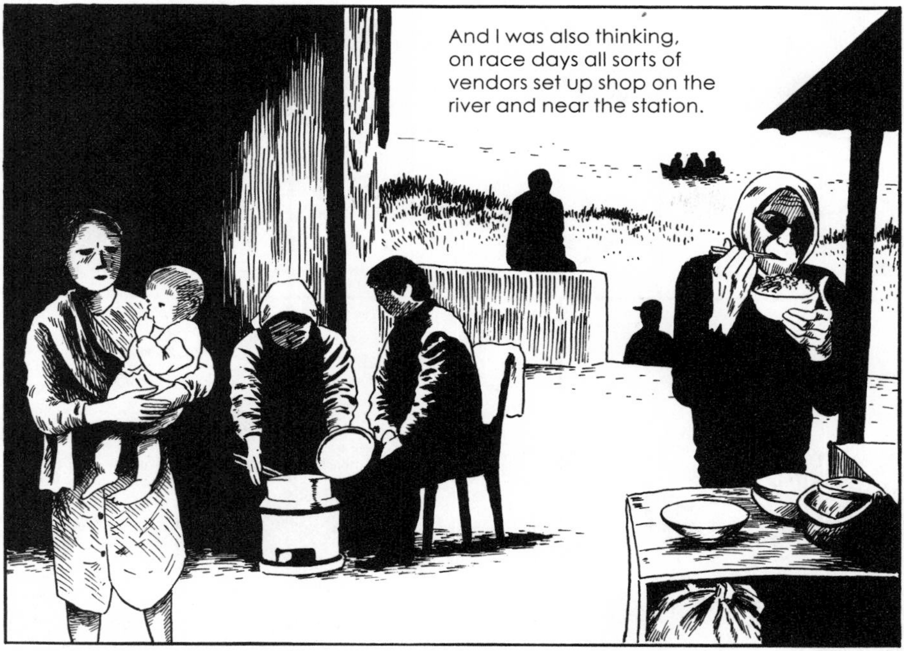
And I was also thinking, on race days all sorts of vendors set up shop on the river and near the station.

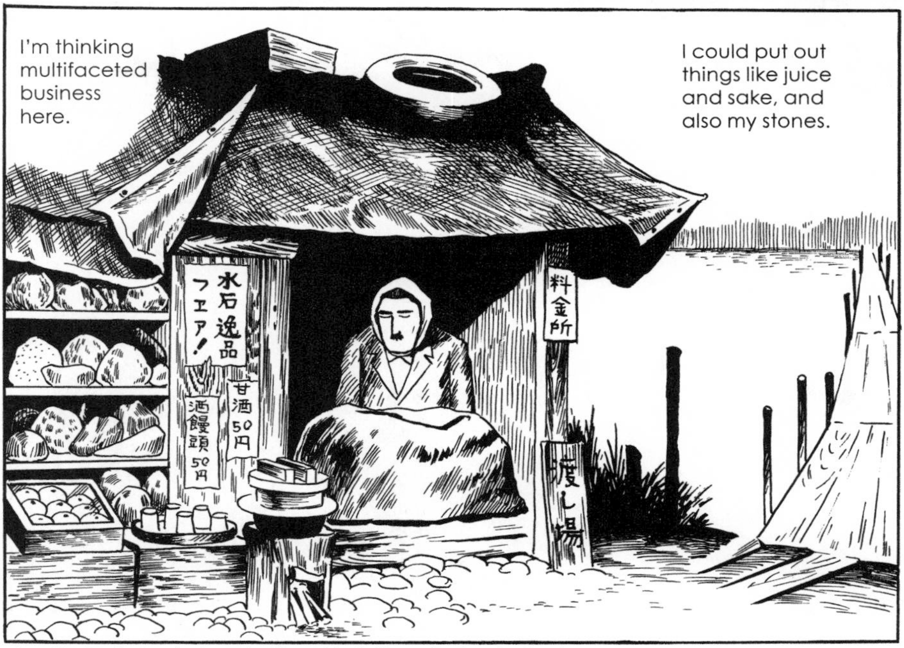
I could put out things like juice and sake, and also my stones.
I'm thinking multifaceted business here.
料金所
水石逸品フェア!
甘酒50円
酒饅頭50円
渡し場

signs: The finest art rocks, Amazake 50 yen, Manju 50 yen, Pay here for Crossing

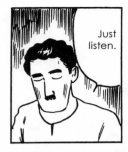

Mmhmm. Stones, huh?
You haven't sold even one yet.
Just listen.
These days, quite a few people come to the river even on days when the track is closed.
People fishing...
Marathon runners...
Baseball players...

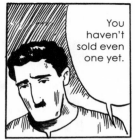

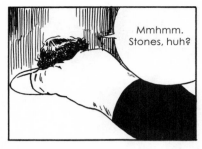

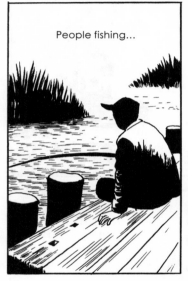

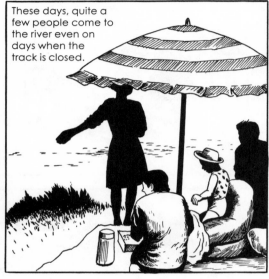

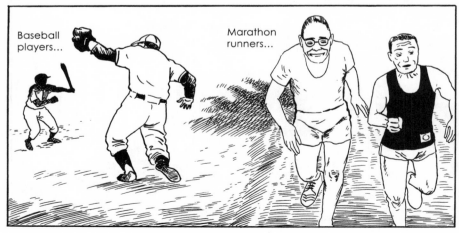

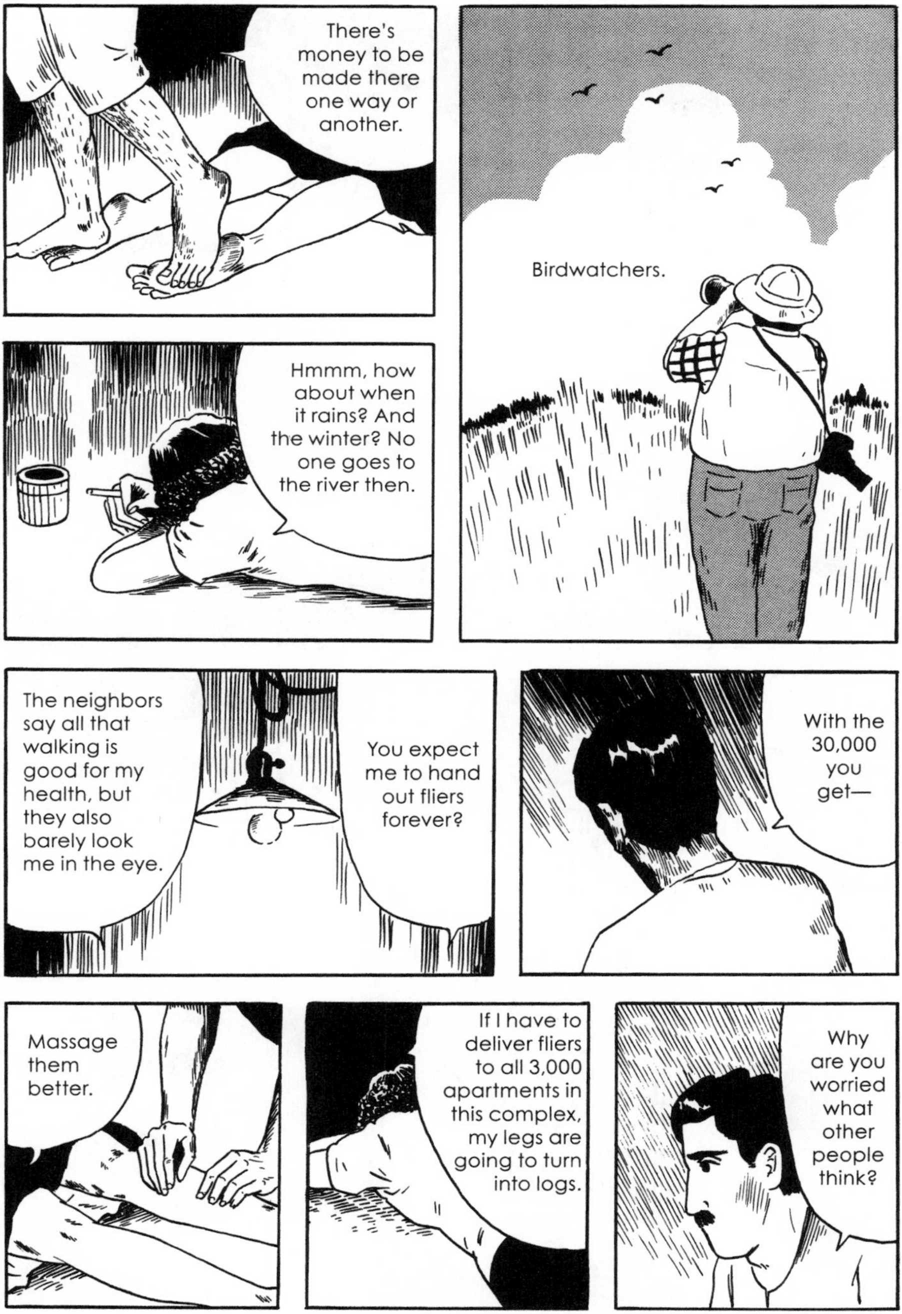
Birdwatchers.
There's money to be made there one way or another.
Hmmm, how about when it rains? And the winter? No one goes to the river then.
With the 30,000 you get—
You expect me to hand out fliers forever?
The neighbors say all that walking is good for my health, but they also barely look me in the eye.
Why are you worried what other people think?
If I have to deliver fliers to all 3,000 apartments in this complex, my legs are going to turn into logs.
Massage them better.

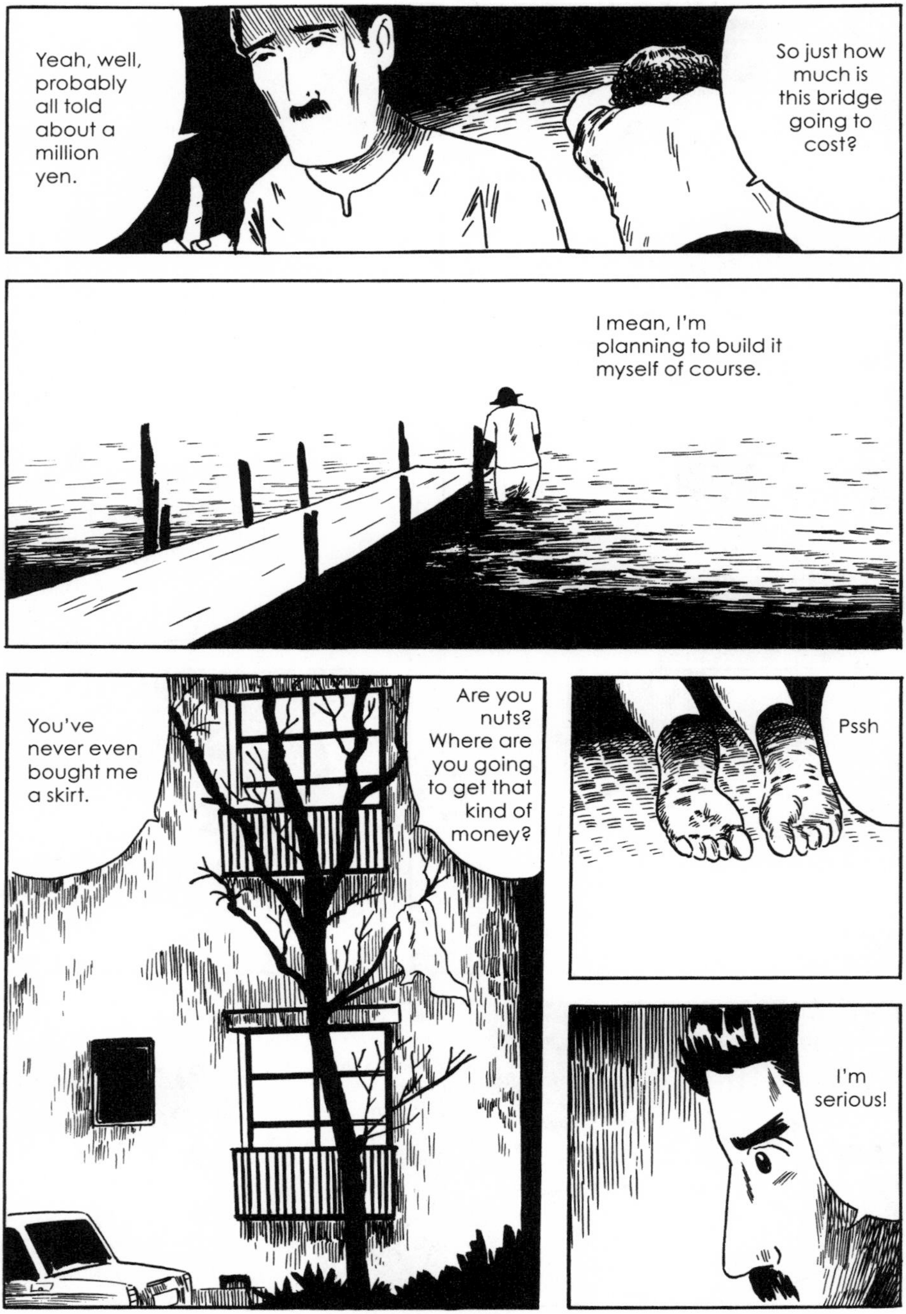
So just how much is this bridge going to cost?
Yeah, well, probably all told about a million yen.
I mean, I'm planning to build it myself of course.
Pssh
I'm serious!
Are you nuts? Where are you going to get that kind of money?
You've never even bought me a skirt.

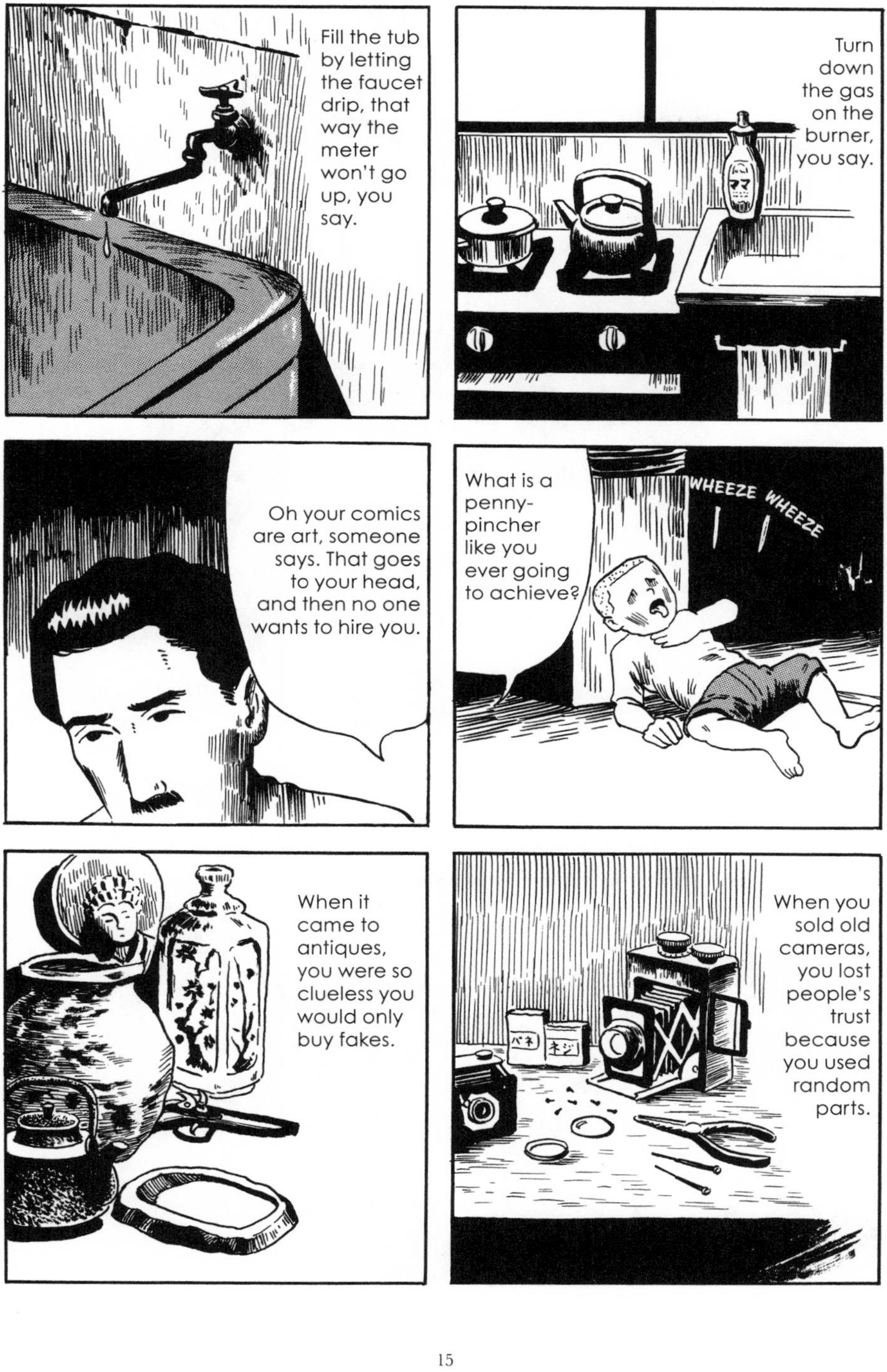
Turn down the gas on the burner, you say.
Fill the tub by letting the faucet drip, that way the meter won't go up, you say.
What is a penny-pincher like you ever going to achieve?
WHEEZE WHEEZE
Oh your comics are art, someone says. That goes to your head, and then no one wants to hire you.
When you sold old cameras, you lost people's trust because you used random parts.
When it came to antiques, you were so clueless you would only buy fakes.

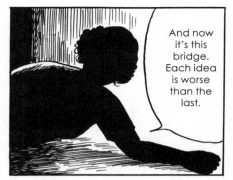

And then stones!
And now it's this bridge. Each idea is worse than the last.
You don't even look the part.
His asthma is acting up
...
WHEEZE
WHEEZE
You're lazy and worth-less.

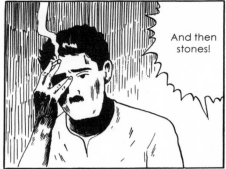

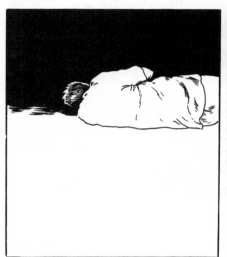

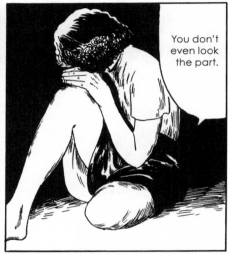

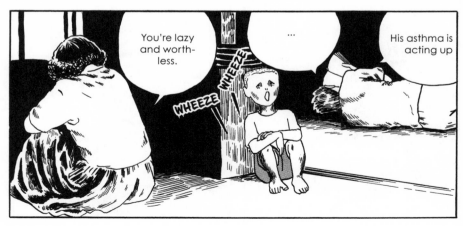

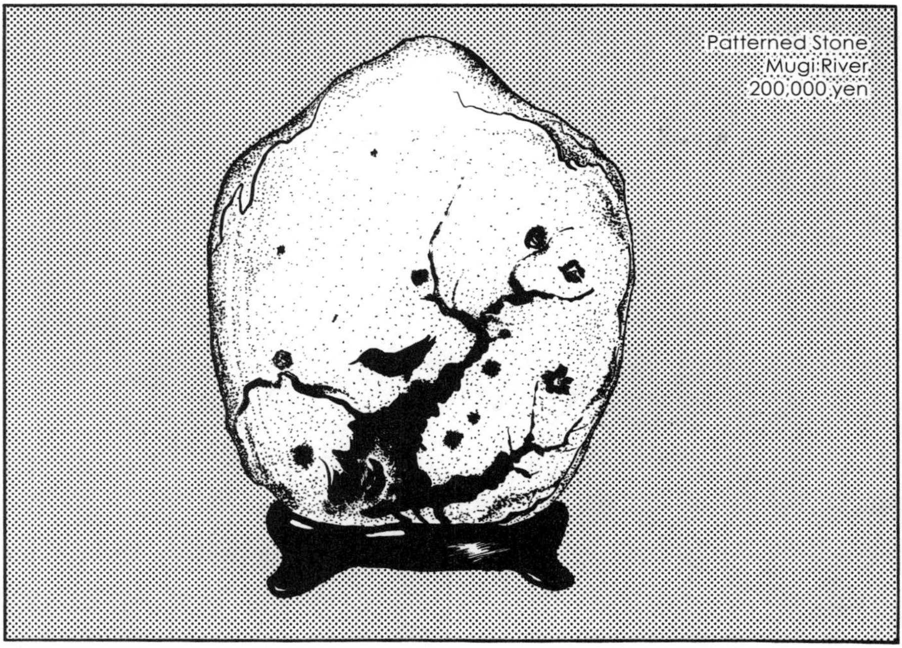
Patterned Stone
Mugi River
200,000 yen

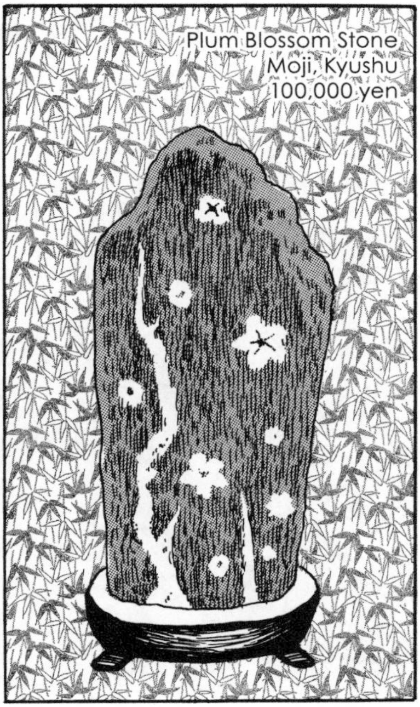
Plum Blossom Stone
Moji, Kyushu
100,000 yen

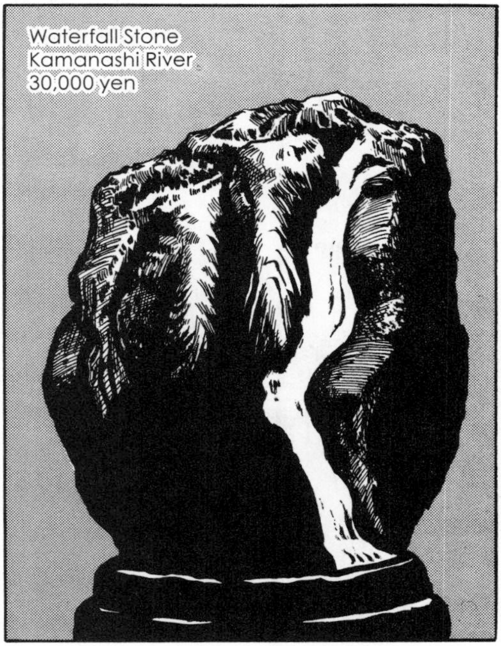
Waterfall Stone
Kamanashi River
30,000 yen

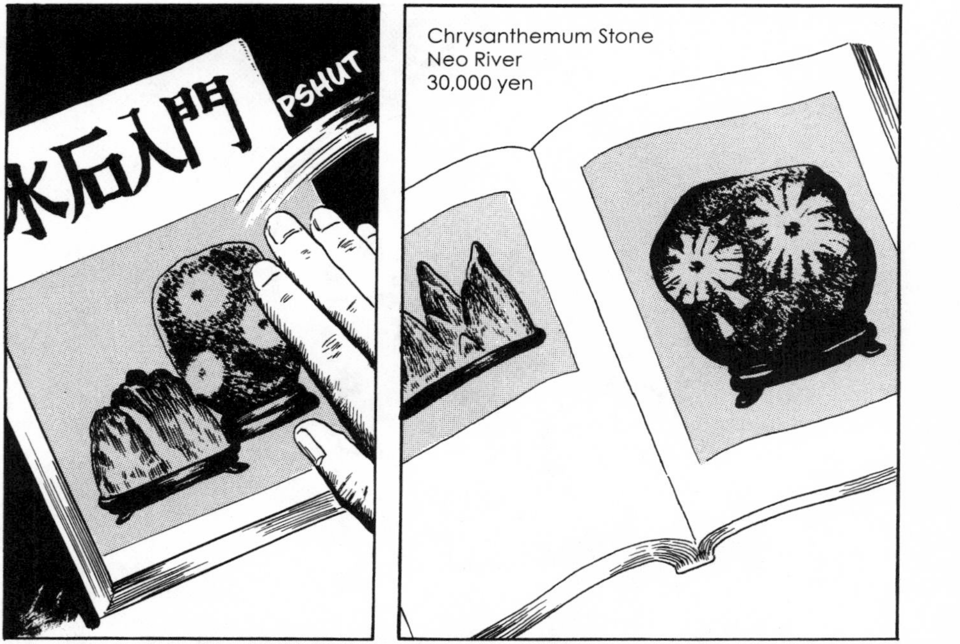
Chrysanthemum Stone
Neo River
30,000 yen
水石入門
PSHUT

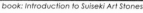

book: Introduction to Suiseki Art Stones

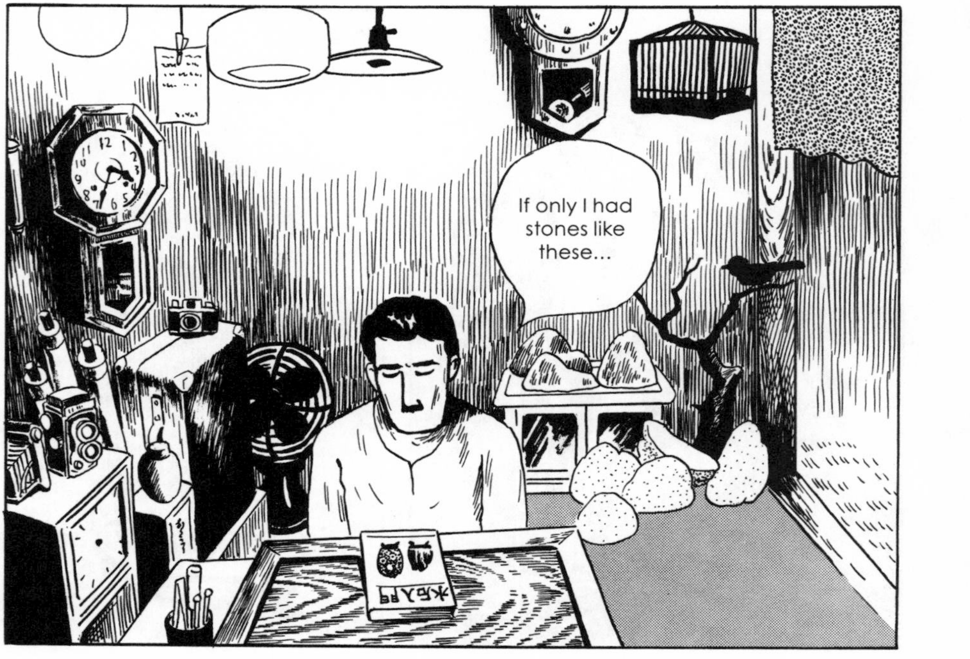
If only I had stones like these...

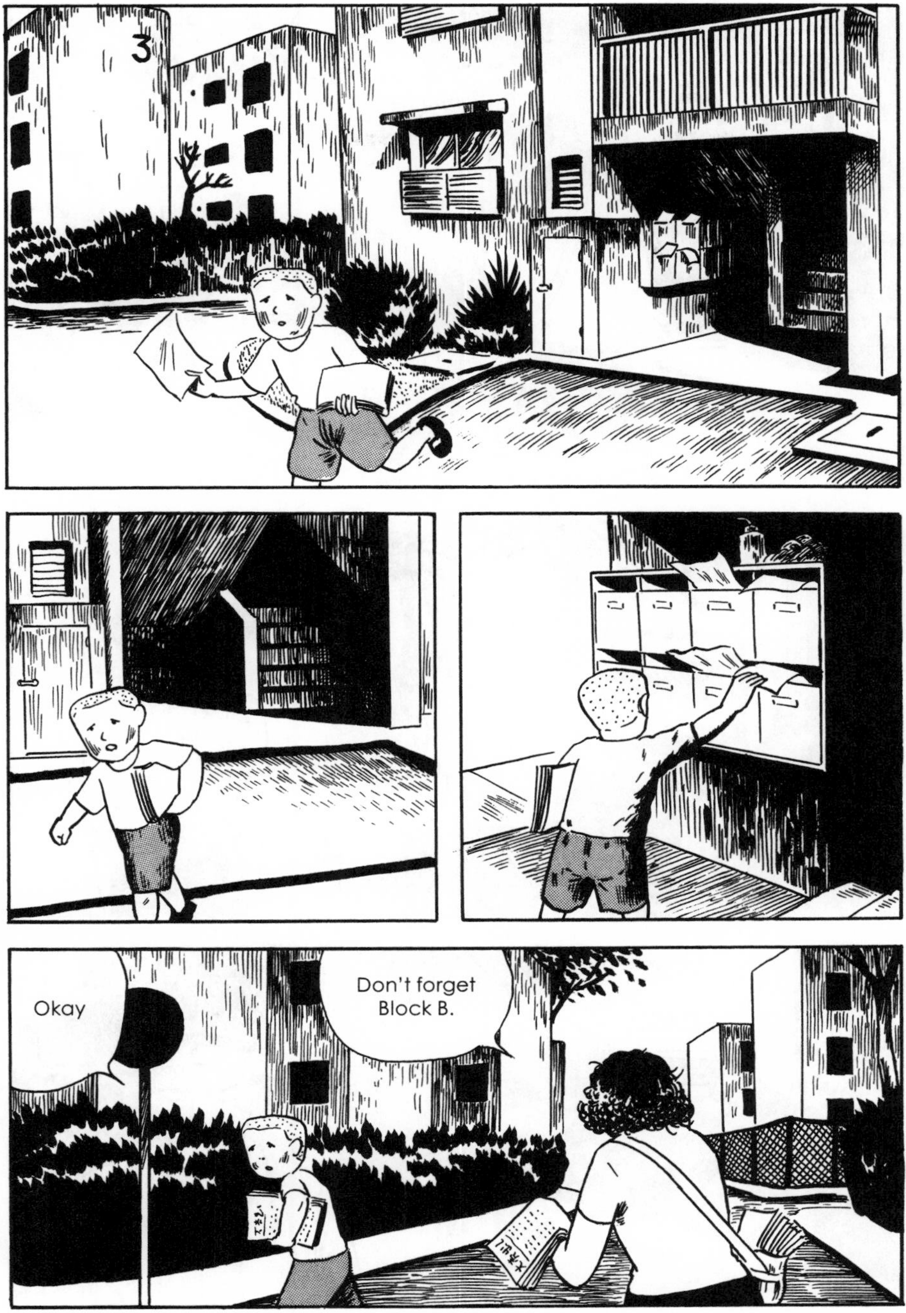
Don't forget Block B.
Okay

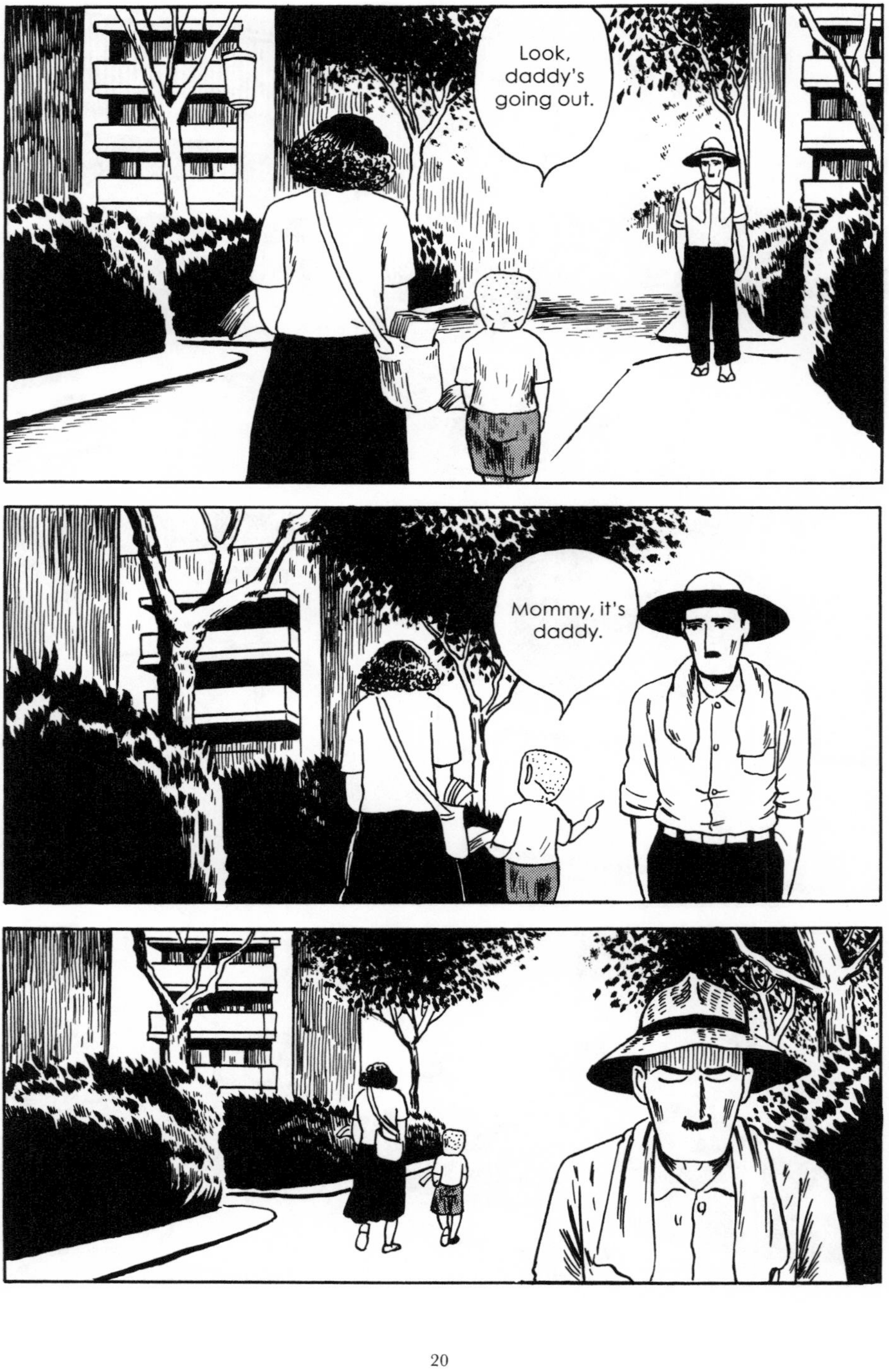
Look, daddy's going out.
Mommy, it's daddy.

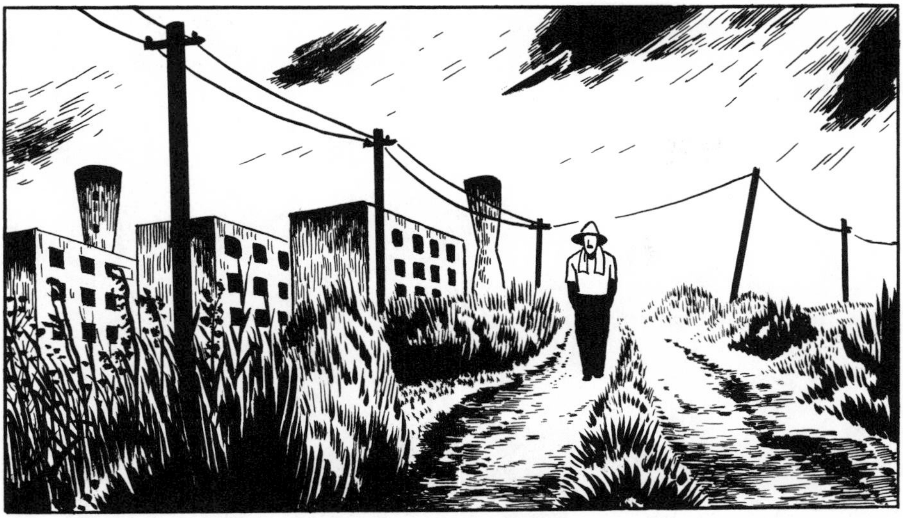

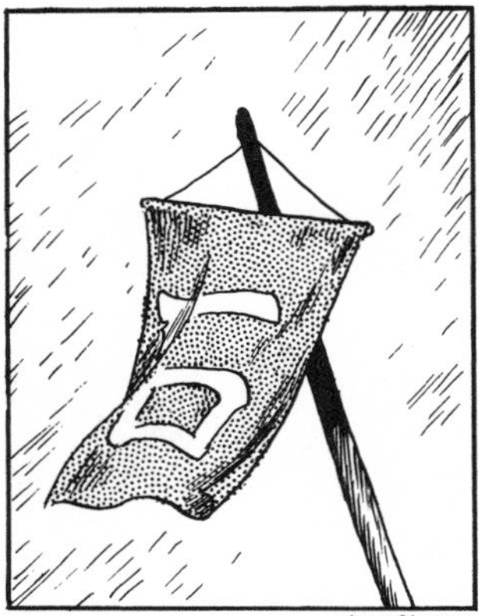

sign: Stones

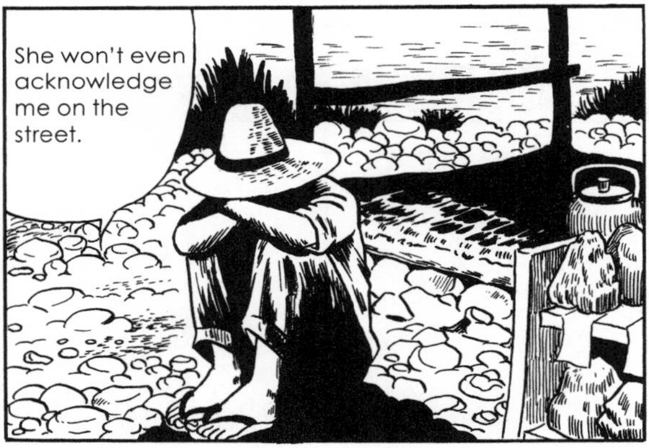
She won't even acknowledge me on the street.

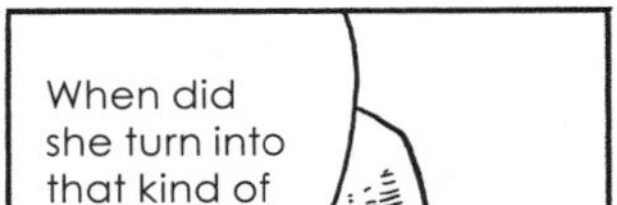
When did she turn into that kind of woman?

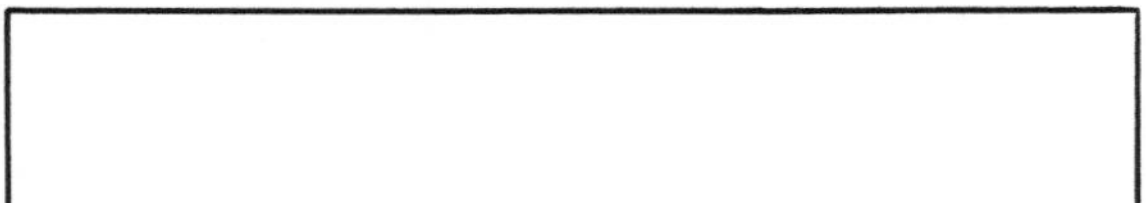

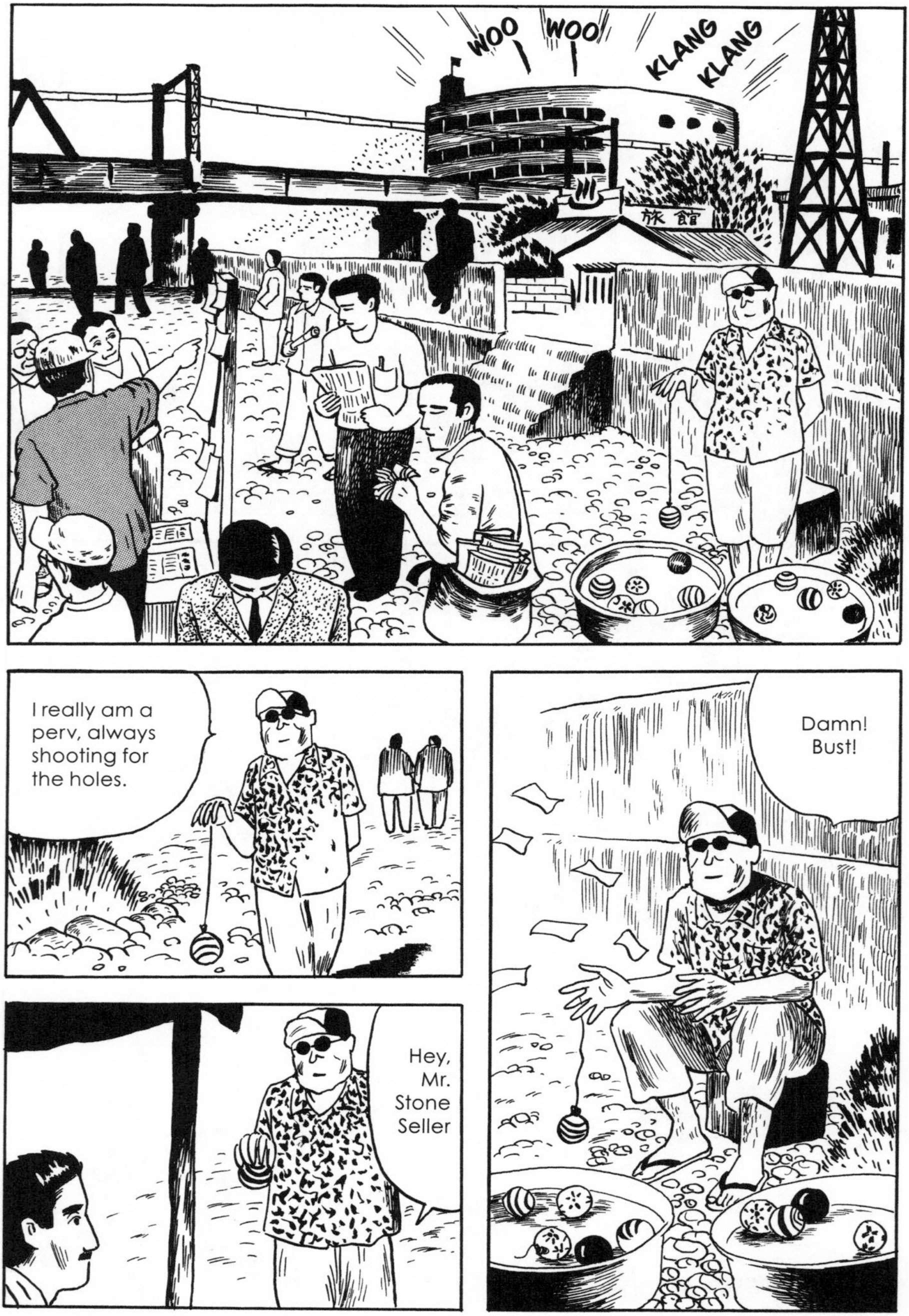
KLANG KLANG
WOO WOO
旅館
Damn! Bust!
I really am a perv, always shooting for the holes.
Hey, Mr. Stone Seller

I just opened up a biz here.
Let's look out for each other, whaddya say?
I've been here for a year already.
Yeah... I've been wondering 'bout that.
These rocks, to me they don't look much different than the rocks along the river here.
That's where I found them.
Ha! I knew it!
They sell?
...
I've seen people sell all sorts of things.
But never nothing that doesn't require a little capital investment.

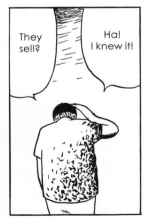

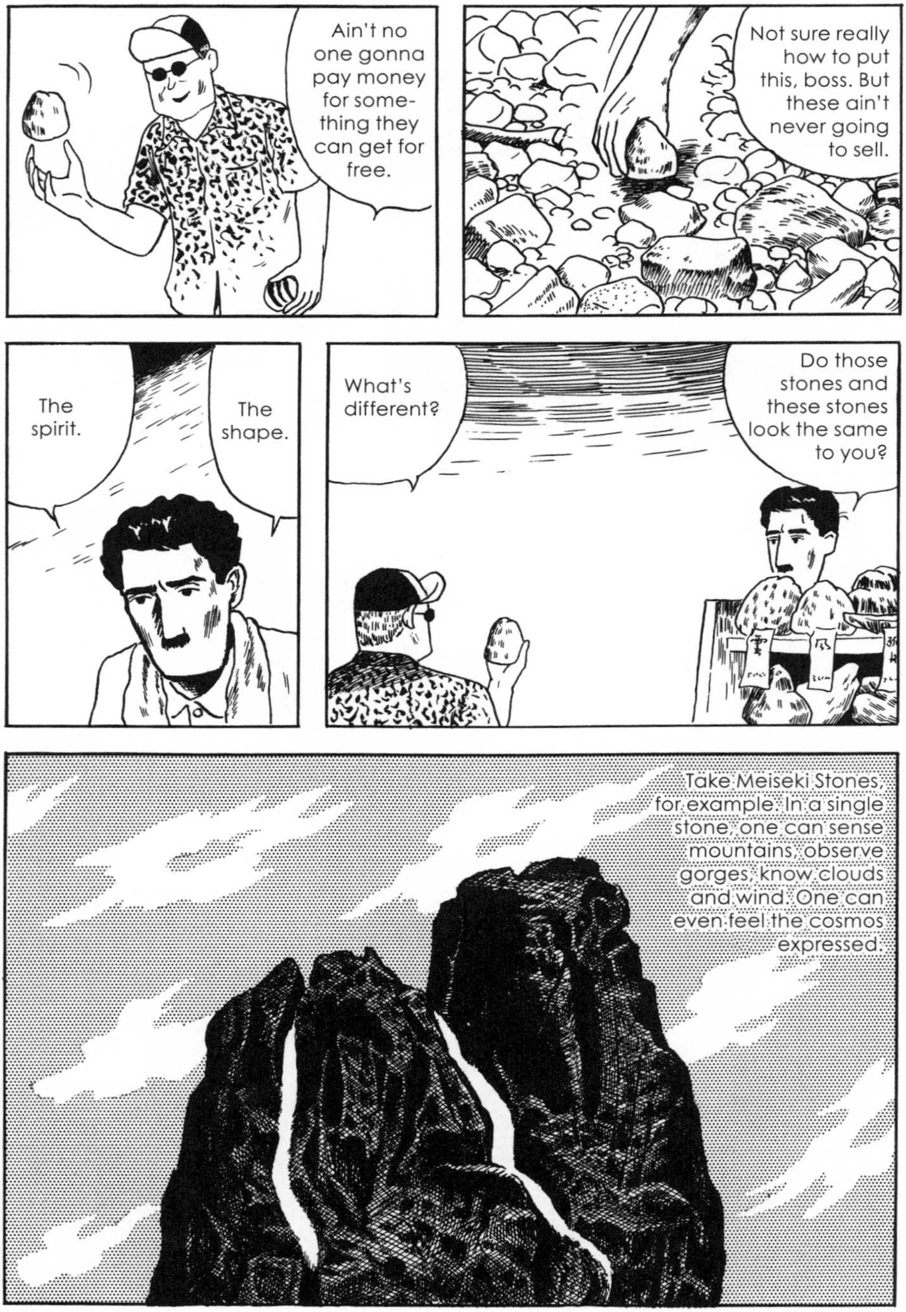
Not sure really how to put this, boss. But these ain't never going to sell.
Ain't no one gonna pay money for some-thing they can get for free.
Do those stones and these stones look the same to you?
What's different?
The shape.
The spirit.
Take Meiseki Stones, for example. In a single stone, one can sense mountains, observe gorges, know clouds and wind. One can even feel the cosmos expressed.

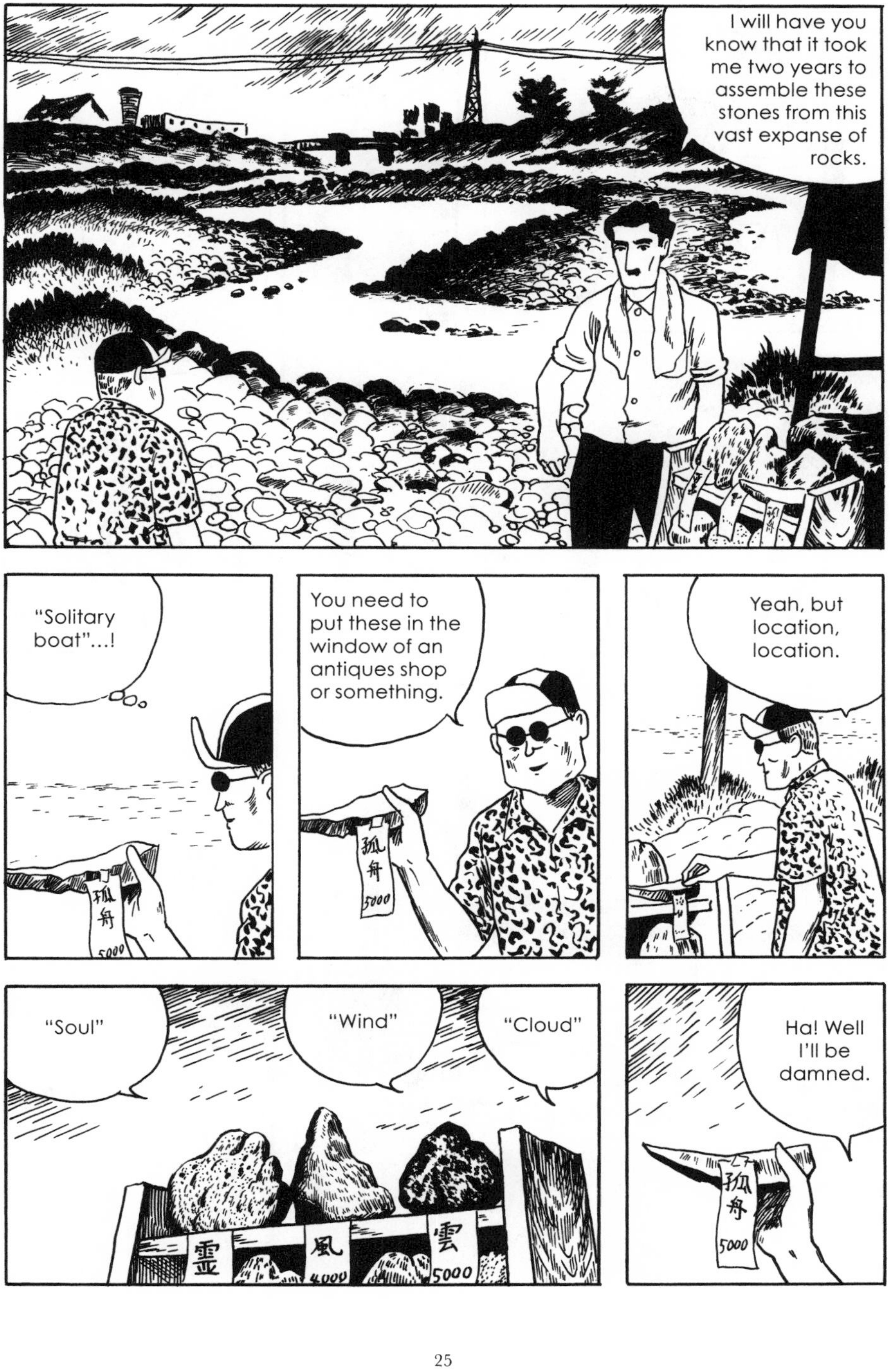
I will have you know that it took me two years to assemble these stones from this vast expanse of rocks.
Yeah, but location, location.
You need to put these in the window of an antiques shop or something.
孤舟
5000
"Solitary boat"...!
孤舟
5000
Ha! Well I'll be damned.
孤舟
5000
"Cloud"
"Wind"
"Soul"
霊
風
雲
4000
5000

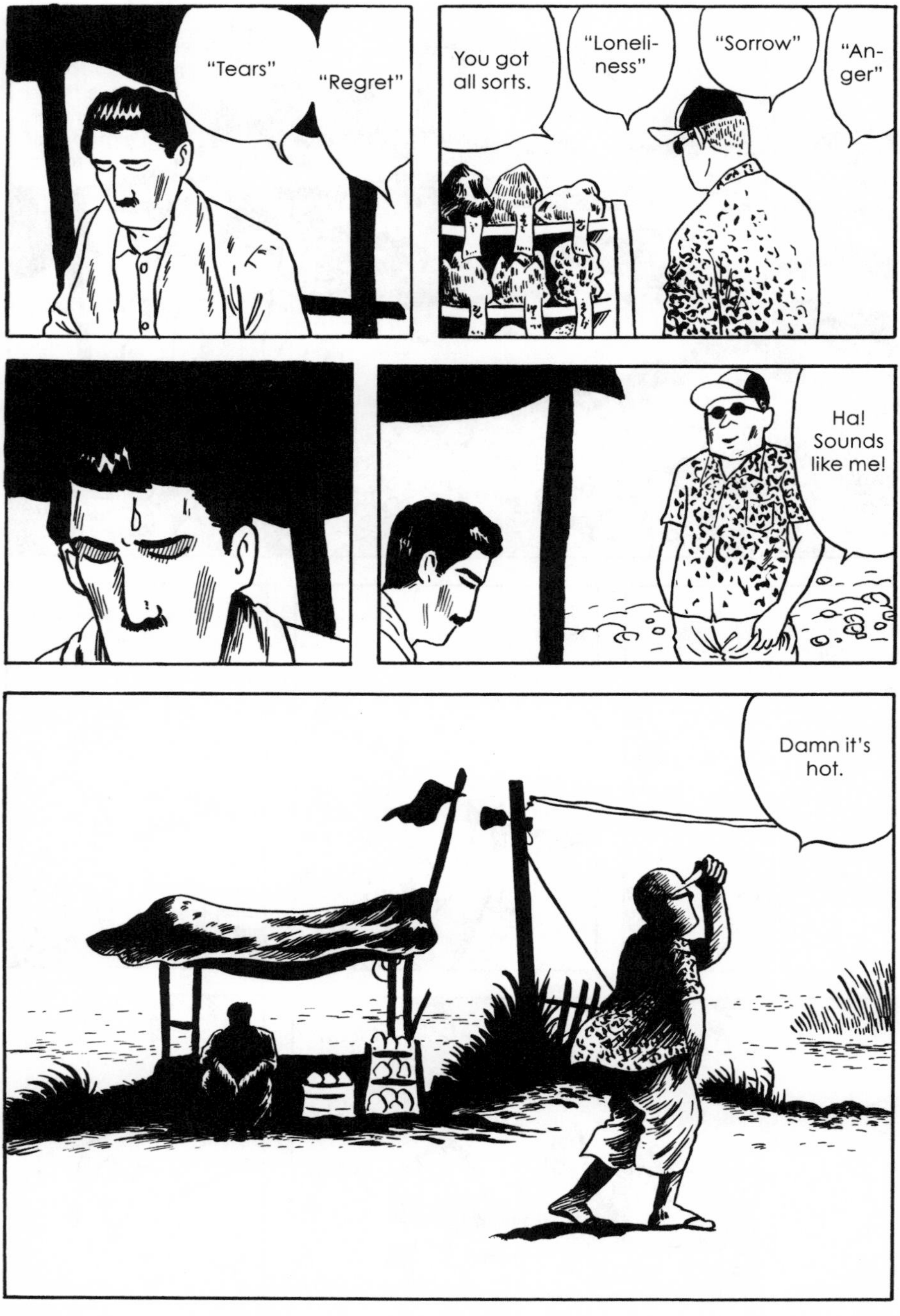
"An-
ger"
"Sorrow"
"Loneli-
ness"
You got
all sorts.
"Regret"
"Tears"
Ha!
Sounds
like me!
Damn it's
hot.

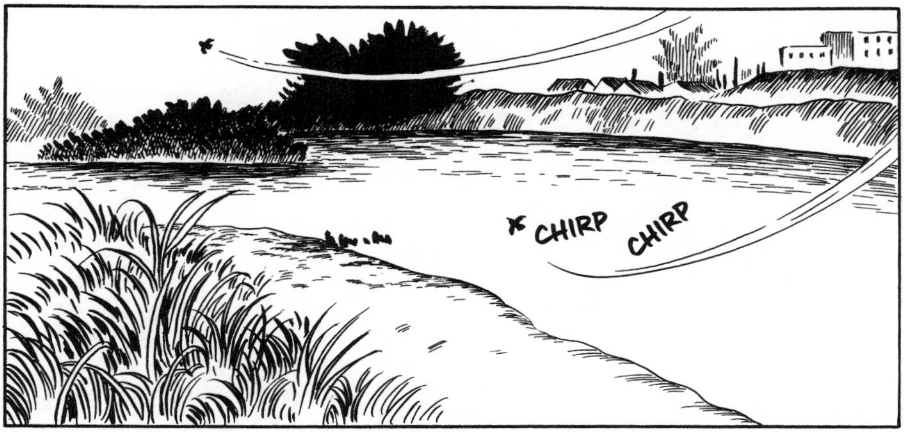
CHIRP
CHIRP

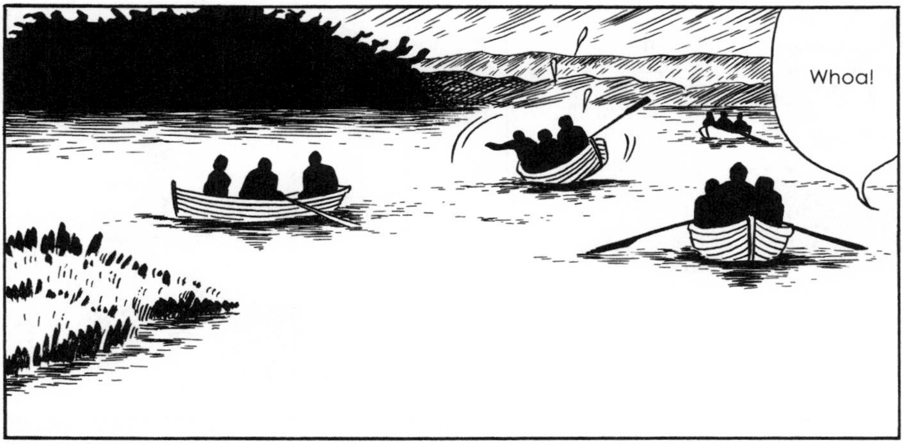
Whoa!

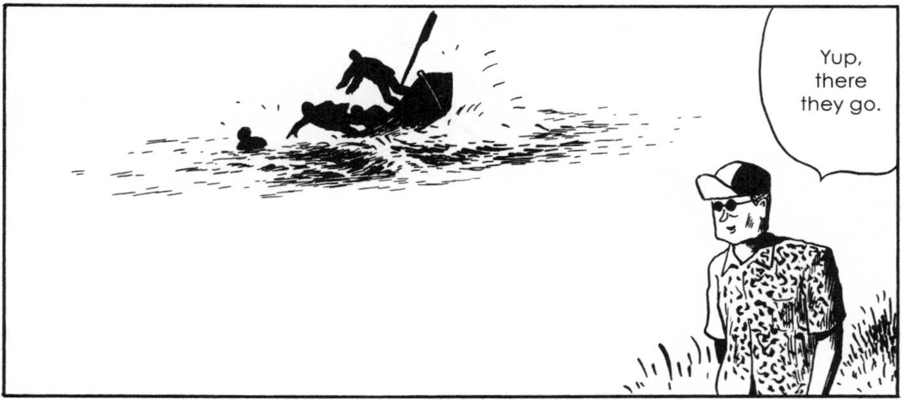
Yup, there they go.

What do those fools expect, four to a boat.
Shit!
It's shallow enough here.
If it's that much trouble, you could just take the train.
The station on the other side is way outside of town.
That's some racket the boat rental is running. An hour minimum at 800 yen, but they're across in three minutes.
Hey! Hurry up!
Problem is, everyone goes one way, so the boats get stuck and it takes time to get them back to the other side.

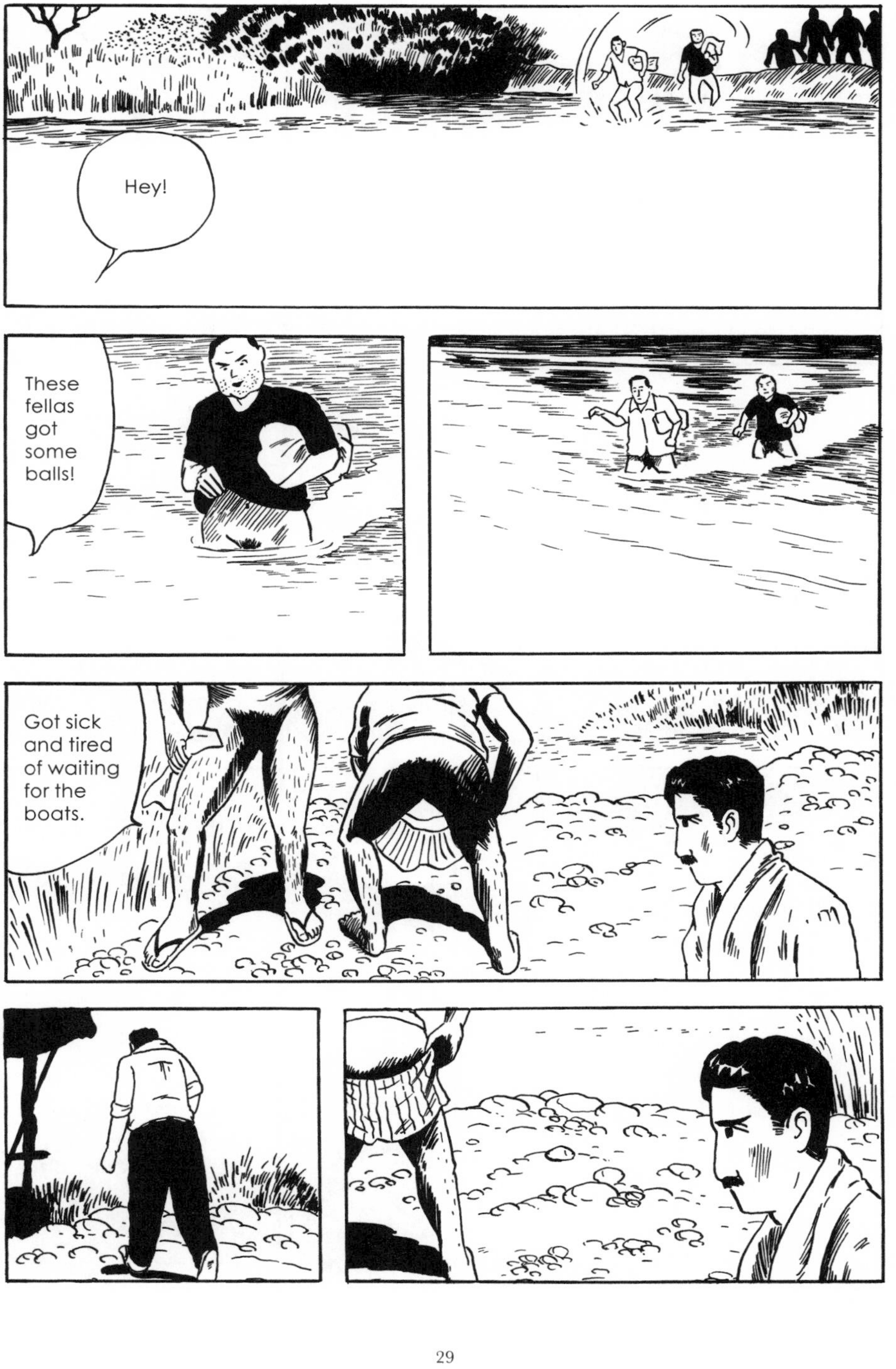
Hey!
These fellas got some balls!
Got sick and tired of waiting for the boats.

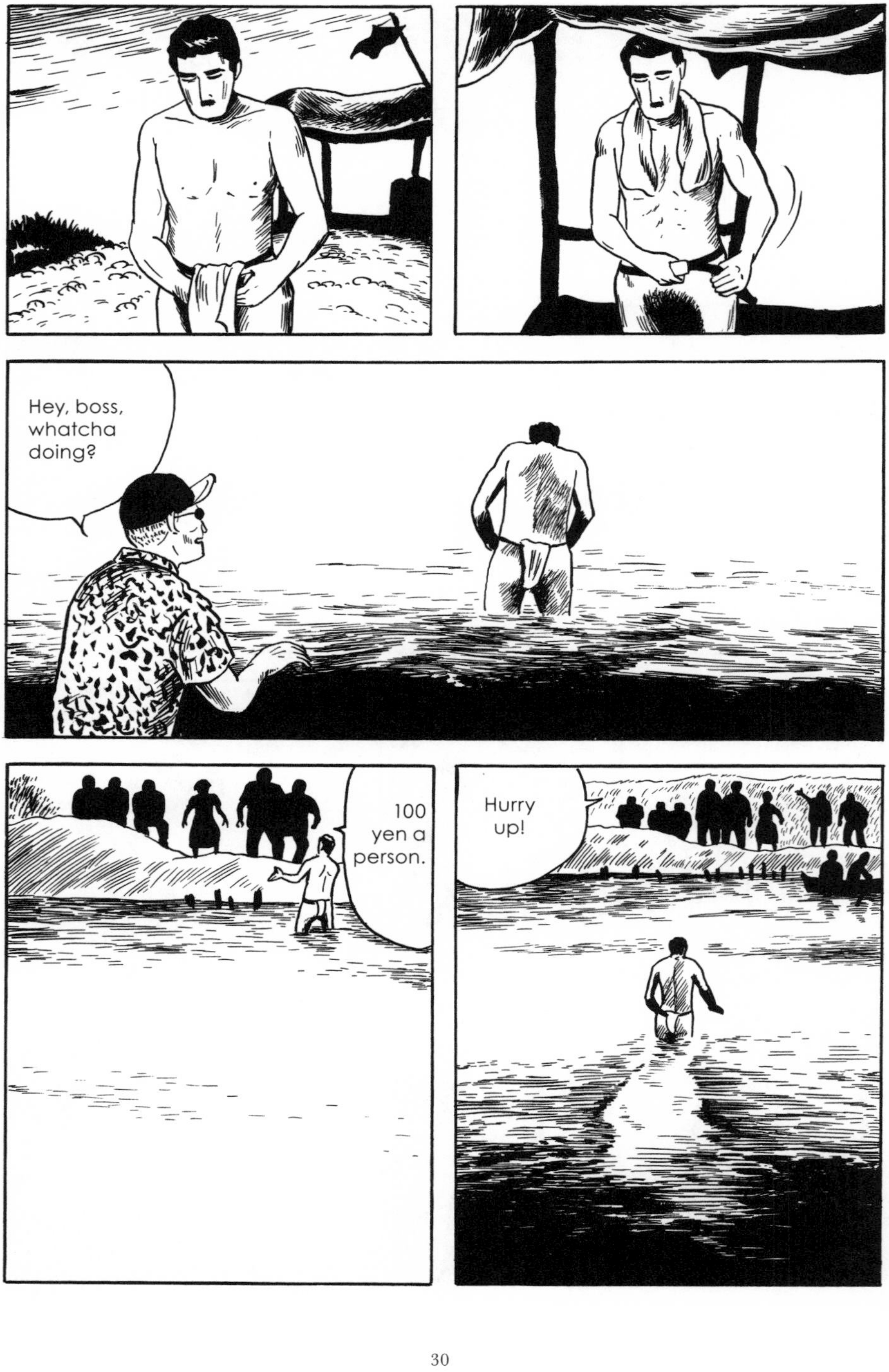
Hey, boss, whatcha doing?
Hurry up!
100 yen a person.

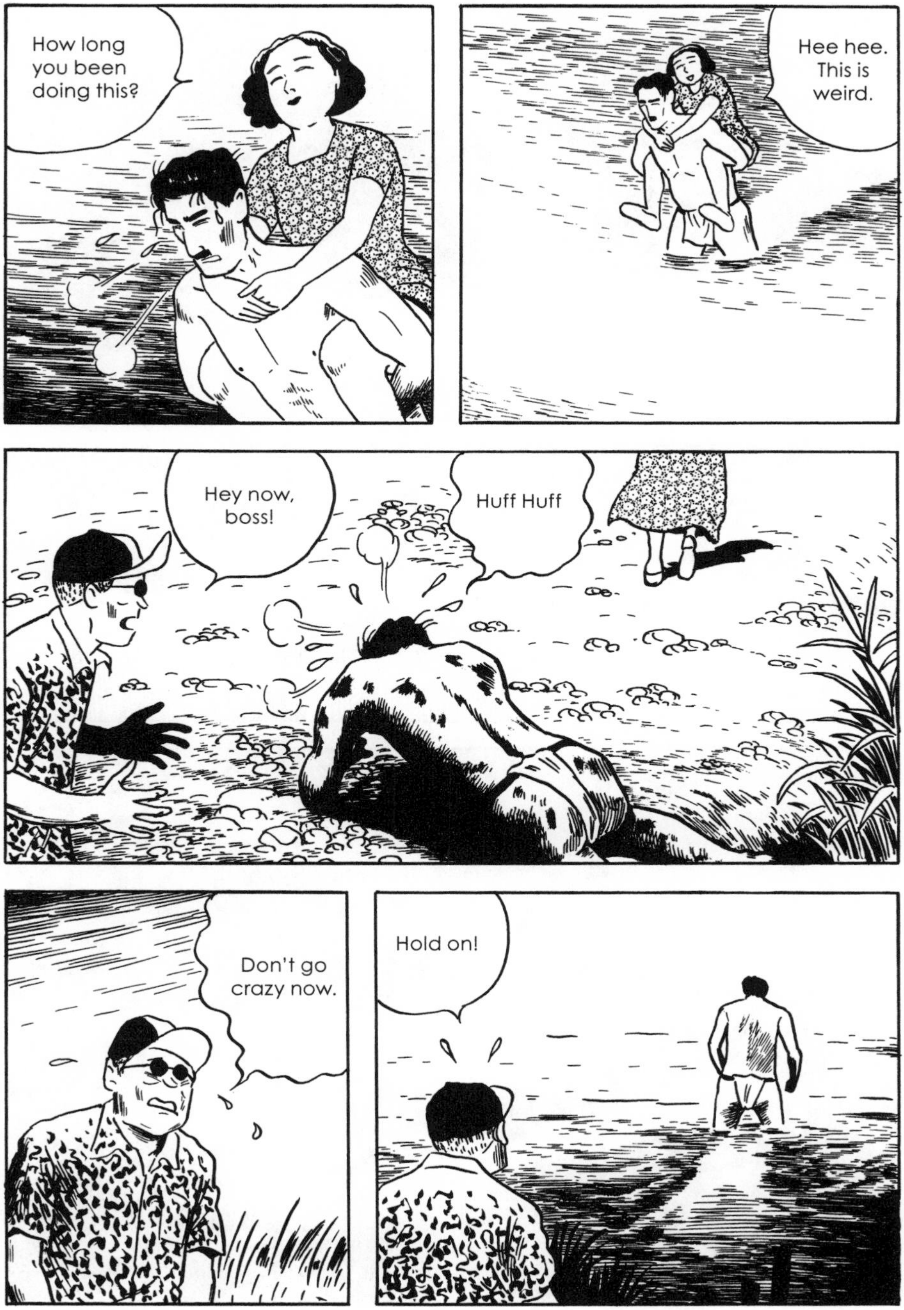
Hee hee. This is weird.
How long you been doing this?
Huff Huff
Hey now, boss!
Hold on!
Don't go crazy now.

 11, 12... 8, 9, 10...

 KPLINK KPLINK

Daddy

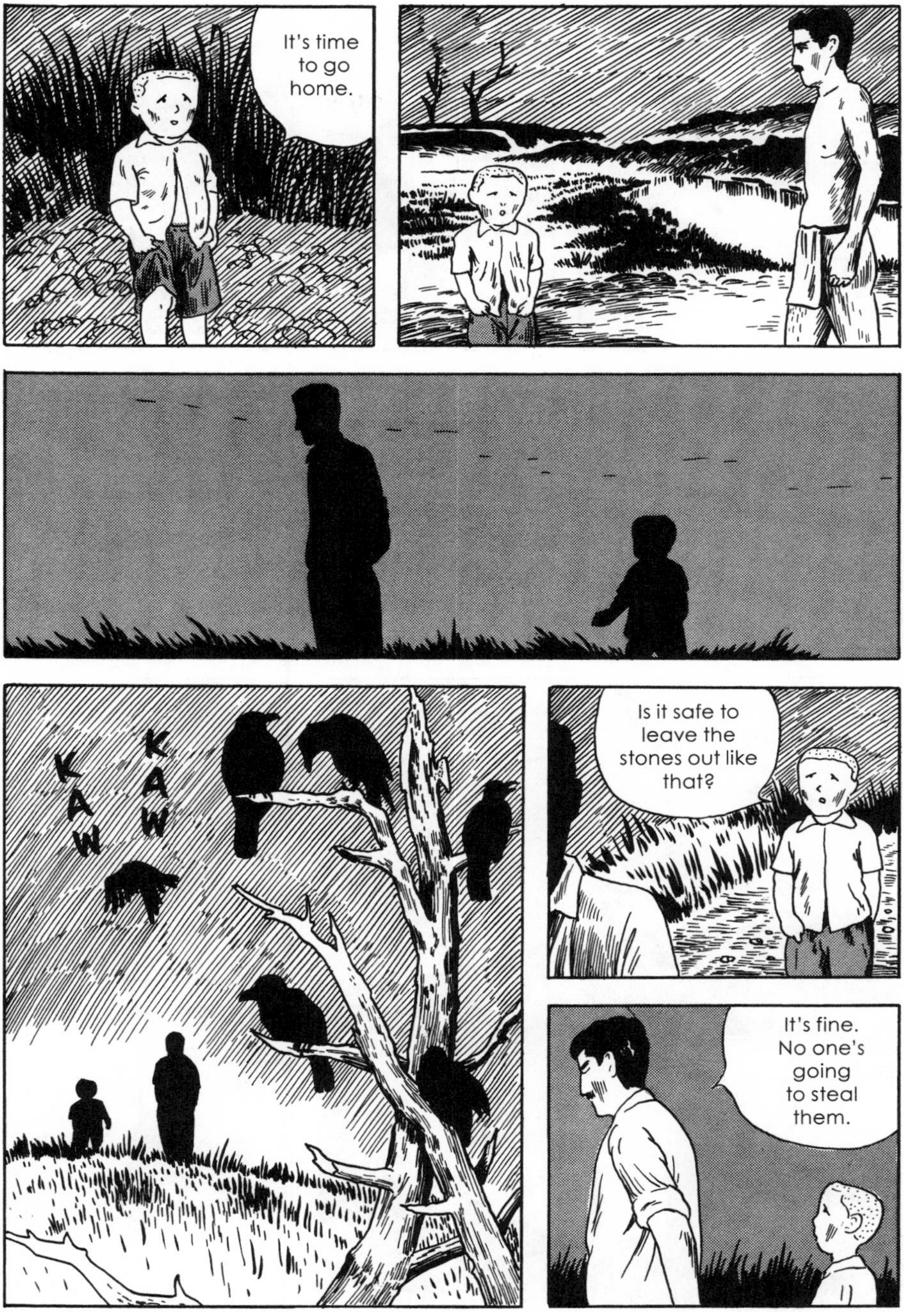
It's time to go home.
Is it safe to leave the stones out like that?
It's fine. No one's going to steal them.
KAW
KAW

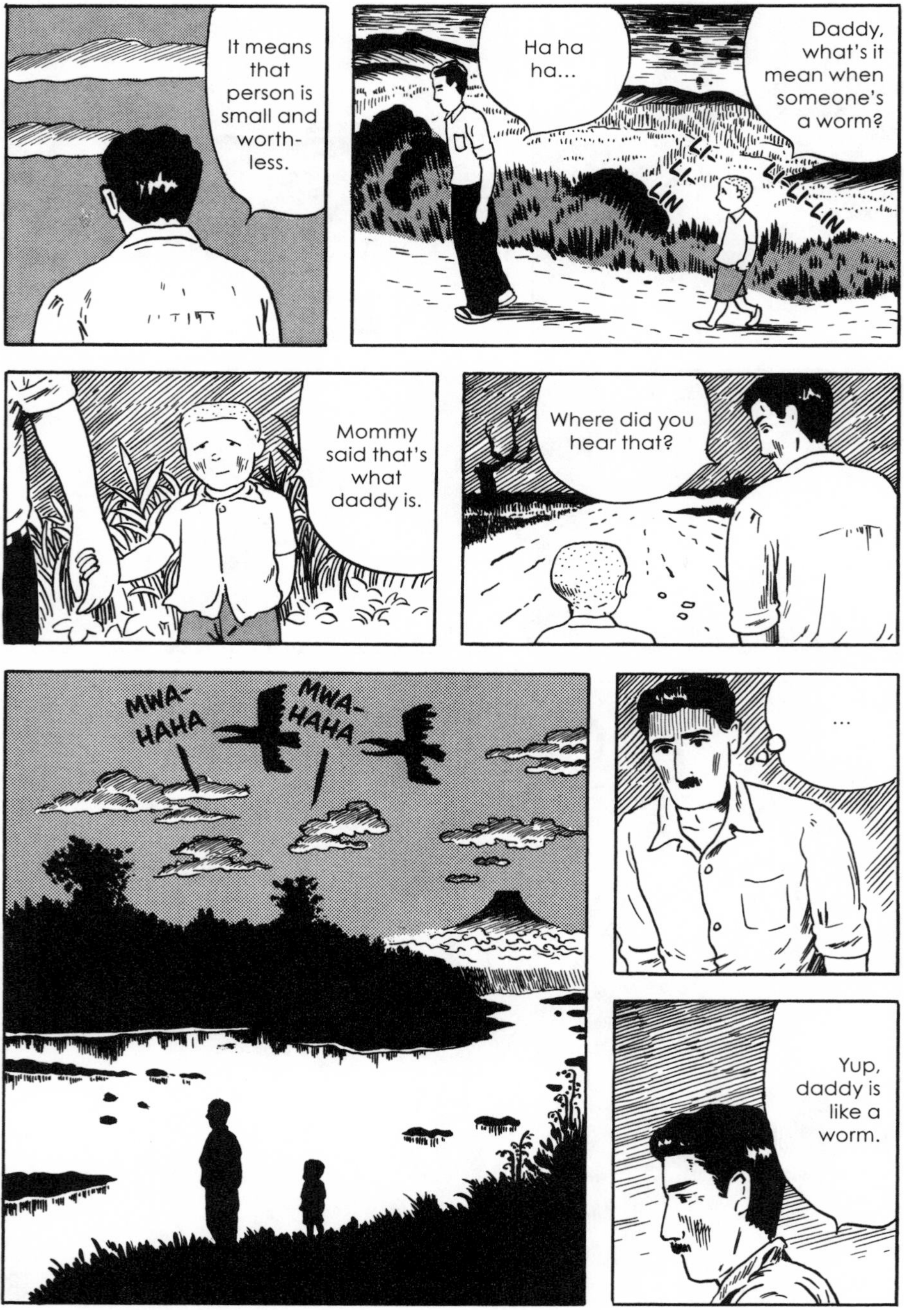
Daddy, what's it mean when someone's a worm?
LI-LI-LIN
LI-LI-LIN
Ha ha ha...
It means that person is small and worth-less.
Where did you hear that?
Mommy said that's what daddy is.
...
Yup, daddy is like a worm.
MWA-HAHA
MWA-HAHA

無能の人

The Man
Without
Talent

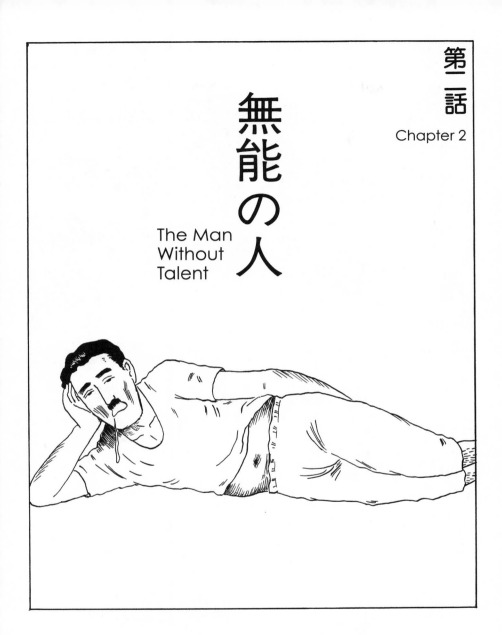

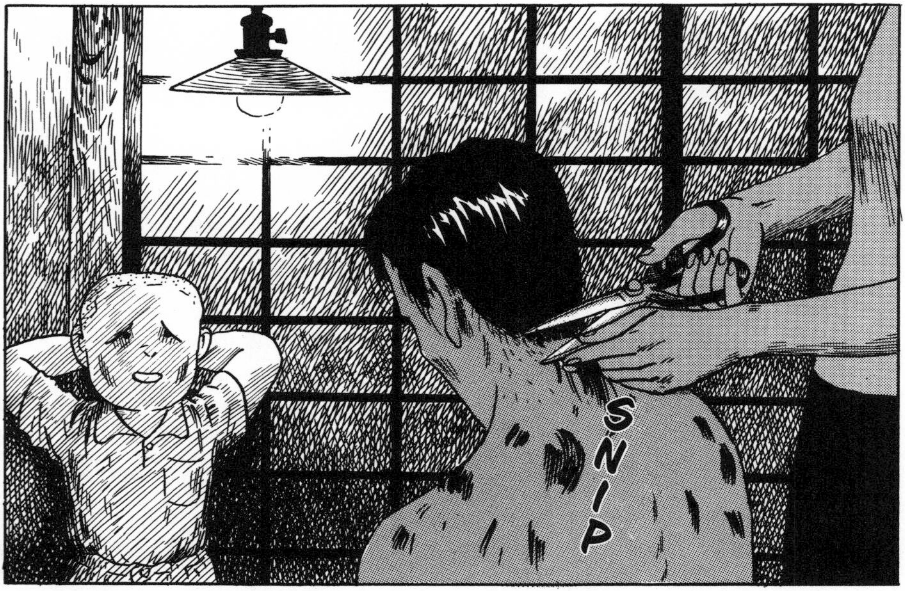
SNIP

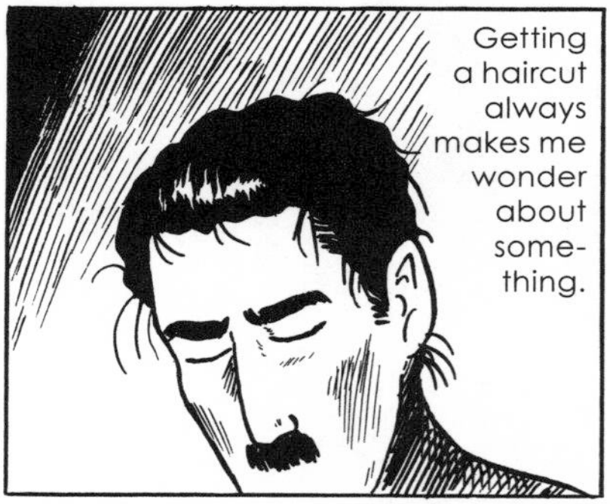
Getting a haircut always makes me wonder about something.

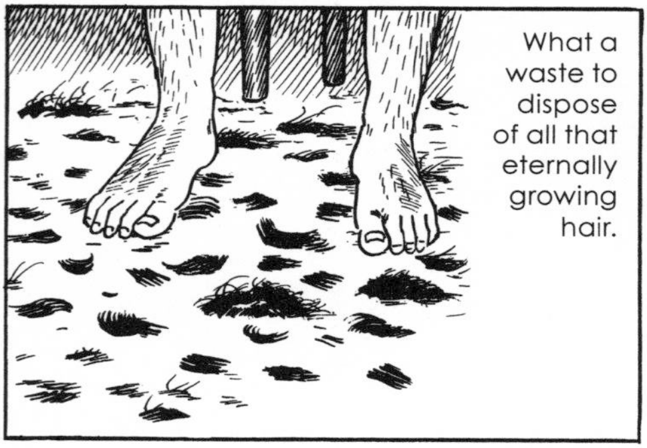
What a waste to dispose of all that eternally growing hair.

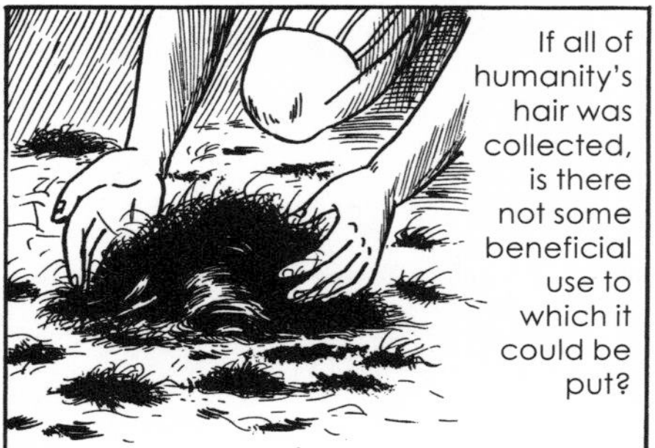
If all of humanity's hair was collected, is there not some beneficial use to which it could be put?

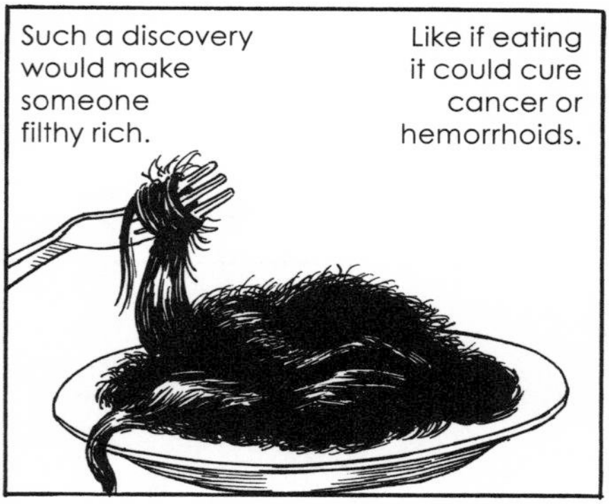
Like if eating it could cure cancer or hemorrhoids.
Such a discovery would make someone filthy rich.

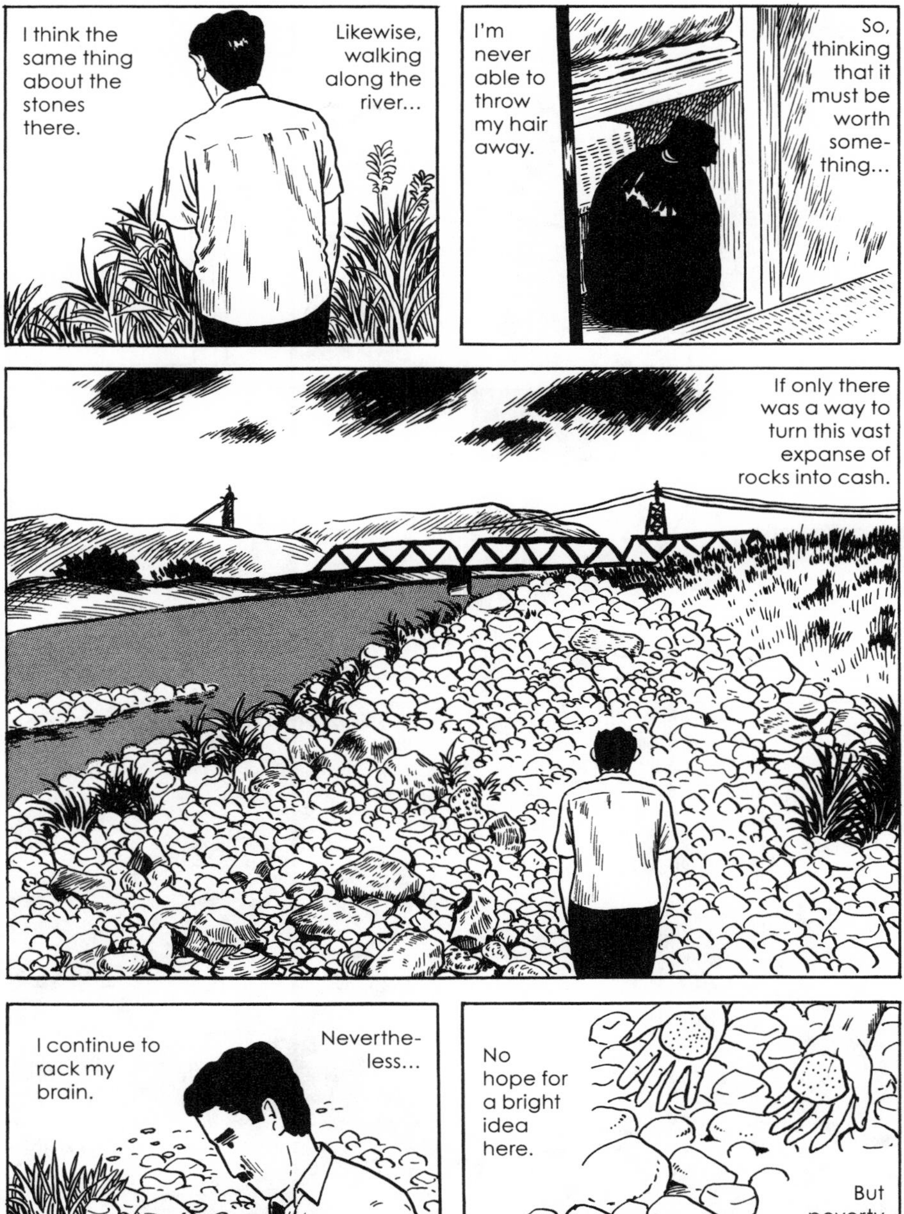
So, thinking that it must be worth something...
I'm never able to throw my hair away.
Likewise, walking along the river...
I think the same thing about the stones there.
If only there was a way to turn this vast expanse of rocks into cash.
No hope for a bright idea here.
But poverty dulls the wit.
Nevertheless...
I continue to rack my brain.

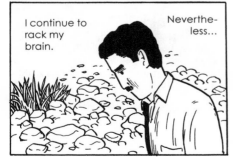

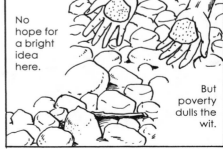

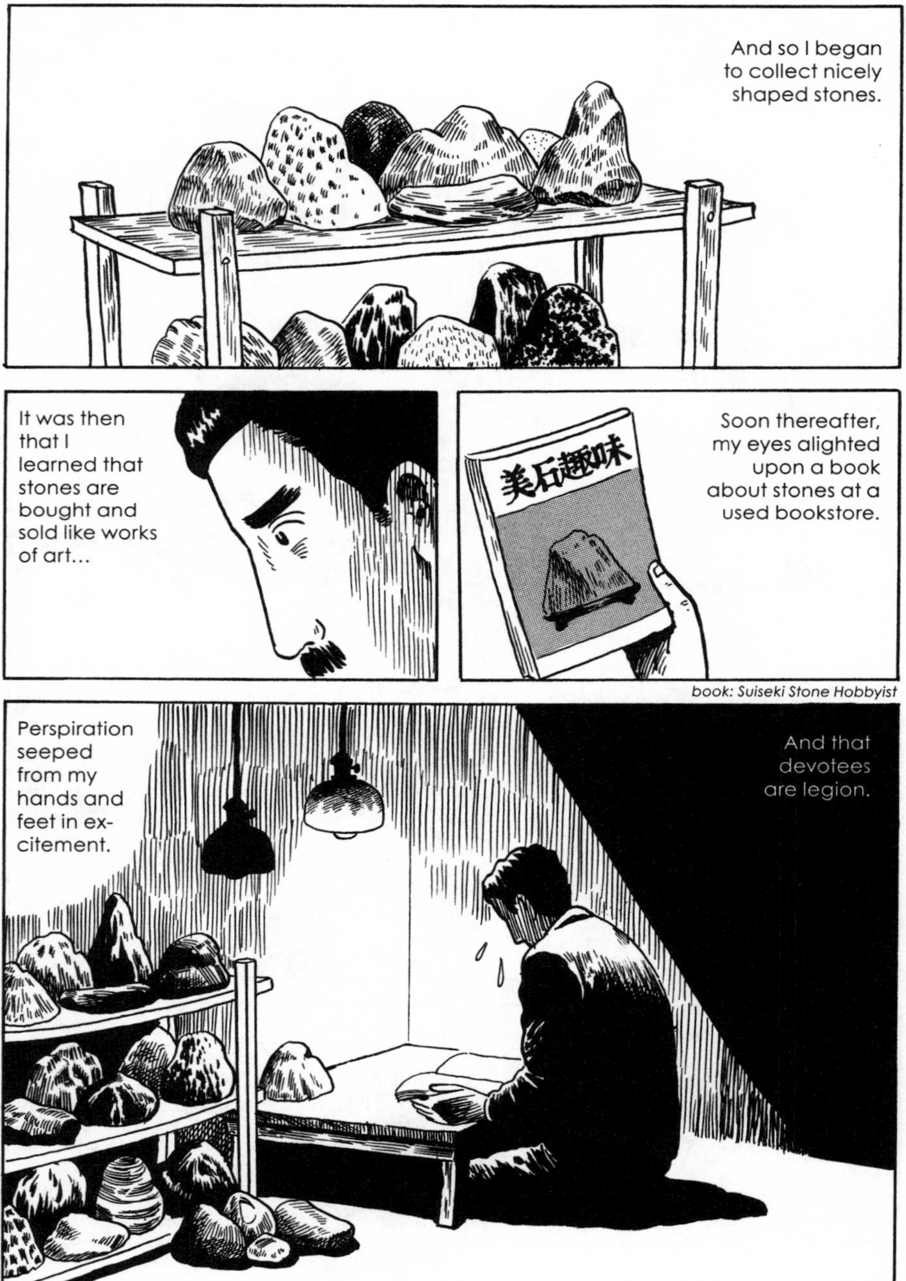
And so I began to collect nicely shaped stones.
Soon thereafter, my eyes alighted upon a book about stones at a used bookstore.
美石趣味
book: Suiseki Stone Hobbyist
It was then that I learned that stones are bought and sold like works of art...
And that devotees are legion.
Perspiration seeped from my hands and feet in excitement.

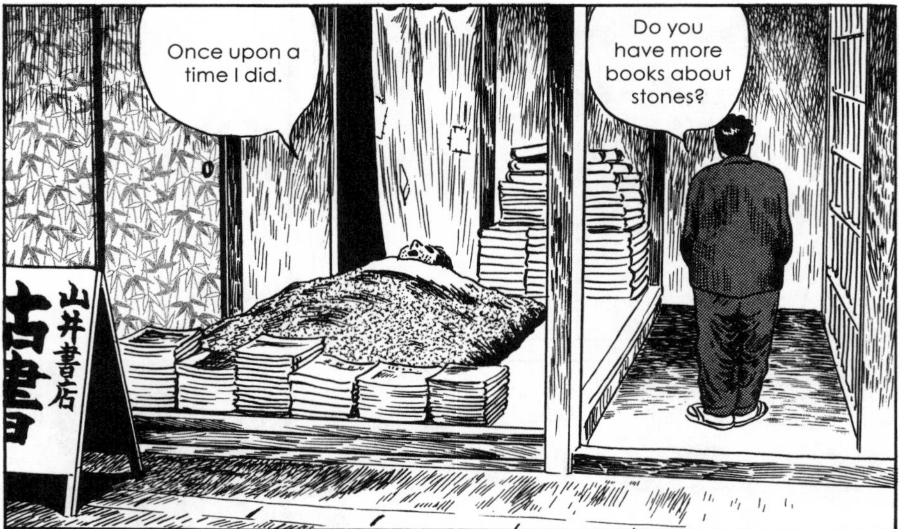
Do you have more books about stones?
Once upon a time I did.
山井書店
古書

sign: Yamai's Vintage Books

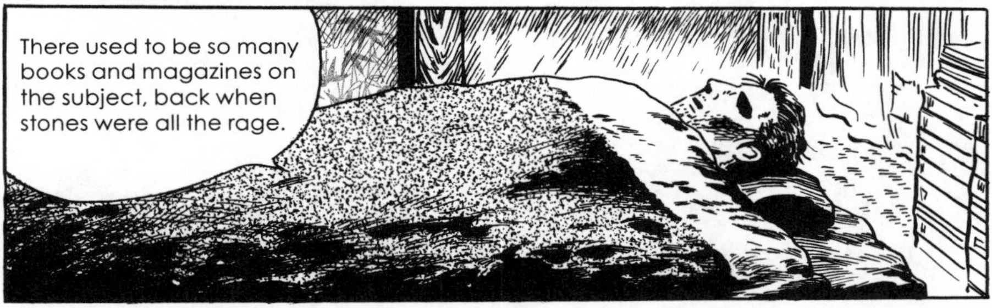
There used to be so many books and magazines on the subject, back when stones were all the rage.

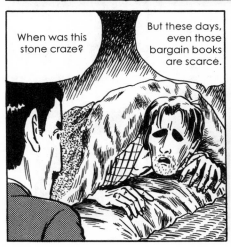

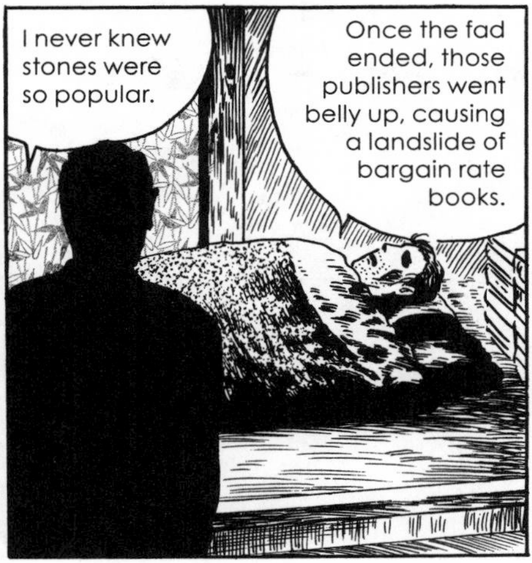
Once the fad ended, those publishers went belly up, causing a landslide of bargain rate books.
I never knew stones were so popular.

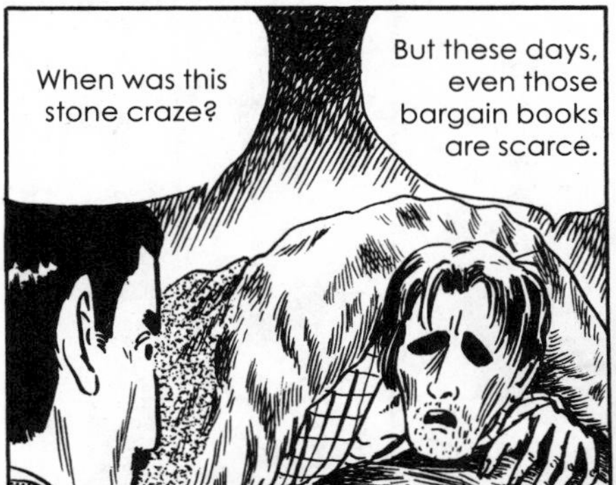
But these days, even those bargain books are scarce.
When was this stone craze?

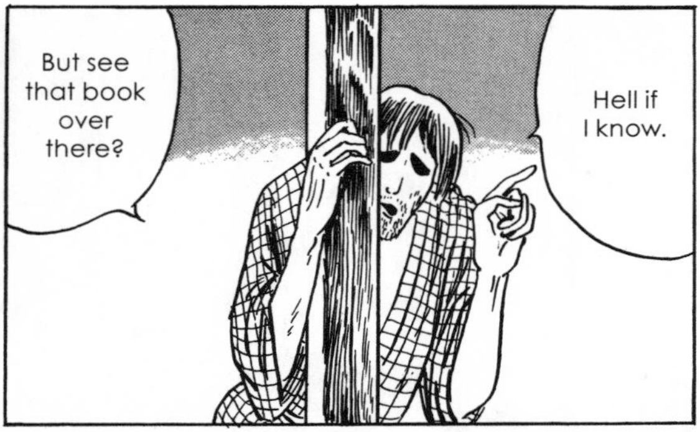
Hell if I know.
But see that book over there?

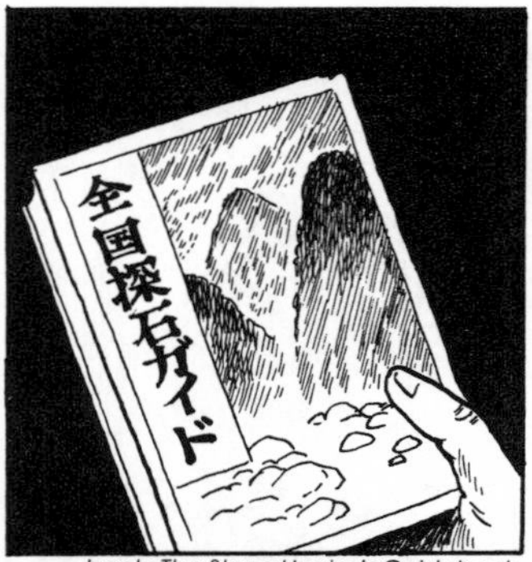
全国探石ガイド
book: The Stone Hunter's Guidebook

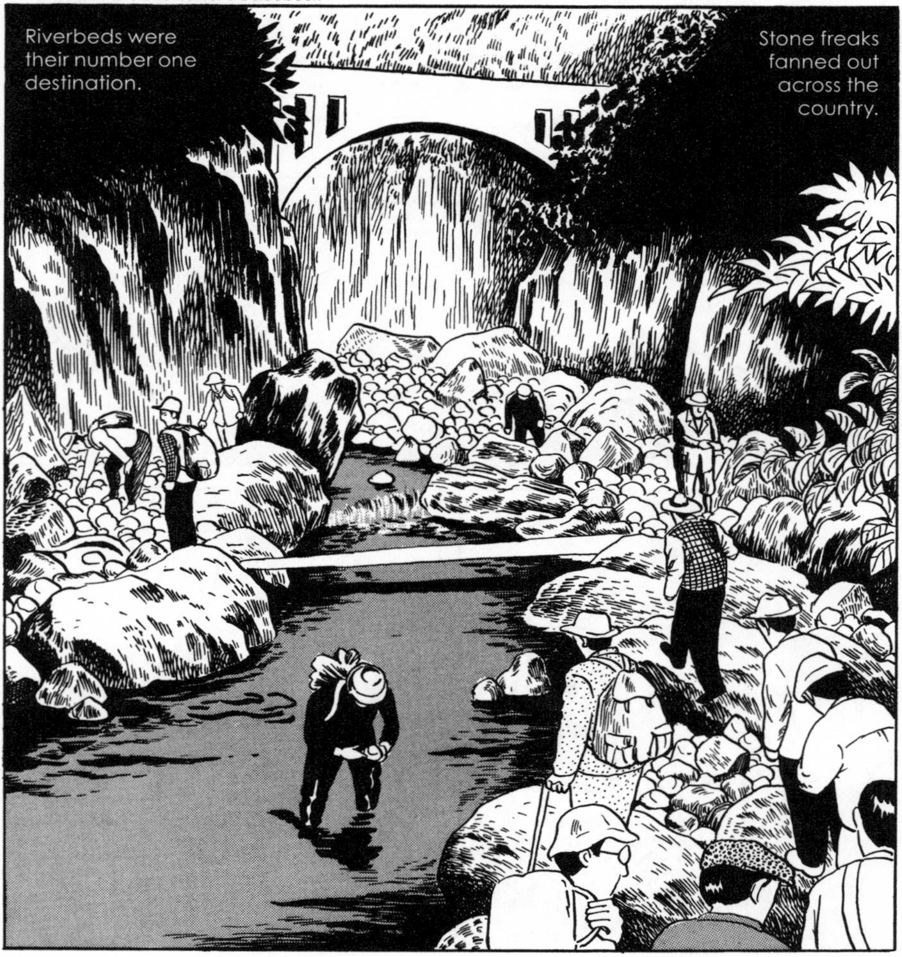
Stone freaks fanned out across the country.
Riverbeds were their number one destination.

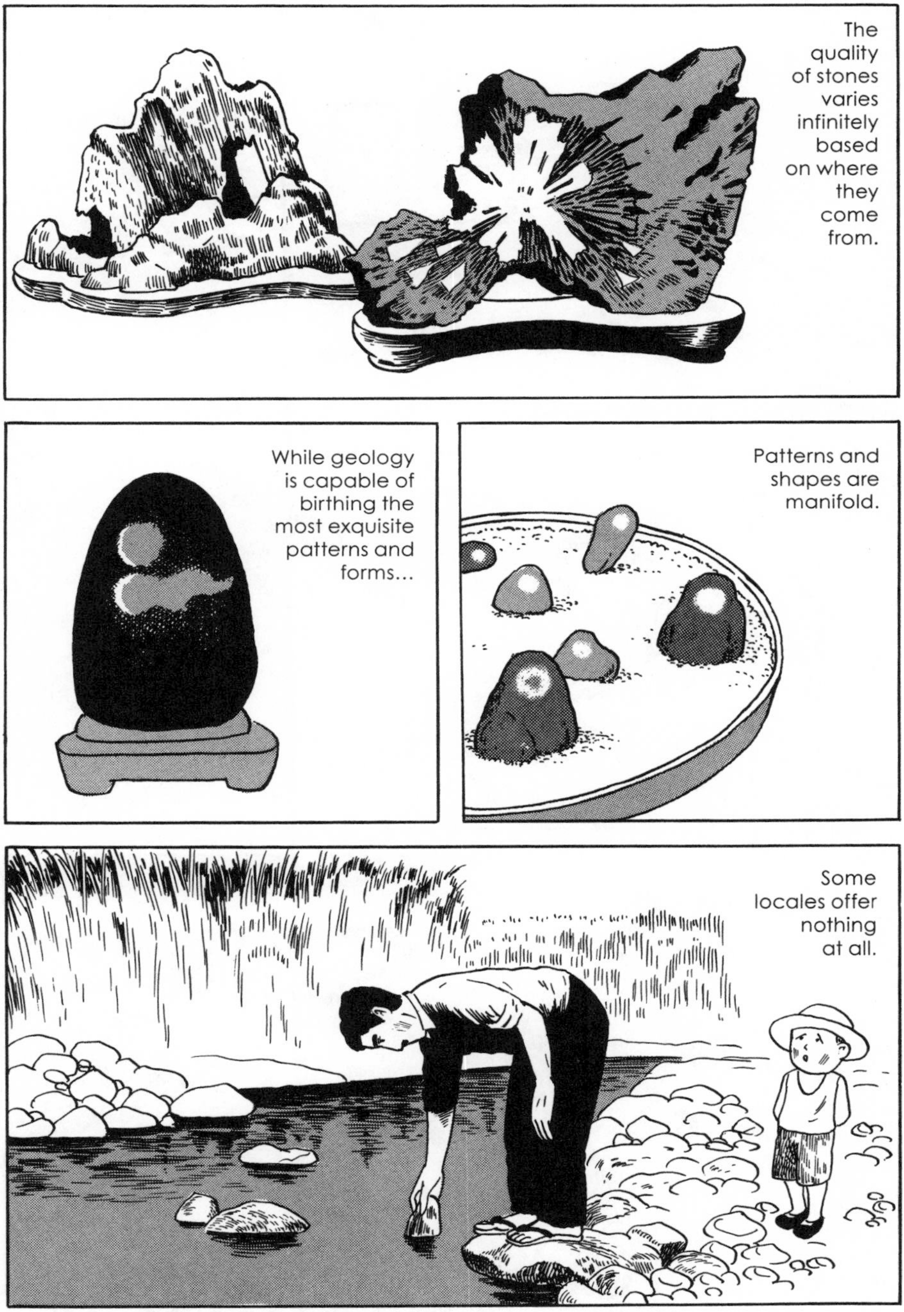
The quality of stones varies infinitely based on where they come from.
Patterns and shapes are manifold.
While geology is capable of birthing the most exquisite patterns and forms...
Some locales offer nothing at all.

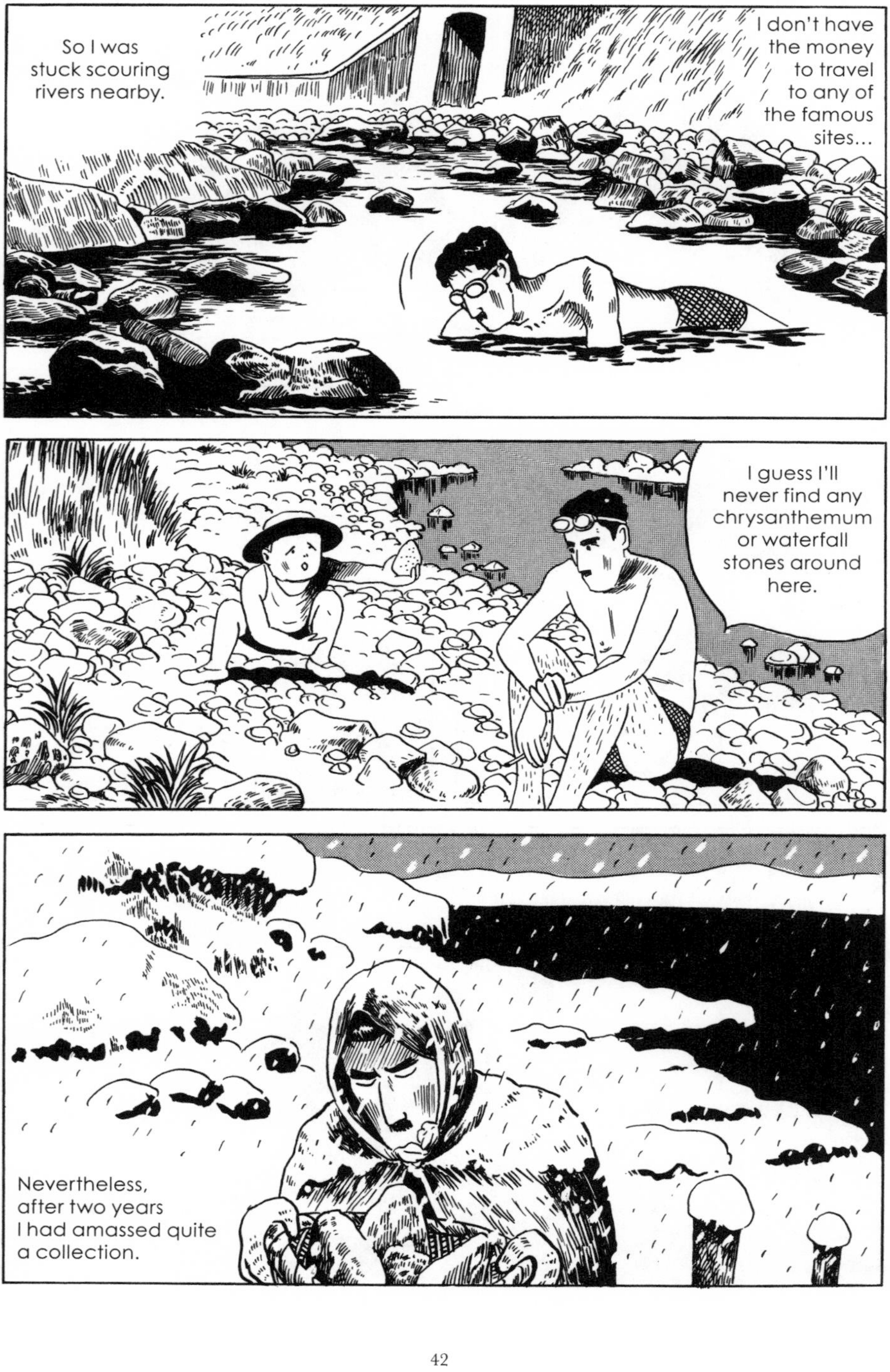
I don't have the money to travel to any of the famous sites…
So I was stuck scouring rivers nearby.
I guess I'll never find any chrysanthemum or waterfall stones around here.
Nevertheless, after two years I had amassed quite a collection.

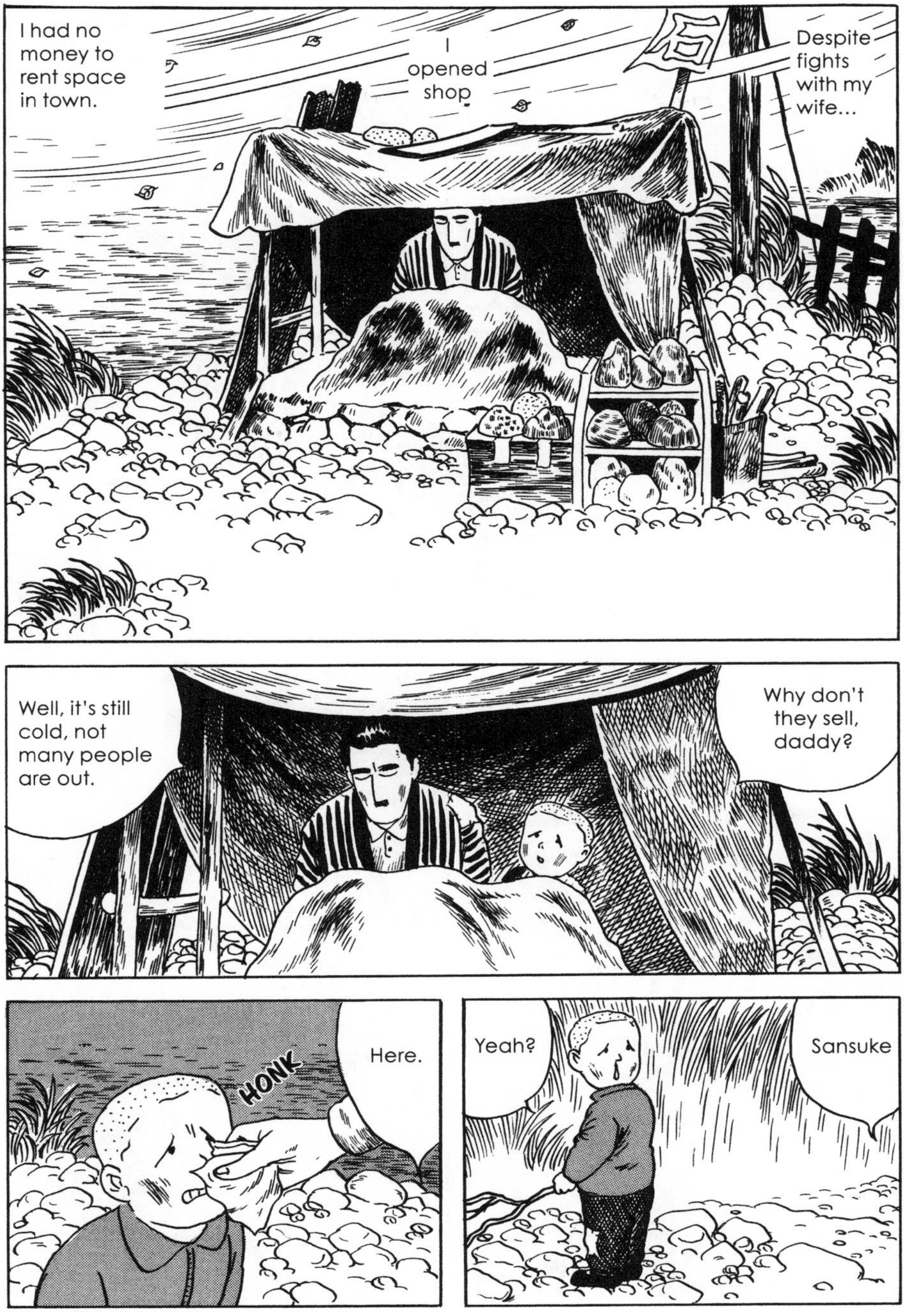
Despite fights with my wife...
I opened shop
I had no money to rent space in town.
Why don't they sell, daddy?
Well, it's still cold, not many people are out.
Sansuke
Yeah?
Here.
HONK

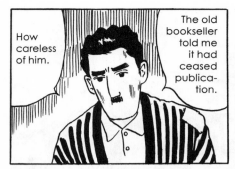

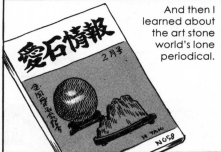

And then I learned about the art stone world's lone periodical.
愛石情報
The old bookseller told me it had ceased publica-tion.
How careless of him.
See the auction ad?
What a find!
Anybody can participate?
It looks like it.
愛石家大集合
第24回
愛石交換会
会費1000円
(飲食代込)
於 新宿H寺
It's being held at H Temple in Shinjuku.
You should apply.
I phoned the sponsor, the Art Stone Fanatics Association.
They agreed to meet me.

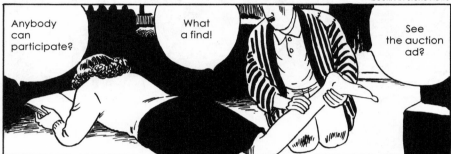

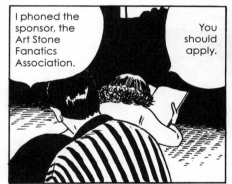

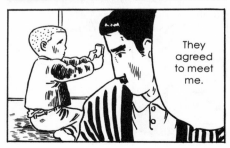

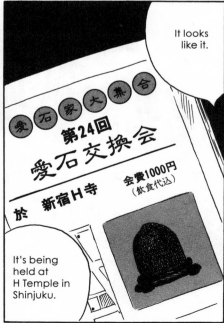

book: Art Stone News

ad: The 24th Art Stone Swap Meet, 1000 yen admission (includes lunch and beverage)

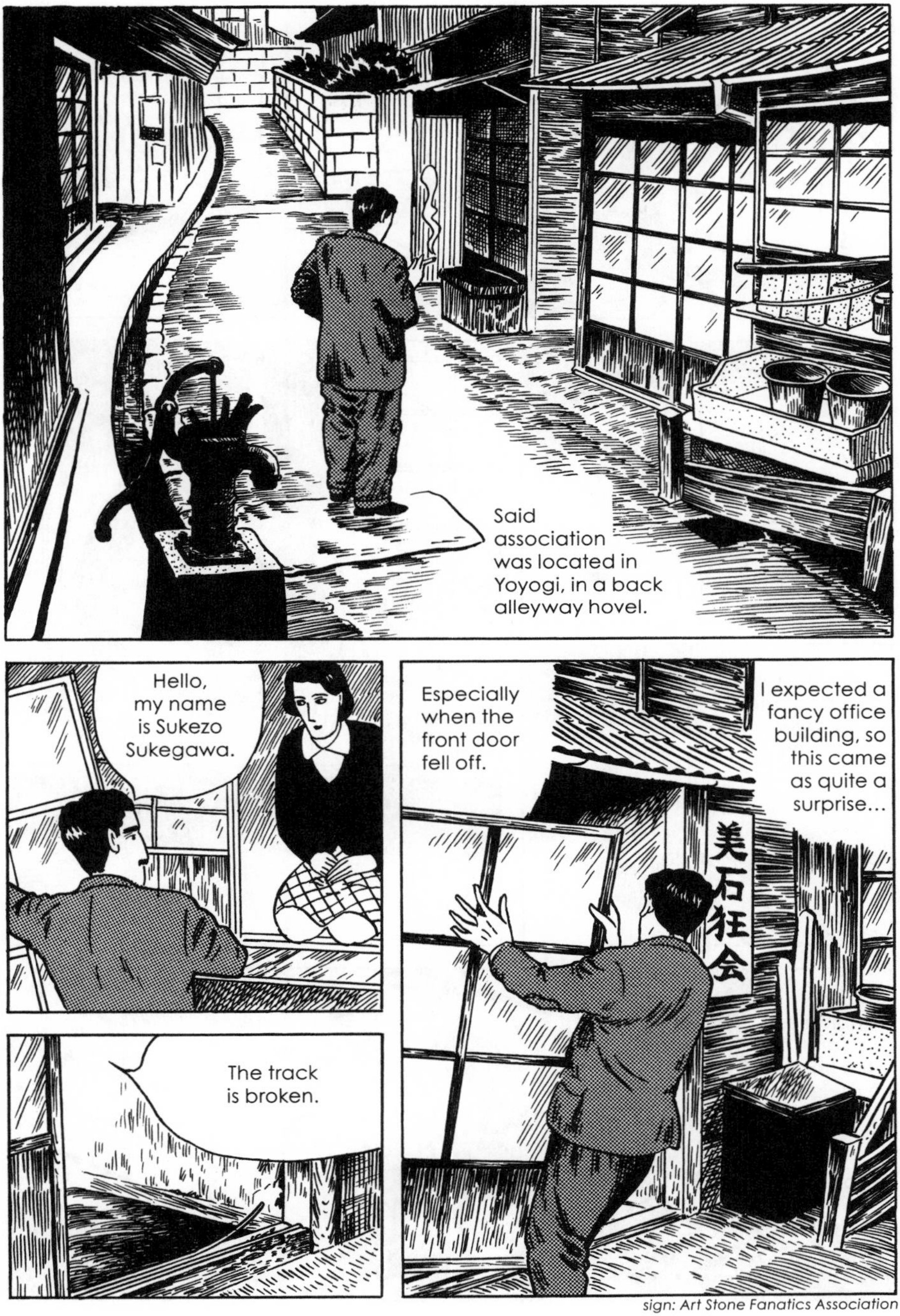
Said association was located in Yoyogi, in a back alleyway hovel.
I expected a fancy office building, so this came as quite a surprise…
Especially when the front door fell off.
美石狂会
Hello, my name is Sukezo Sukegawa.
The track is broken.

sign: Art Stone Fanatics Association

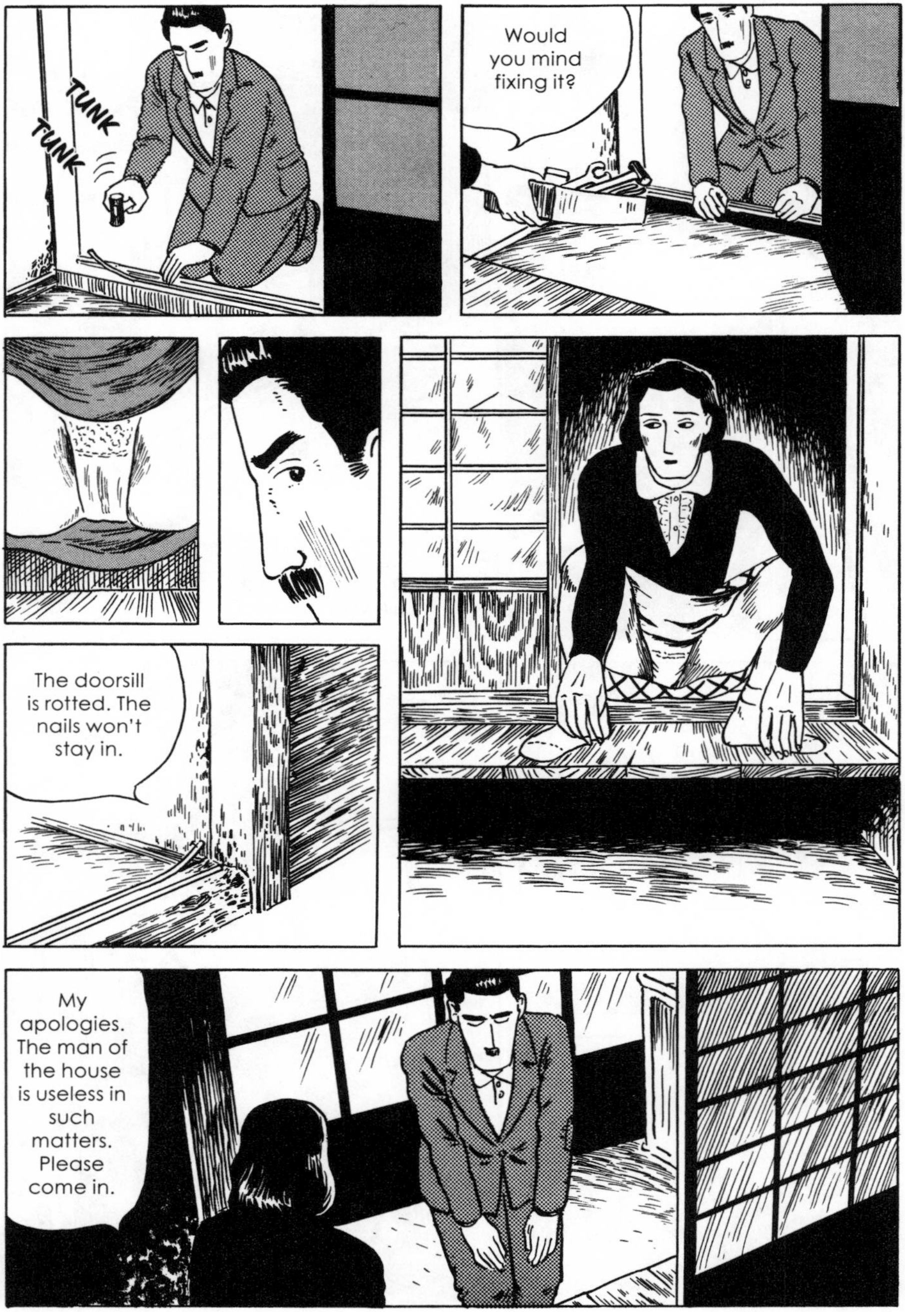
Would you mind fixing it?
TUNK
TUNK
The doorsill is rotted. The nails won't stay in.
My apologies. The man of the house is useless in such matters. Please come in.

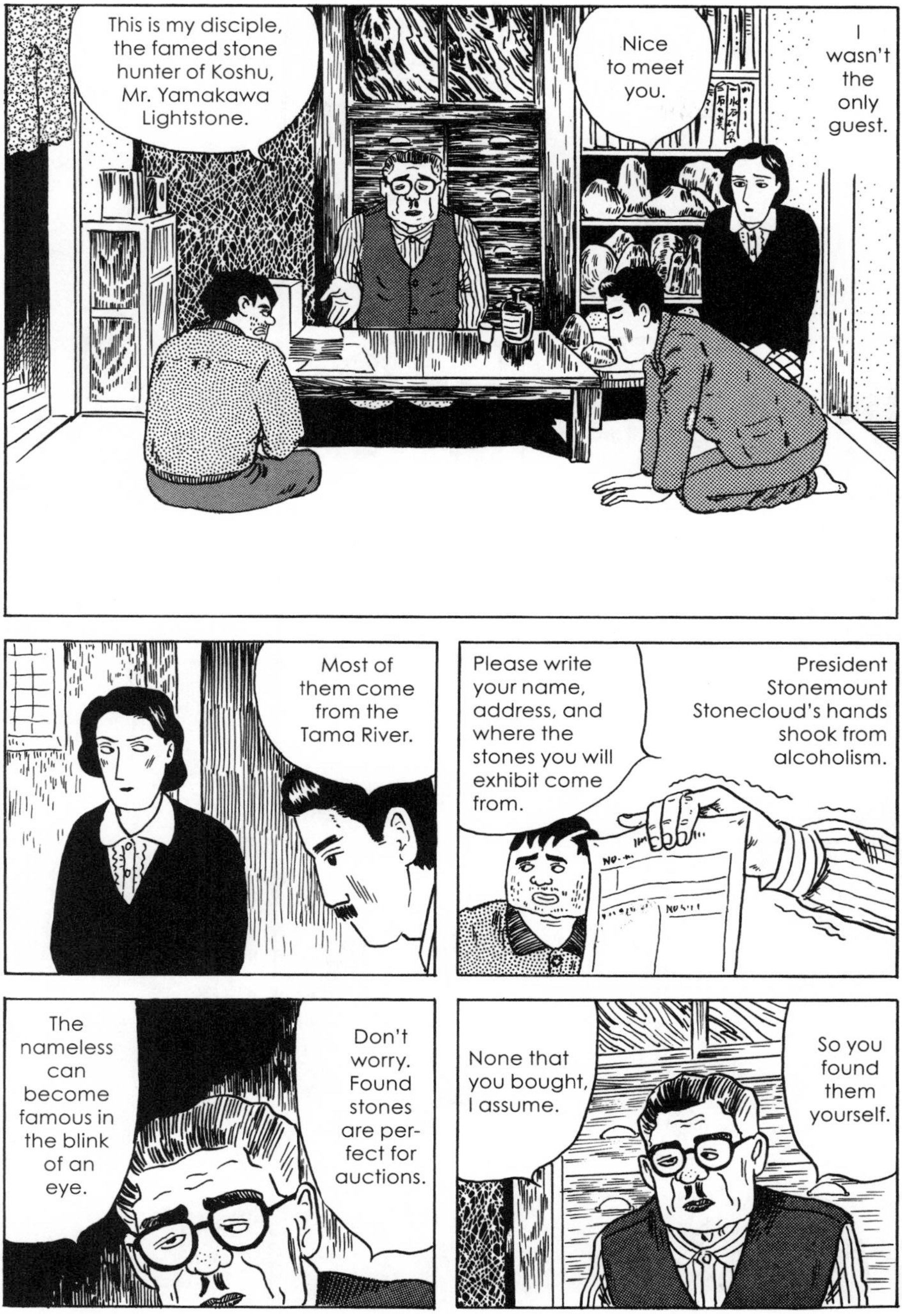
I wasn't the only guest.
Nice to meet you.
This is my disciple, the famed stone hunter of Koshu, Mr. Yamakawa Lightstone.
President Stonemount Stonecloud's hands shook from alcoholism.
Please write your name, address, and where the stones you will exhibit come from.
Most of them come from the Tama River.
So you found them yourself.
None that you bought, I assume.
Don't worry. Found stones are per-fect for auctions.
The nameless can become famous in the blink of an eye.

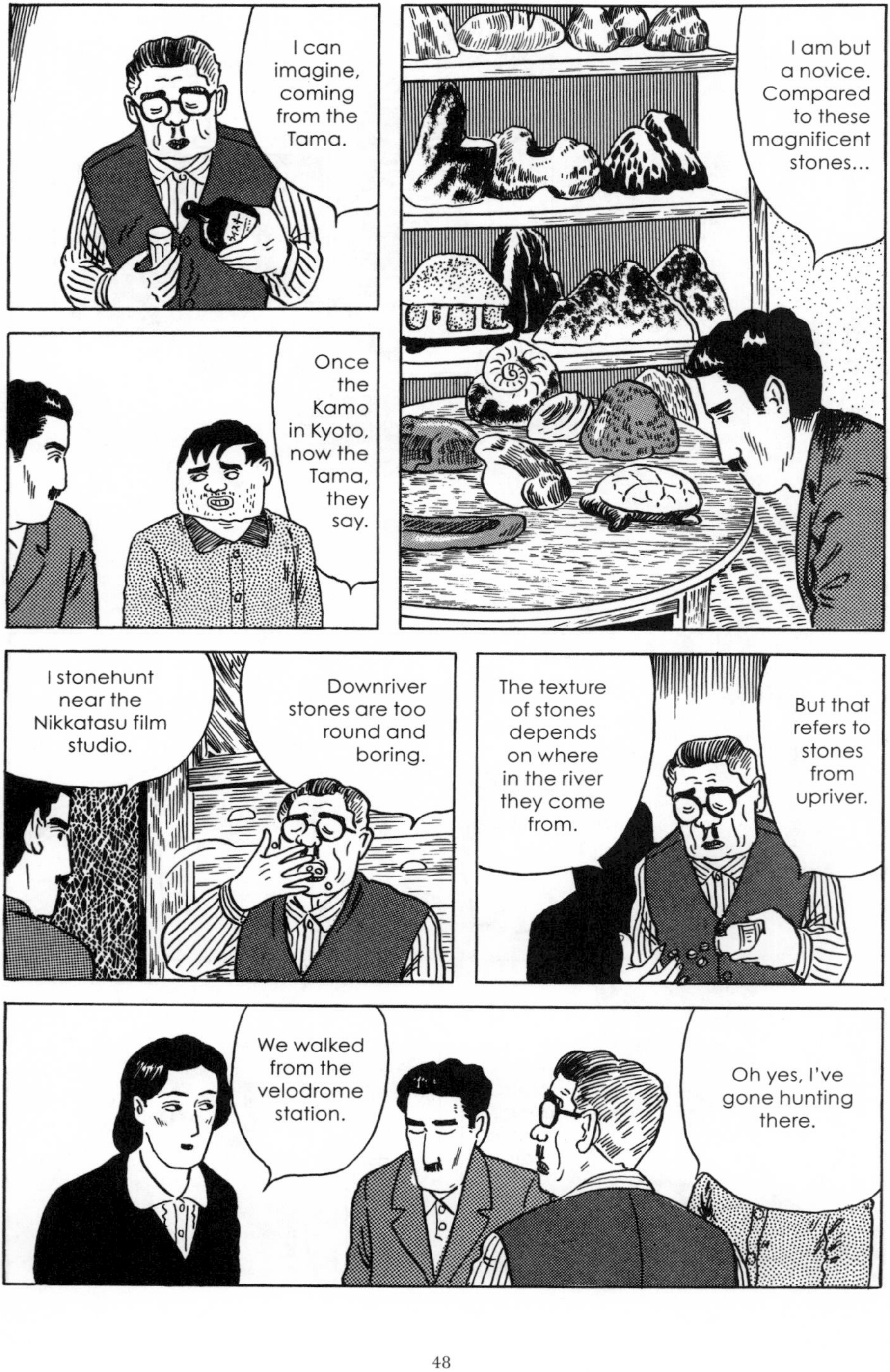

I can imagine, coming from the Tama.
I am but a novice. Compared to these magnificent stones...
Once the Kamo in Kyoto, now the Tama, they say.
I stonehunt near the Nikkatasu film studio.
Downriver stones are too round and boring.
The texture of stones depends on where in the river they come from.
But that refers to stones from upriver.
We walked from the velodrome station.
Oh yes, I've gone hunting there.

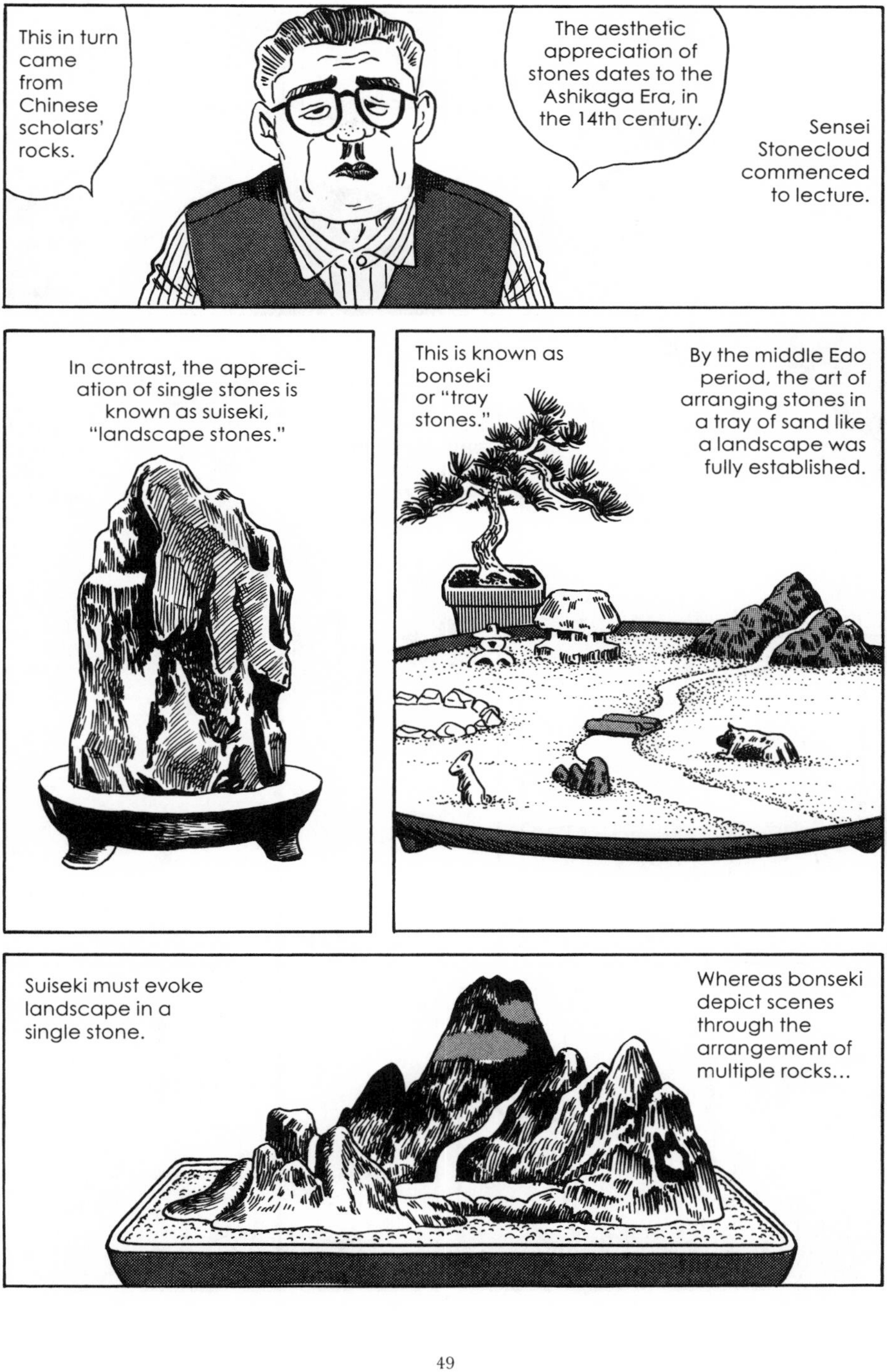
Sensei Stonecloud commenced to lecture.
The aesthetic appreciation of stones dates to the Ashikaga Era, in the 14th century.
This in turn came from Chinese scholars' rocks.
By the middle Edo period, the art of arranging stones in a tray of sand like a landscape was fully established.
This is known as bonseki or "tray stones."
In contrast, the appreciation of single stones is known as suiseki, "landscape stones."
Whereas bonseki depict scenes through the arrangement of multiple rocks...
Suiseki must evoke landscape in a single stone.

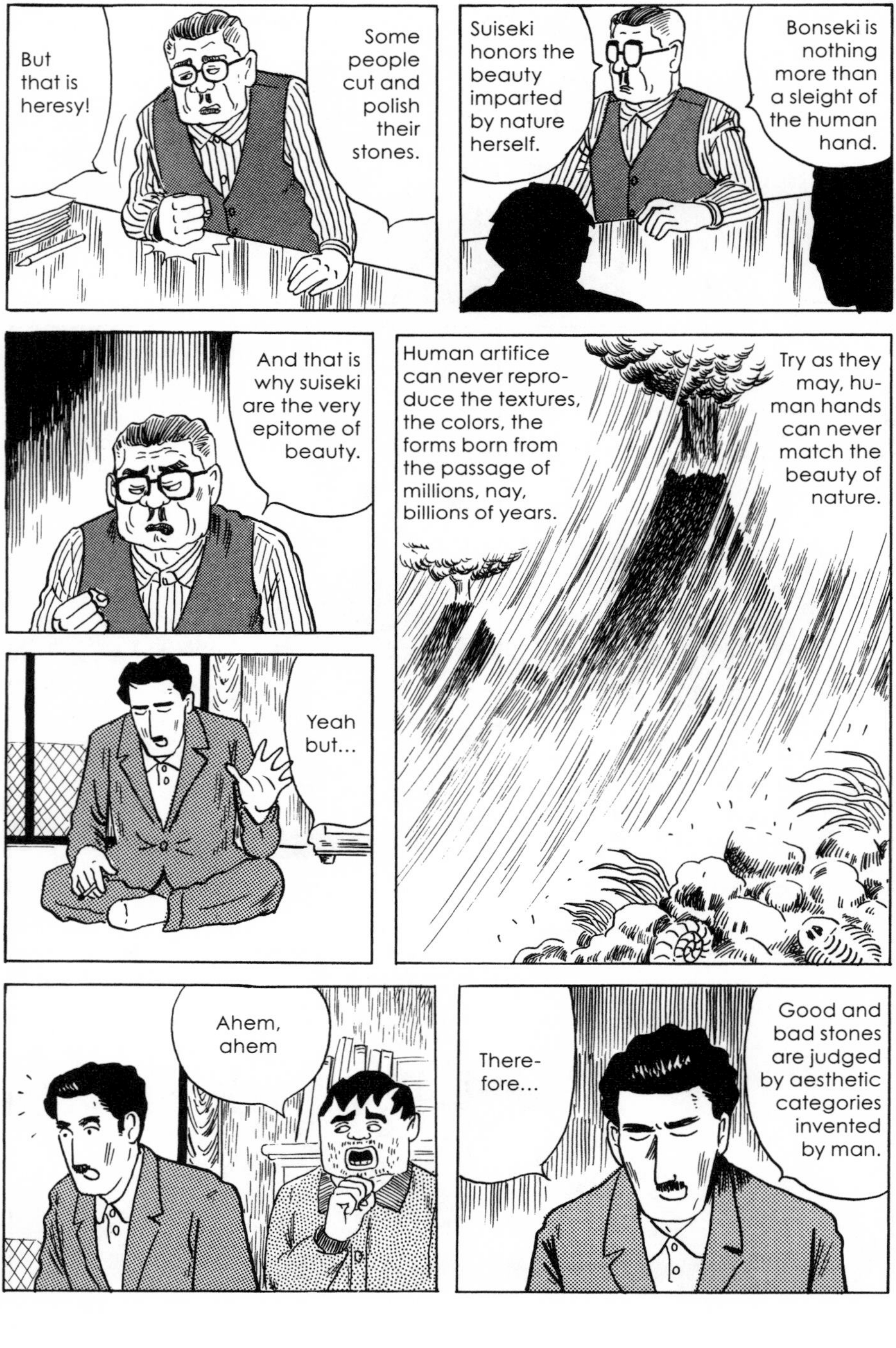
Bonseki is nothing more than a sleight of the human hand.
Suiseki honors the beauty imparted by nature herself.
Some people cut and polish their stones.
But that is heresy!
Try as they may, human hands can never match the beauty of nature.
Human artifice can never reproduce the textures, the colors, the forms born from the passage of millions, nay, billions of years.
And that is why suiseki are the very epitome of beauty.
Yeah but...
Good and bad stones are judged by aesthetic categories invented by man.
There-fore...
Ahem, ahem

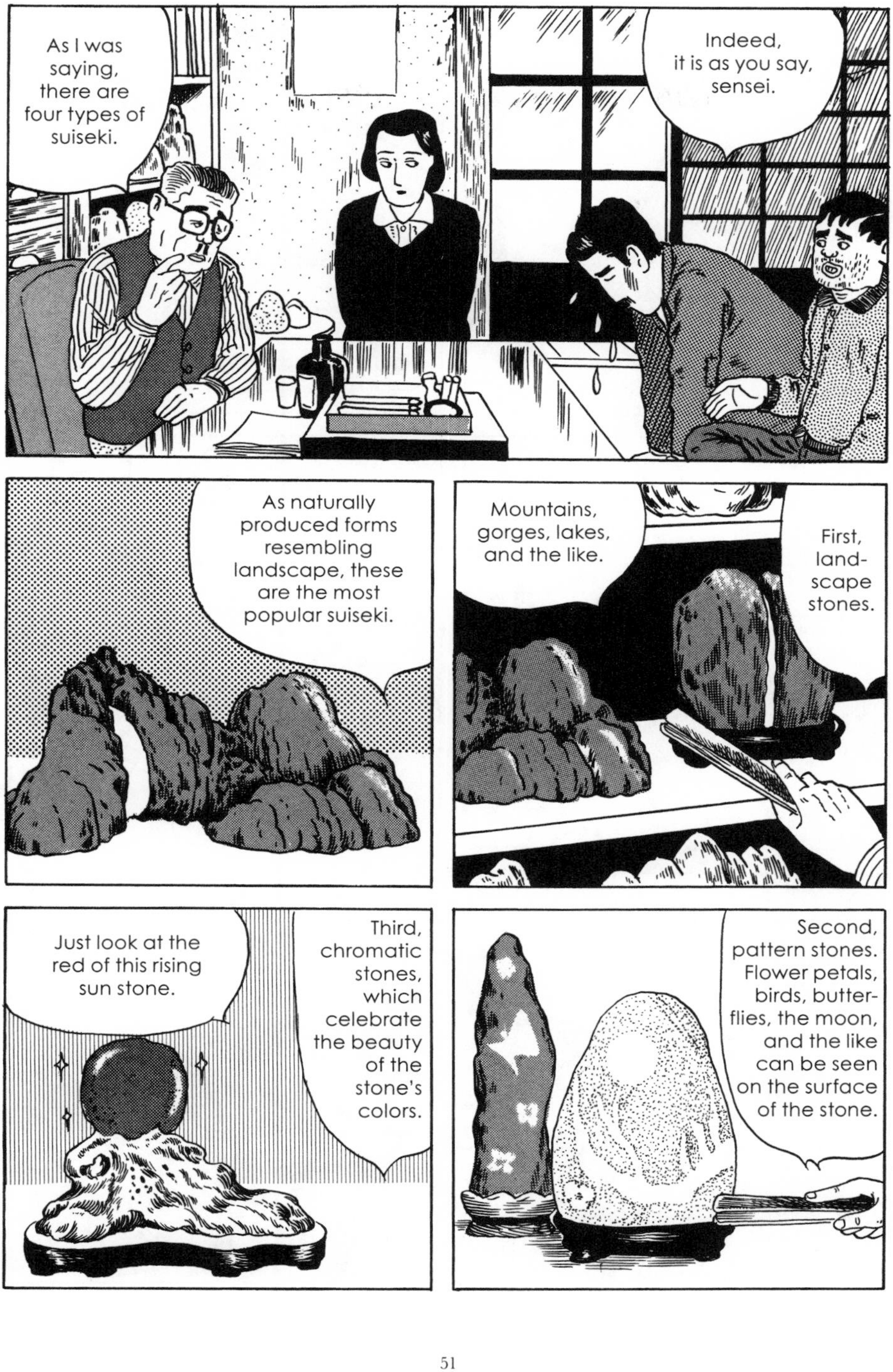
Indeed, it is as you say, sensei.
As I was saying, there are four types of suiseki.
First, land-scape stones.
Mountains, gorges, lakes, and the like.
As naturally produced forms resembling landscape, these are the most popular suiseki.
Second, pattern stones. Flower petals, birds, butter-flies, the moon, and the like can be seen on the surface of the stone.
Third, chromatic stones, which celebrate the beauty of the stone's colors.
Just look at the red of this rising sun stone.

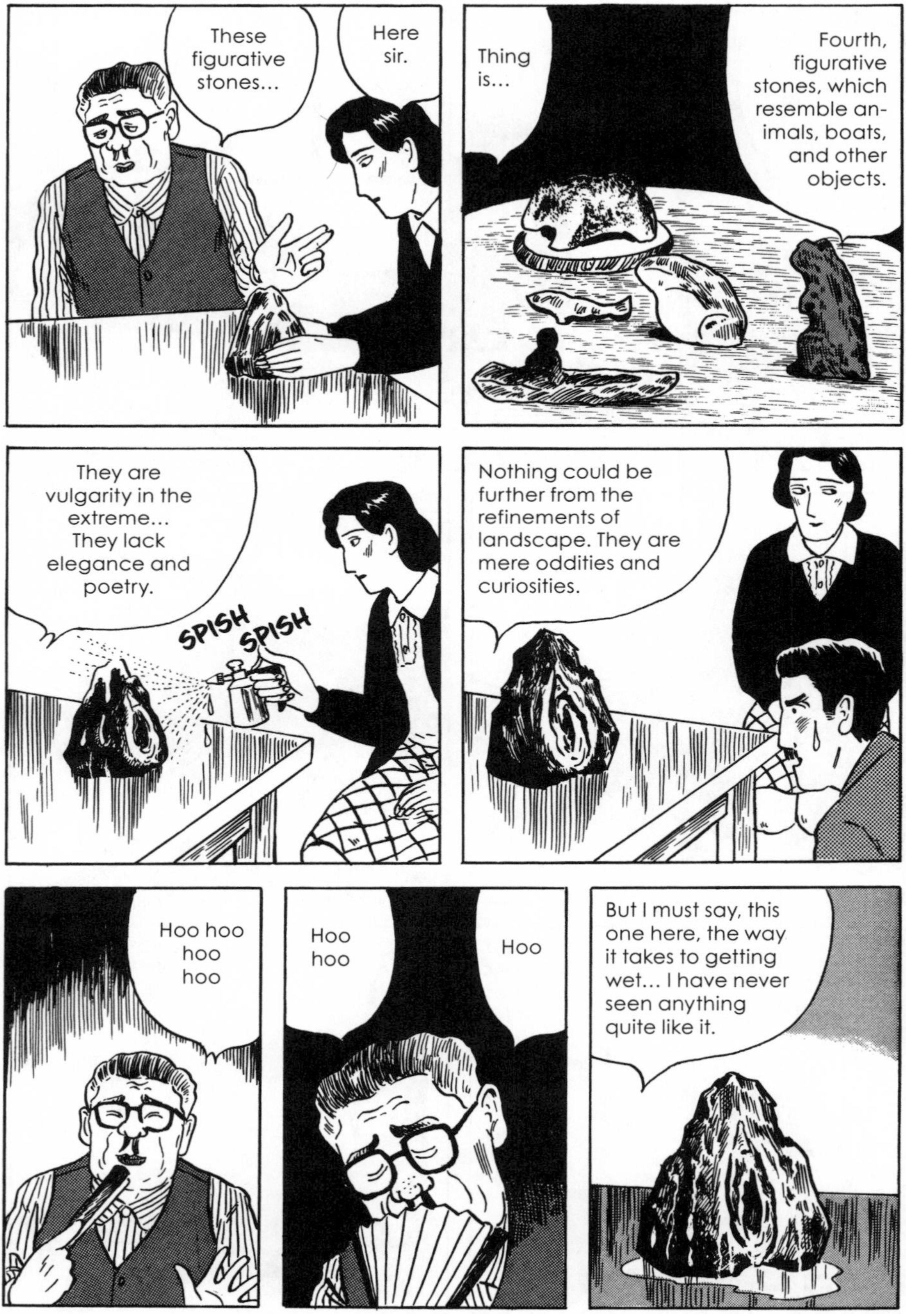

Fourth, figurative stones, which resemble animals, boats, and other objects.
Thing is...
Here sir.
These figurative stones...
Nothing could be further from the refinements of landscape. They are mere oddities and curiosities.
They are vulgarity in the extreme... They lack elegance and poetry.
SPISH
SPISH
But I must say, this one here, the way it takes to getting wet... I have never seen anything quite like it.
Hoo
Hoo hoo
Hoo hoo hoo hoo

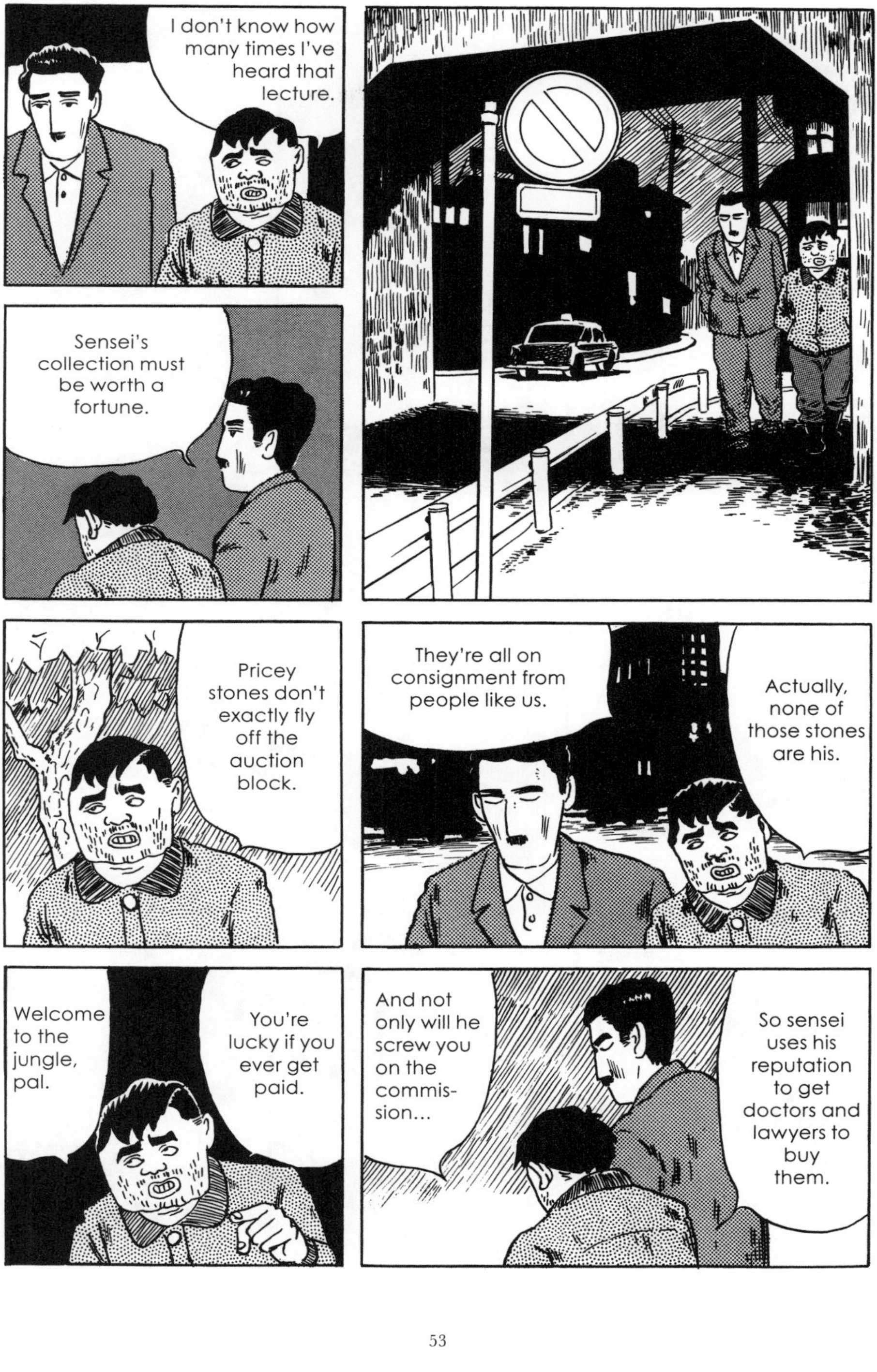

I don't know how many times I've heard that lecture.
Sensei's collection must be worth a fortune.
Actually, none of those stones are his.
They're all on consignment from people like us.
Pricey stones don't exactly fly off the auction block.
So sensei uses his reputation to get doctors and lawyers to buy them.
And not only will he screw you on the commis-sion...
You're lucky if you ever get paid.
Welcome to the jungle, pal.

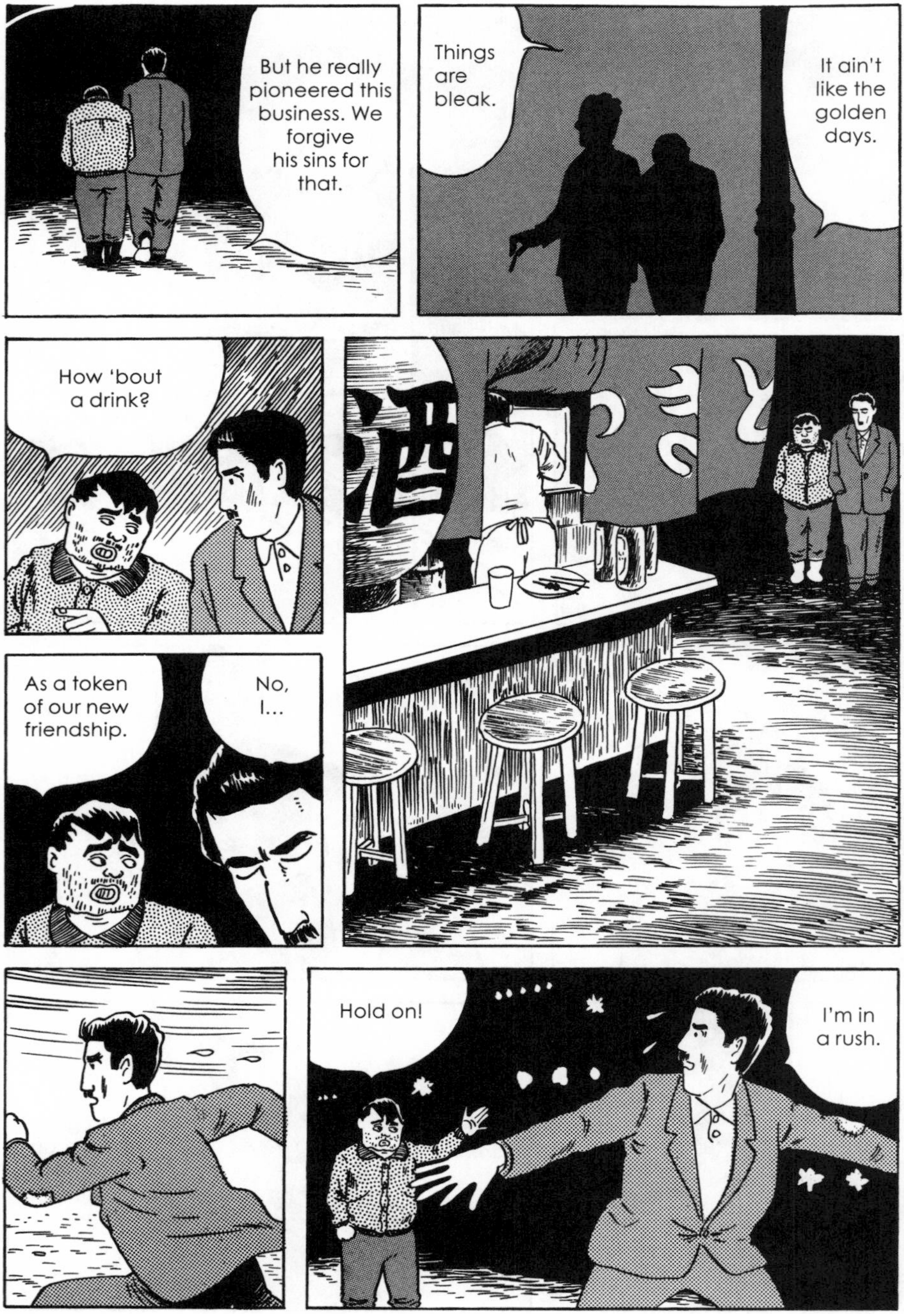
It ain't like the golden days.
Things are bleak.
But he really pioneered this business. We forgive his sins for that.
No, I...
How 'bout a drink?
As a token of our new friendship.
I'm in a rush.
Hold on!

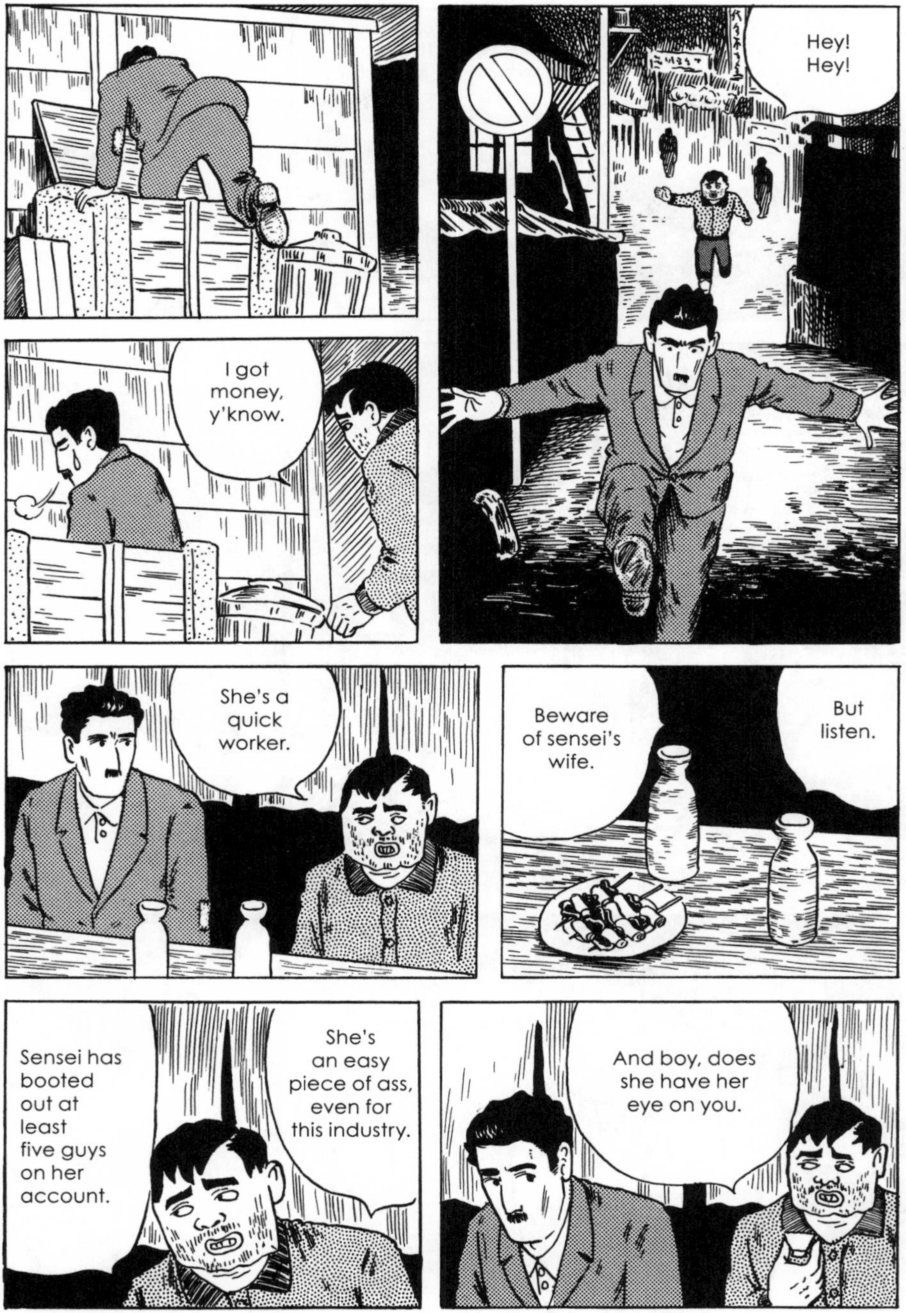
Hey! Hey!
I got money, y'know.
But listen.
Beware of sensei's wife.
She's a quick worker.
And boy, does she have her eye on you.
She's an easy piece of ass, even for this industry.
Sensei has booted out at least five guys on her account.

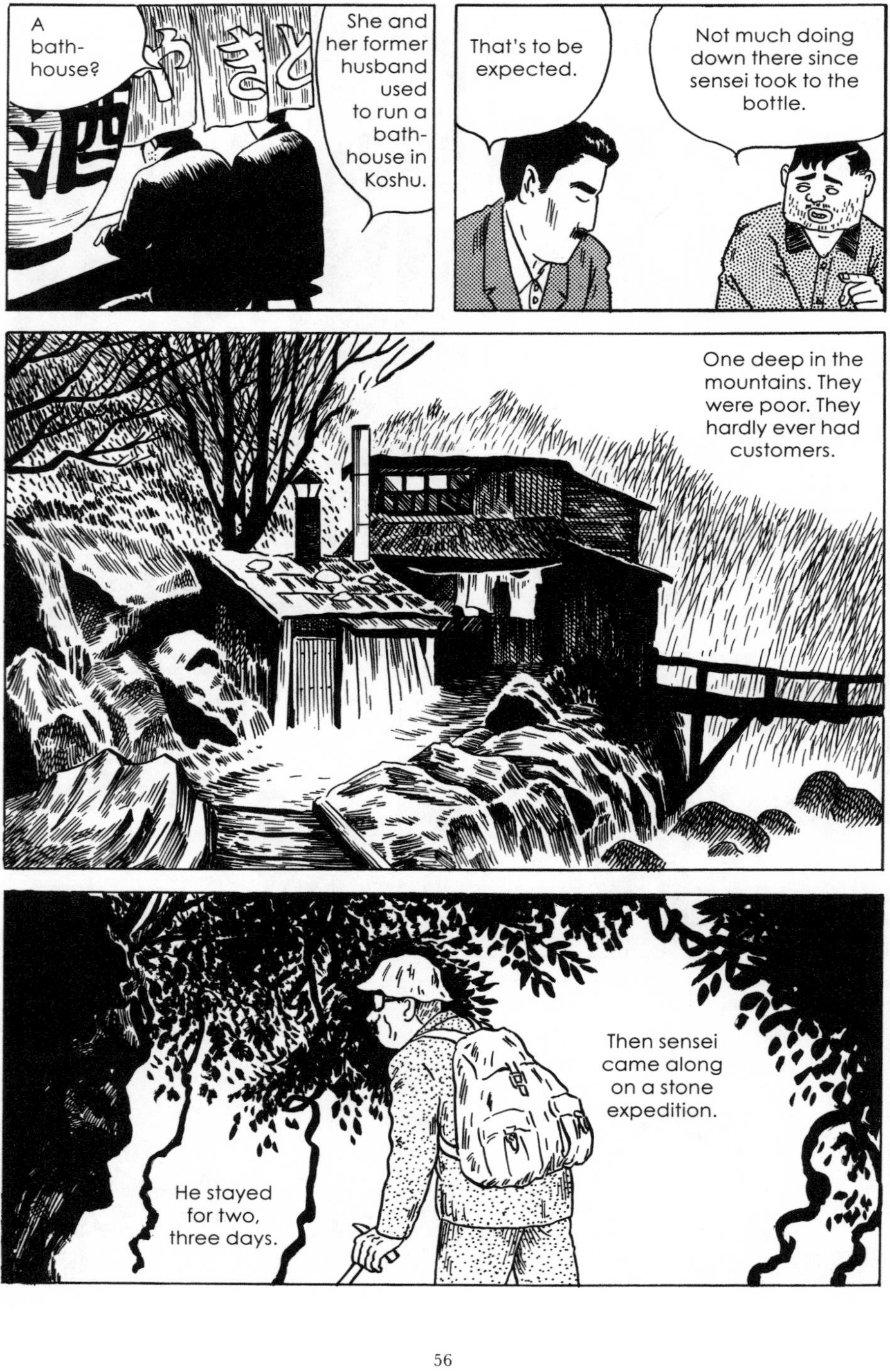
Not much doing down there since sensei took to the bottle.
That's to be expected.
She and her former husband used to run a bath-house in Koshu.
A bath-house?
One deep in the mountains. They were poor. They hardly ever had customers.
Then sensei came along on a stone expedition.
He stayed for two, three days.

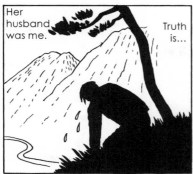

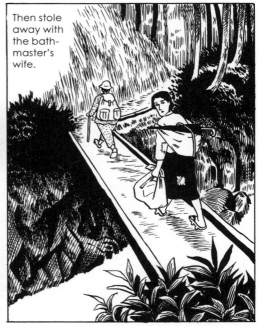

Then stole away with the bath-master's wife.
Truth is...
Her husband was me.
WAAAA
Time and again, I went to sensei's to get her back.
Before I knew it, he was teaching me rocks.
Our life in the mountains was miserable. We trapped snakes, made bird nesting boxes and dispos-able chopsticks

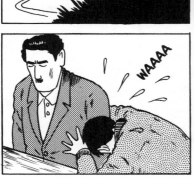

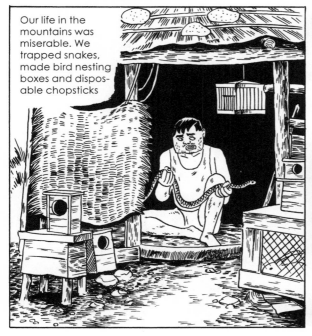

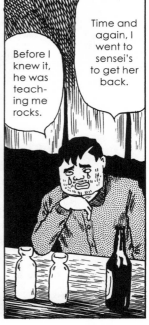

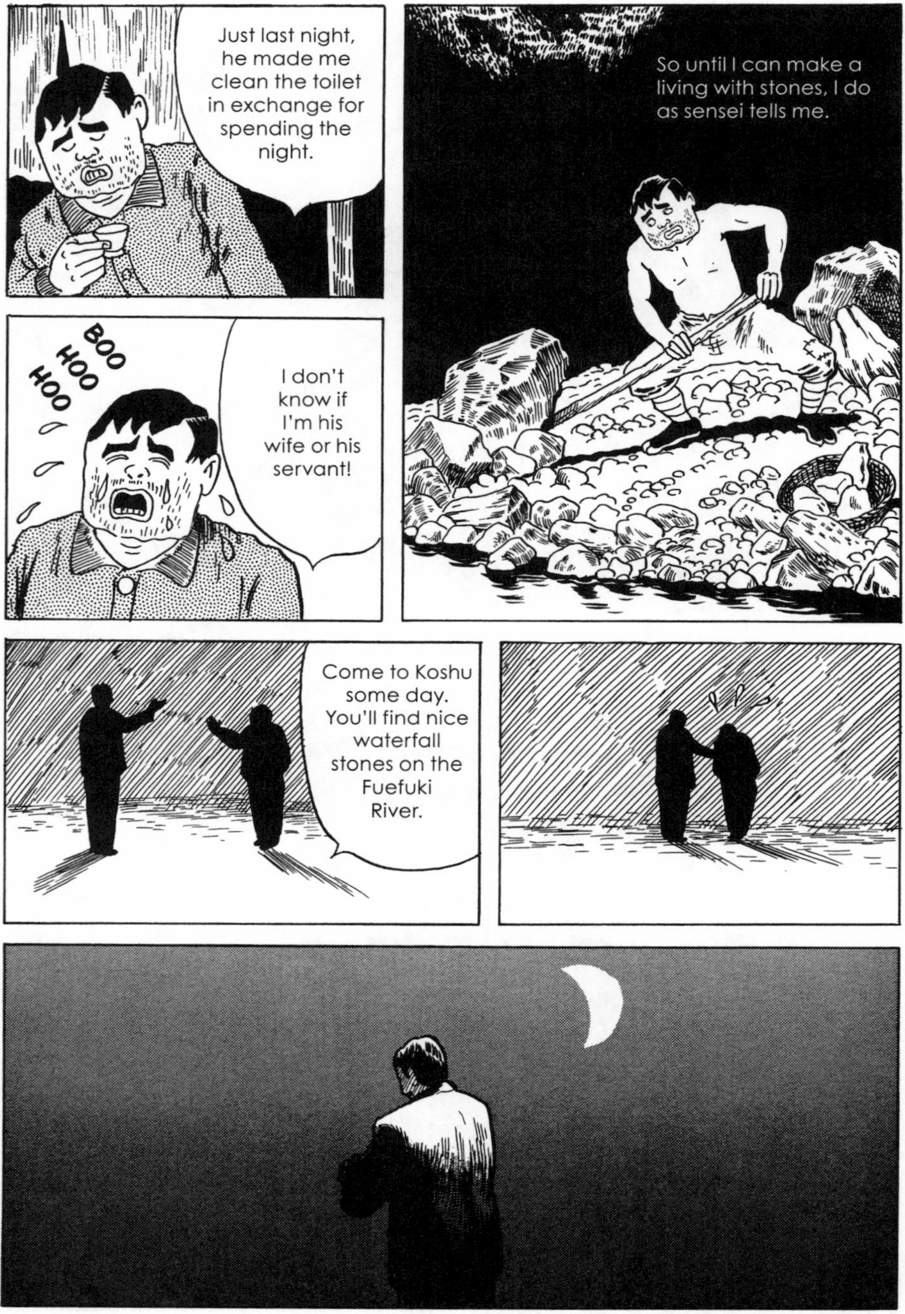
Just last night, he made me clean the toilet in exchange for spending the night.
BOO HOO HOO
I don't know if I'm his wife or his servant!
So until I can make a living with stones, I do as sensei tells me.
Come to Koshu some day. You'll find nice waterfall stones on the Fuefuki River.

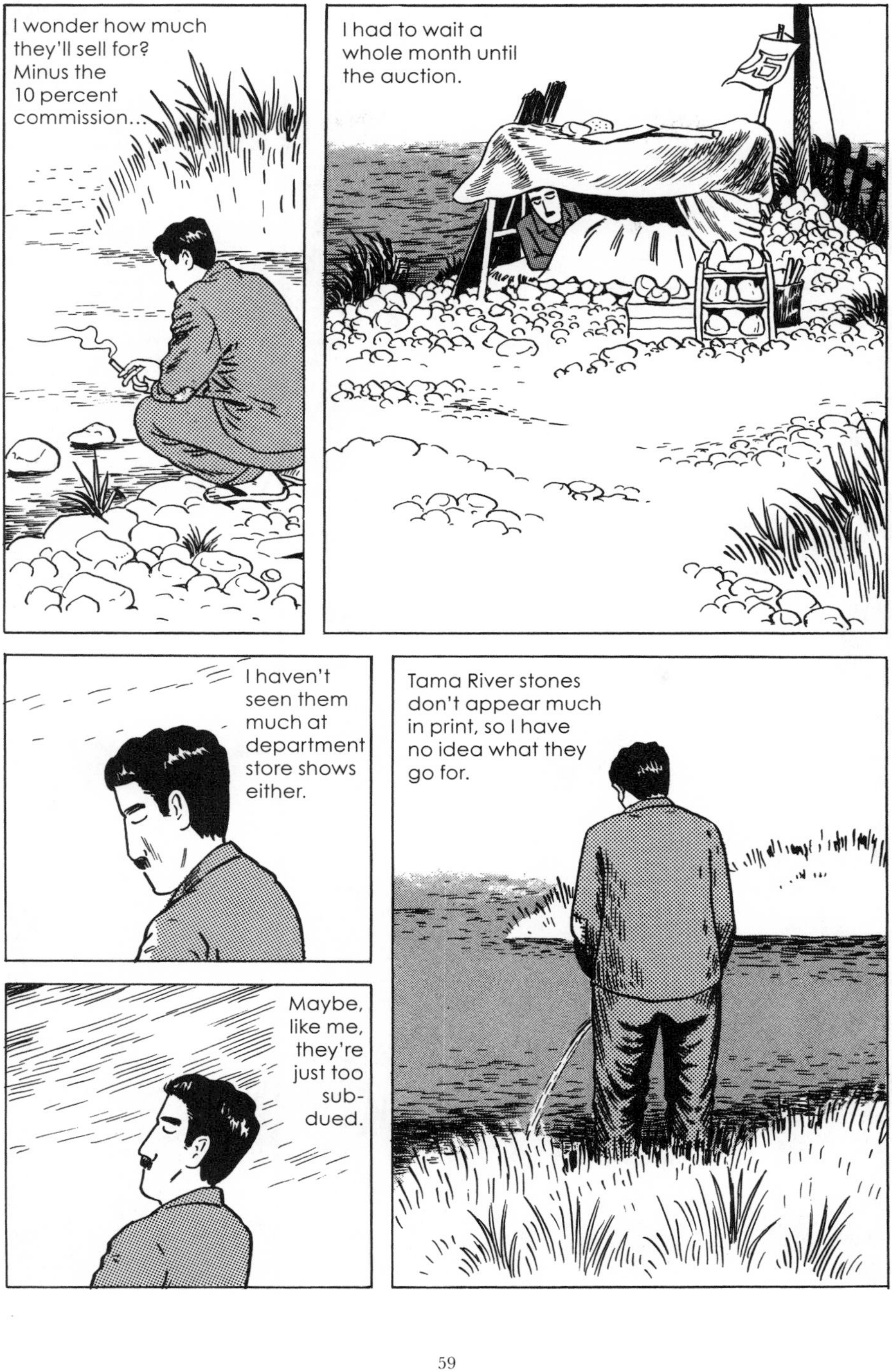
I had to wait a whole month until the auction.
I wonder how much they'll sell for? Minus the 10 percent commission...
Tama River stones don't appear much in print, so I have no idea what they go for.
I haven't seen them much at department store shows either.
Maybe, like me, they're just too sub-dued.

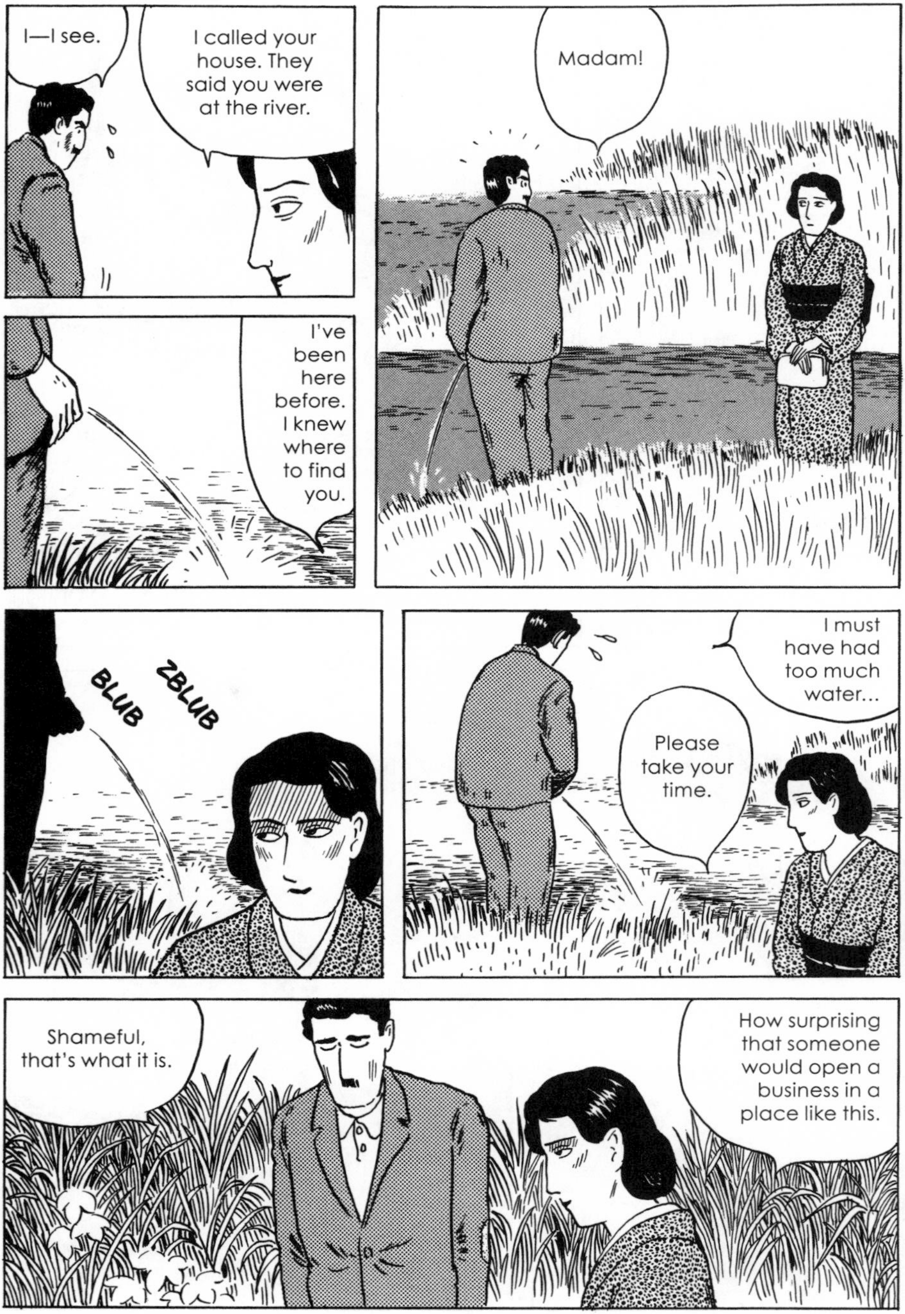
Madam!
I called your house. They said you were at the river.
I—I see.
I've been here before. I knew where to find you.
I must have had too much water...
Please take your time.
ZBLUB
BLUB
How surprising that someone would open a business in a place like this.
Shameful, that's what it is.

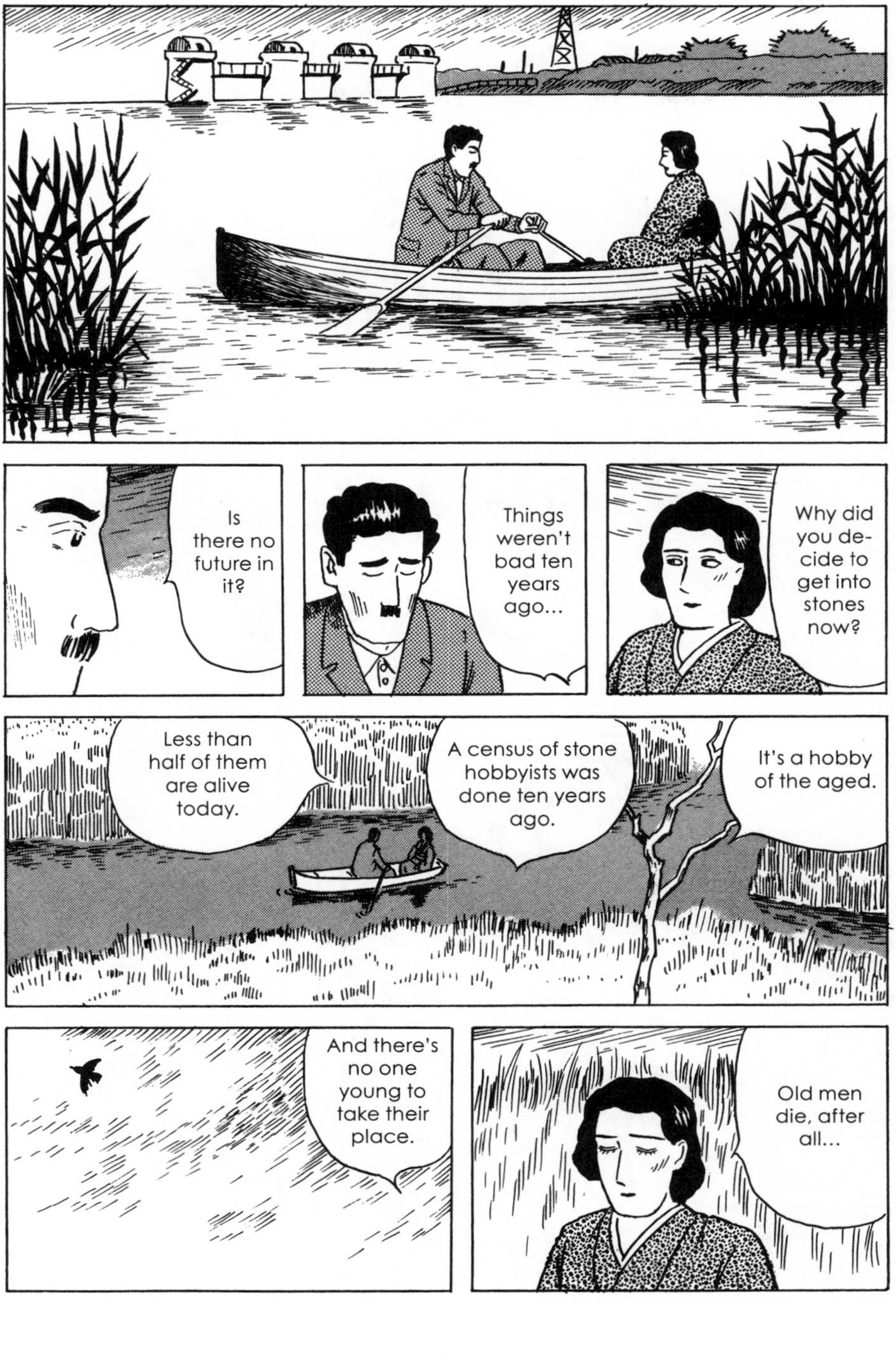
Why did you decide to get into stones now?
Things weren't bad ten years ago...
Is there no future in it?
It's a hobby of the aged.
A census of stone hobbyists was done ten years ago.
Less than half of them are alive today.
Old men die, after all...
And there's no one young to take their place.

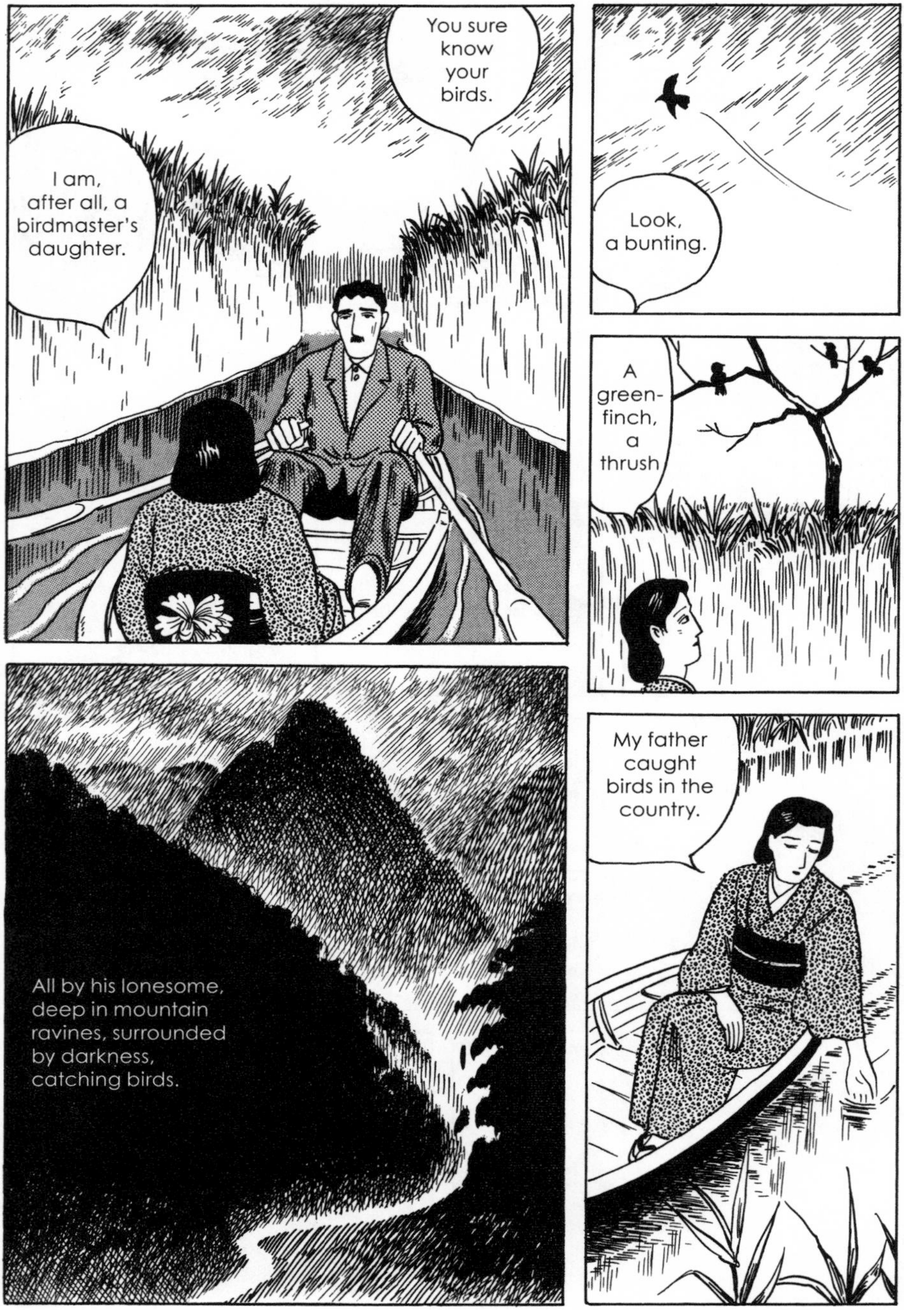
Look, a bunting.
A greenfinch, a thrush
You sure know your birds.
I am, after all, a birdmaster's daughter.
My father caught birds in the country.
All by his lonesome, deep in mountain ravines, surrounded by darkness, catching birds.

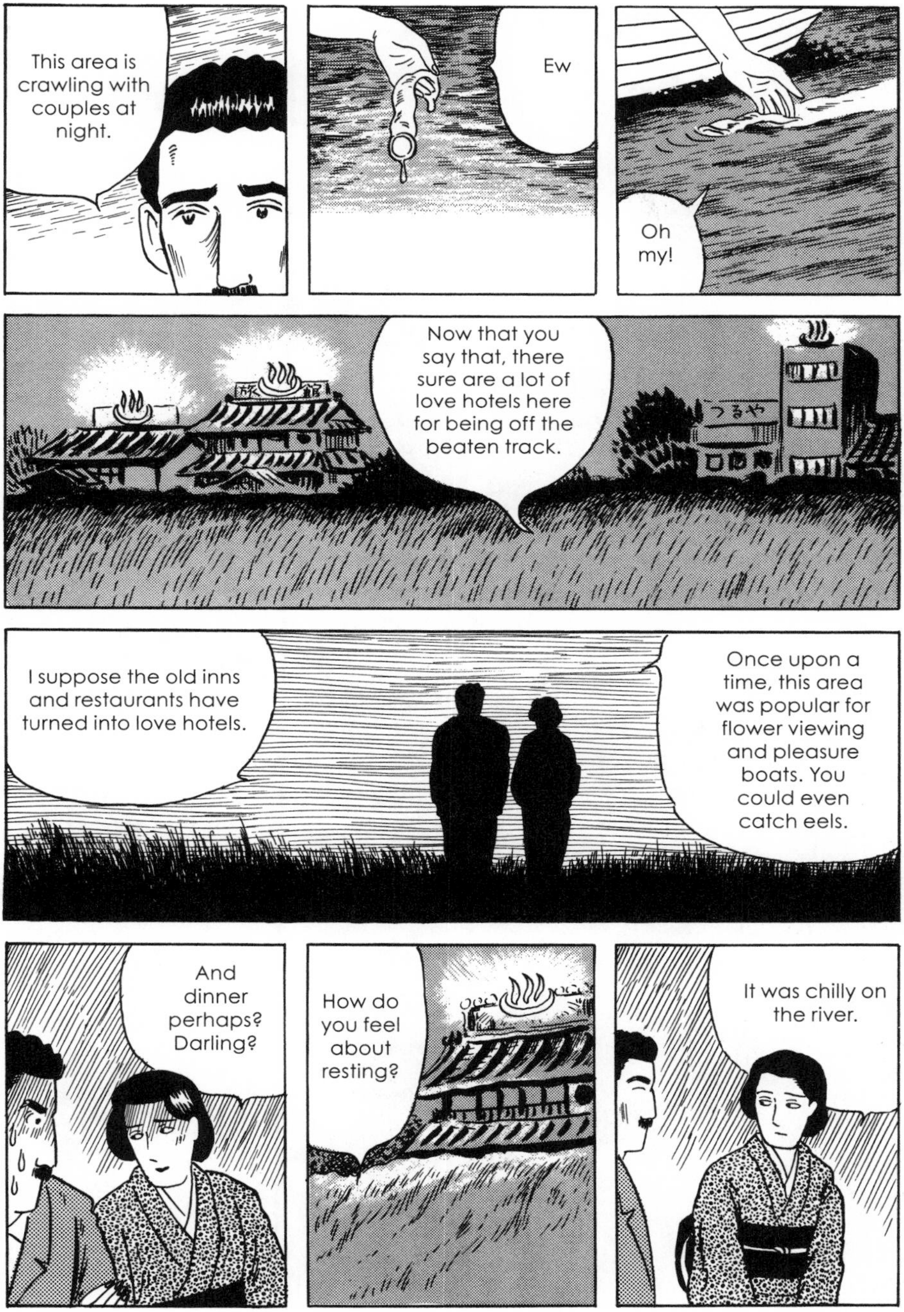
Oh my!
Ew
This area is crawling with couples at night.
Now that you say that, there sure are a lot of love hotels here for being off the beaten track.
つるや
Once upon a time, this area was popular for flower viewing and pleasure boats. You could even catch eels.
I suppose the old inns and restaurants have turned into love hotels.
It was chilly on the river.
How do you feel about resting?
And dinner perhaps? Darling?

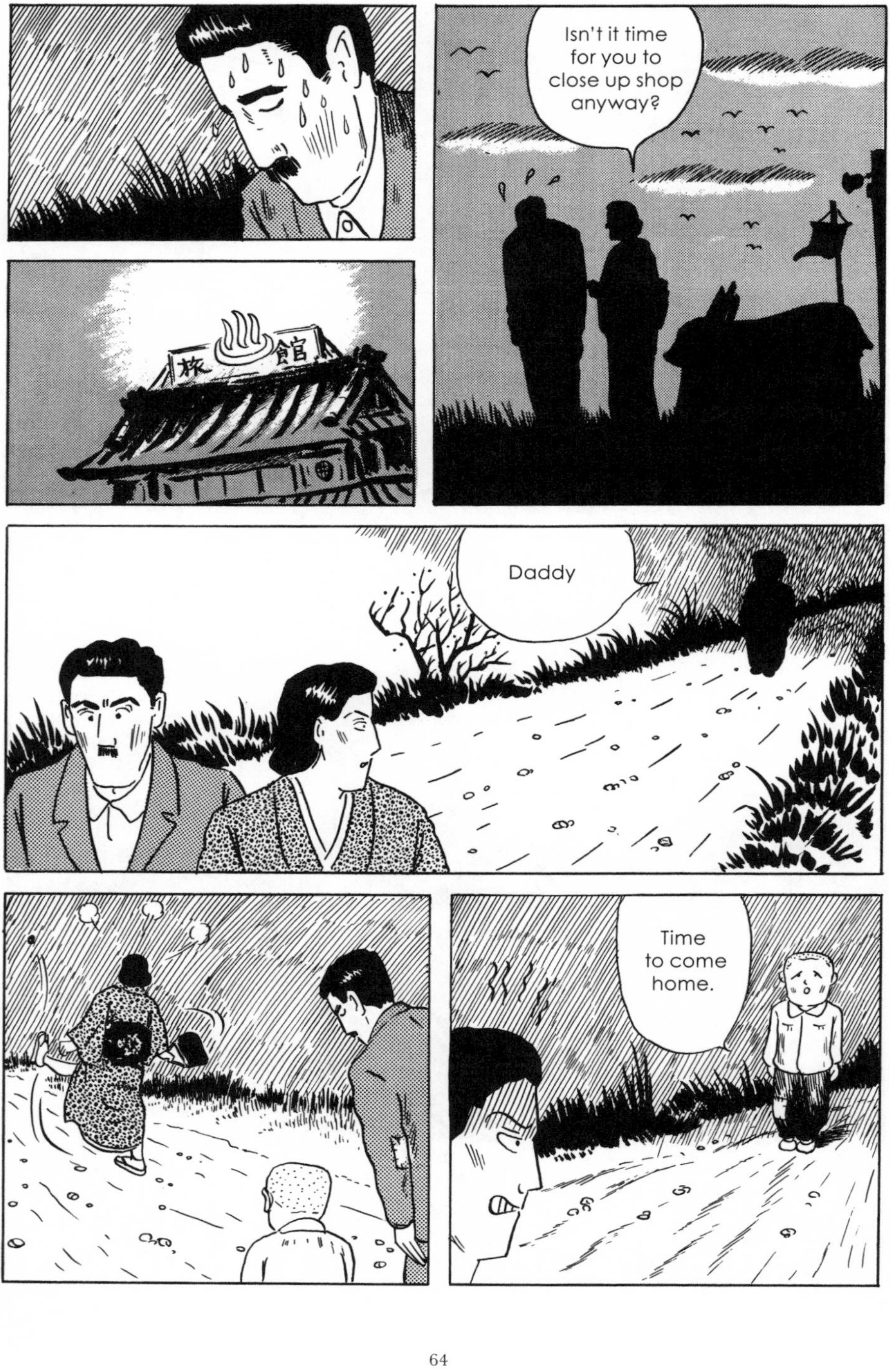

Isn't it time for you to close up shop anyway?
旅館
Daddy
Time to come home.

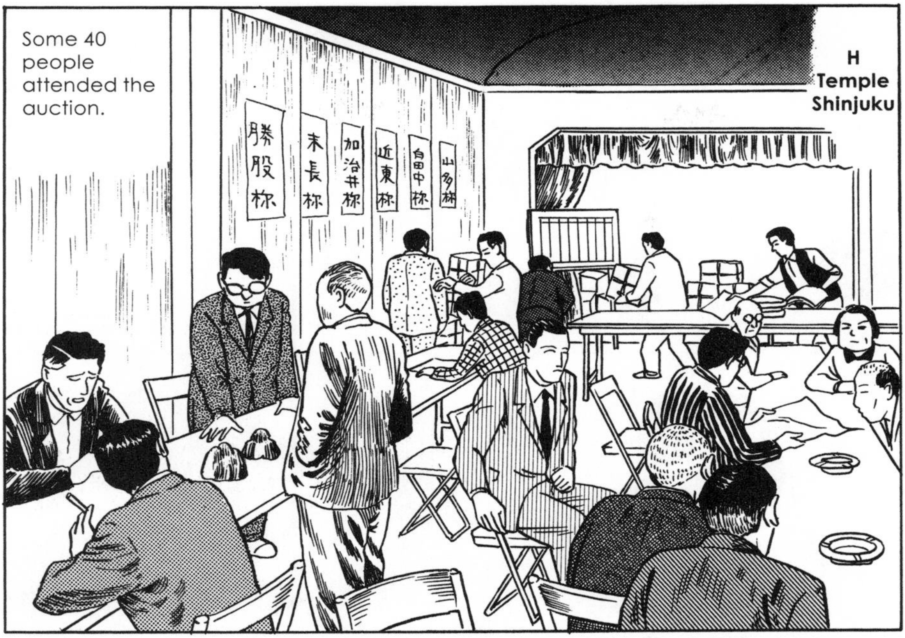
H Temple Shinjuku
Some 40 people attended the auction.
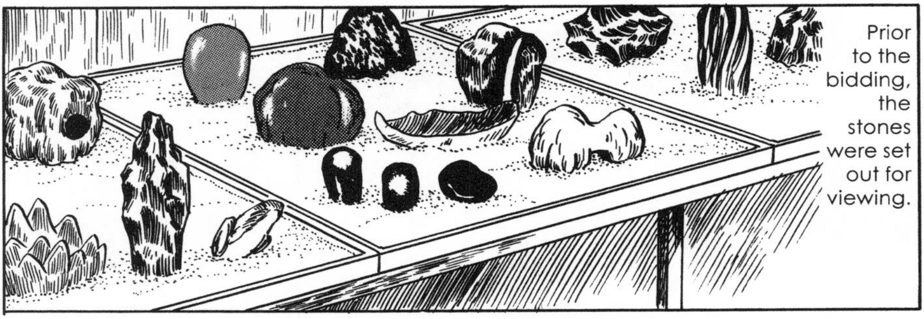
Prior to the bidding, the stones were set out for viewing.
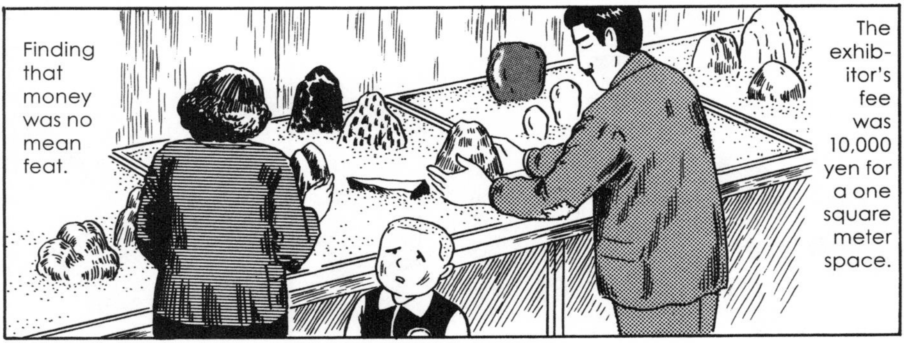
The exhibitor's fee was 10,000 yen for a one square meter space.
Finding that money was no mean feat.

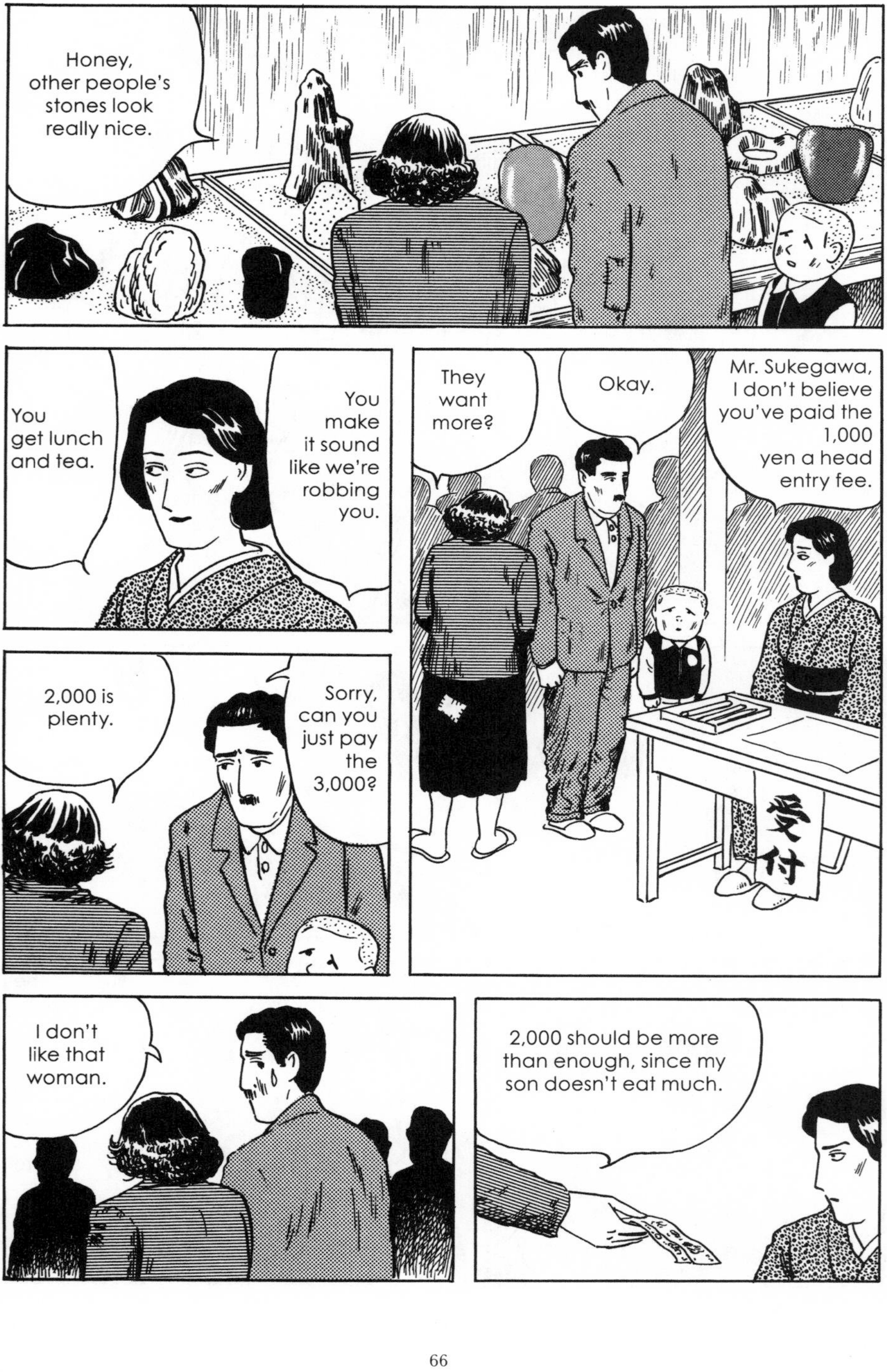
Honey, other people's stones look really nice.
Mr. Sukegawa, I don't believe you've paid the 1,000 yen a head entry fee.
受付
Okay.
They want more?
You make it sound like we're robbing you.
You get lunch and tea.
Sorry, can you just pay the 3,000?
2,000 is plenty.
2,000 should be more than enough, since my son doesn't eat much.
I don't like that woman.

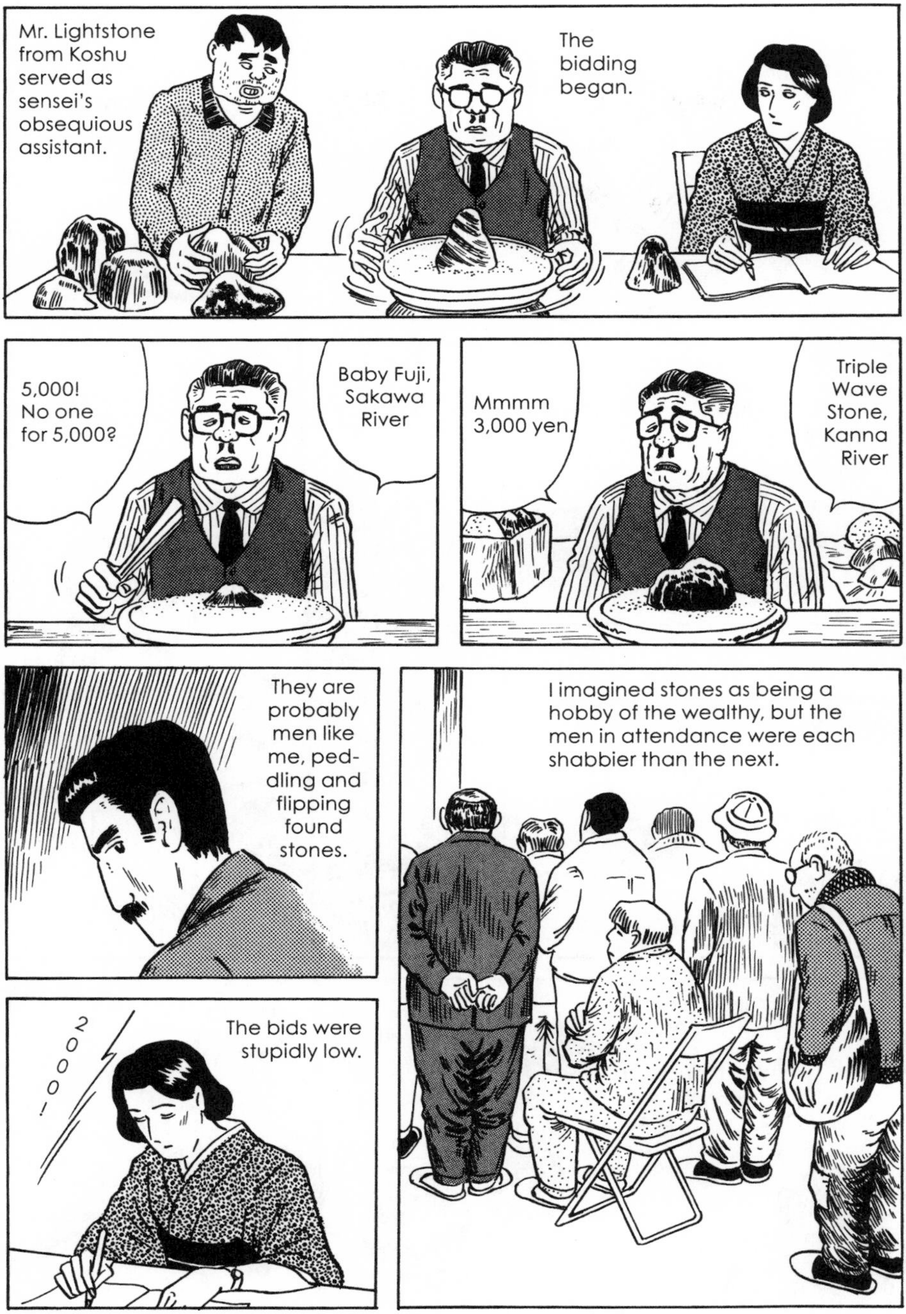

Mr. Lightstone from Koshu served as sensei's obsequious assistant.
The bidding began.
Triple Wave Stone, Kanna River
Mmmm 3,000 yen.
Baby Fuji, Sakawa River
5,000! No one for 5,000?
I imagined stones as being a hobby of the wealthy, but the men in attendance were each shabbier than the next.
They are probably men like me, ped-dling and flipping found stones.
The bids were stupidly low.
2000!

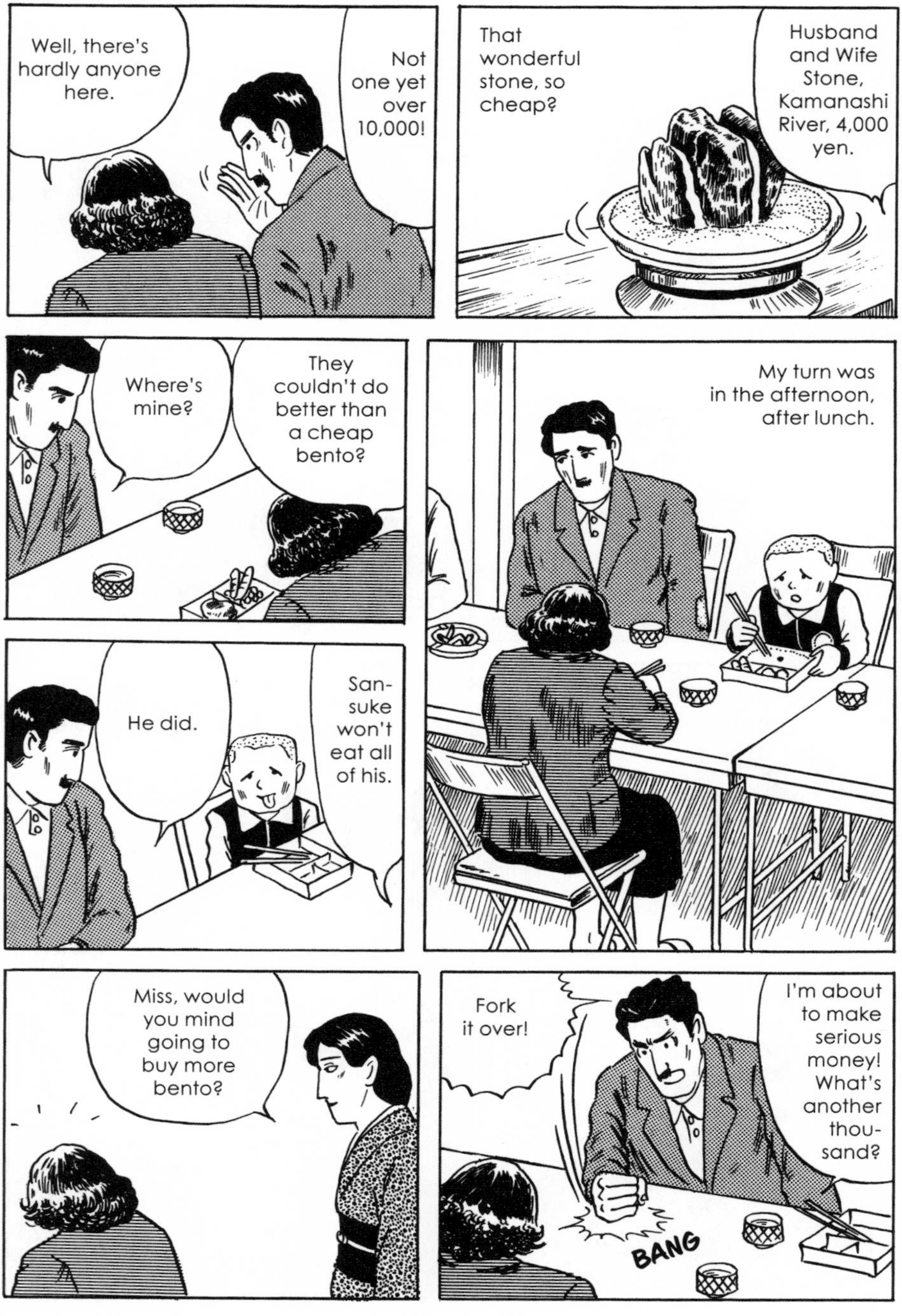
Husband and Wife Stone, Kamanashi River, 4,000 yen.
That wonderful stone, so cheap?
Not one yet over 10,000!
Well, there's hardly anyone here.
My turn was in the afternoon, after lunch.
They couldn't do better than a cheap bento?
Where's mine?
San-suke won't eat all of his.
He did.
I'm about to make serious money! What's another thou-sand?
Fork it over!
BANG
Miss, would you mind going to buy more bento?

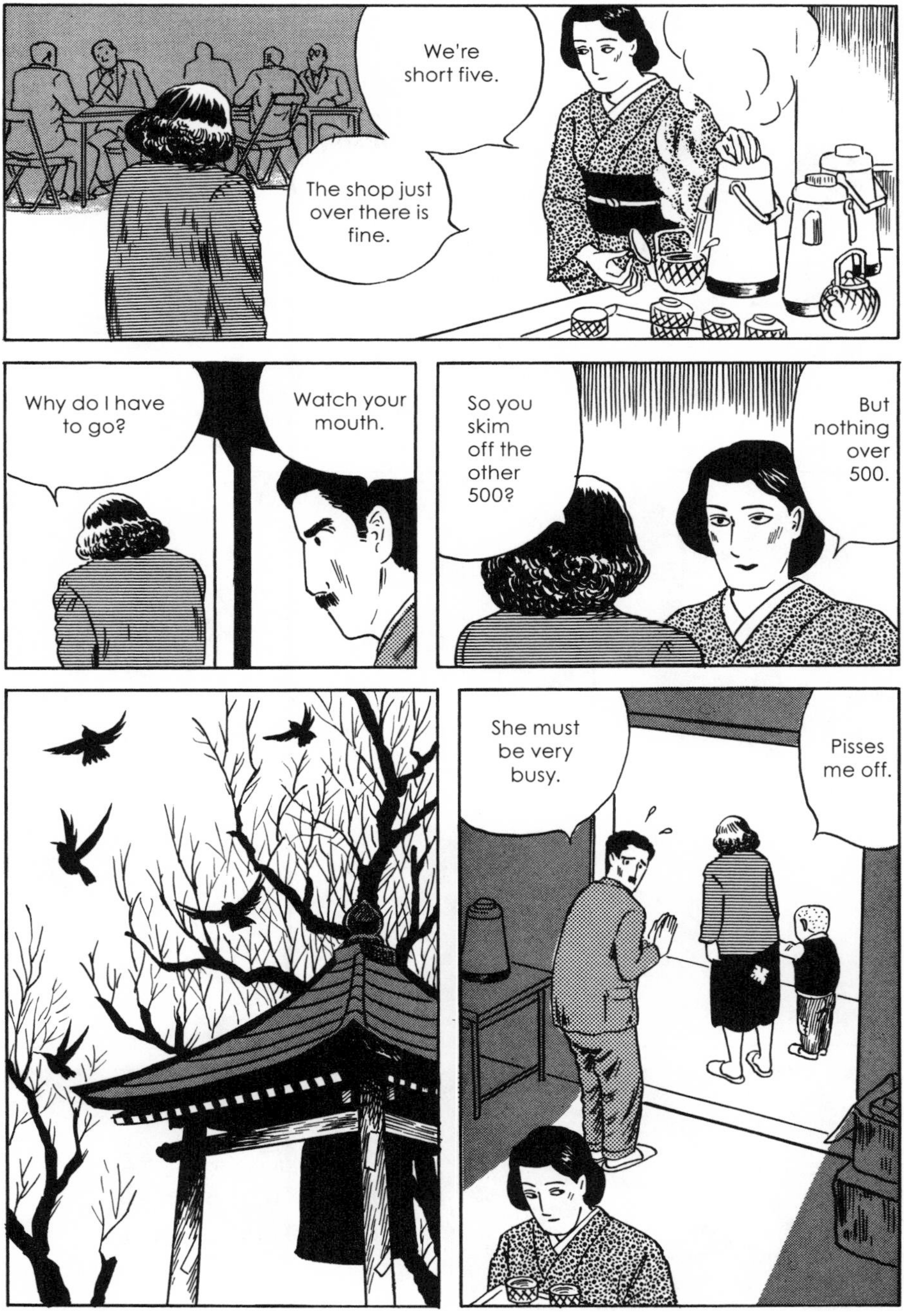
We're short five.
The shop just over there is fine.
But nothing over 500.
So you skim off the other 500?
Watch your mouth.
Why do I have to go?
Pisses me off.
She must be very busy.

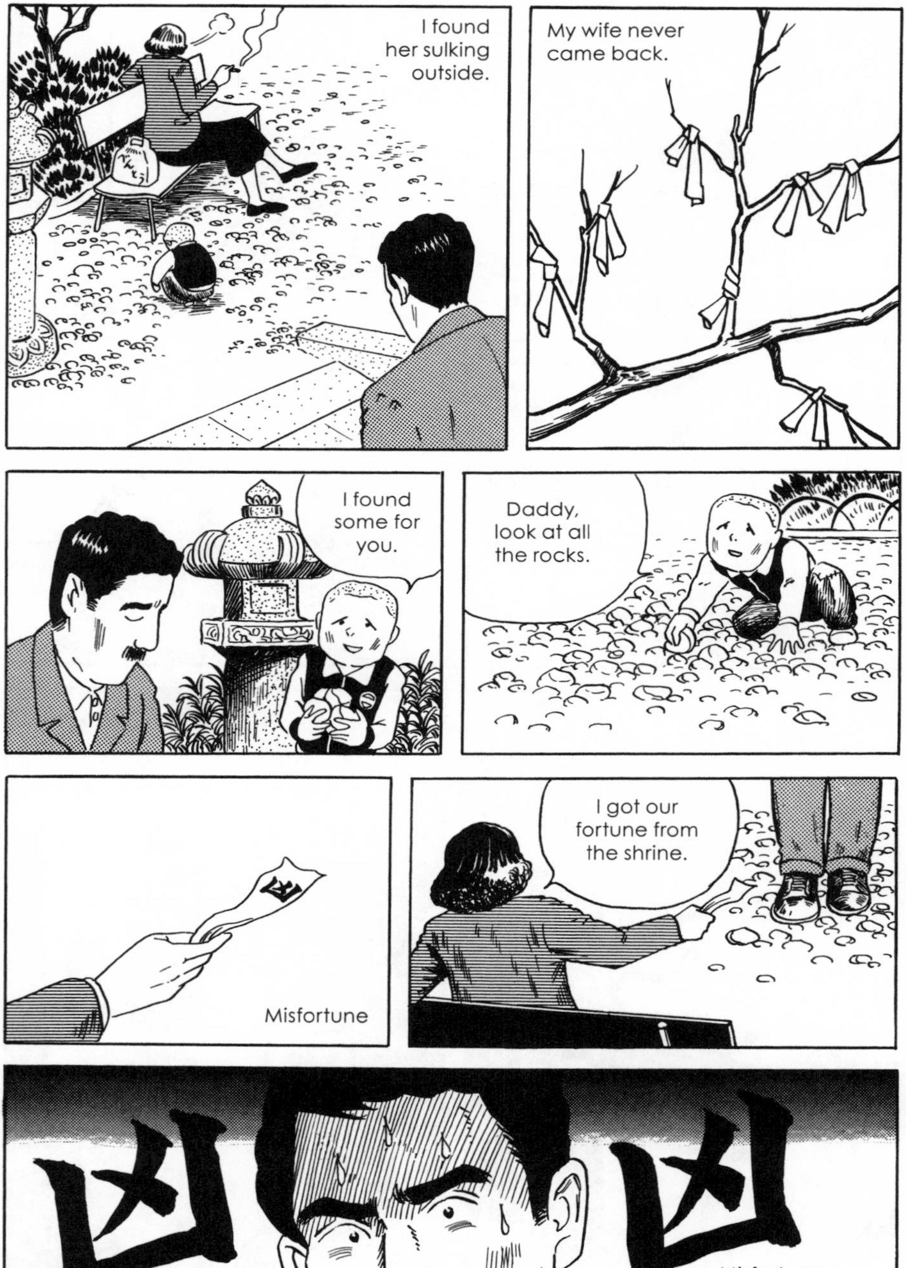
My wife never came back.
I found her sulking outside.
Daddy, look at all the rocks.
I found some for you.
I got our fortune from the shrine.
凶
Misfortune
凶
Misfortune
凶
Misfortune

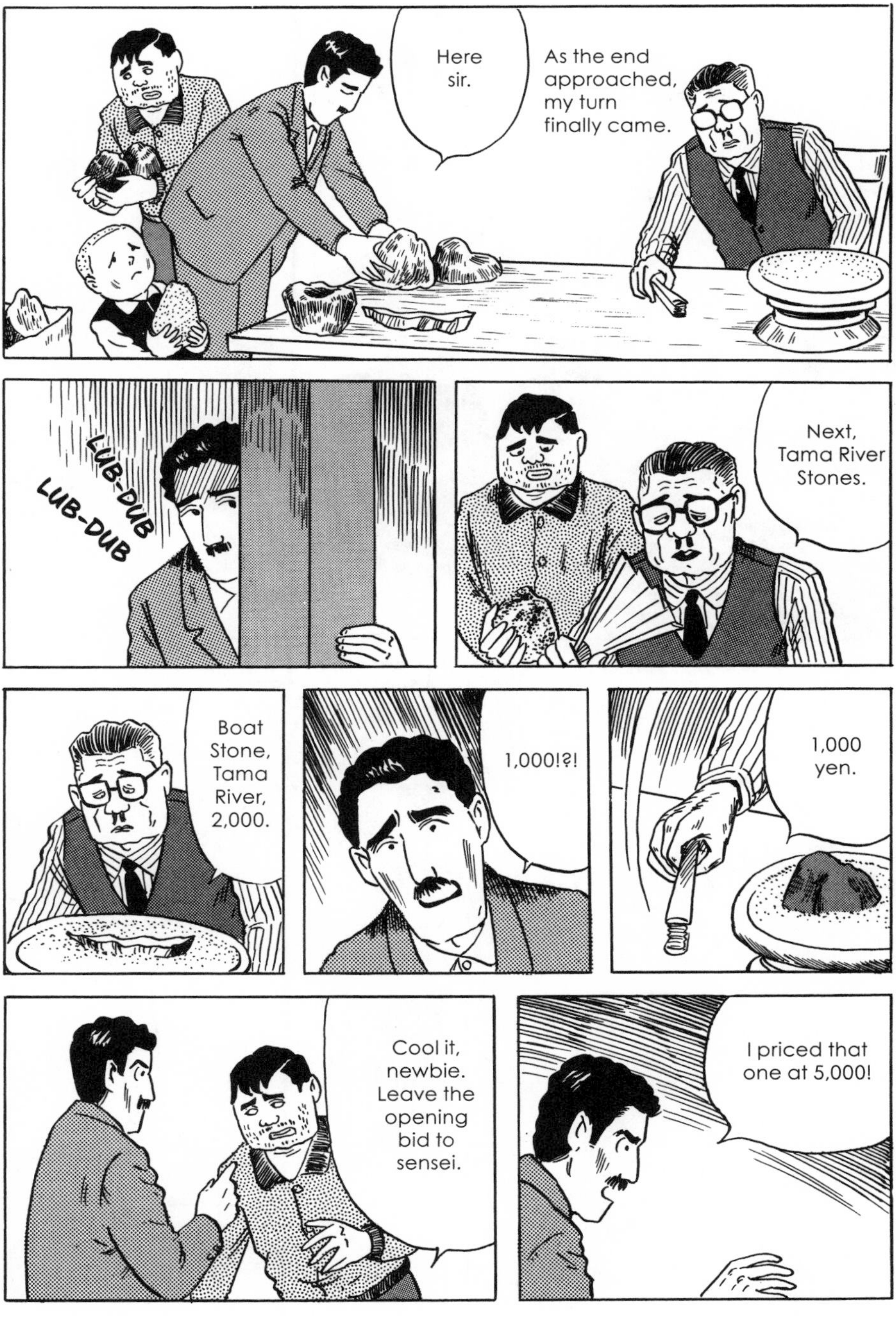

As the end approached, my turn finally came.
Here sir.
Next, Tama River Stones.
LUB-DUB
LUB-DUB
1,000 yen.
1,000!?!
Boat Stone, Tama River, 2,000.
I priced that one at 5,000!
Cool it, newbie. Leave the opening bid to sensei.

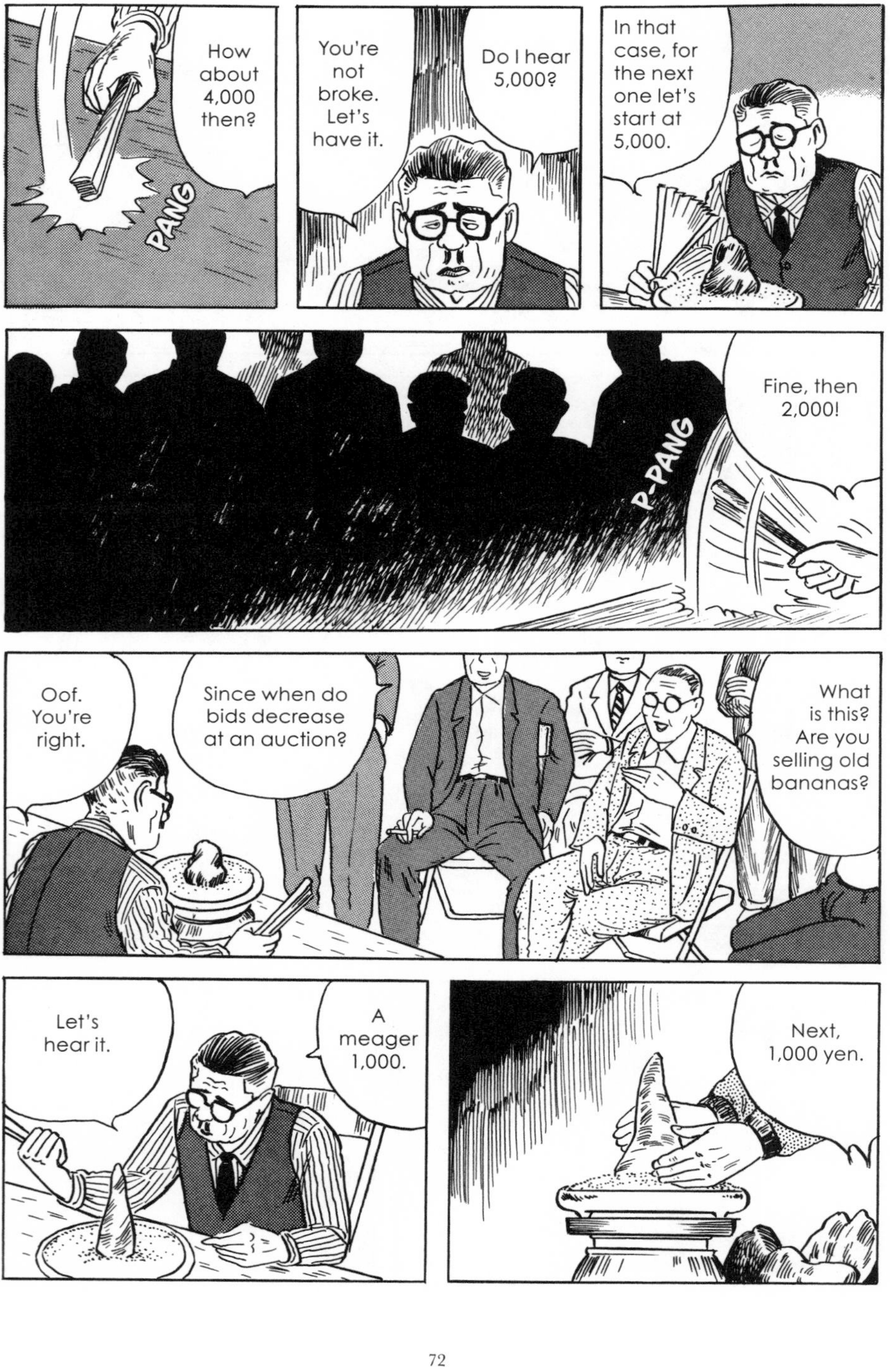
In that case, for the next one let's start at 5,000.
Do I hear 5,000?
You're not broke. Let's have it.
How about 4,000 then?
PANG
Fine, then 2,000!
P-PANG
What is this? Are you selling old bananas?
Since when do bids decrease at an auction?
Oof. You're right.
Next, 1,000 yen.
A meager 1,000.
Let's hear it.

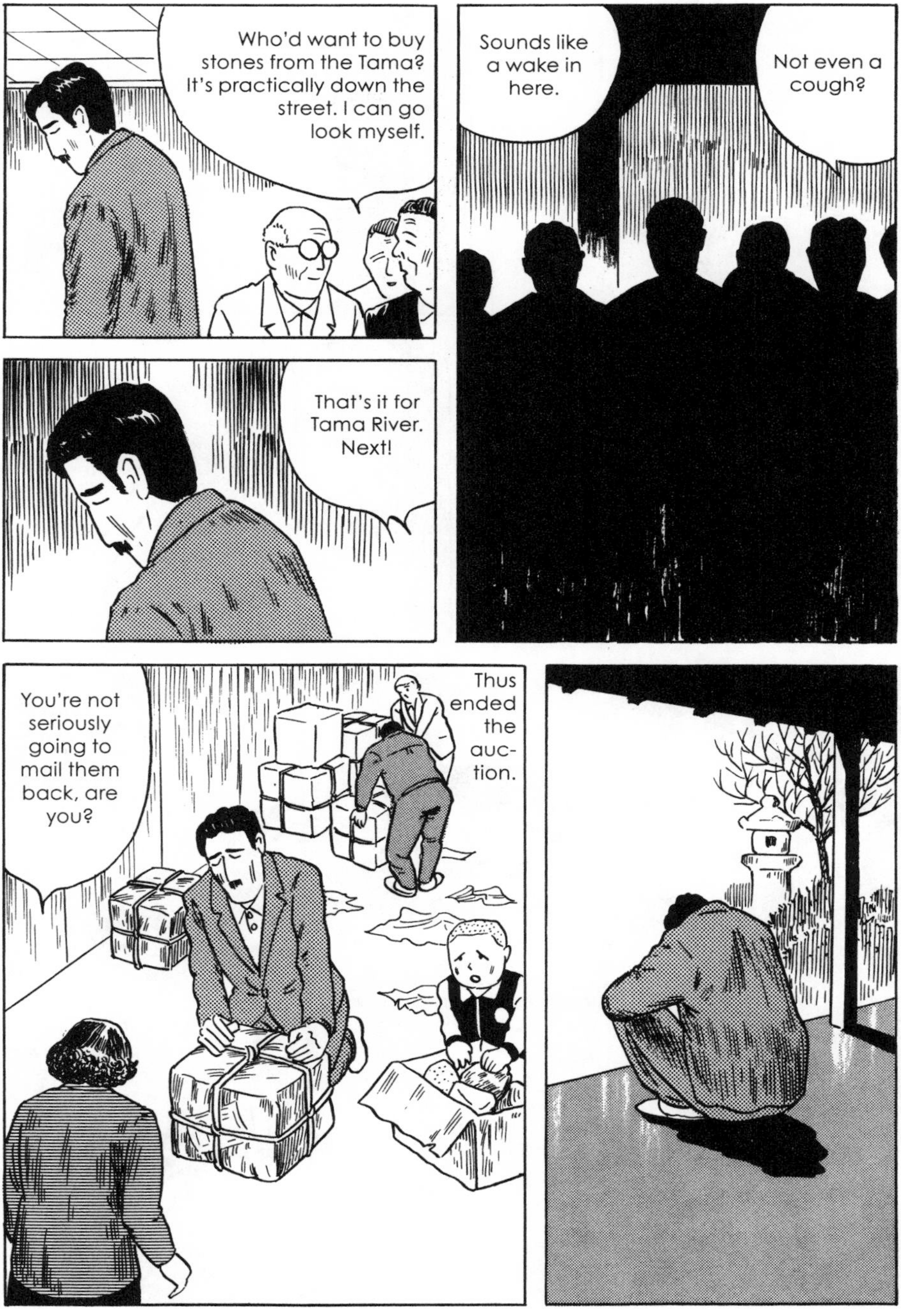
Not even a cough?
Sounds like a wake in here.
Who'd want to buy stones from the Tama? It's practically down the street. I can go look myself.
That's it for Tama River. Next!
Thus ended the auction.
You're not seriously going to mail them back, are you?

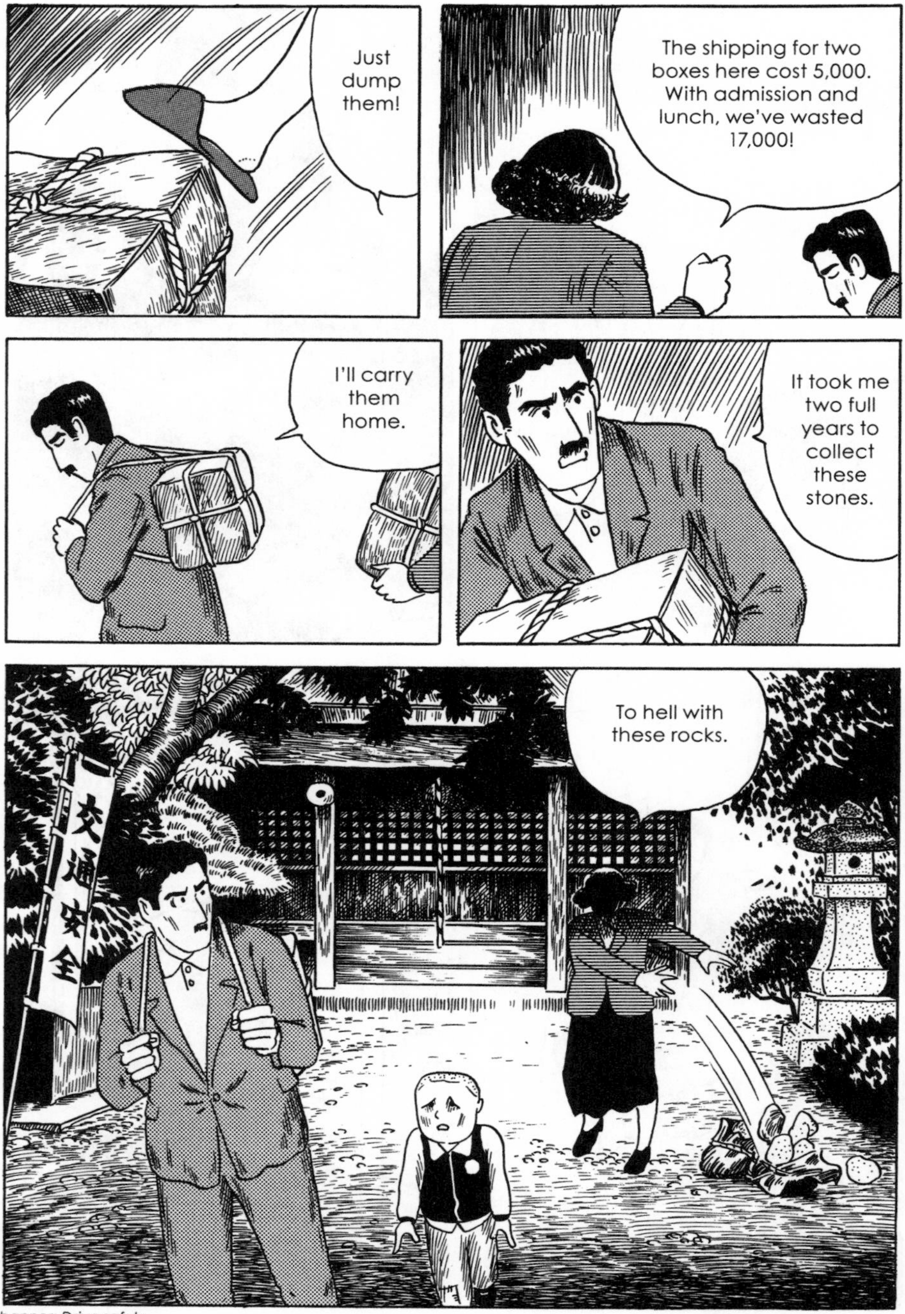
The shipping for two boxes here cost 5,000. With admission and lunch, we've wasted 17,000!
Just dump them!
It took me two full years to collect these stones.
I'll carry them home.
To hell with these rocks.
交通安全

banner: Drive safely

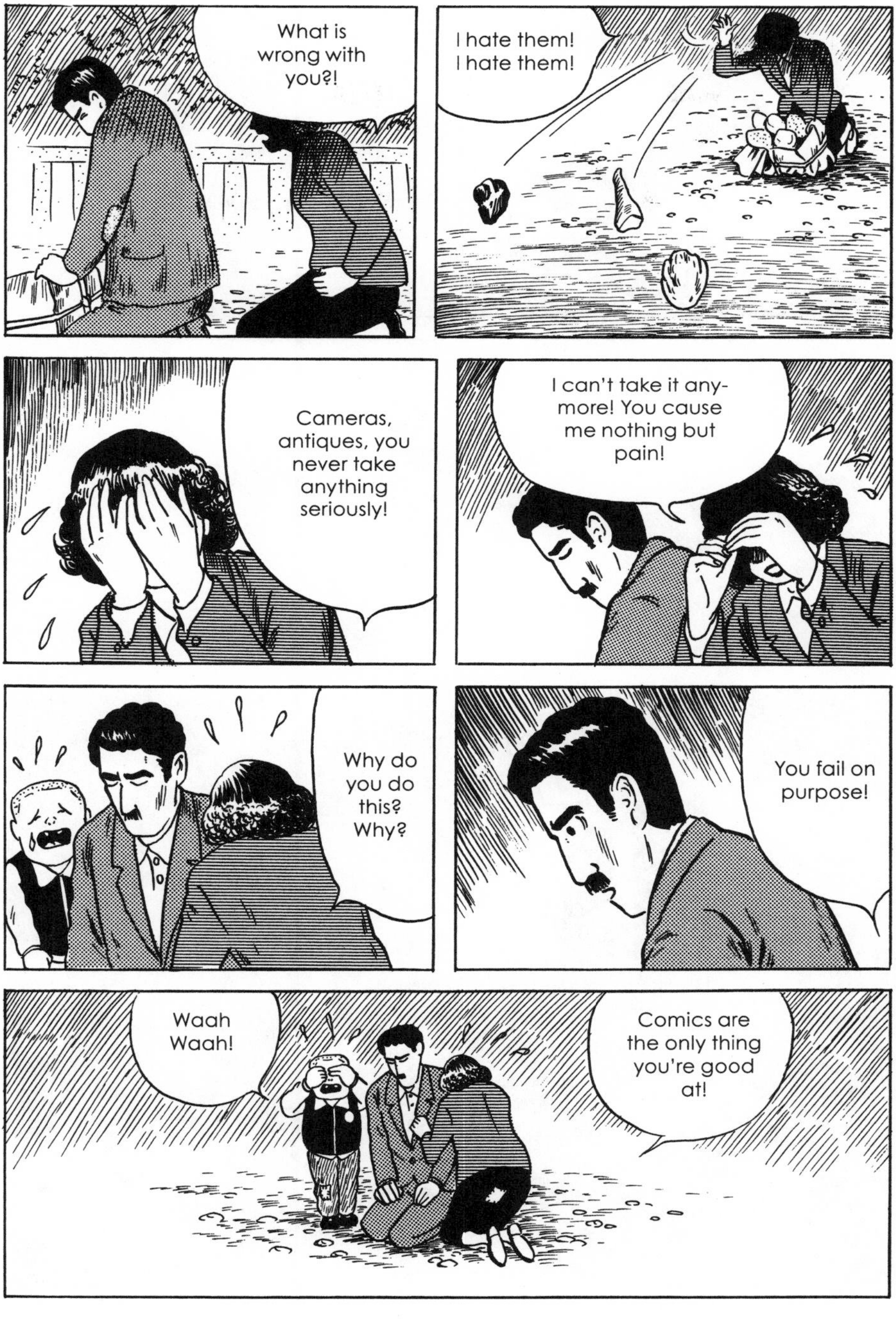
I hate them! I hate them!
What is wrong with you?!
I can't take it any-more! You cause me nothing but pain!
Cameras, antiques, you never take anything seriously!
You fail on purpose!
Why do you do this? Why?
Comics are the only thing you're good at!
Waah Waah!

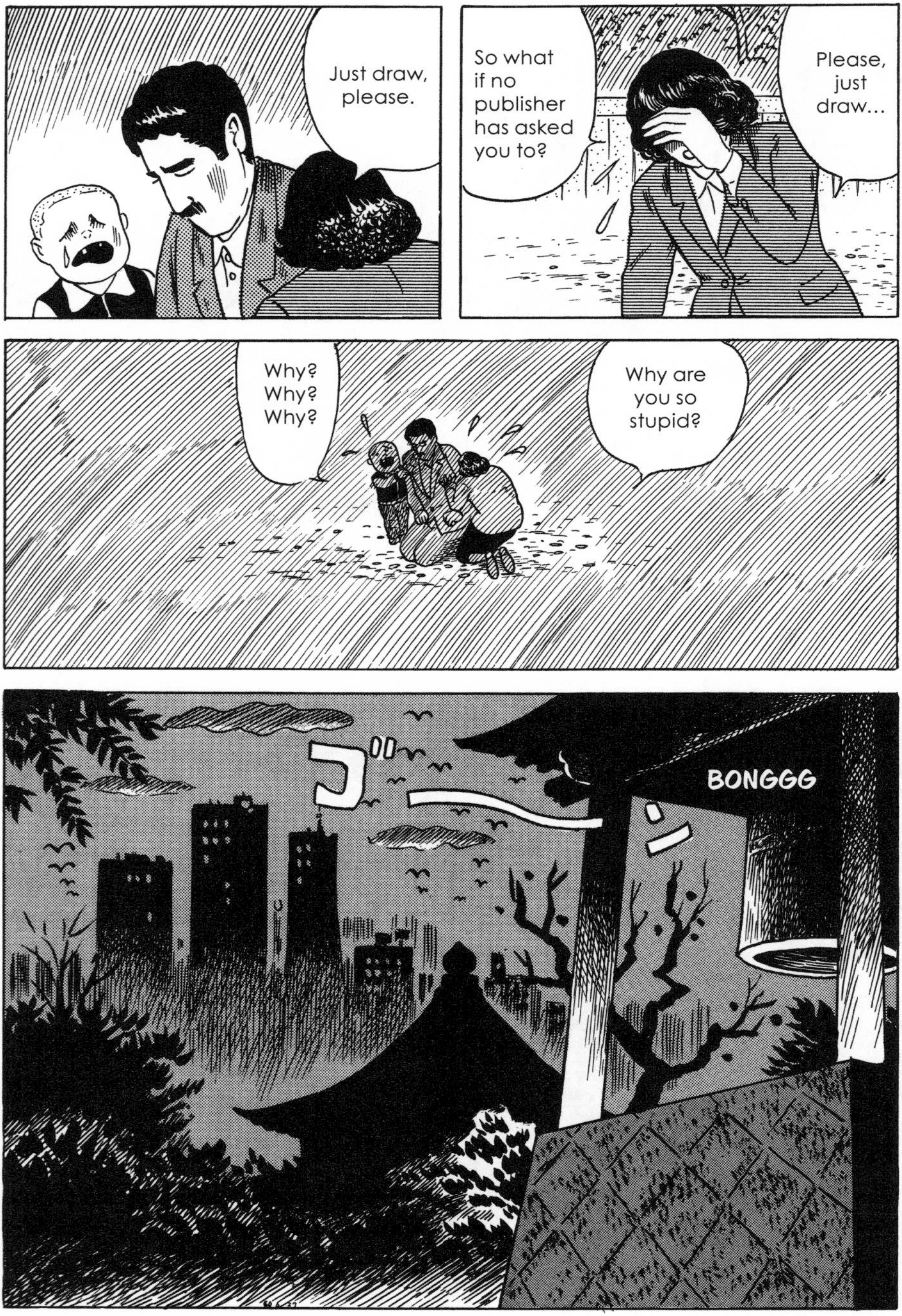
Please, just draw…
So what if no publisher has asked you to?
Just draw, please.
Why are you so stupid?
Why? Why? Why?
ゴーン
BONGGG

第三話
Chapter 3

鳥師
The Bird Master

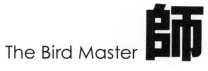

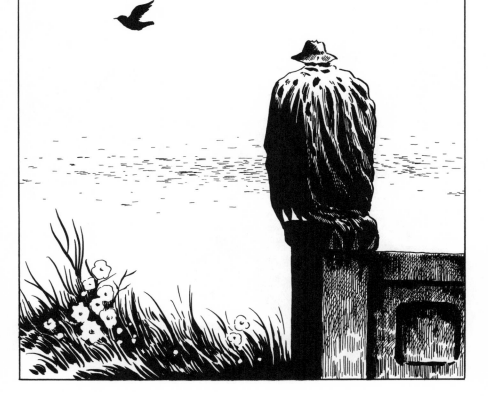

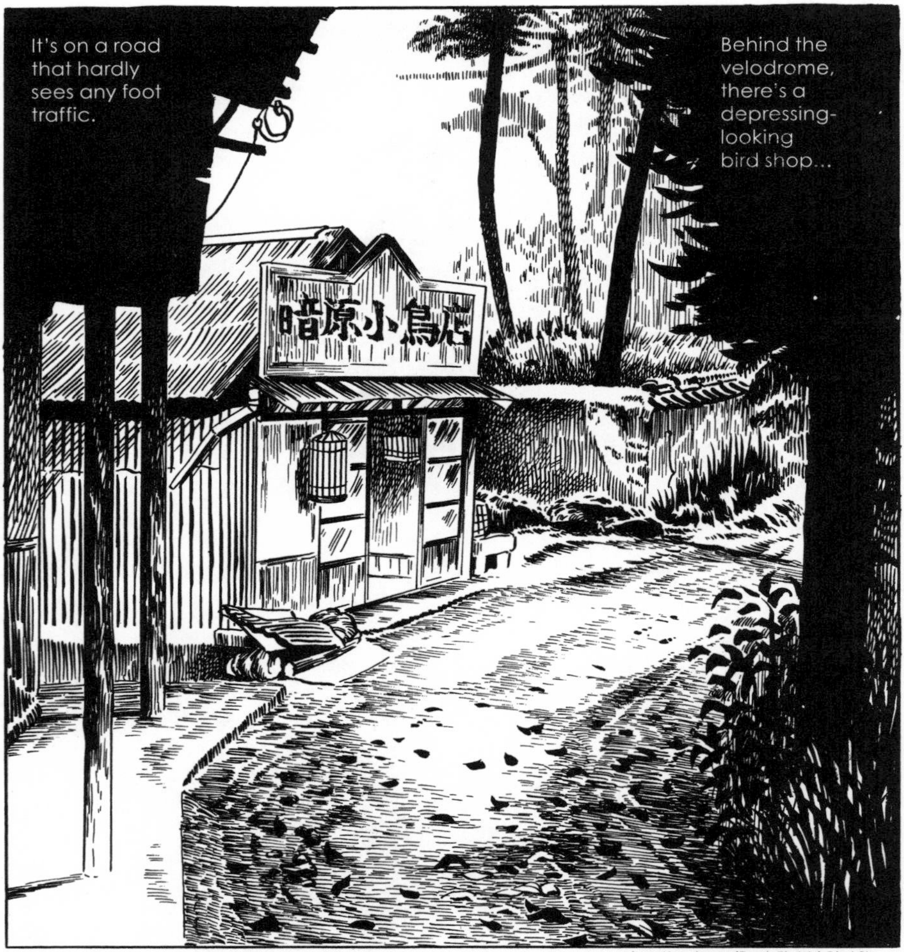
Behind the velodrome, there's a depressing-looking bird shop...
It's on a road that hardly sees any foot traffic.
暗原小鳥店
sign: Kurahara (Dark Fields) Bird Shop

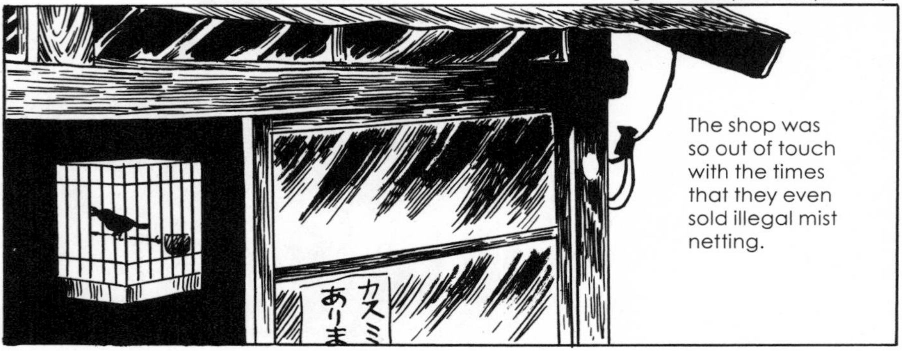
The shop was so out of touch with the times that they even sold illegal mist netting.
カスミ
ありま

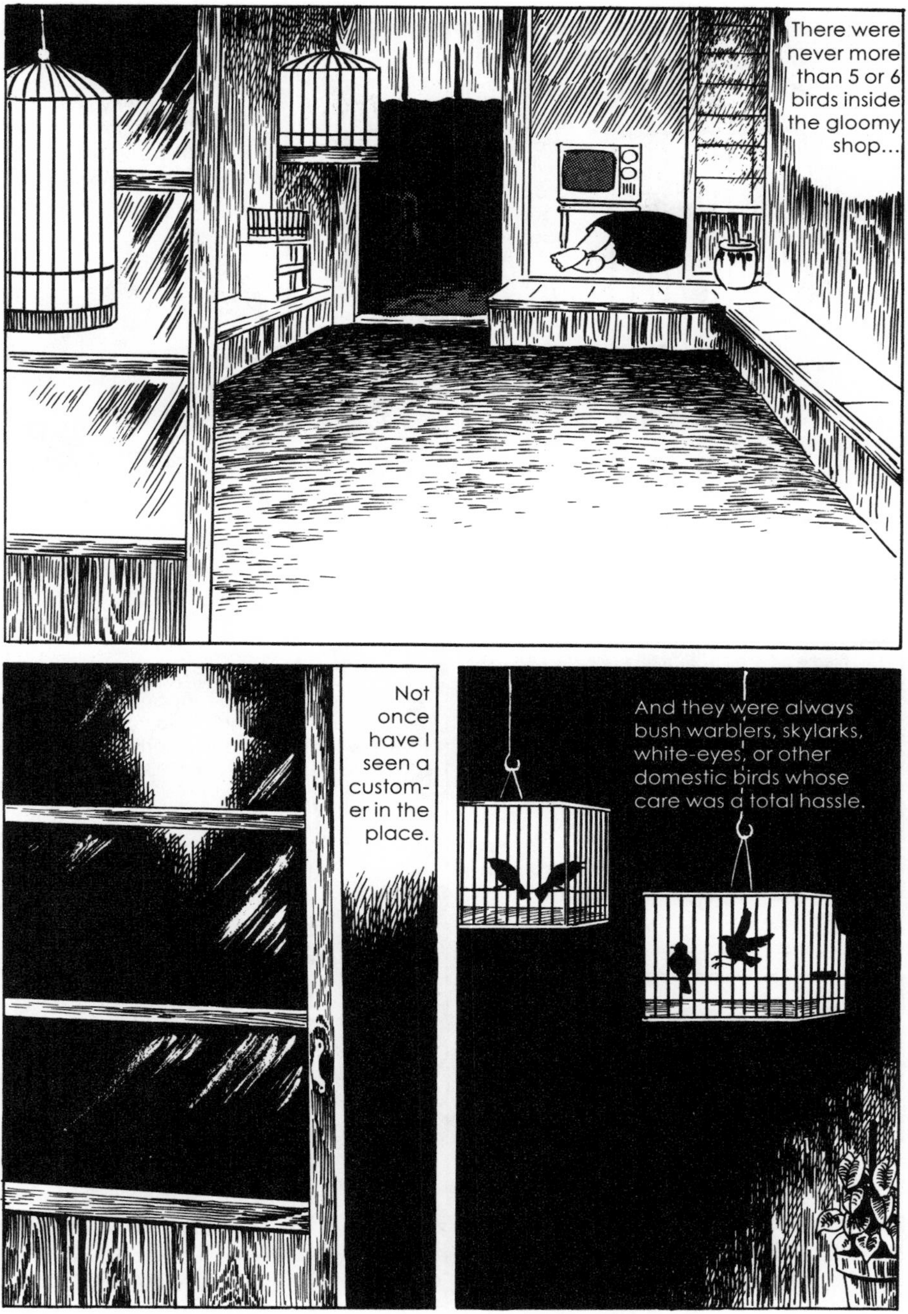
There were never more than 5 or 6 birds inside the gloomy shop...
And they were always bush warblers, skylarks, white-eyes, or other domestic birds whose care was a total hassle.
Not once have I seen a custom-er in the place.

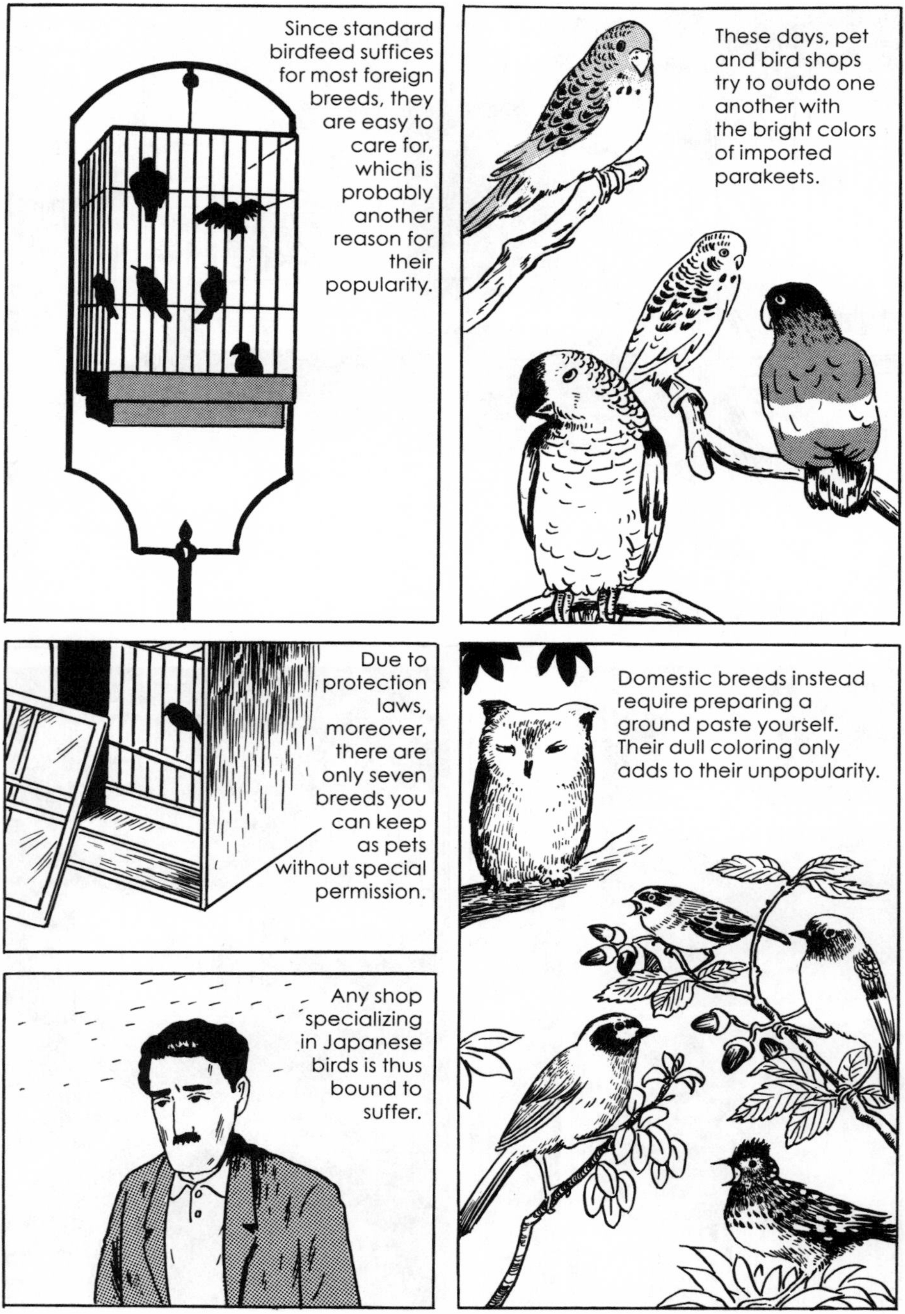
These days, pet and bird shops try to outdo one another with the bright colors of imported parakeets.
Since standard birdfeed suffices for most foreign breeds, they are easy to care for, which is probably another reason for their popularity.
Domestic breeds instead require preparing a ground paste yourself. Their dull coloring only adds to their unpopularity.
Due to protection laws, moreover, there are only seven breeds you can keep as pets without special permission.
Any shop specializing in Japanese birds is thus bound to suffer.

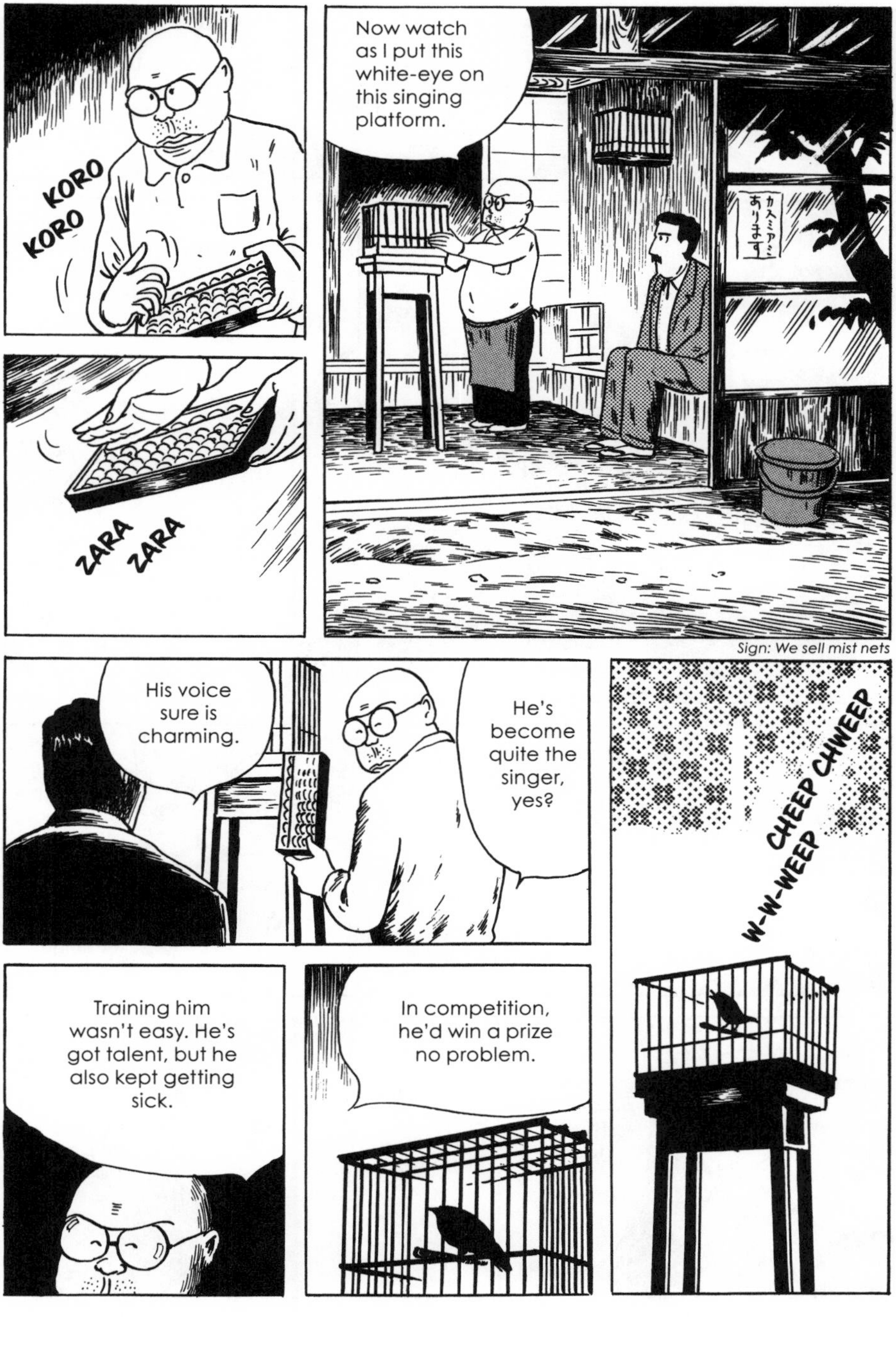
Now watch as I put this white-eye on this singing platform.
カスミアミあります
KORO KORO
ZARA ZARA
CHEEP CHWEEP
W-W-WEEP
He's become quite the singer, yes?
His voice sure is charming.
In competition, he'd win a prize no problem.
Training him wasn't easy. He's got talent, but he also kept getting sick.
Sign: We sell mist nets

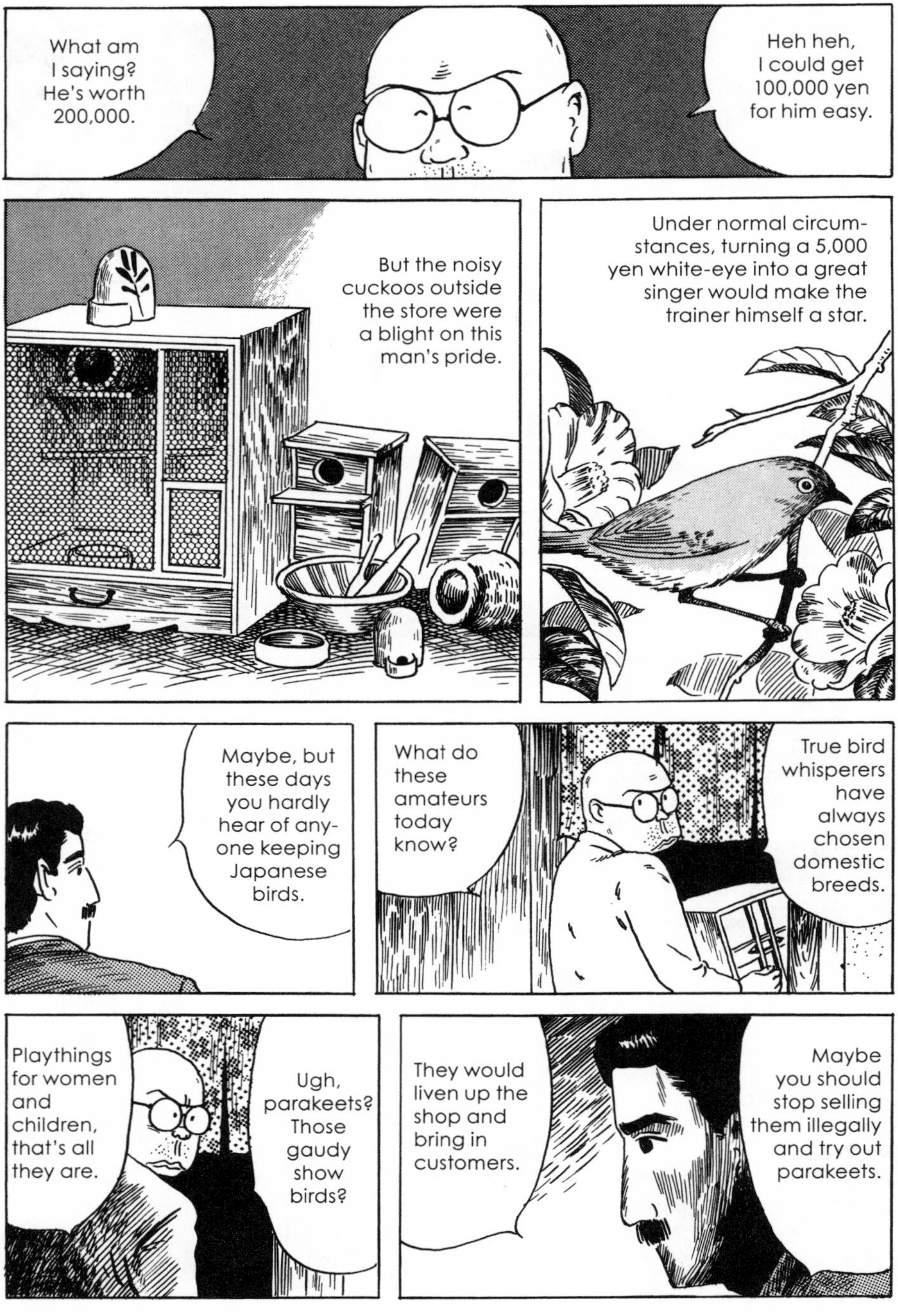
Heh heh, I could get 100,000 yen for him easy.
What am I saying? He's worth 200,000.
Under normal circum-stances, turning a 5,000 yen white-eye into a great singer would make the trainer himself a star.
But the noisy cuckoos outside the store were a blight on this man's pride.
True bird whisperers have always chosen domestic breeds.
What do these amateurs today know?
Maybe, but these days you hardly hear of any-one keeping Japanese birds.
Maybe you should stop selling them illegally and try out parakeets.
They would liven up the shop and bring in customers.
Ugh, parakeets? Those gaudy show birds?
Playthings for women and children, that's all they are.

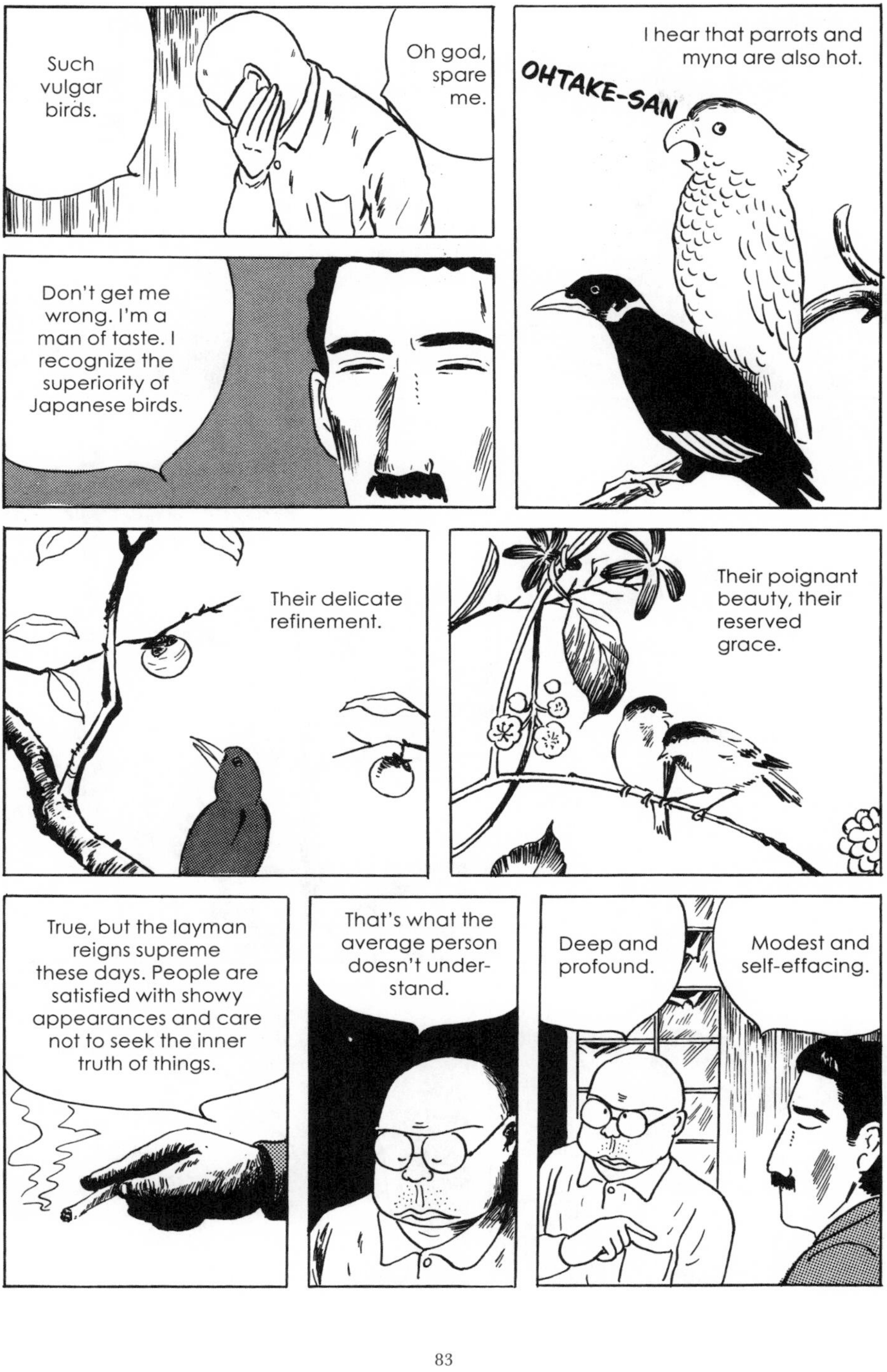
I hear that parrots and myna are also hot.
OHTAKE-SAN
Oh god, spare me.
Such vulgar birds.
Don't get me wrong. I'm a man of taste. I recognize the superiority of Japanese birds.
Their poignant beauty, their reserved grace.
Their delicate refinement.
Modest and self-effacing.
Deep and profound.
That's what the average person doesn't under-stand.
True, but the layman reigns supreme these days. People are satisfied with showy appearances and care not to seek the inner truth of things.

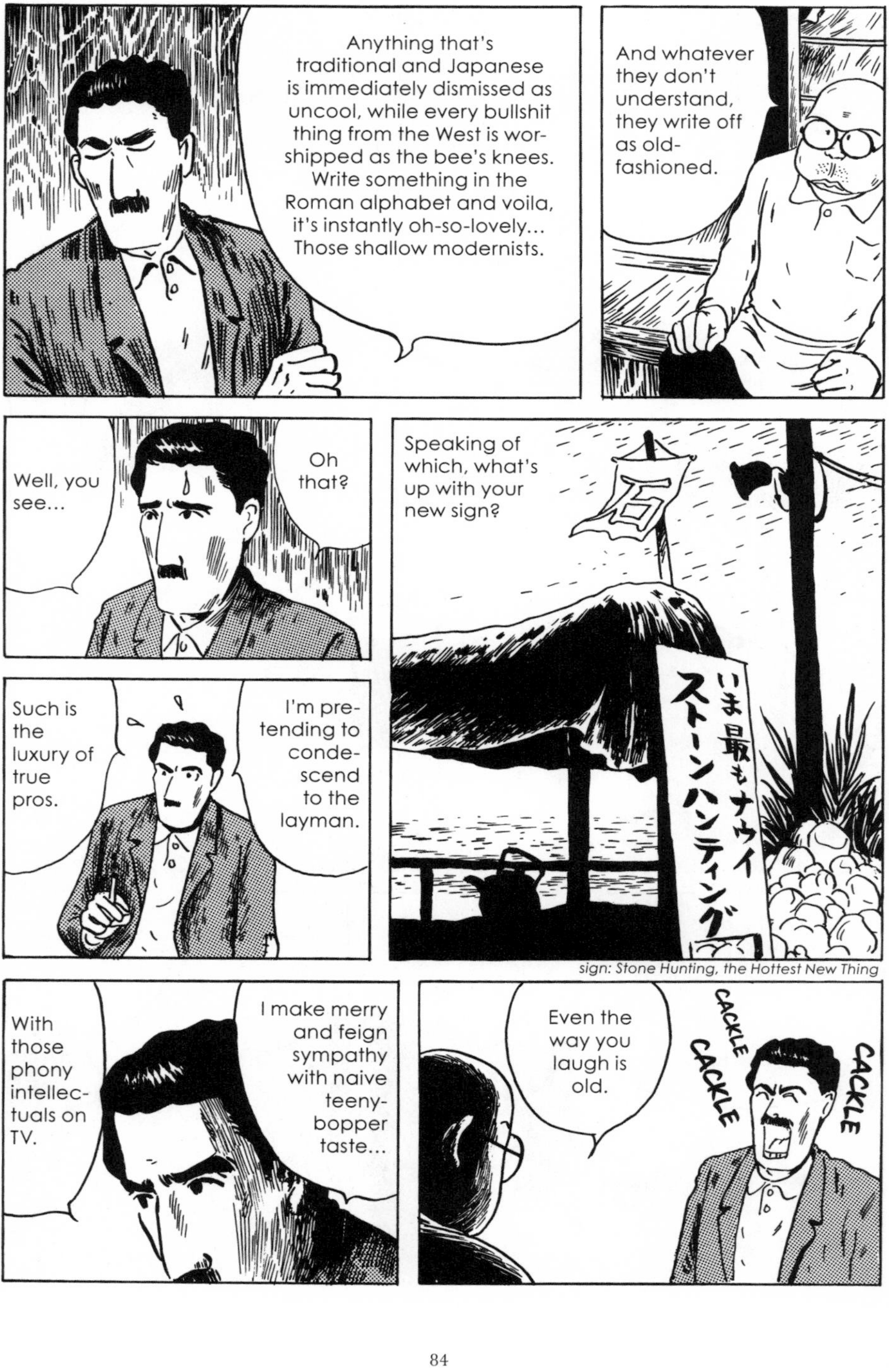
And whatever they don't understand, they write off as old-fashioned.
Anything that's traditional and Japanese is immediately dismissed as uncool, while every bullshit thing from the West is wor-shipped as the bee's knees. Write something in the Roman alphabet and voila, it's instantly oh-so-lovely… Those shallow modernists.
Speaking of which, what's up with your new sign?
石
いま最もナウイ
ストーンハンティング
Oh that?
Well, you see…
I'm pre-tending to conde-scend to the layman.
Such is the luxury of true pros.
Even the way you laugh is old.
CACKLE CACKLE
CACKLE CACKLE
I make merry and feign sympathy with naive teeny-bopper taste…
With those phony intellec-tuals on TV.
sign: Stone Hunting, the Hottest New Thing

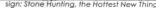

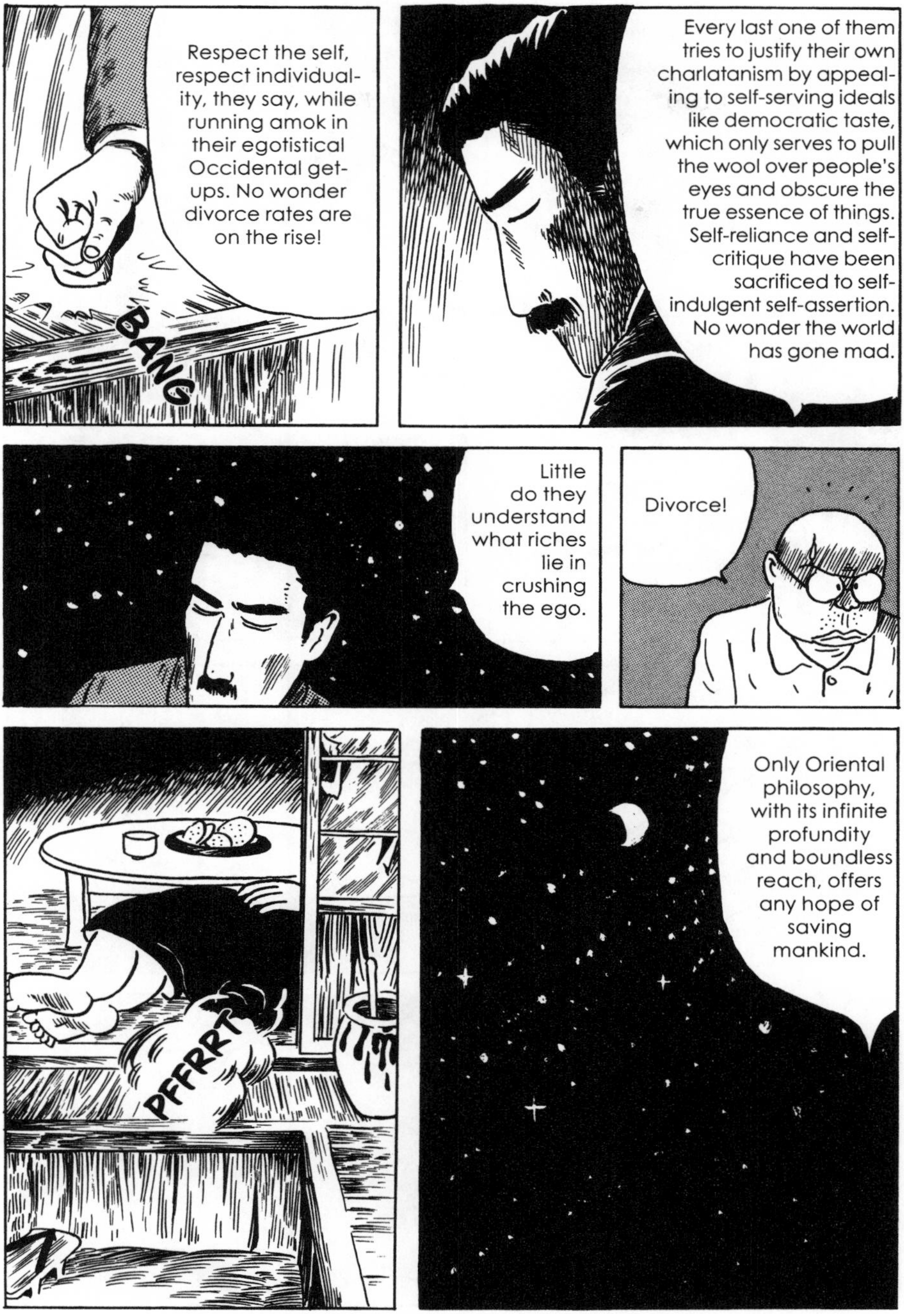
Every last one of them tries to justify their own charlatanism by appealing to self-serving ideals like democratic taste, which only serves to pull the wool over people's eyes and obscure the true essence of things. Self-reliance and self-critique have been sacrificed to self-indulgent self-assertion. No wonder the world has gone mad.
Respect the self, respect individuality, they say, while running amok in their egotistical Occidental get-ups. No wonder divorce rates are on the rise!
BANG
Divorce!
Little do they understand what riches lie in crushing the ego.
Only Oriental philosophy, with its infinite profundity and boundless reach, offers any hope of saving mankind.
PFFRRT

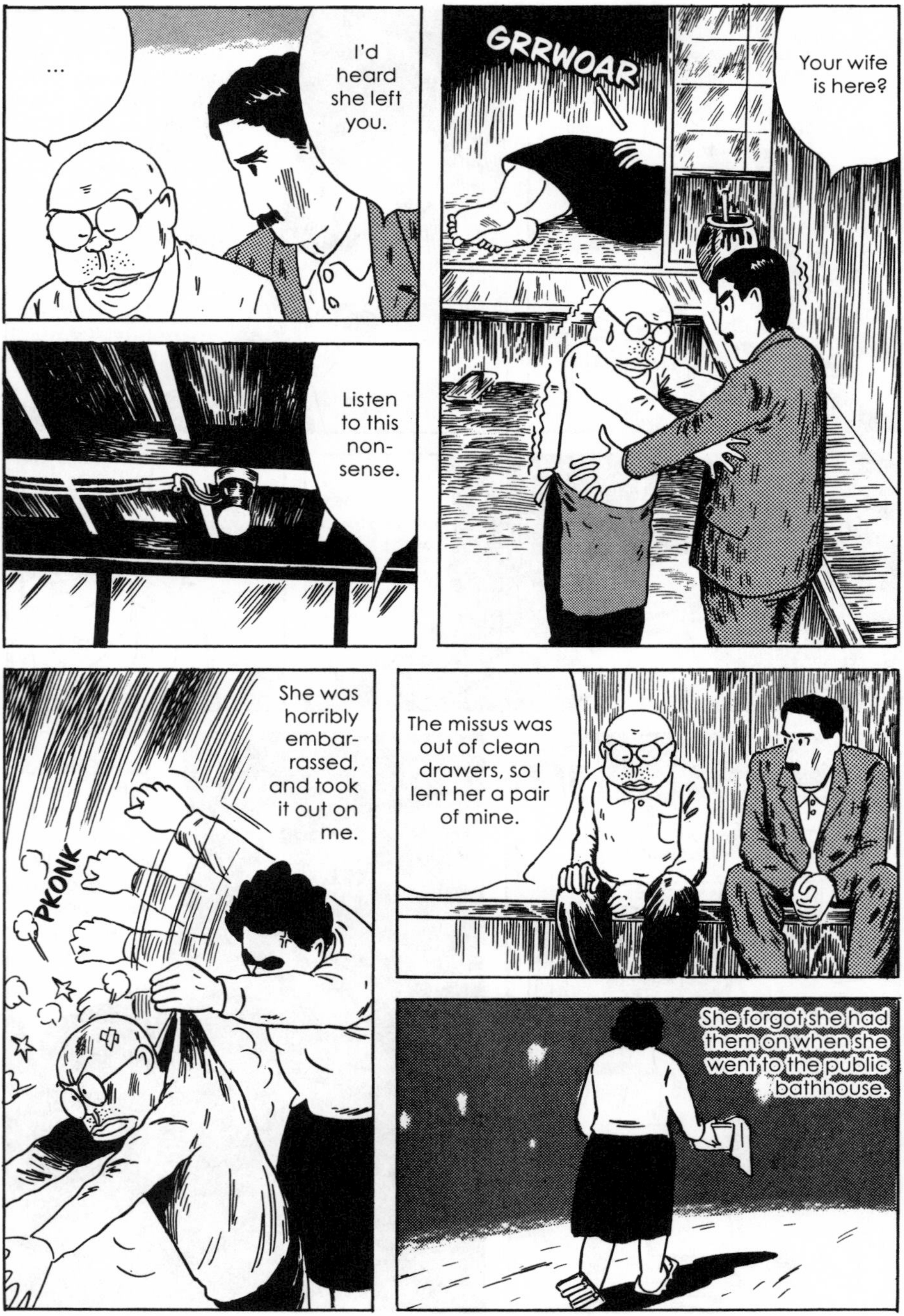
GRRWOAR
Your wife is here?
I'd heard she left you.
...
Listen to this nonsense.
The missus was out of clean drawers, so I lent her a pair of mine.
She forgot she had them on when she went to the public bathhouse.
She was horribly embarrassed, and took it out on me.
PKONK

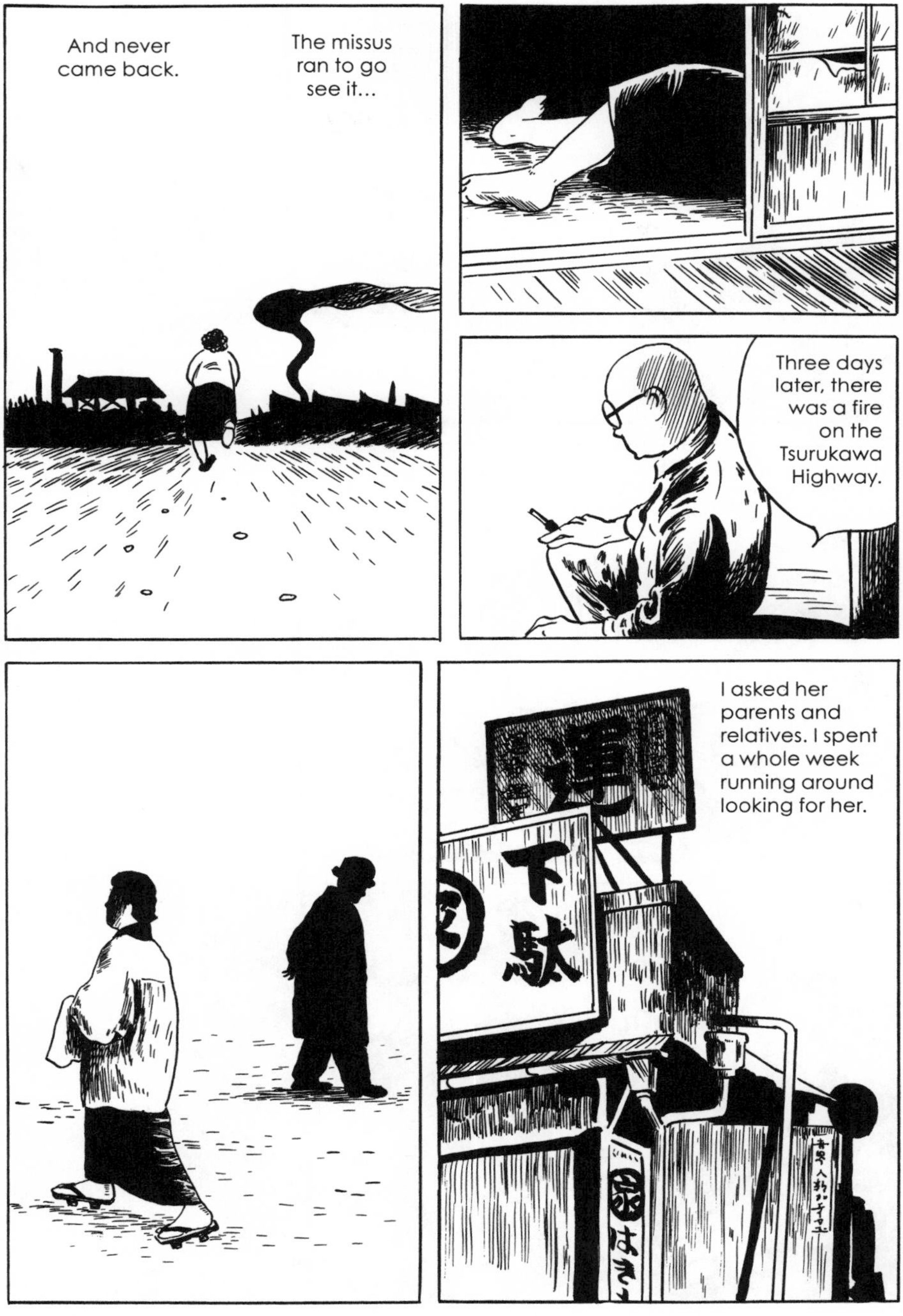
Three days later, there was a fire on the Tsurukawa Highway.
The missus ran to go see it...
And never came back.
I asked her parents and relatives. I spent a whole week running around looking for her.
下駄

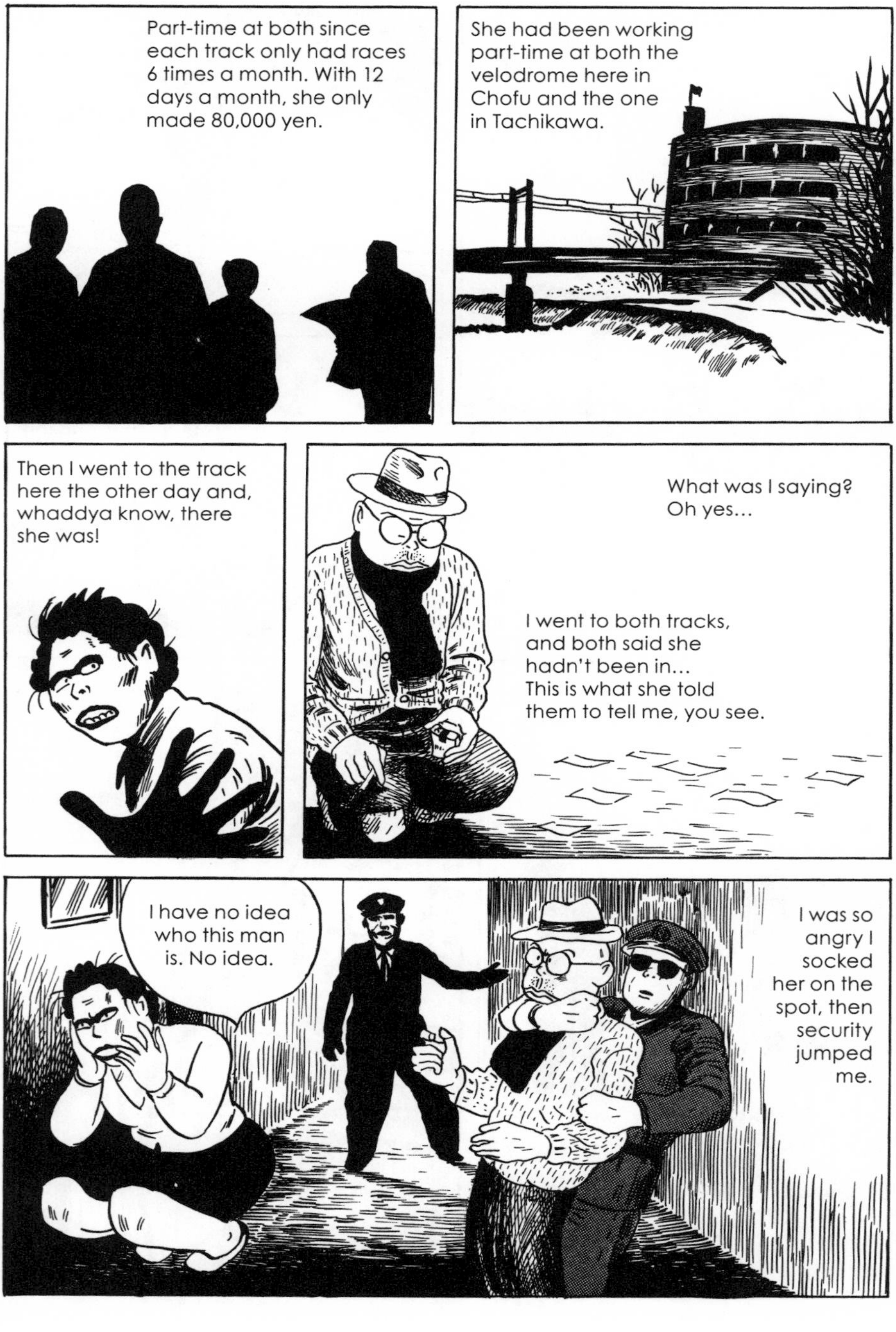
She had been working part-time at both the velodrome here in Chofu and the one in Tachikawa.
Part-time at both since each track only had races 6 times a month. With 12 days a month, she only made 80,000 yen.
What was I saying? Oh yes...
I went to both tracks, and both said she hadn't been in... This is what she told them to tell me, you see.
Then I went to the track here the other day and, whaddya know, there she was!
I was so angry I socked her on the spot, then security jumped me.
I have no idea who this man is. No idea.

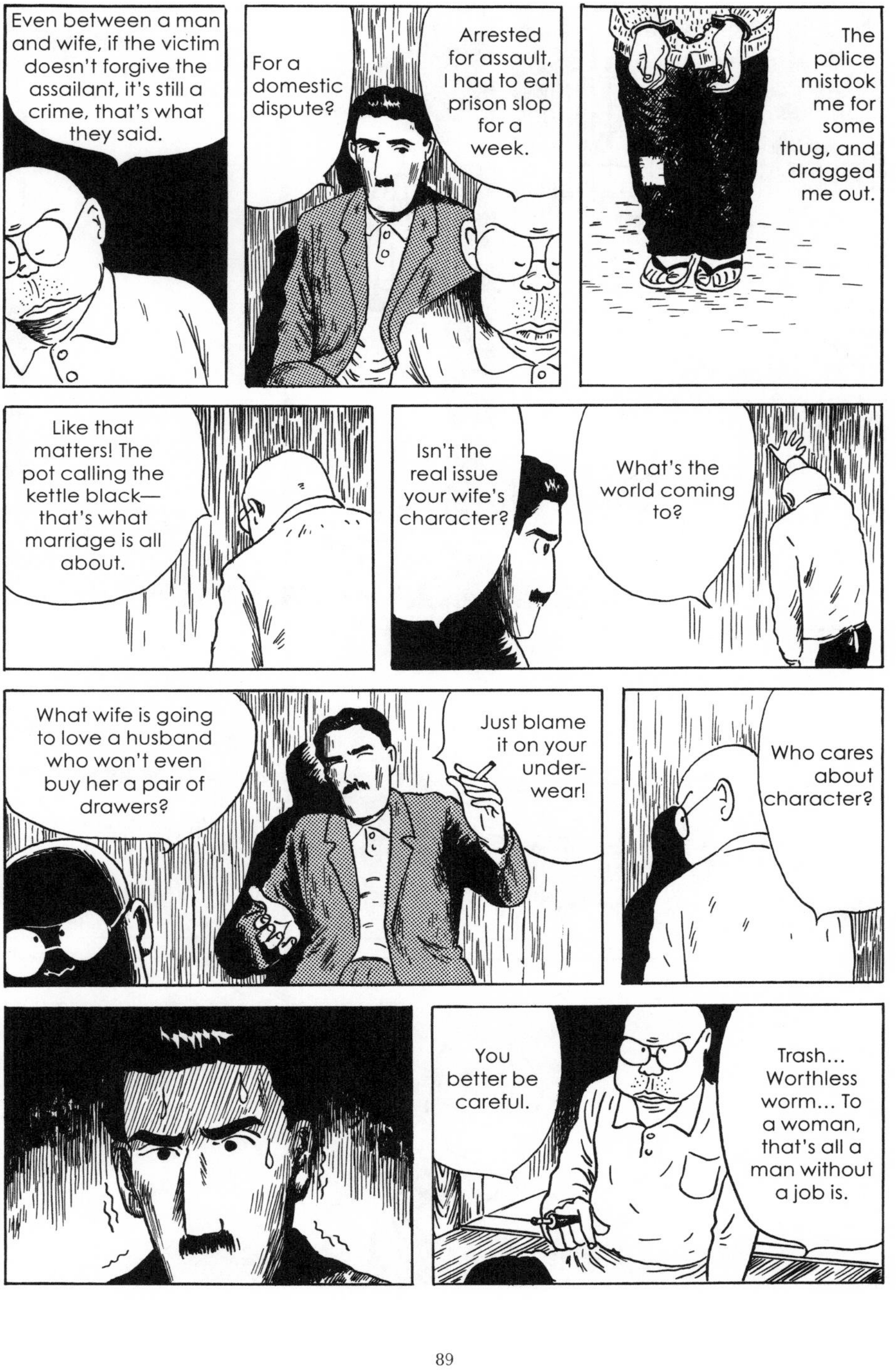
The police mistook me for some thug, and dragged me out.
Arrested for assault, I had to eat prison slop for a week.
For a domestic dispute?
Even between a man and wife, if the victim doesn't forgive the assailant, it's still a crime, that's what they said.
What's the world coming to?
Isn't the real issue your wife's character?
Like that matters! The pot calling the kettle black—that's what marriage is all about.
Who cares about character?
Just blame it on your under-wear!
What wife is going to love a husband who won't even buy her a pair of drawers?
Trash... Worthless worm... To a woman, that's all a man without a job is.
You better be careful.

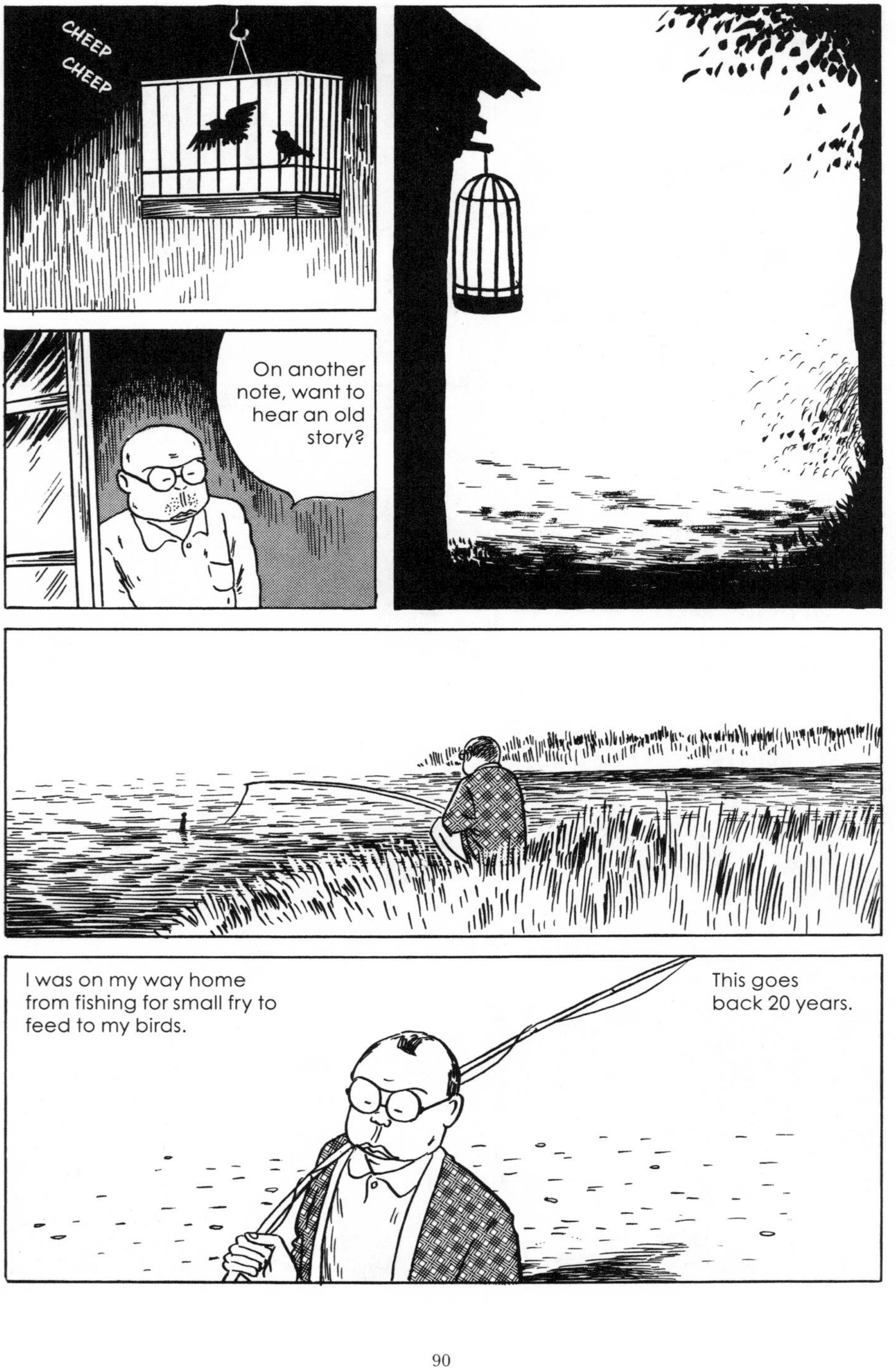
CHEEP CHEEP
On another note, want to hear an old story?
This goes back 20 years.
I was on my way home from fishing for small fry to feed to my birds.

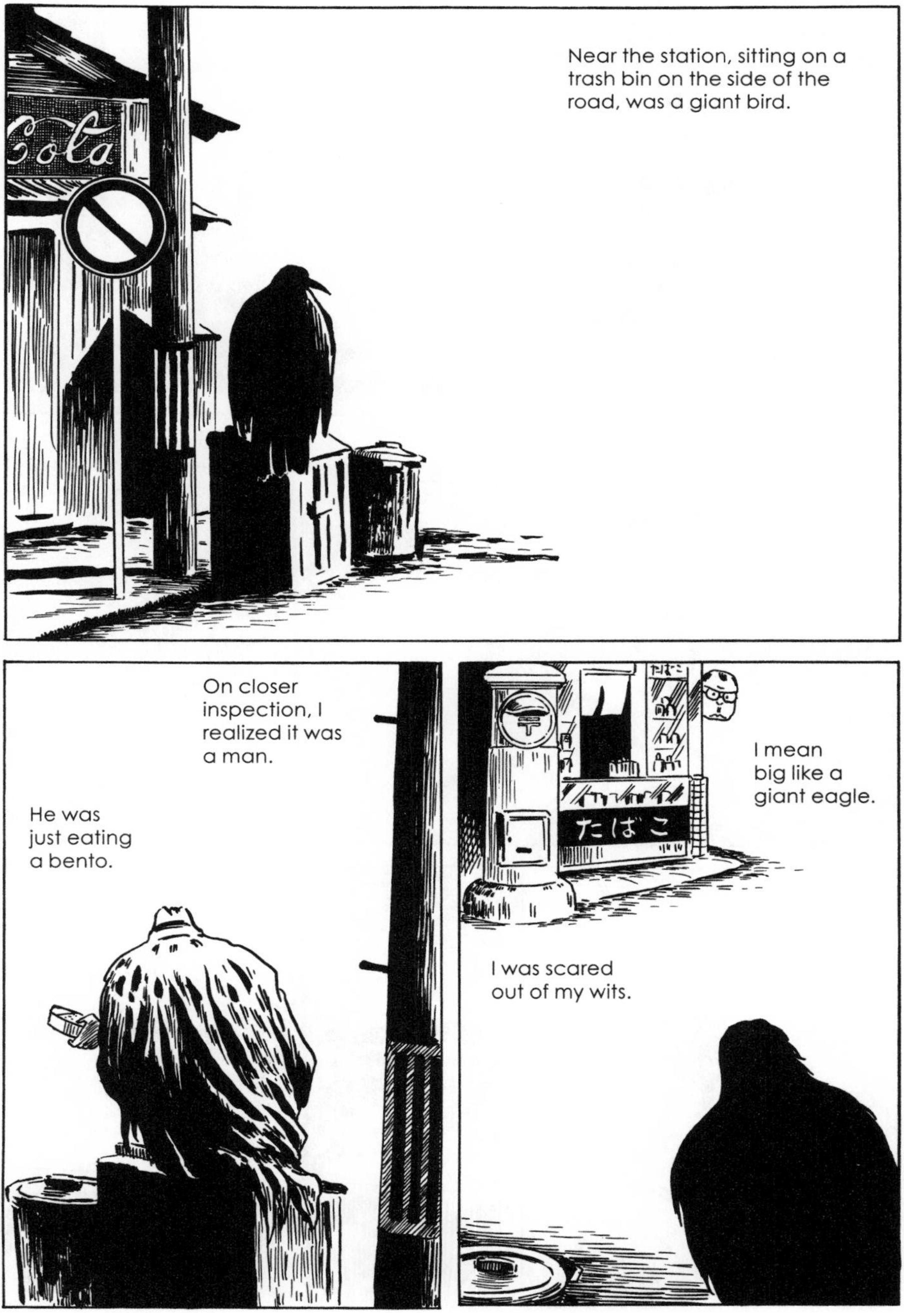
Cola
Near the station, sitting on a trash bin on the side of the road, was a giant bird.
たばこ
I mean big like a giant eagle.
I was scared out of my wits.
On closer inspection, I realized it was a man.
He was just eating a bento.

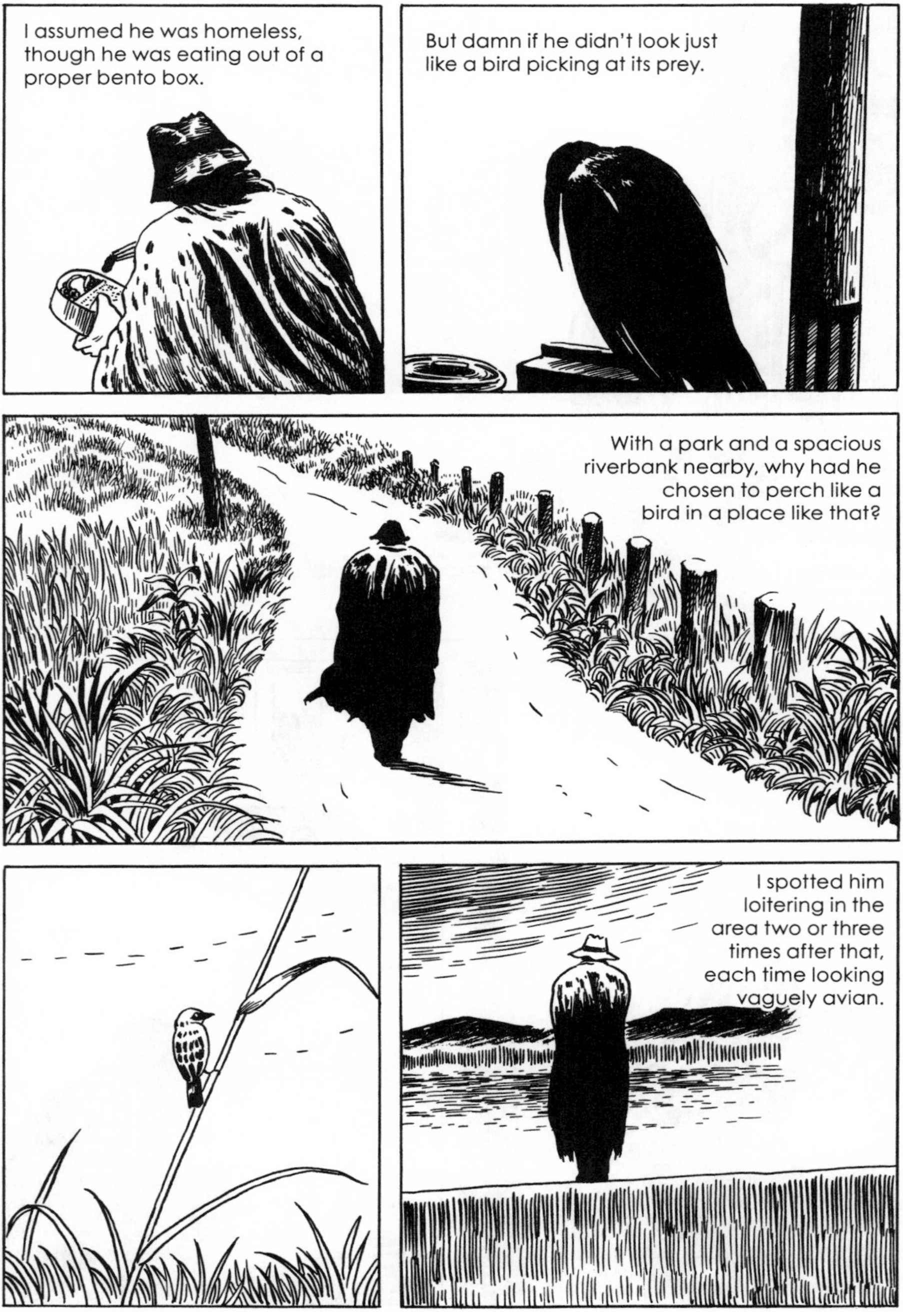
I assumed he was homeless, though he was eating out of a proper bento box.
But damn if he didn't look just like a bird picking at its prey.
With a park and a spacious riverbank nearby, why had he chosen to perch like a bird in a place like that?
I spotted him loitering in the area two or three times after that, each time looking vaguely avian.

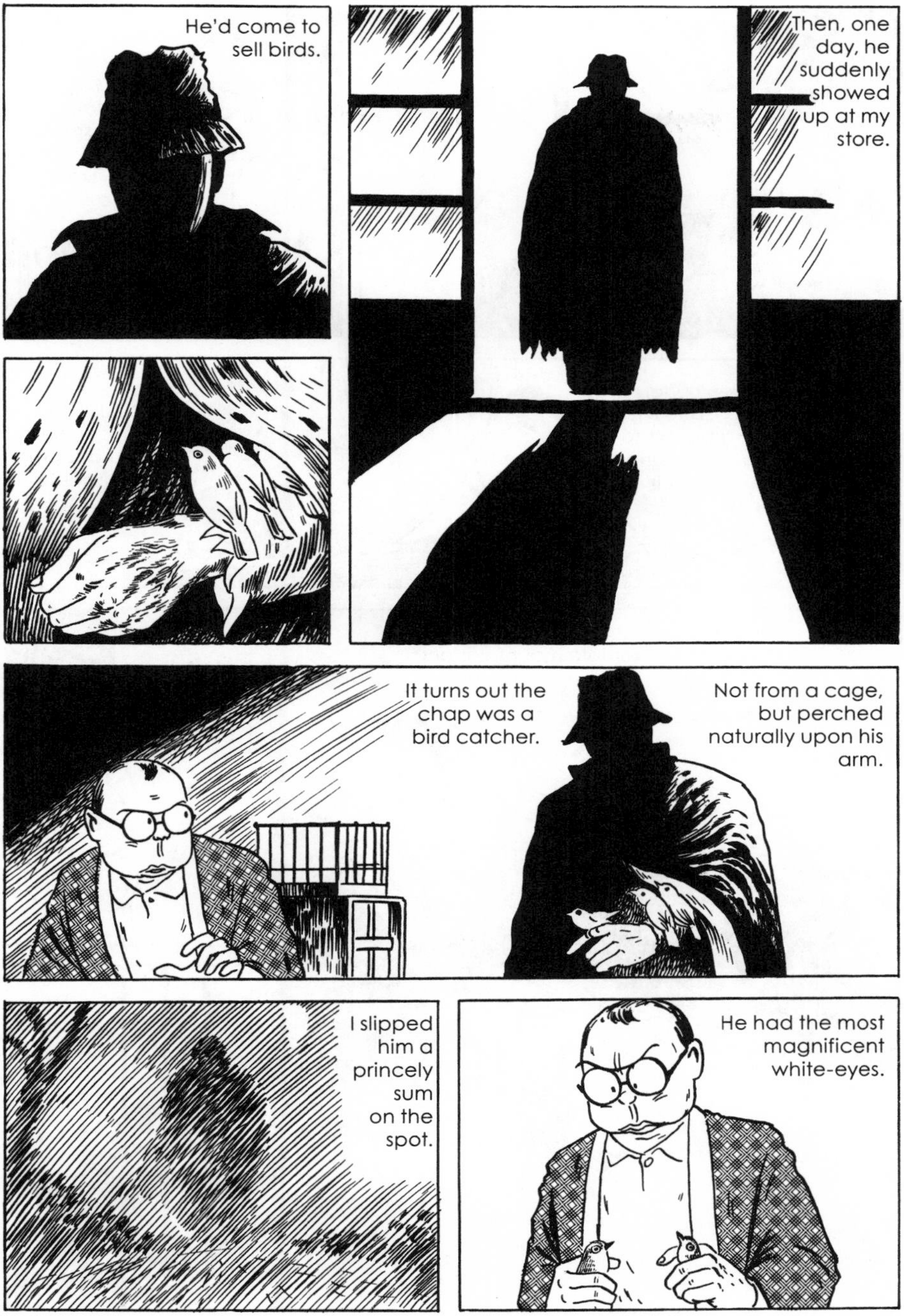
Then, one day, he suddenly showed up at my store.
He'd come to sell birds.
Not from a cage, but perched naturally upon his arm.
It turns out the chap was a bird catcher.
He had the most magnificent white-eyes.
I slipped him a princely sum on the spot.

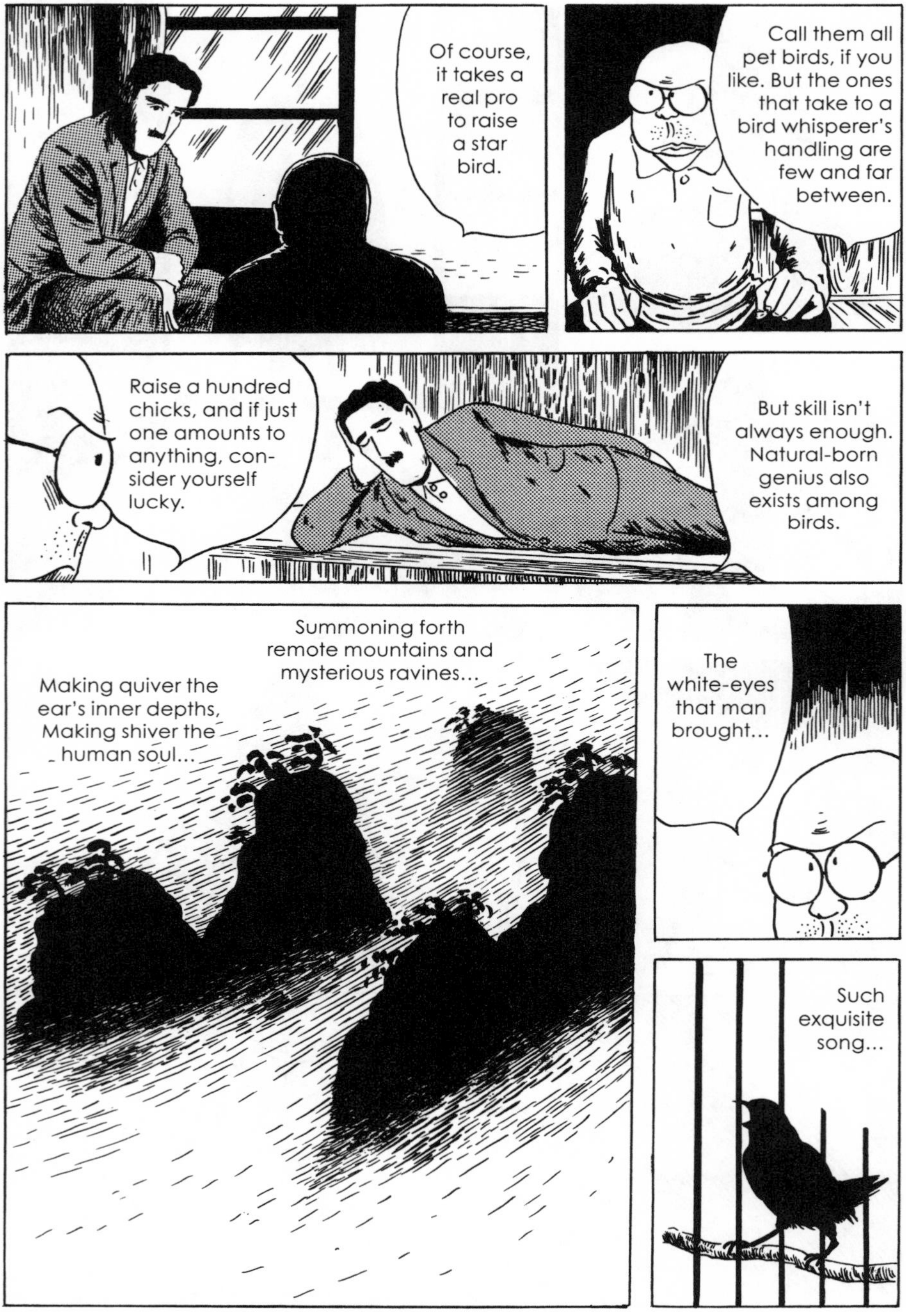
Call them all pet birds, if you like. But the ones that take to a bird whisperer's handling are few and far between.
Of course, it takes a real pro to raise a star bird.
But skill isn't always enough. Natural-born genius also exists among birds.
Raise a hundred chicks, and if just one amounts to anything, consider yourself lucky.
The white-eyes that man brought...
Such exquisite song...
Summoning forth remote mountains and mysterious ravines...
Making quiver the ear's inner depths, Making shiver the human soul...

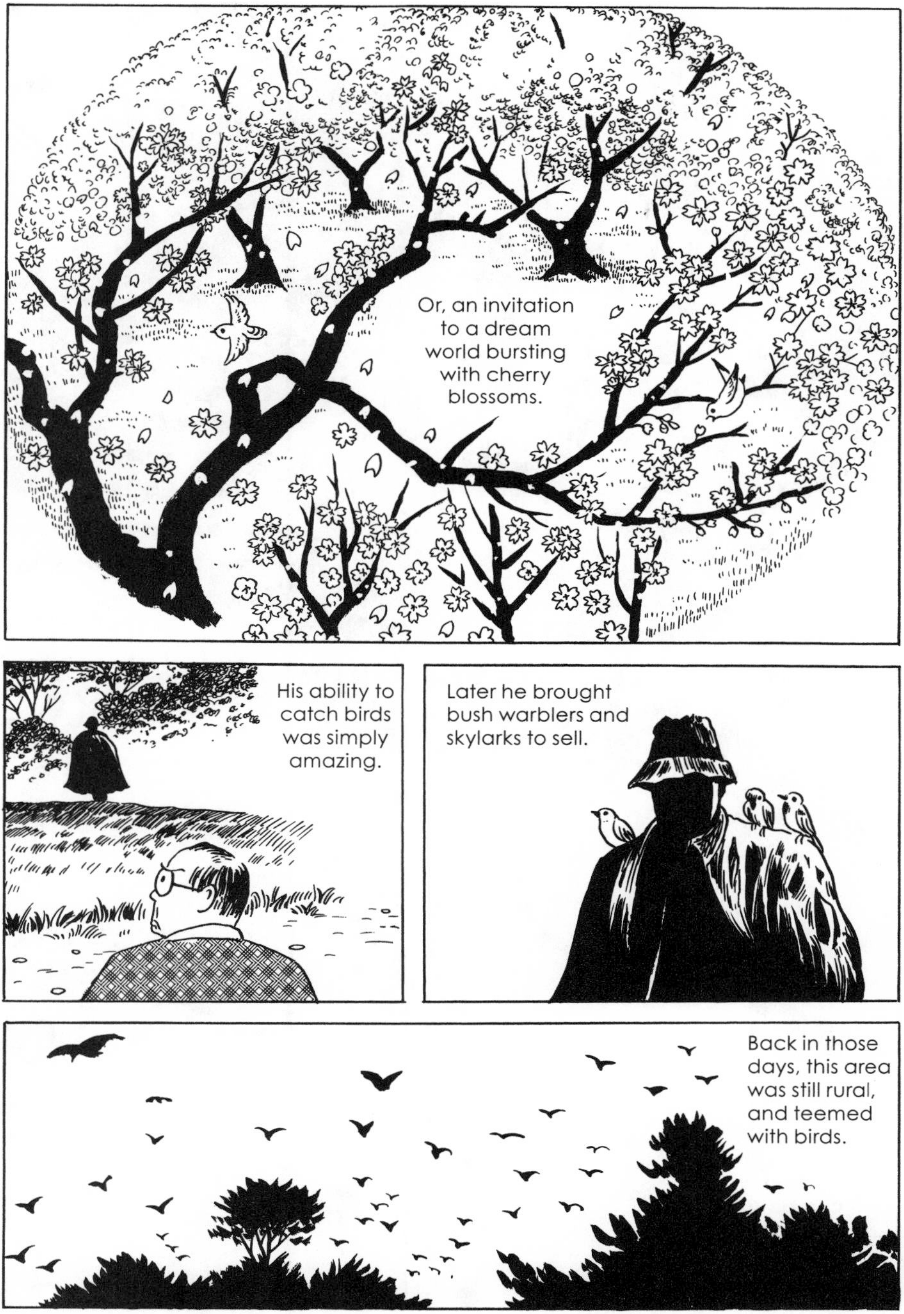
Or, an invitation to a dream world bursting with cherry blossoms.
Later he brought bush warblers and skylarks to sell.
His ability to catch birds was simply amazing.
Back in those days, this area was still rural, and teemed with birds.

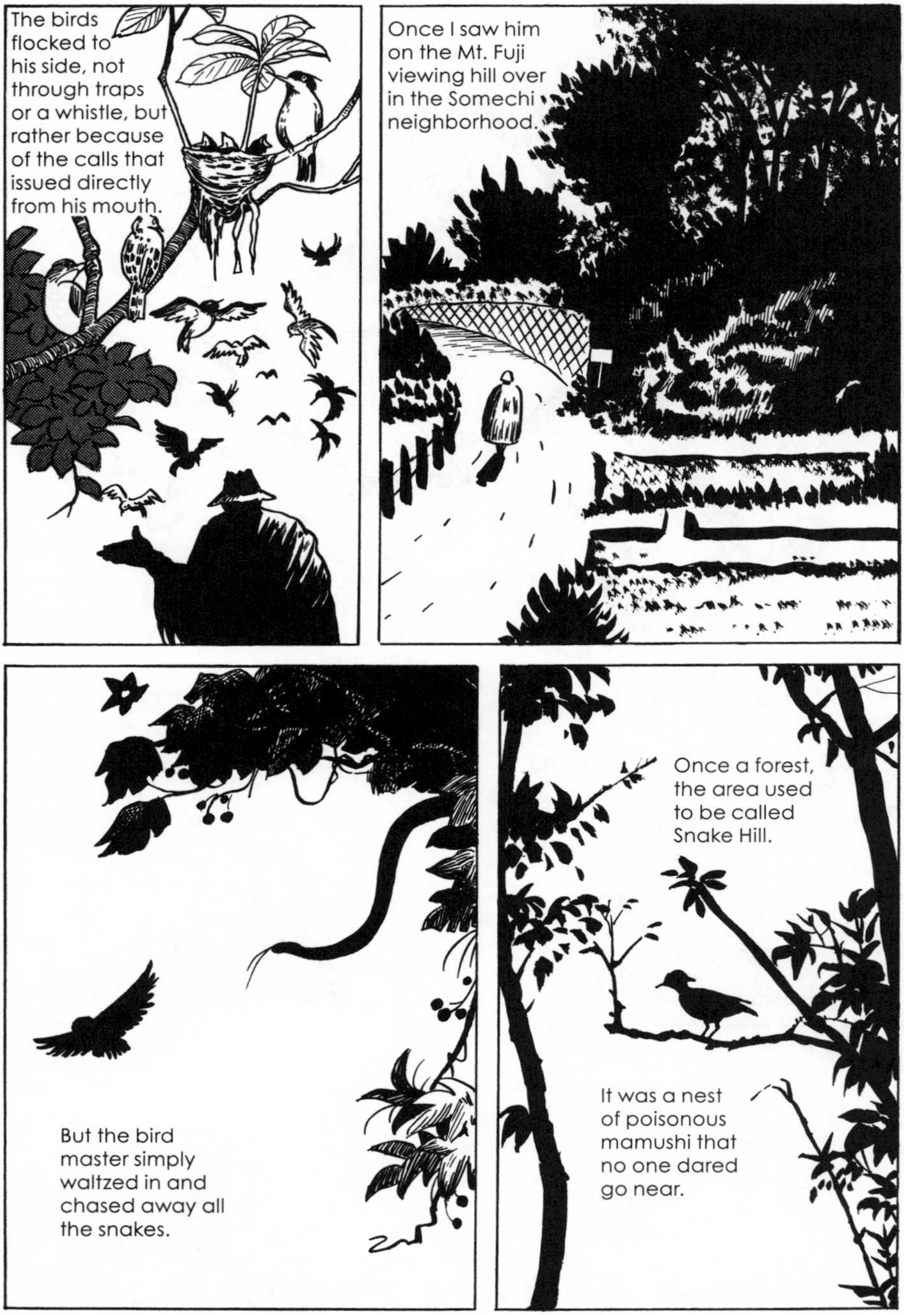
Once I saw him on the Mt. Fuji viewing hill over in the Somechi neighborhood.
The birds flocked to his side, not through traps or a whistle, but rather because of the calls that issued directly from his mouth.
Once a forest, the area used to be called Snake Hill.
It was a nest of poisonous mamushi that no one dared go near.
But the bird master simply waltzed in and chased away all the snakes.

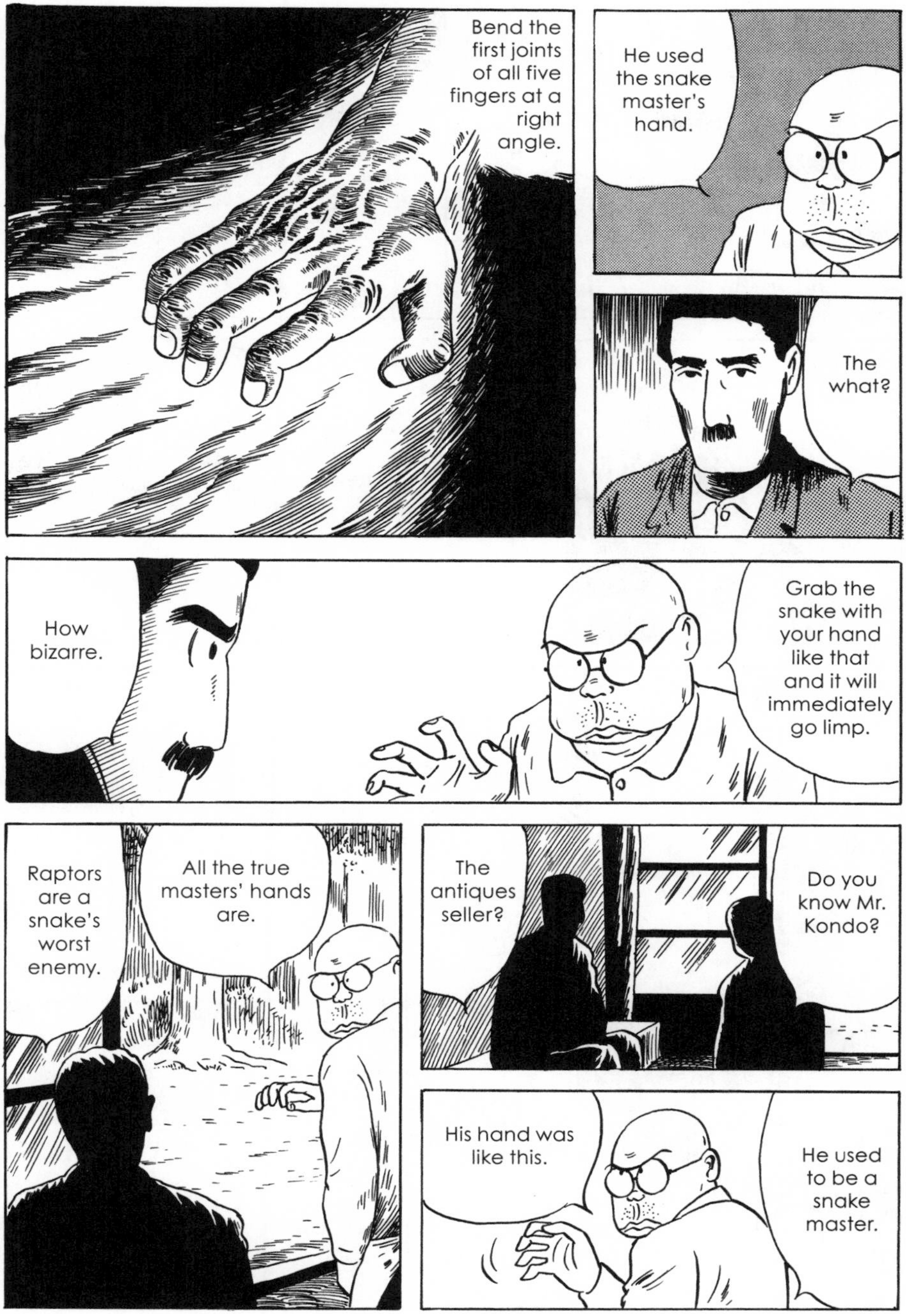
He used the snake master's hand.
The what?
Bend the first joints of all five fingers at a right angle.
Grab the snake with your hand like that and it will immediately go limp.
How bizarre.
Do you know Mr. Kondo?
The antiques seller?
He used to be a snake master.
His hand was like this.
All the true masters' hands are.
Raptors are a snake's worst enemy.

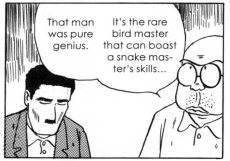

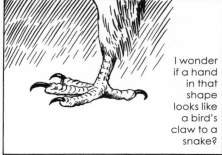

I wonder if a hand in that shape looks like a bird's claw to a snake?
That man was pure genius.
It's the rare bird master that can boast a snake master's skills...
Still, I wonder what brought him to this town...
He looked like a vagabond, that much I knew. But where he lived or who he was, I never found out.
Thanks to him, we almost had a war in the bird market here.
Mr. Sekimoto, who runs the rice shop in your complex, his obsession with white-eyes just about ruined him.
Once he gets worked up, he gets furious.
I was wrong about you!
Zero loyalty! Zero humanity!

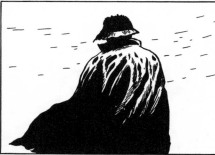

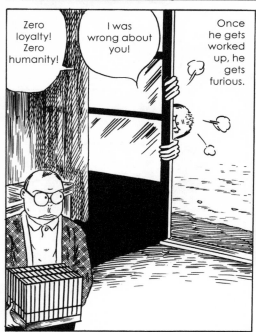

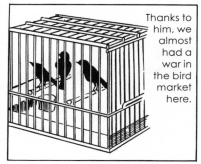

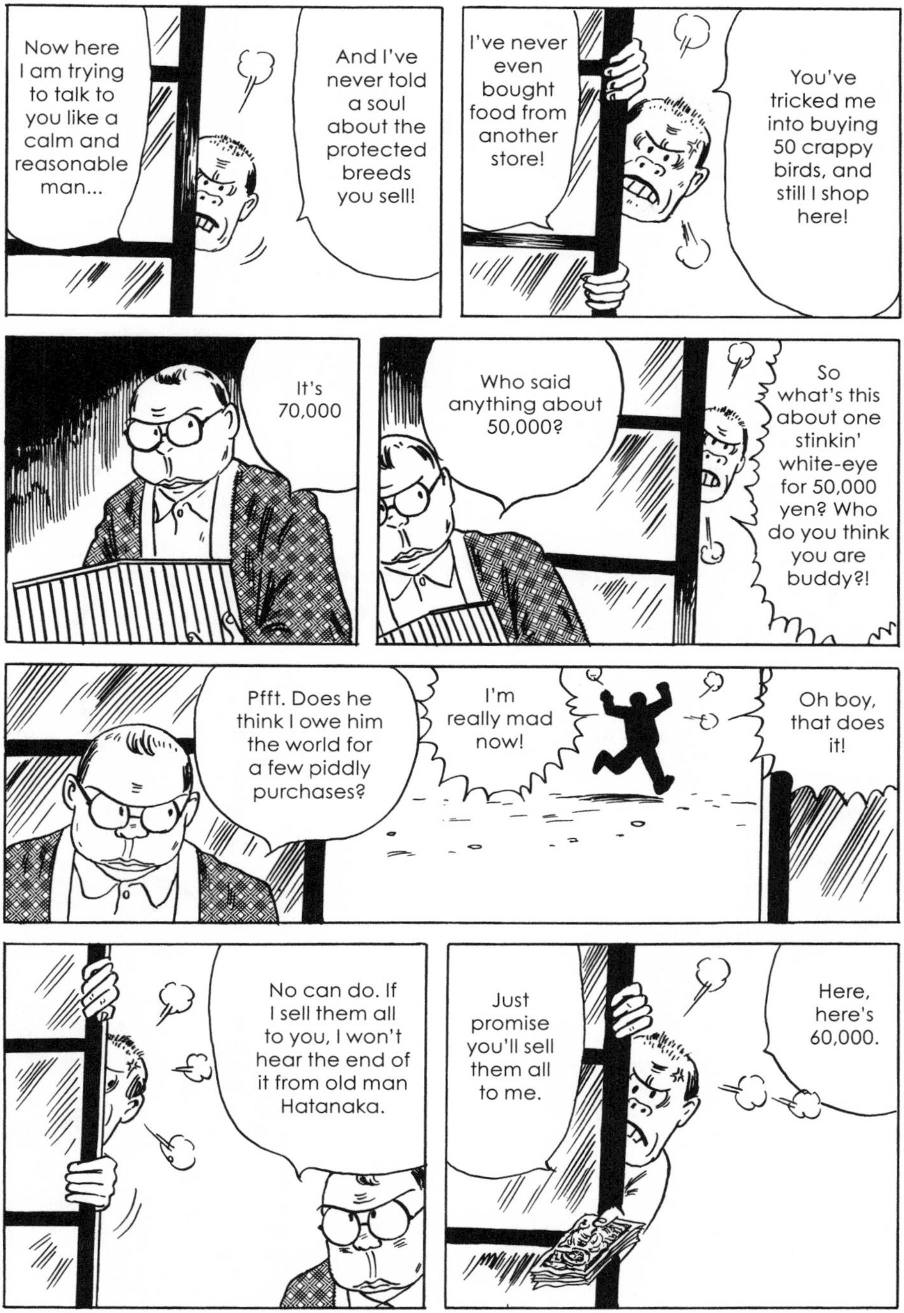
You've tricked me into buying 50 crappy birds, and still I shop here!
I've never even bought food from another store!
And I've never told a soul about the protected breeds you sell!
Now here I am trying to talk to you like a calm and reasonable man...
So what's this about one stinkin' white-eye for 50,000 yen? Who do you think you are buddy?!
Who said anything about 50,000?
It's 70,000
Oh boy, that does it!
I'm really mad now!
Pfft. Does he think I owe him the world for a few piddly purchases?
Here, here's 60,000.
Just promise you'll sell them all to me.
No can do. If I sell them all to you, I won't hear the end of it from old man Hatanaka.

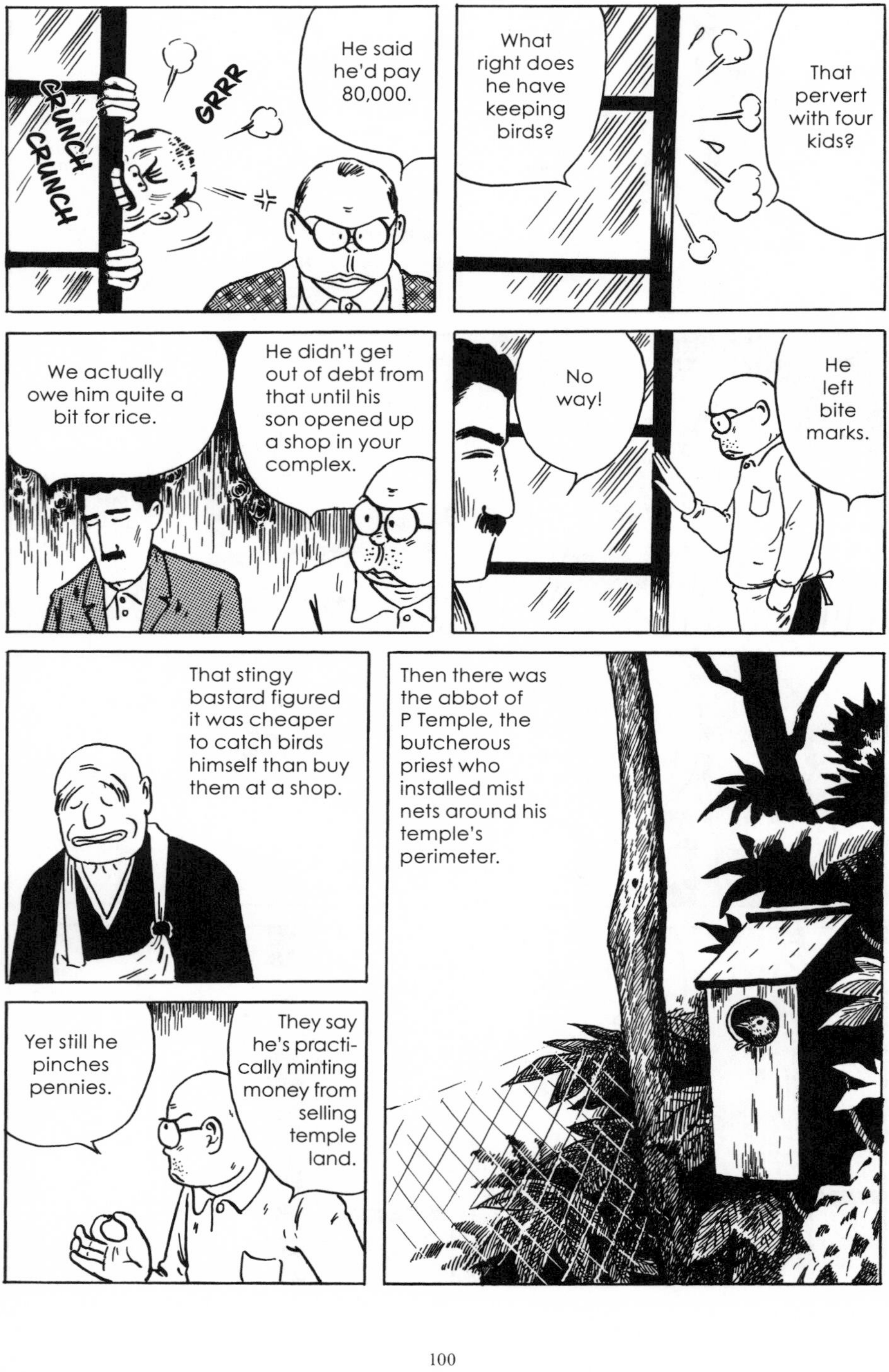
That pervert with four kids?
What right does he have keeping birds?
He said he'd pay 80,000.
GRRR
CRUNCH CRUNCH
He left bite marks.
No way!
He didn't get out of debt from that until his son opened up a shop in your complex.
We actually owe him quite a bit for rice.
Then there was the abbot of P Temple, the butcherous priest who installed mist nets around his temple's perimeter.
That stingy bastard figured it was cheaper to catch birds himself than buy them at a shop.
They say he's practically minting money from selling temple land.
Yet still he pinches pennies.

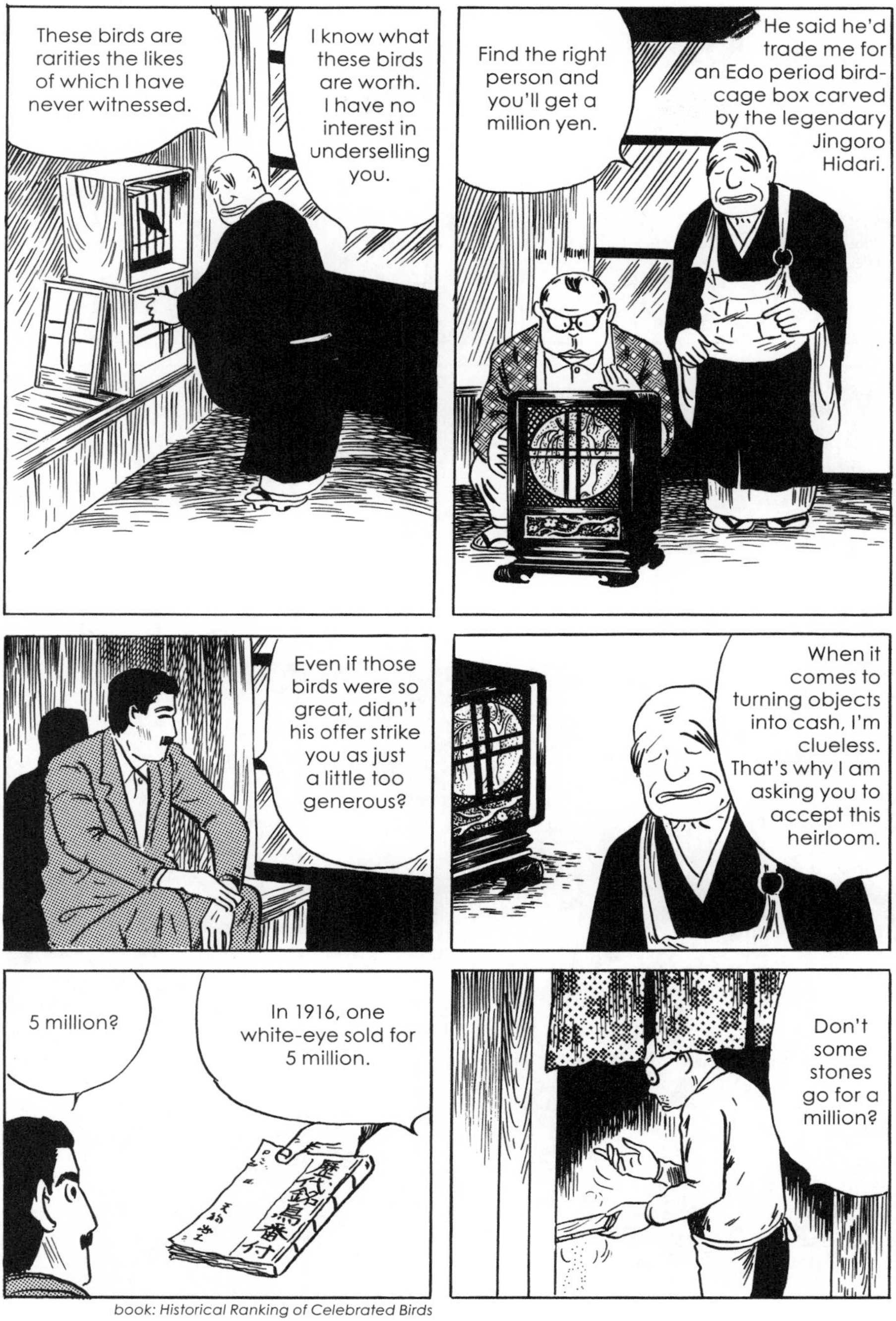
He said he'd trade me for an Edo period bird-cage box carved by the legendary Jingoro Hidari.
Find the right person and you'll get a million yen.
I know what these birds are worth. I have no interest in underselling you.
These birds are rarities the likes of which I have never witnessed.
When it comes to turning objects into cash, I'm clueless. That's why I am asking you to accept this heirloom.
Even if those birds were so great, didn't his offer strike you as just a little too generous?
Don't some stones go for a million?
In 1916, one white-eye sold for 5 million.
5 million?
歴代銘鳥番付

book: *Historical Ranking of Celebrated Birds*

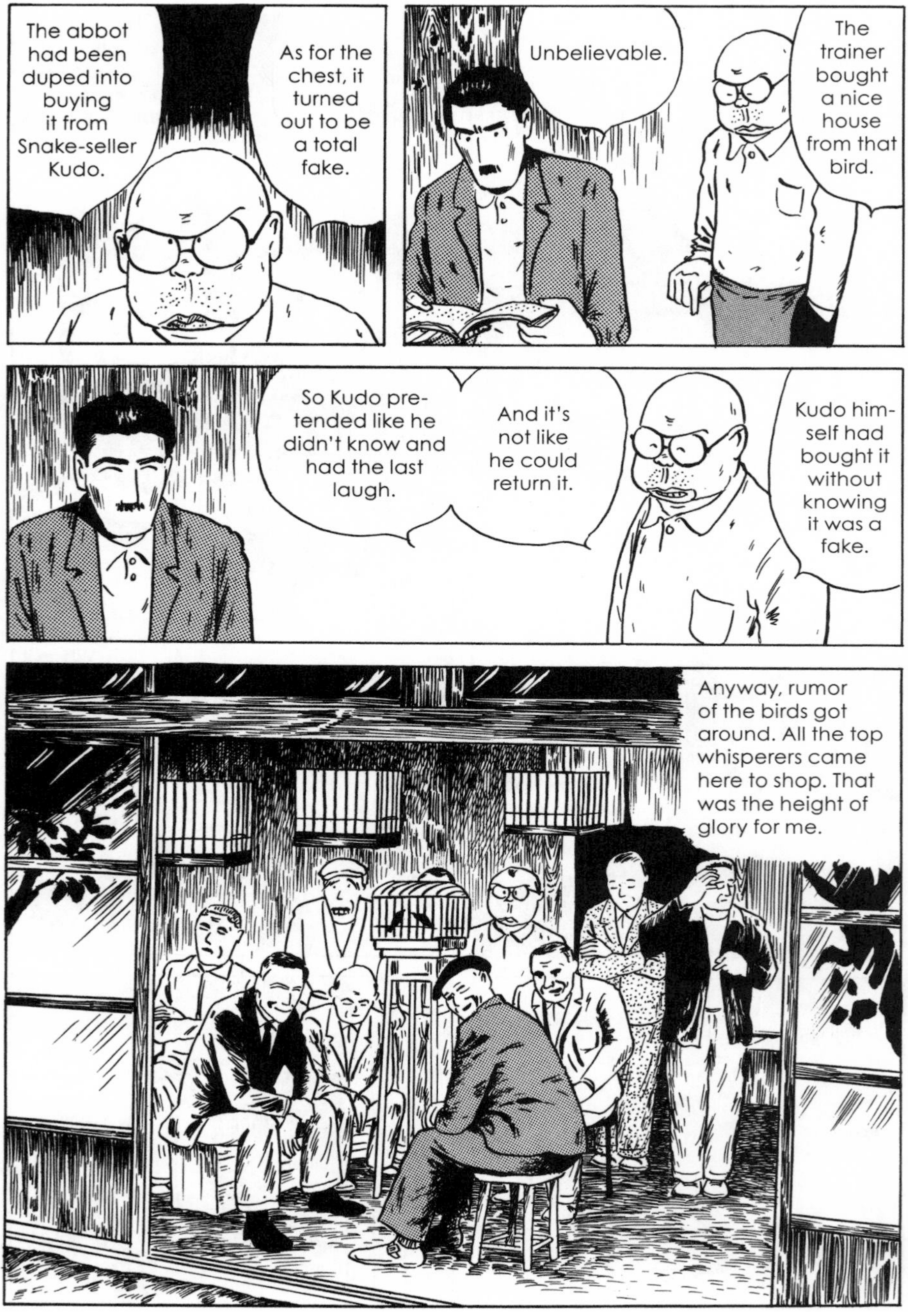
The trainer bought a nice house from that bird.
Unbelievable.
As for the chest, it turned out to be a total fake.
The abbot had been duped into buying it from Snake-seller Kudo.
Kudo him-self had bought it without knowing it was a fake.
And it's not like he could return it.
So Kudo pre-tended like he didn't know and had the last laugh.
Anyway, rumor of the birds got around. All the top whisperers came here to shop. That was the height of glory for me.

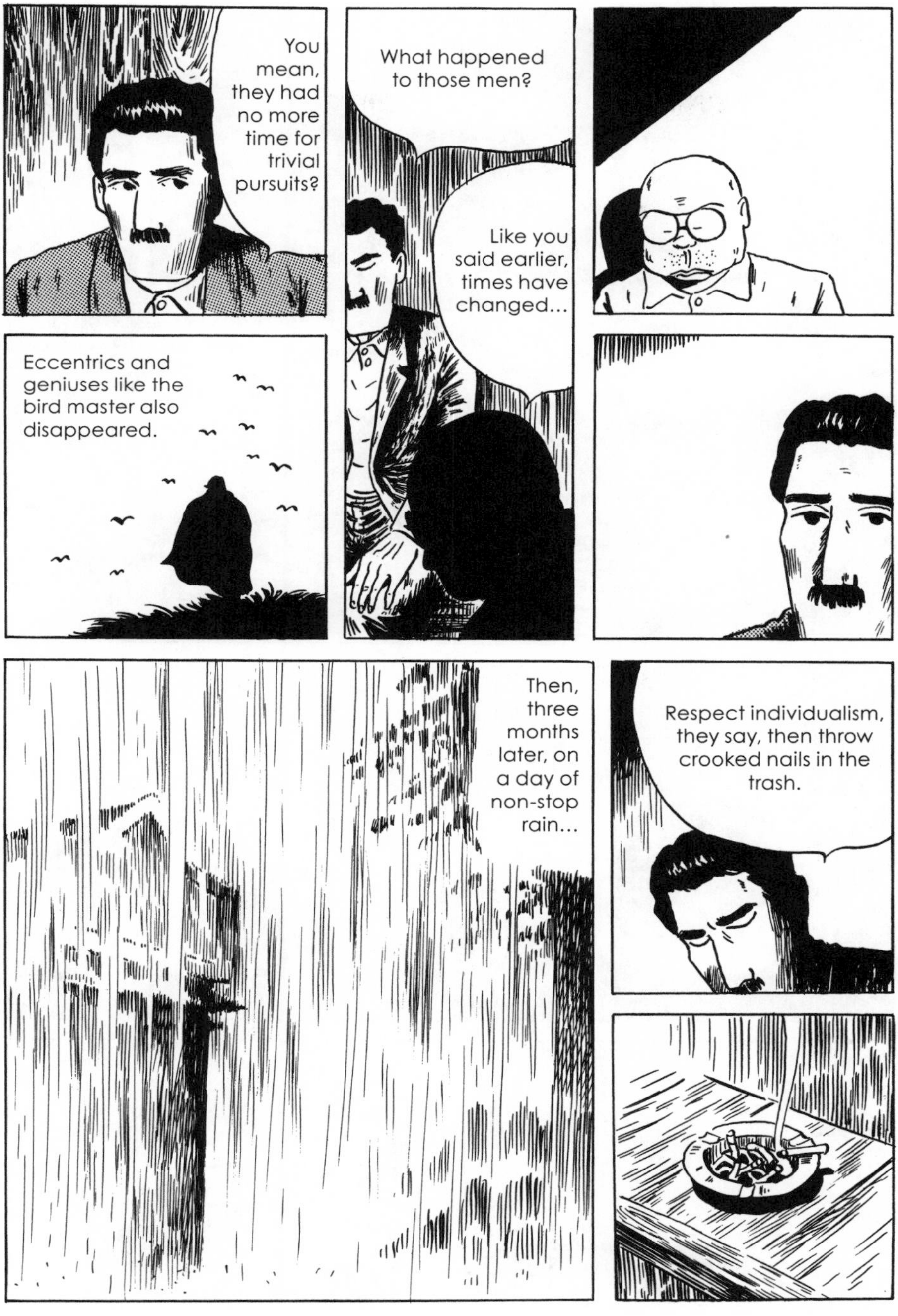
What happened to those men?
Like you said earlier, times have changed...
You mean, they had no more time for trivial pursuits?
Eccentrics and geniuses like the bird master also disappeared.
Respect individualism, they say, then throw crooked nails in the trash.
Then, three months later, on a day of non-stop rain...

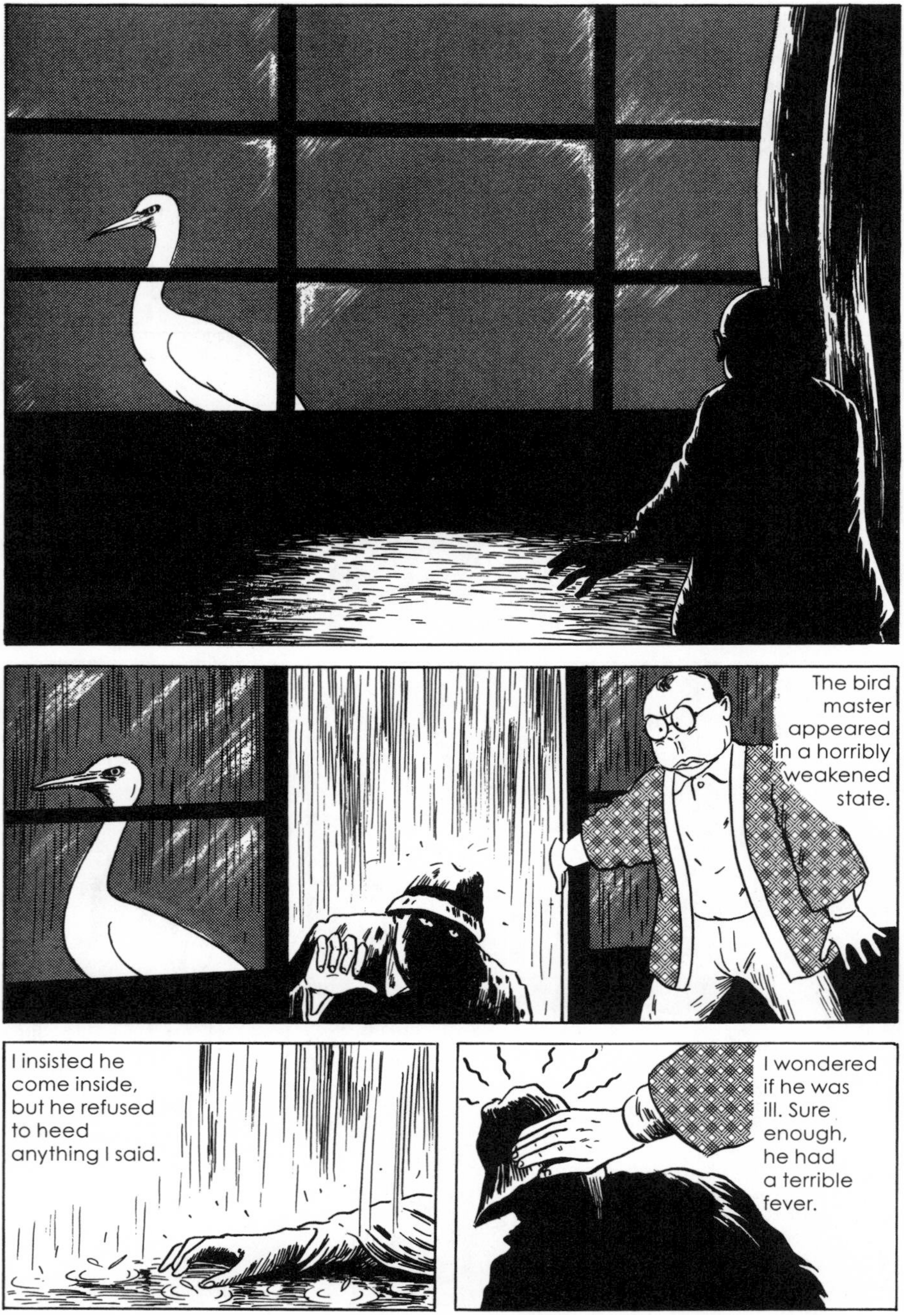
The bird master appeared in a horribly weakened state.
I wondered if he was ill. Sure enough, he had a terrible fever.
I insisted he come inside, but he refused to heed anything I said.

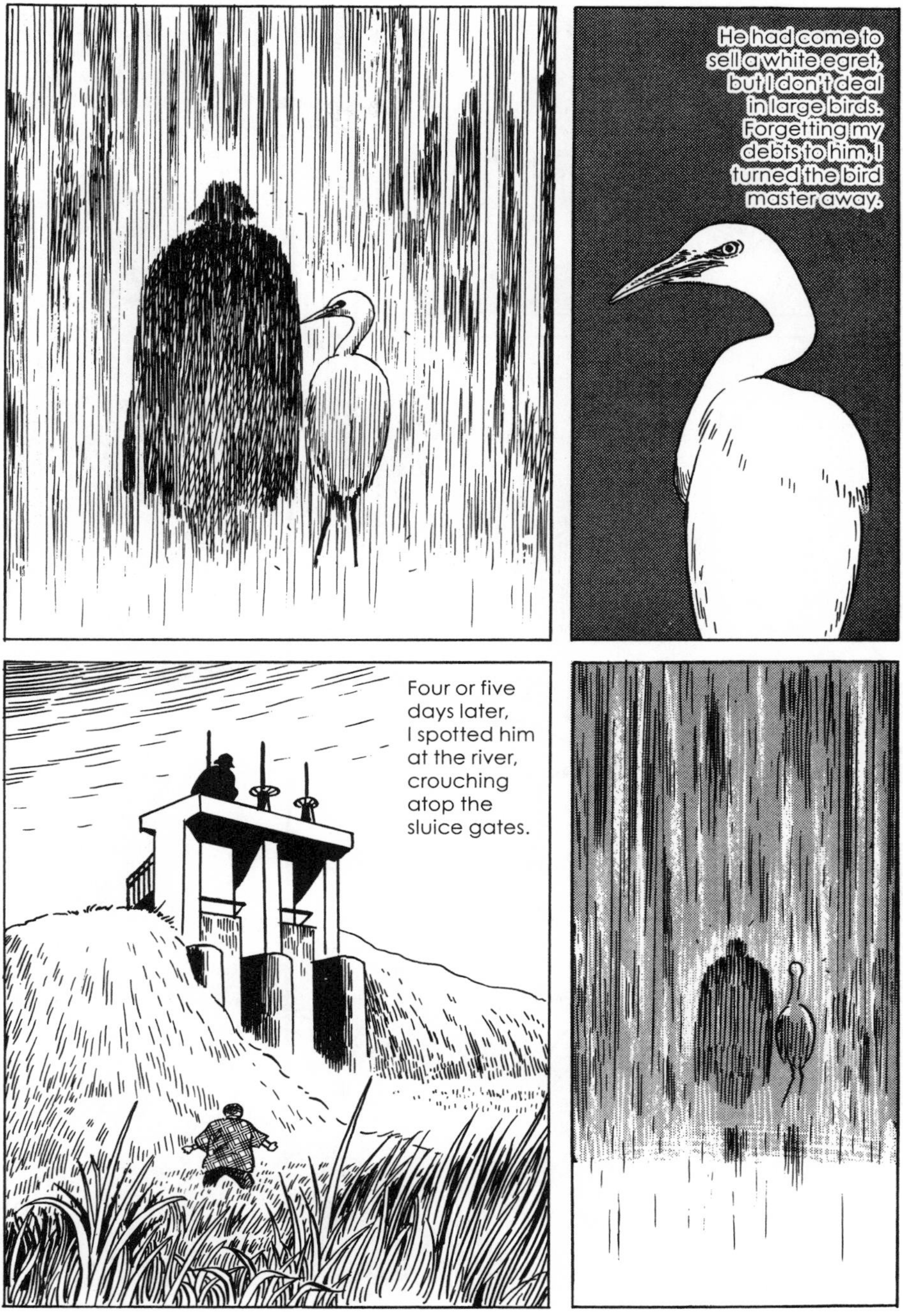
He had come to sell a white egret, but I don't deal in large birds. Forgetting my debts to him, I turned the bird master away.
Four or five days later, I spotted him at the river, crouching atop the sluice gates.

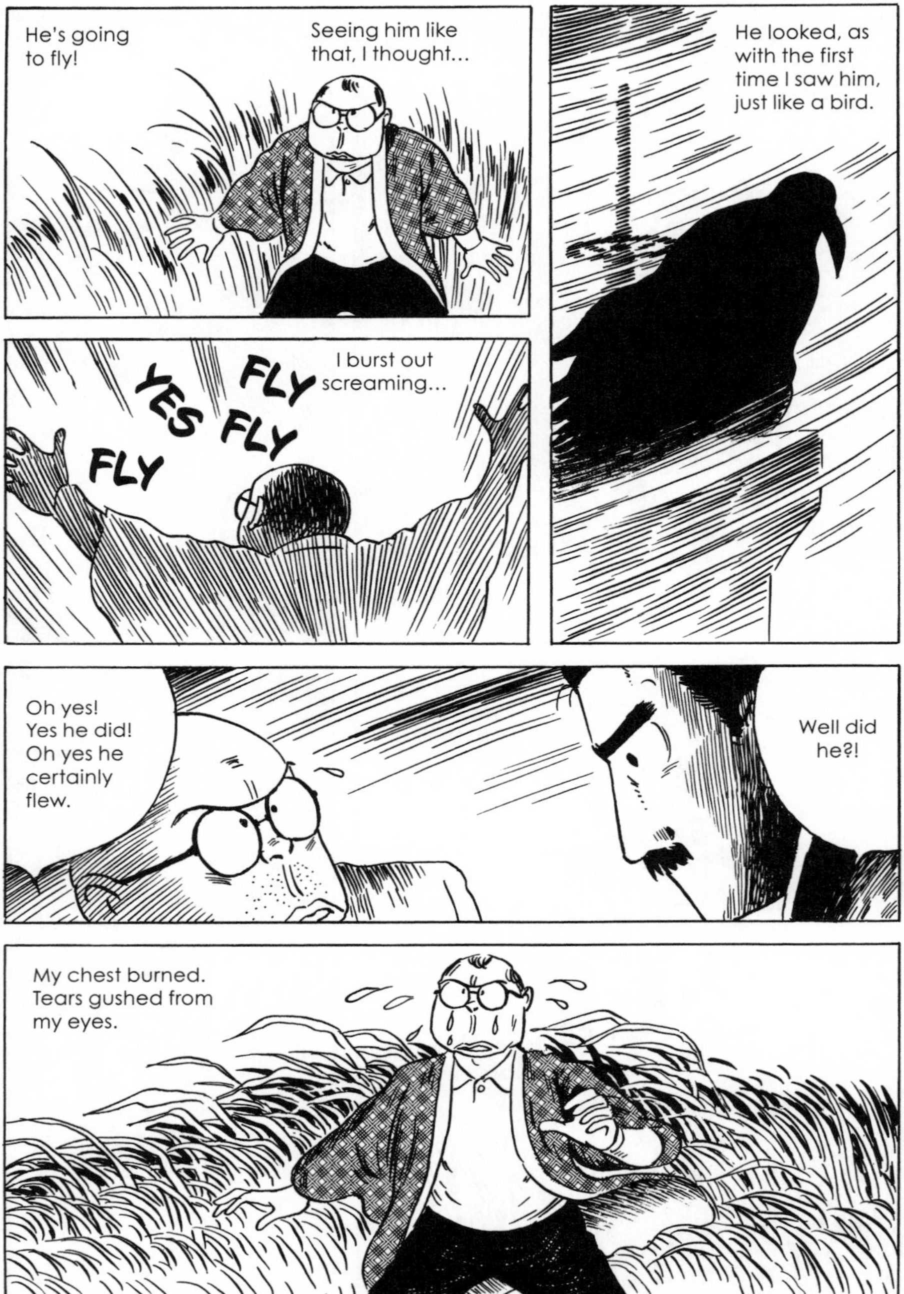
He looked, as with the first time I saw him, just like a bird.
Seeing him like that, I thought...
He's going to fly!
I burst out screaming...
FLY
YES FLY
FLY
Well did he?!
Oh yes! Yes he did! Oh yes he certainly flew.
My chest burned. Tears gushed from my eyes.

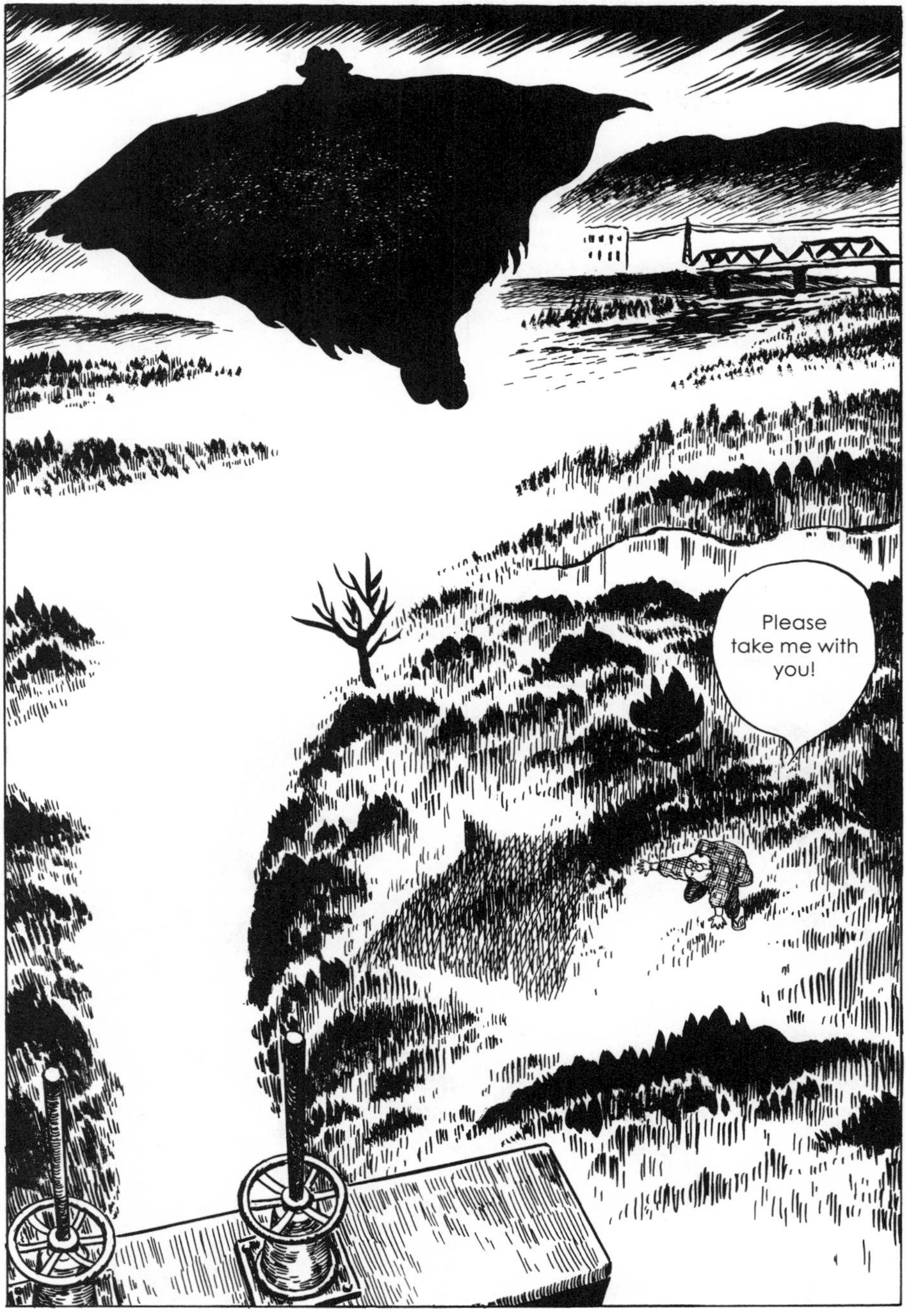
Please take me with you!

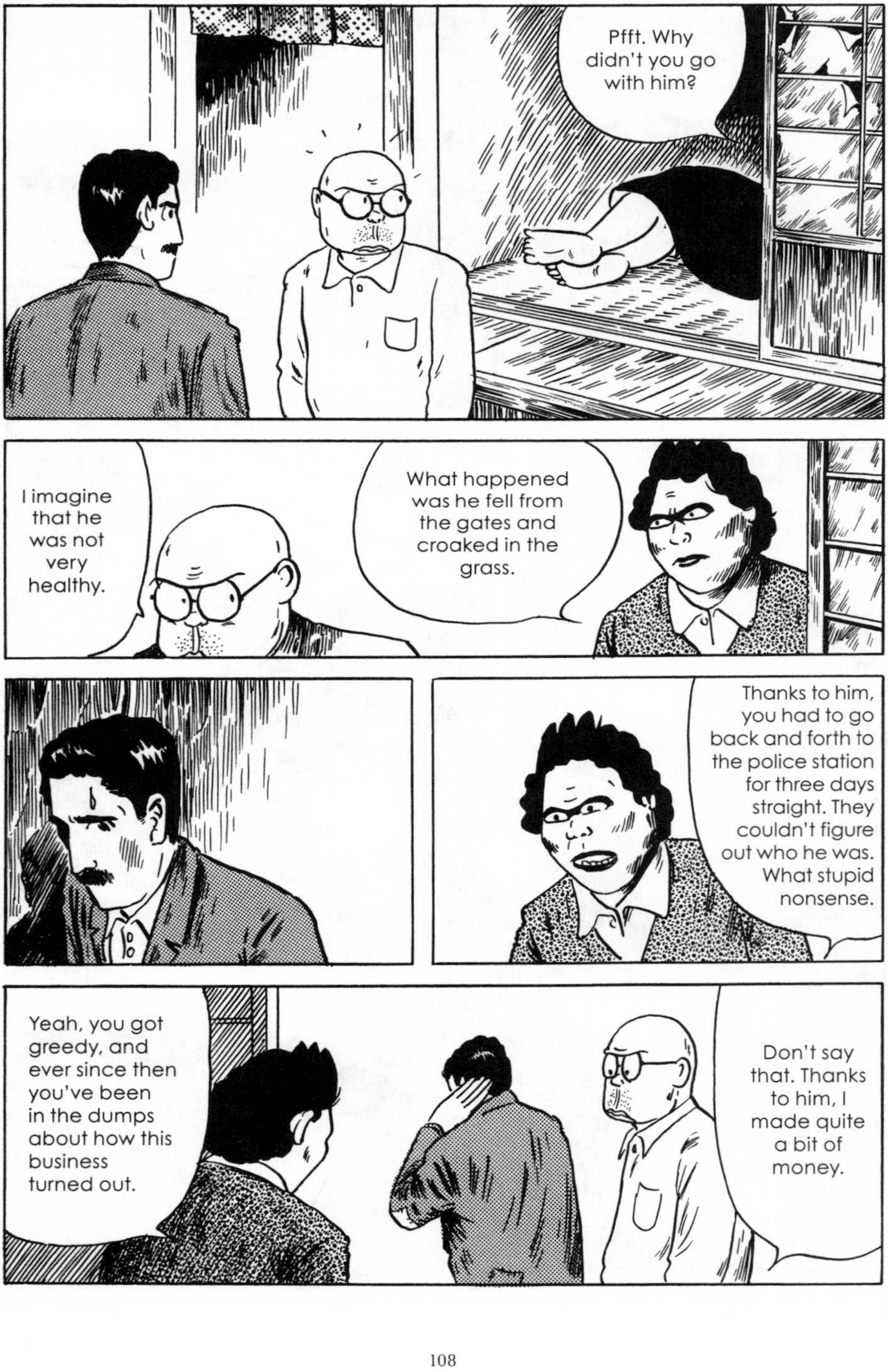
Pfft. Why didn't you go with him?
What happened was he fell from the gates and croaked in the grass.
I imagine that he was not very healthy.
Thanks to him, you had to go back and forth to the police station for three days straight. They couldn't figure out who he was. What stupid nonsense.
Don't say that. Thanks to him, I made quite a bit of money.
Yeah, you got greedy, and ever since then you've been in the dumps about how this business turned out.

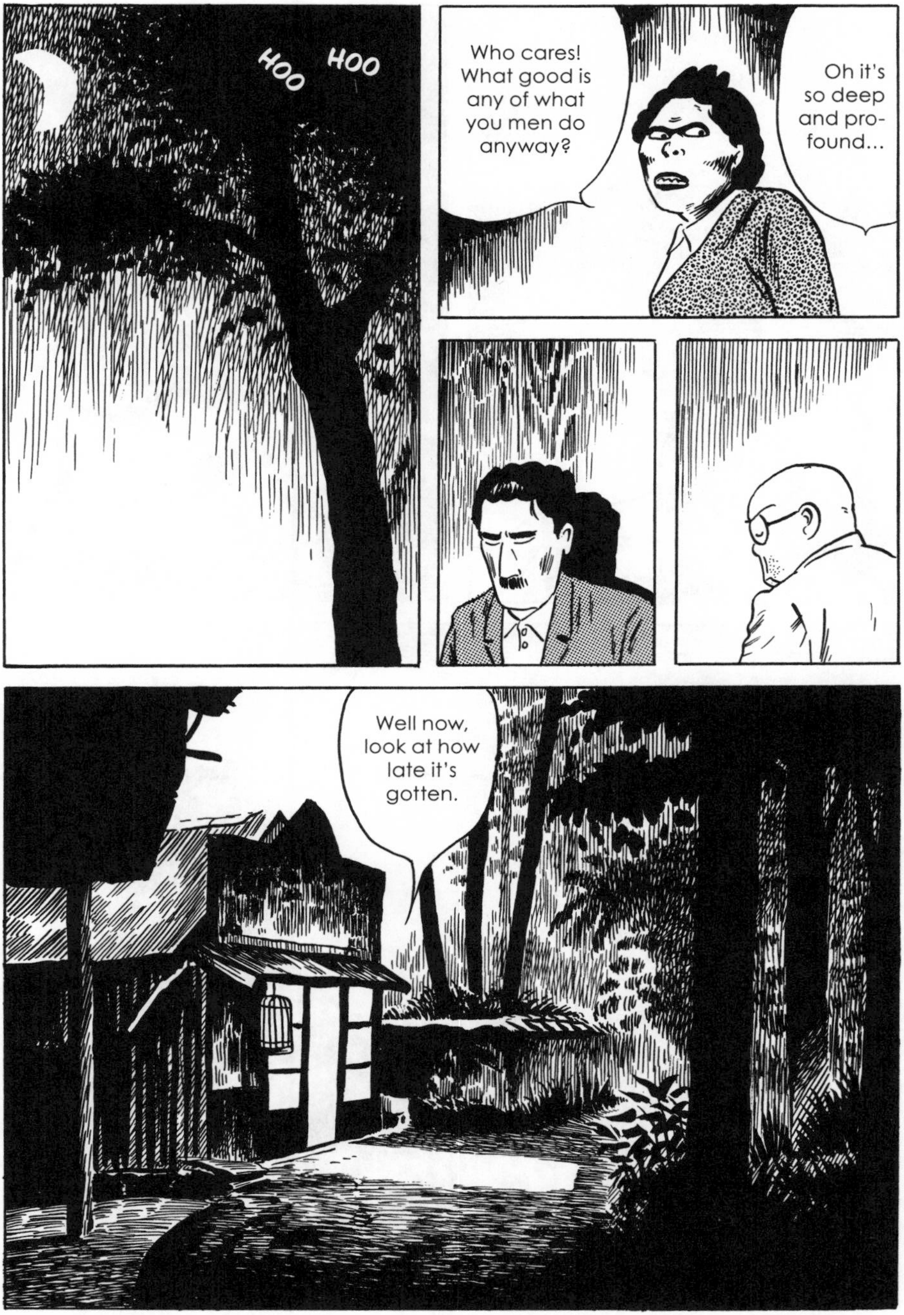
Oh it's so deep and pro-found...
Who cares! What good is any of what you men do anyway?
HOO HOO
Well now, look at how late it's gotten.

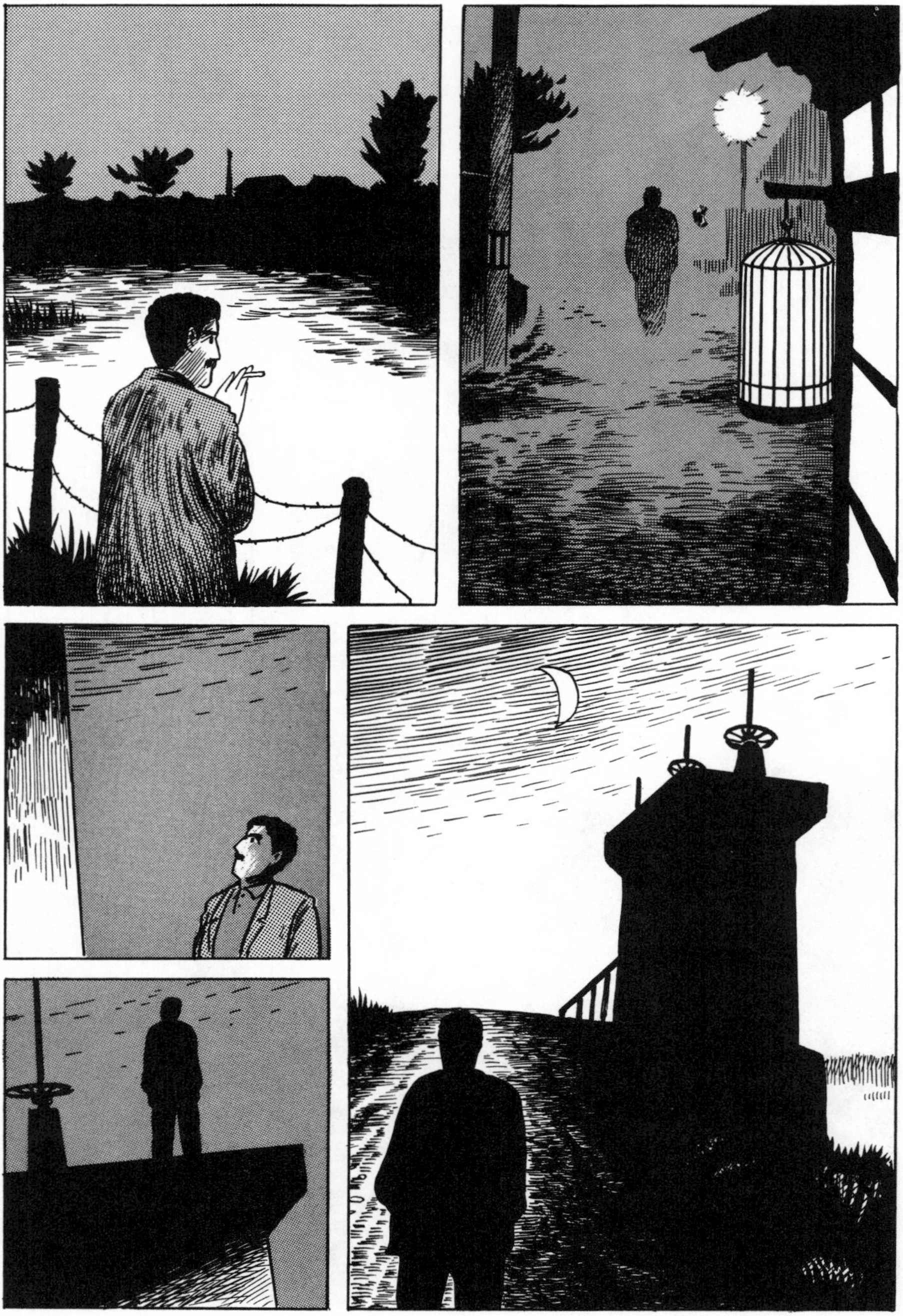

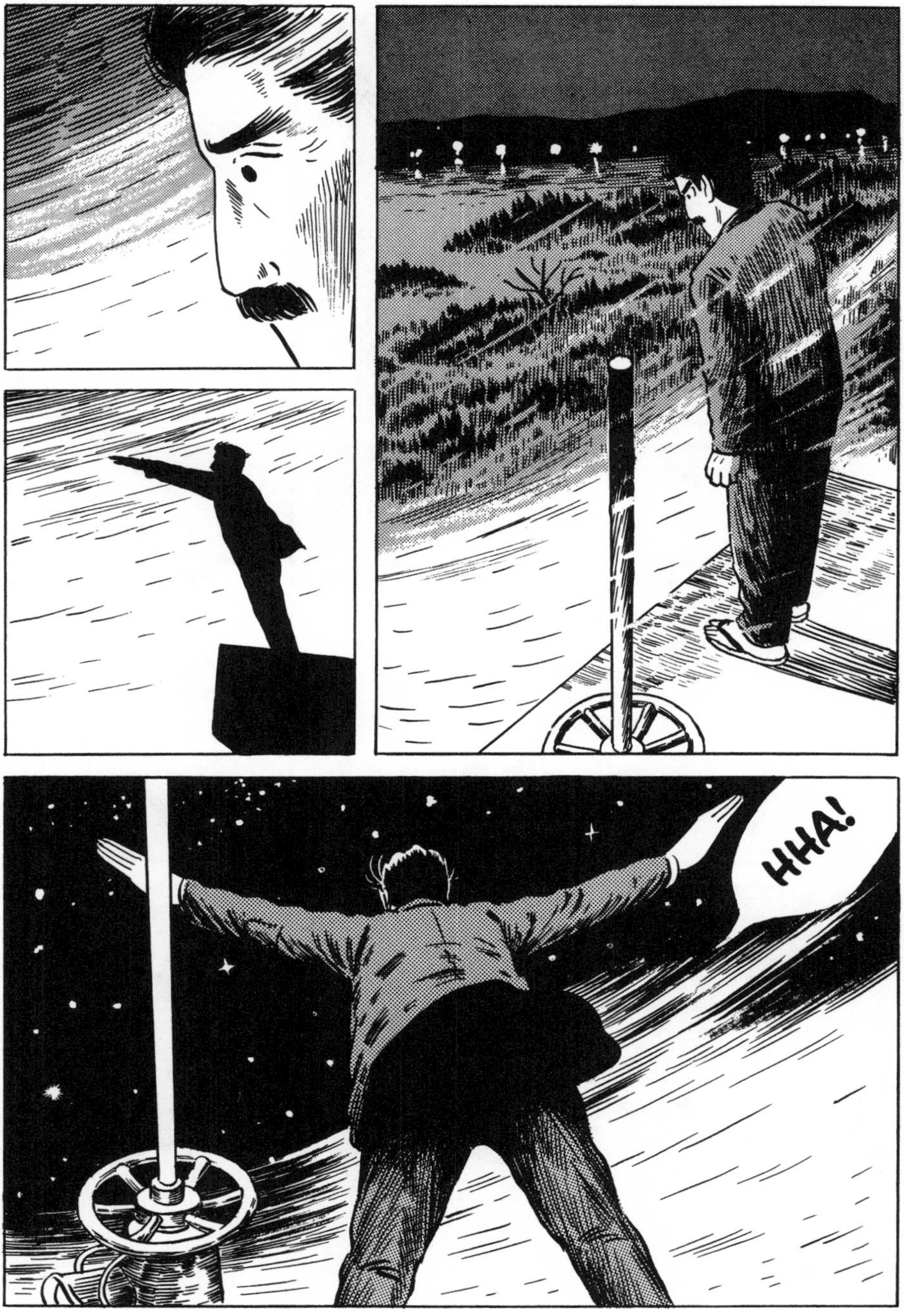
HHA!

Daddy
It's time to come home.

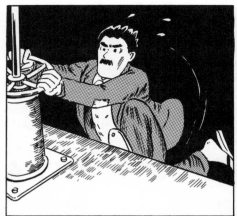

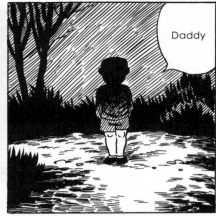

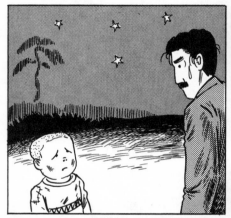

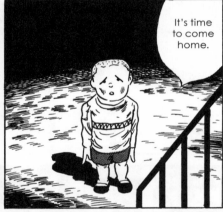

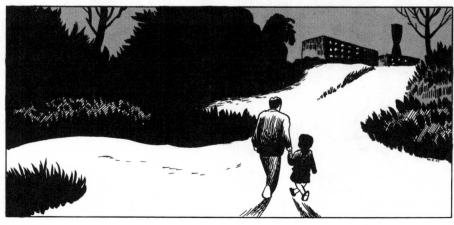

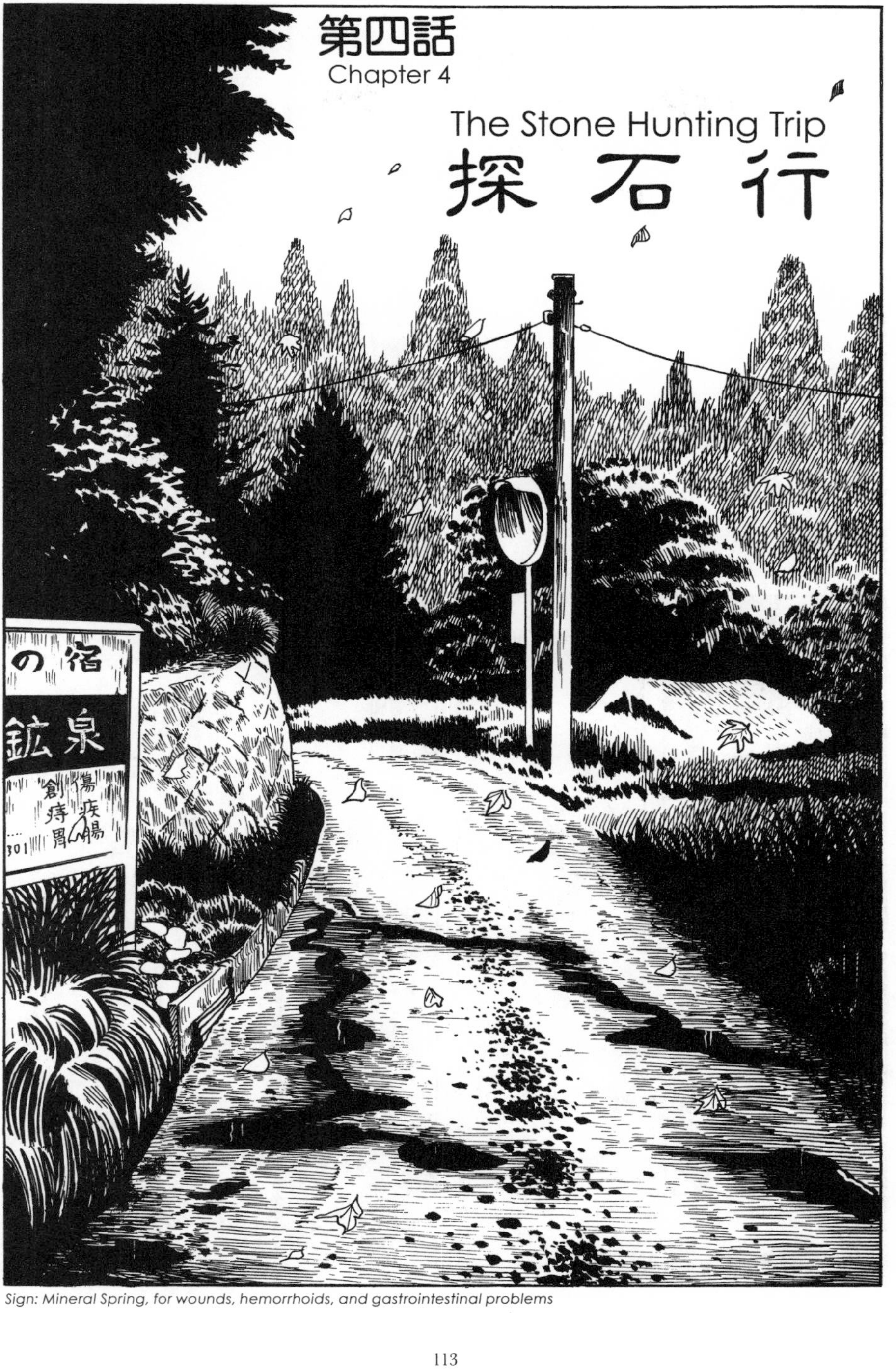
第四話
Chapter 4
The Stone Hunting Trip
探石行
の宿
鉱泉
創傷
痔疾
胃腸
301
Sign: Mineral Spring, for wounds, hemorrhoids, and gastrointestinal problems

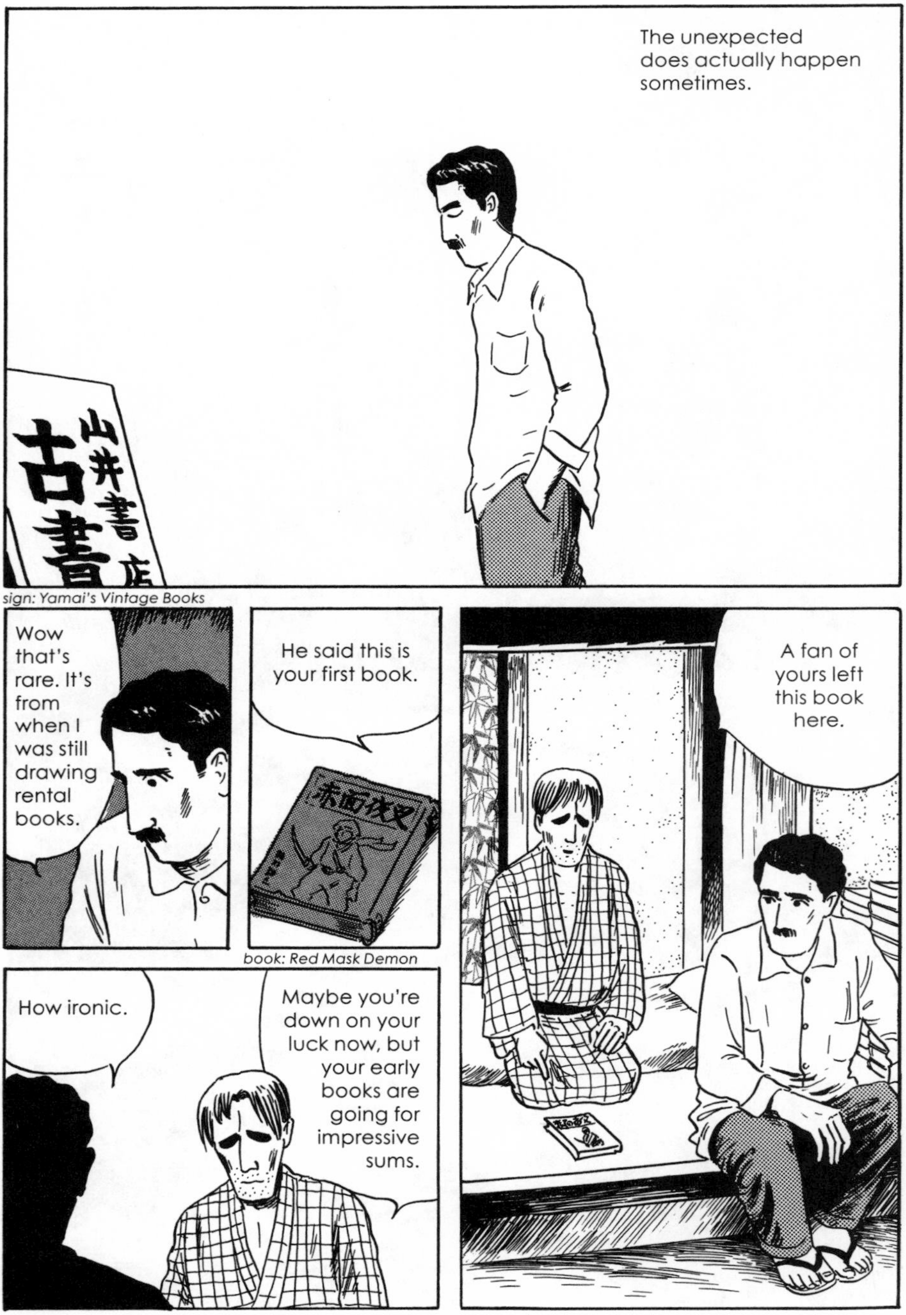
The unexpected does actually happen sometimes.
山井書店
古書
sign: Yamai's Vintage Books
A fan of yours left this book here.
He said this is your first book.
book: Red Mask Demon
Wow that's rare. It's from when I was still drawing rental books.
Maybe you're down on your luck now, but your early books are going for impressive sums.
How ironic.

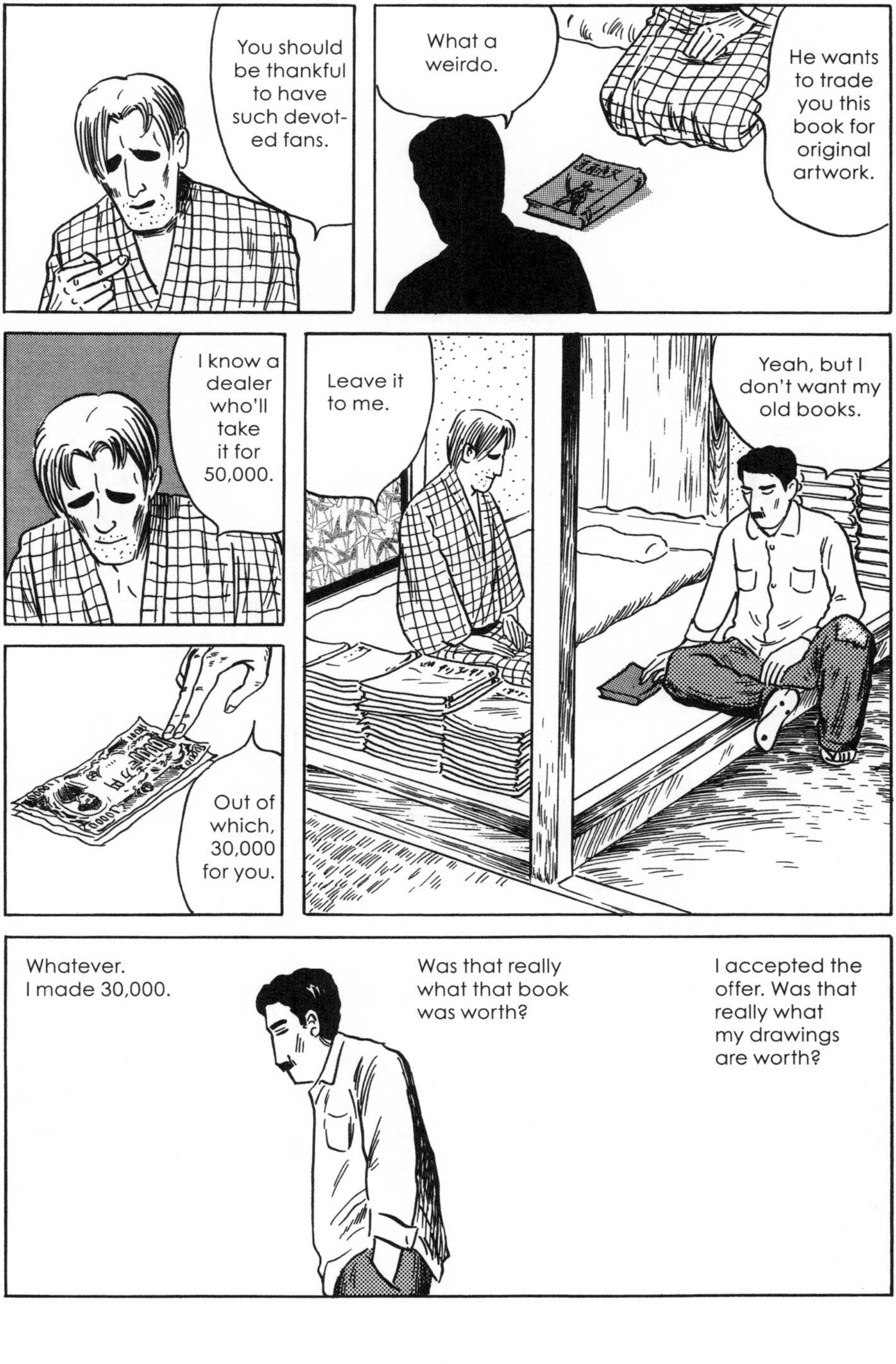
He wants to trade you this book for original artwork.
What a weirdo.
You should be thankful to have such devoted fans.
Yeah, but I don't want my old books.
Leave it to me.
I know a dealer who'll take it for 50,000.
Out of which, 30,000 for you.
I accepted the offer. Was that really what my drawings are worth?
Was that really what that book was worth?
Whatever. I made 30,000.

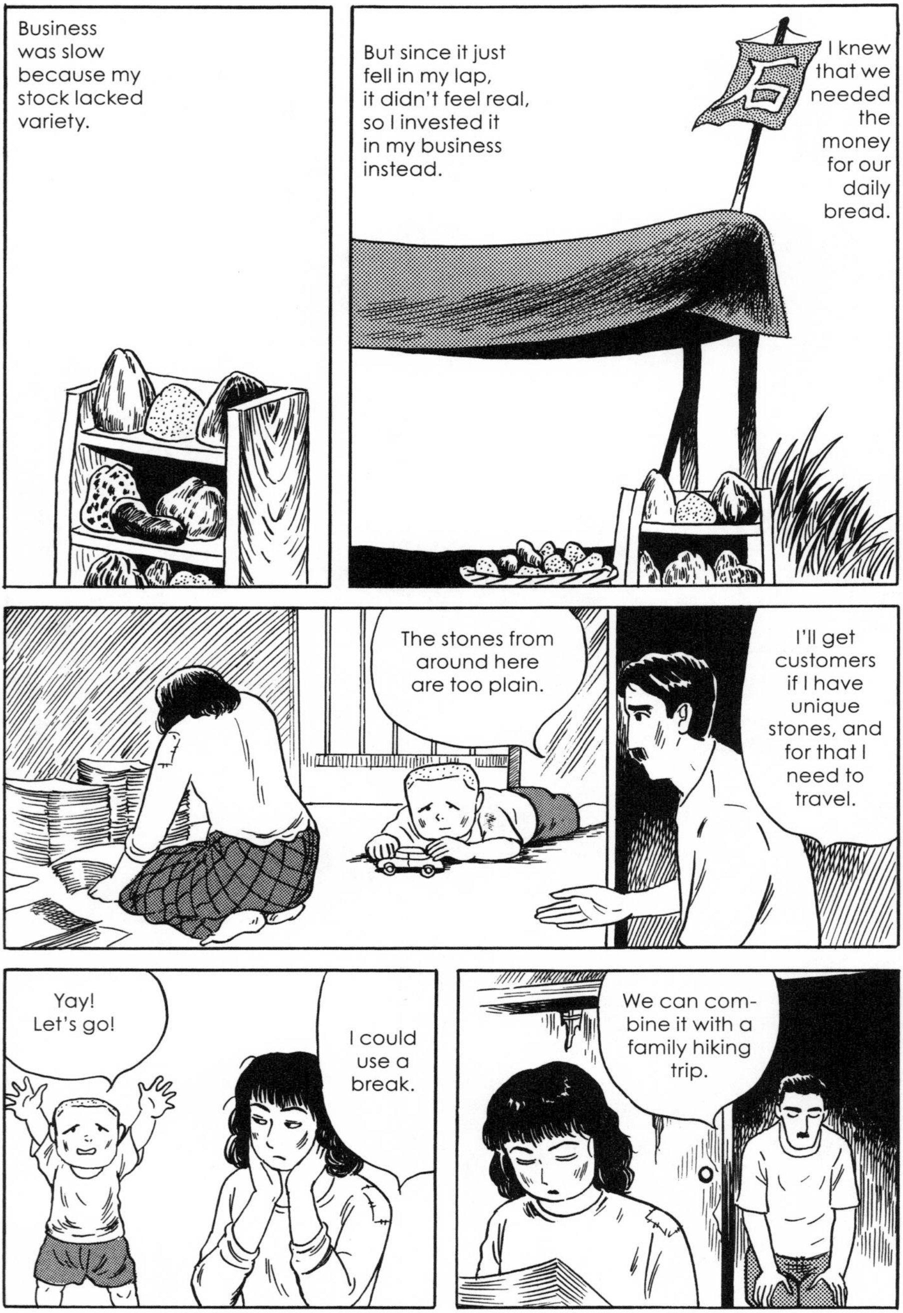
I knew that we needed the money for our daily bread.
But since it just fell in my lap, it didn't feel real, so I invested it in my business instead.
Business was slow because my stock lacked variety.
I'll get customers if I have unique stones, and for that I need to travel.
The stones from around here are too plain.
We can combine it with a family hiking trip.
I could use a break.
Yay! Let's go!

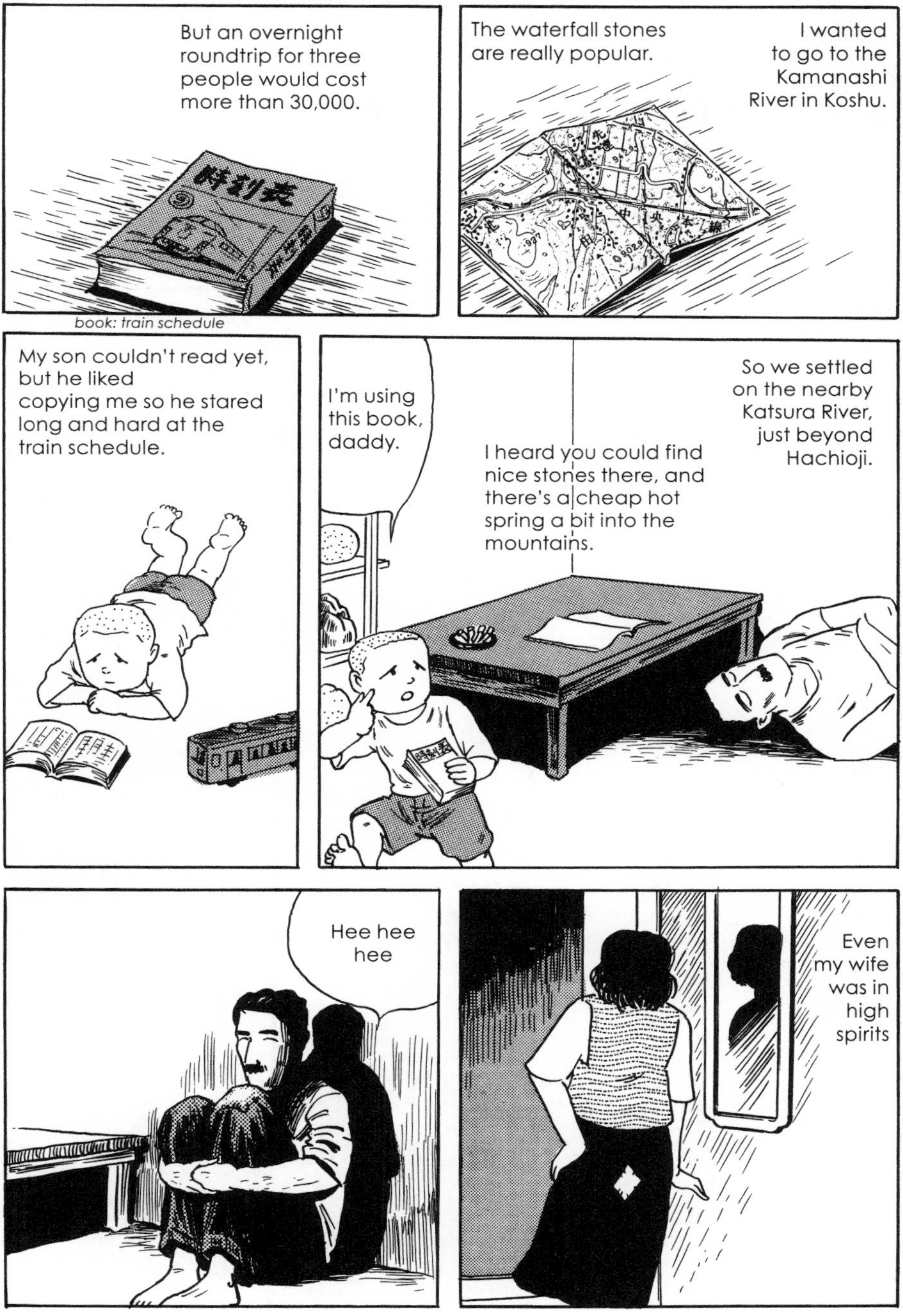
I wanted to go to the Kamanashi River in Koshu.
The waterfall stones are really popular.
But an overnight roundtrip for three people would cost more than 30,000.
book: train schedule
So we settled on the nearby Katsura River, just beyond Hachioji.
I heard you could find nice stones there, and there's a cheap hot spring a bit into the mountains.
I'm using this book, daddy.
My son couldn't read yet, but he liked copying me so he stared long and hard at the train schedule.
Even my wife was in high spirits
Hee hee hee

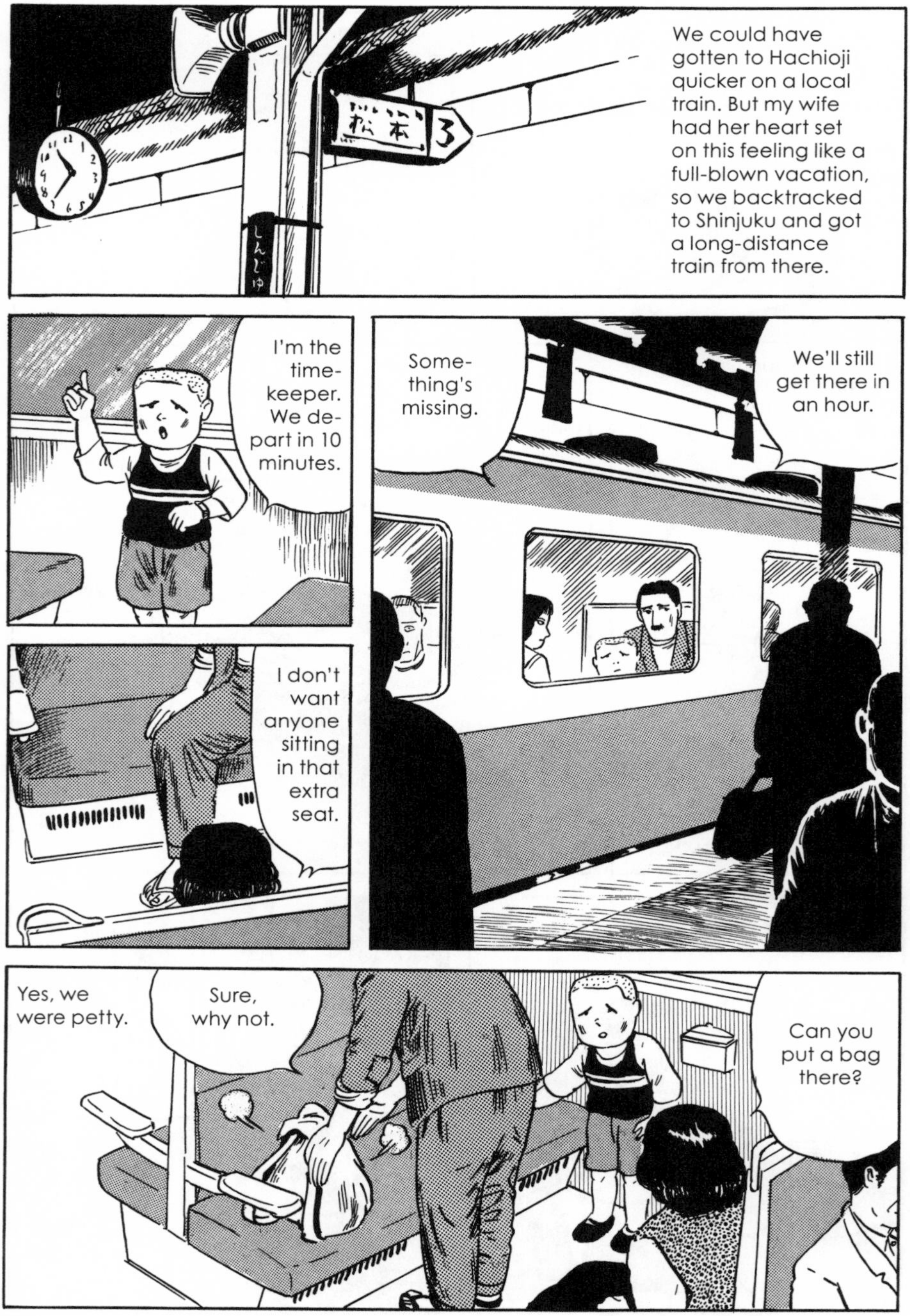

We could have gotten to Hachioji quicker on a local train. But my wife had her heart set on this feeling like a full-blown vacation, so we backtracked to Shinjuku and got a long-distance train from there.
We'll still get there in an hour.
Some-thing's missing.
I'm the time-keeper. We de-part in 10 minutes.
I don't want anyone sitting in that extra seat.
Can you put a bag there?
Sure, why not.
Yes, we were petty.

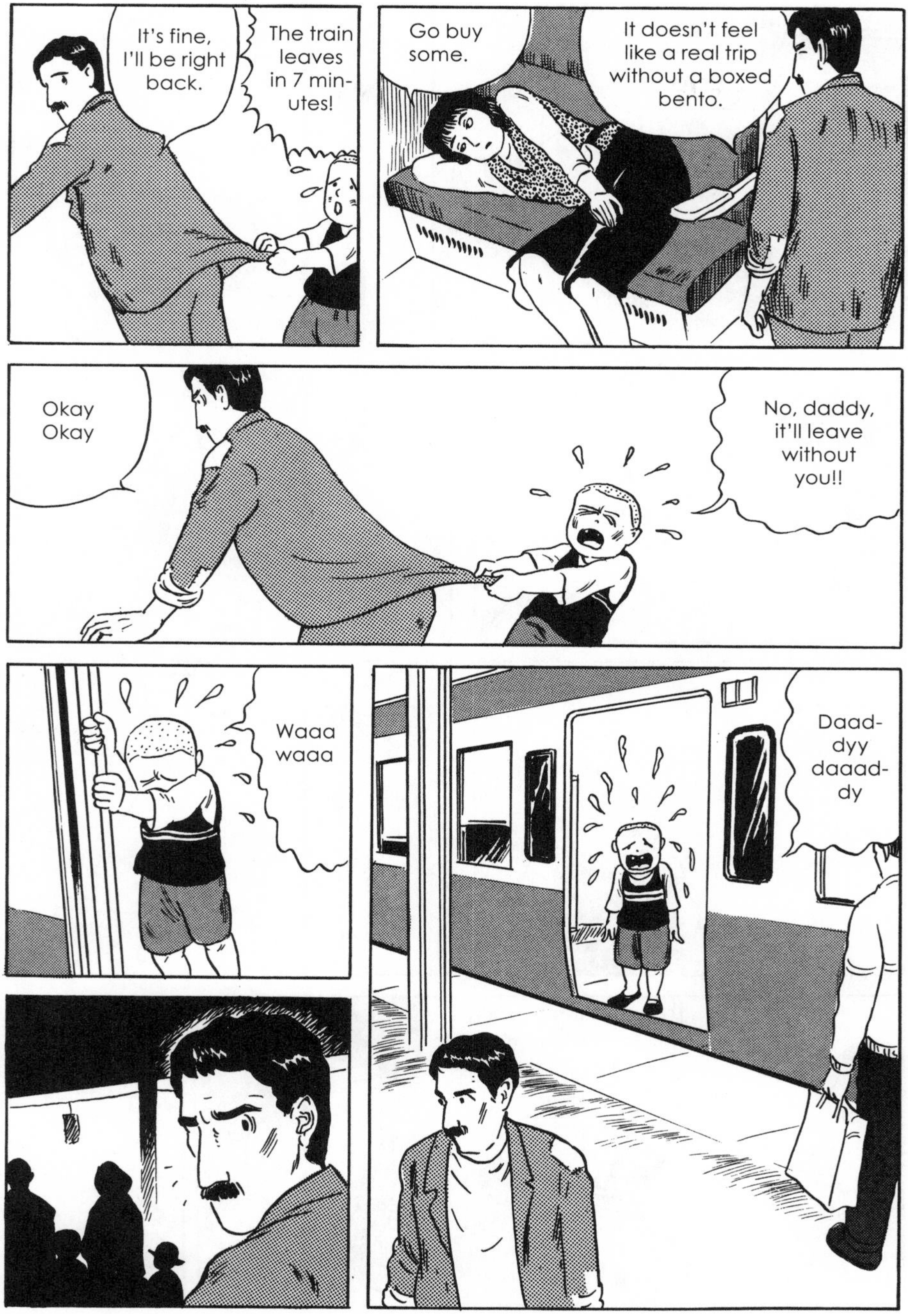

It doesn't feel like a real trip without a boxed bento.
Go buy some.
The train leaves in 7 min-utes!
It's fine, I'll be right back.
No, daddy, it'll leave without you!!
Okay Okay
Daad-dyy daaad-dy
Waaa waaa

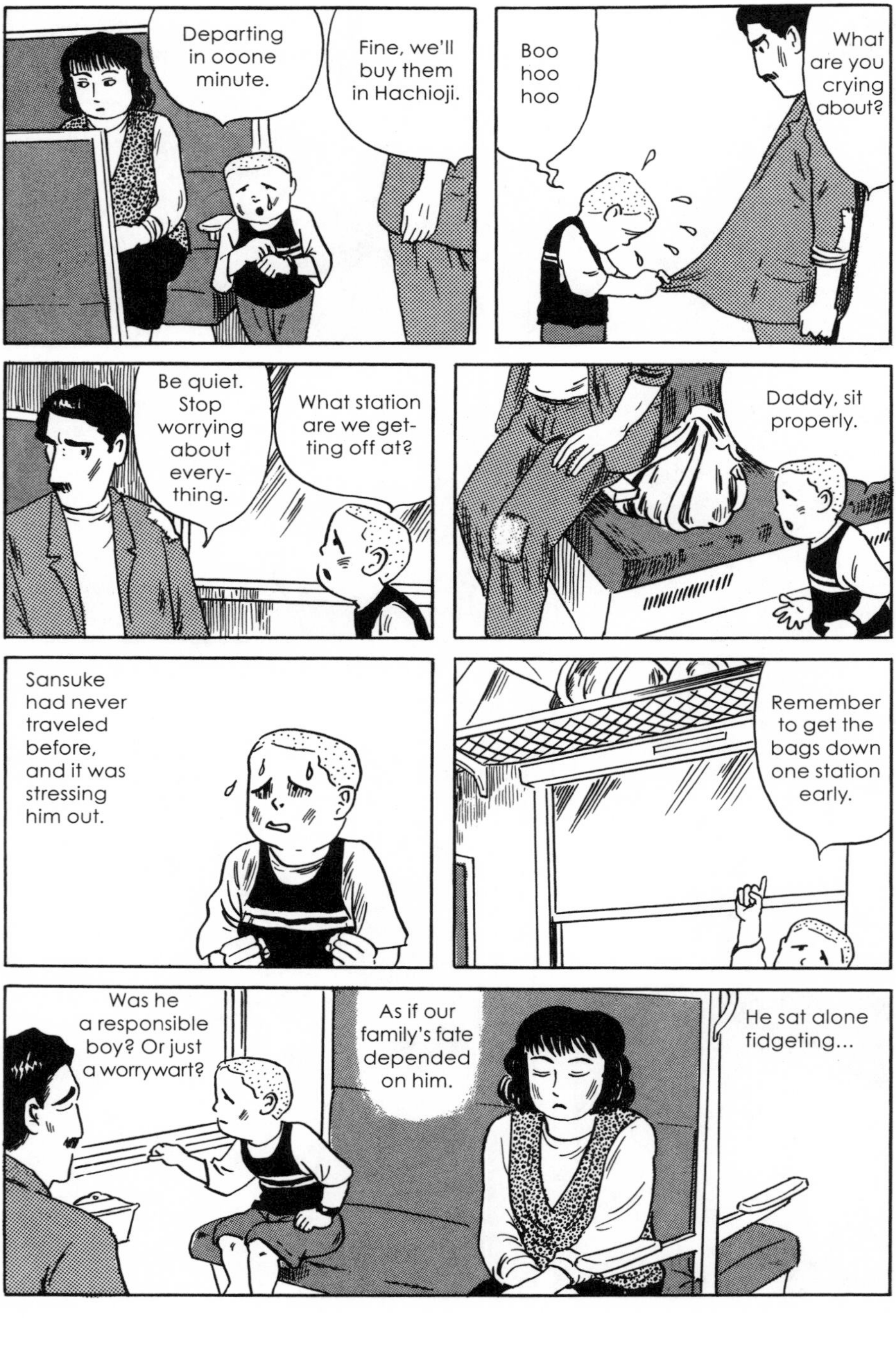
What are you crying about?
Boo hoo hoo
Fine, we'll buy them in Hachioji.
Departing in ooone minute.
Daddy, sit properly.
What station are we get-ting off at?
Be quiet. Stop worrying about every-thing.
Remember to get the bags down one station early.
Sansuke had never traveled before, and it was stressing him out.
He sat alone fidgeting…
As if our family's fate depended on him.
Was he a responsible boy? Or just a worrywart?

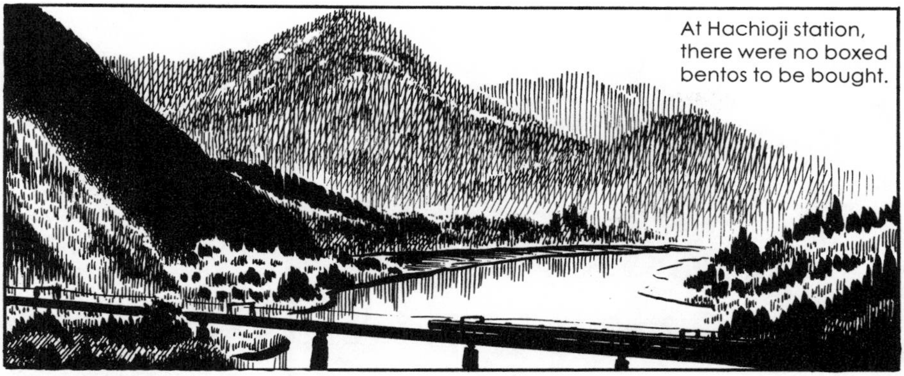
At Hachioji station, there were no boxed bentos to be bought.

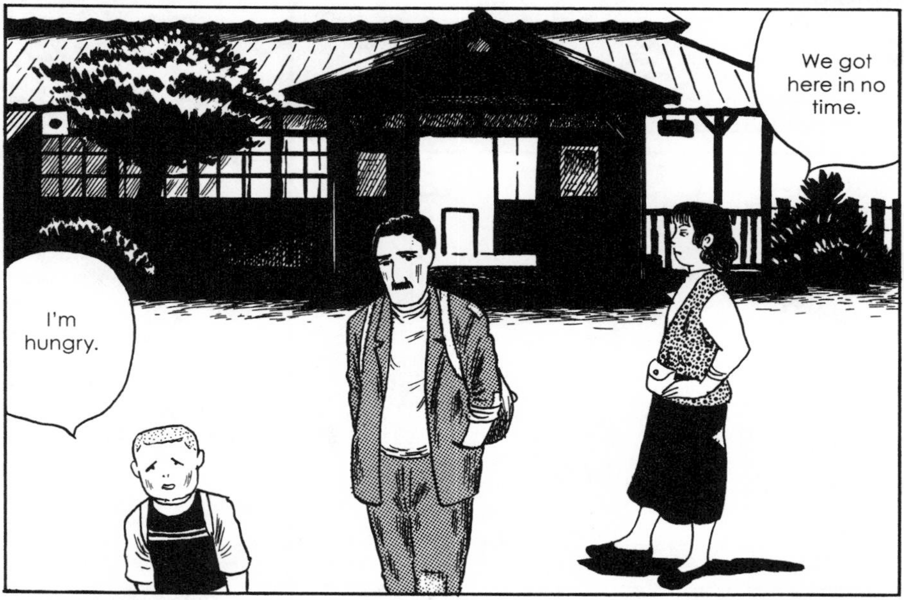
We got here in no time.
I'm hungry.

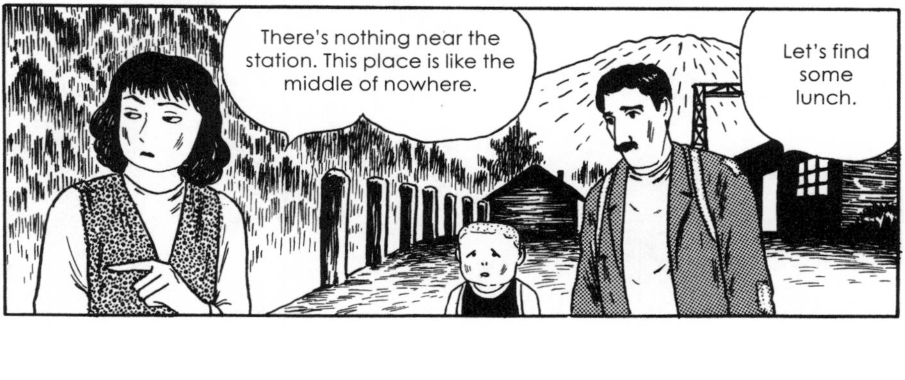
Let's find some lunch.
There's nothing near the station. This place is like the middle of nowhere.

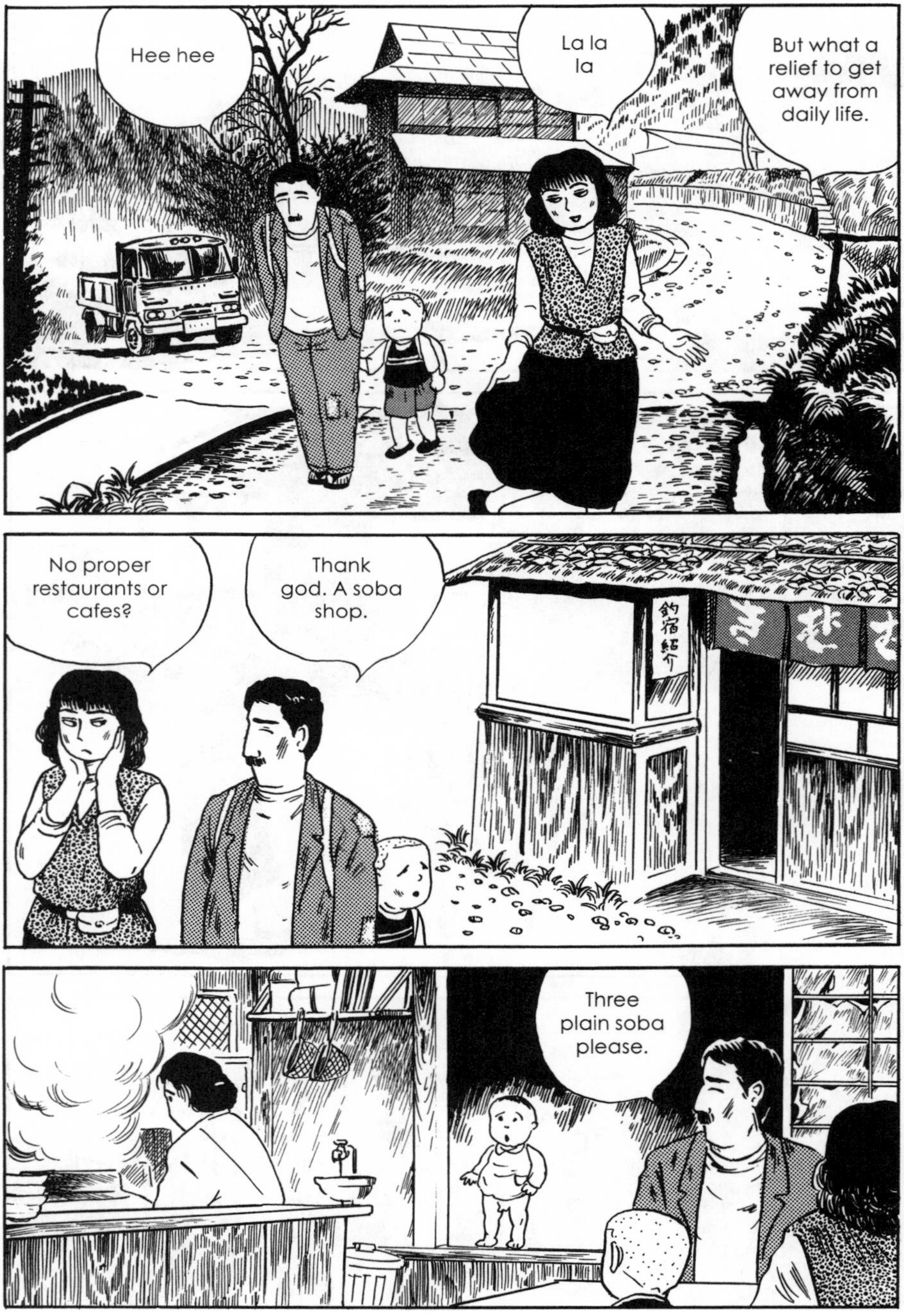
But what a relief to get away from daily life.
La la la
Hee hee
釣宿紹介
Thank god. A soba shop.
No proper restaurants or cafes?
Three plain soba please.

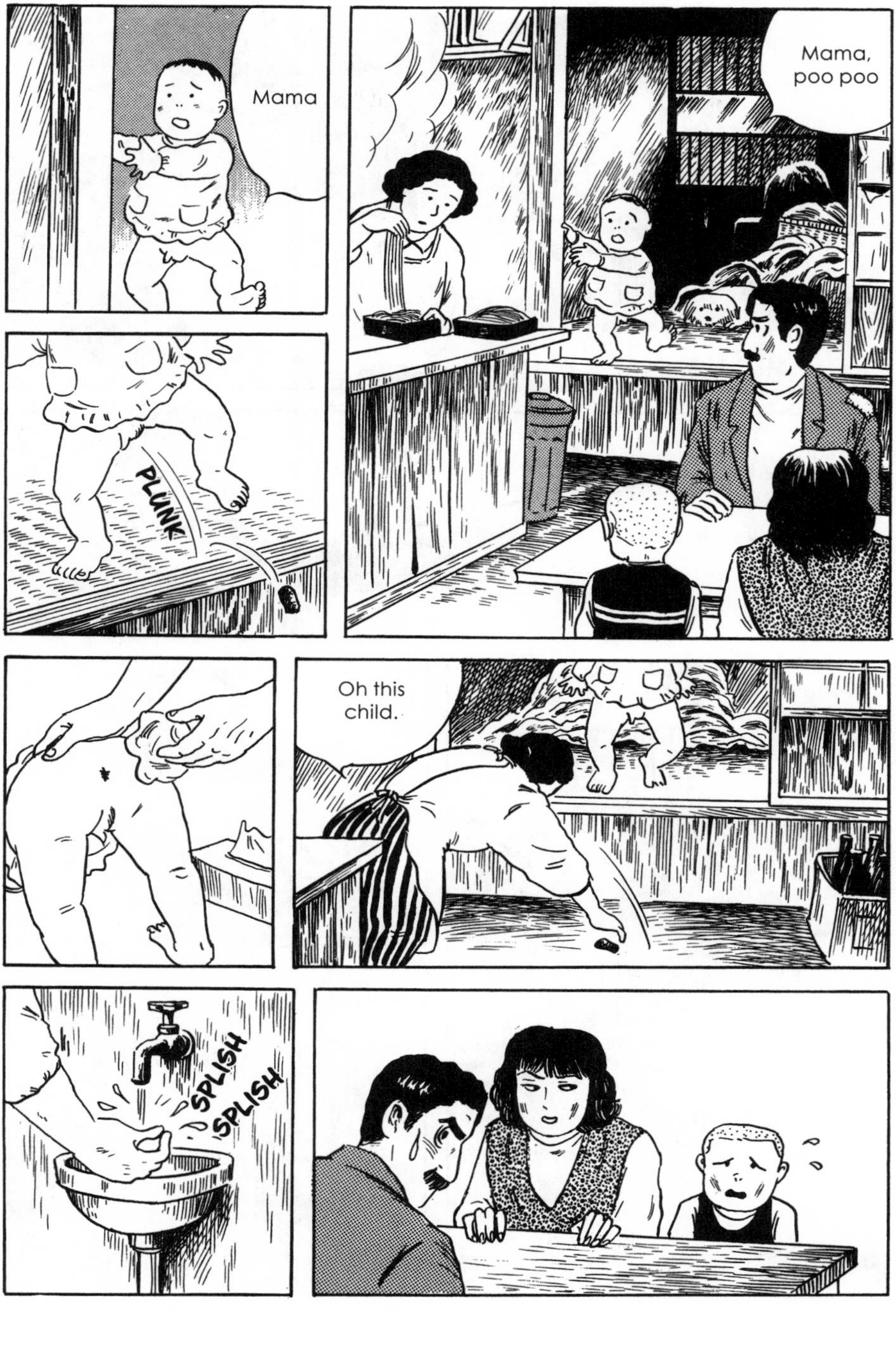
Mama, poo poo
Mama
PLUNK
Oh this child.
SPLISH SPLISH

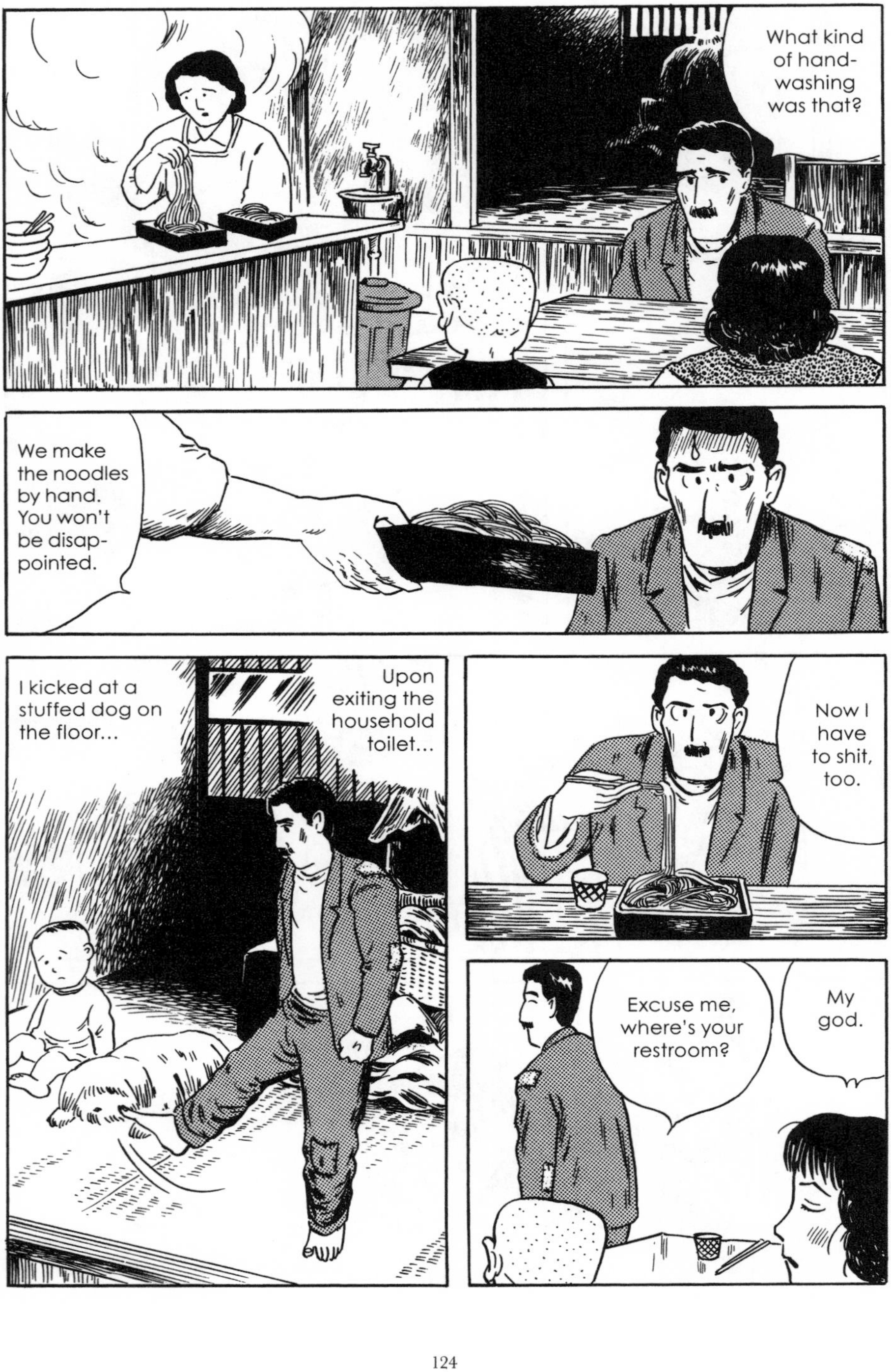
What kind of hand-washing was that?
We make the noodles by hand. You won't be disappointed.
Now I have to shit, too.
My god.
Excuse me, where's your restroom?
Upon exiting the household toilet...
I kicked at a stuffed dog on the floor...

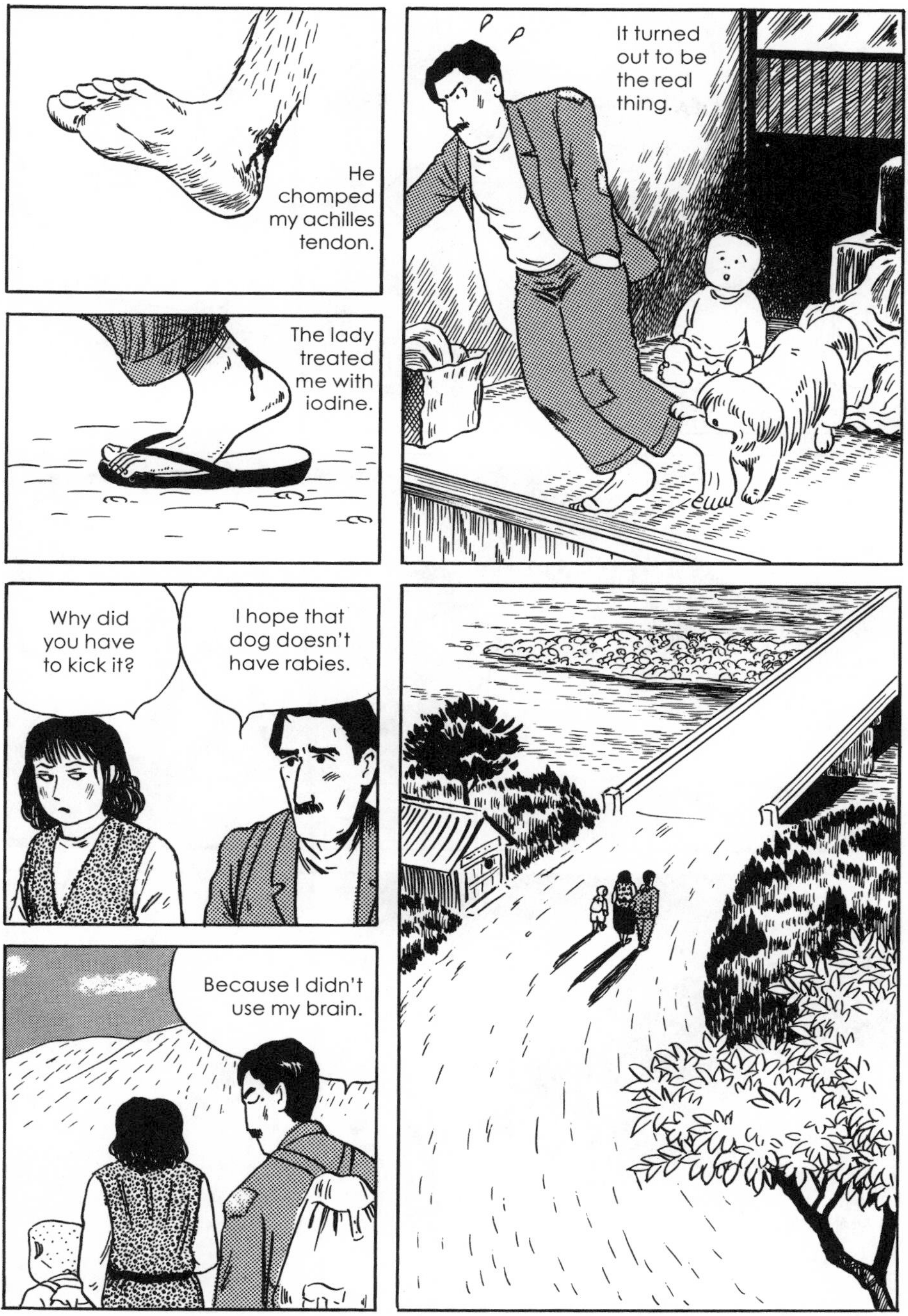
It turned out to be the real thing.
He chomped my achilles tendon.
The lady treated me with iodine.
I hope that dog doesn't have rabies.
Why did you have to kick it?
Because I didn't use my brain.

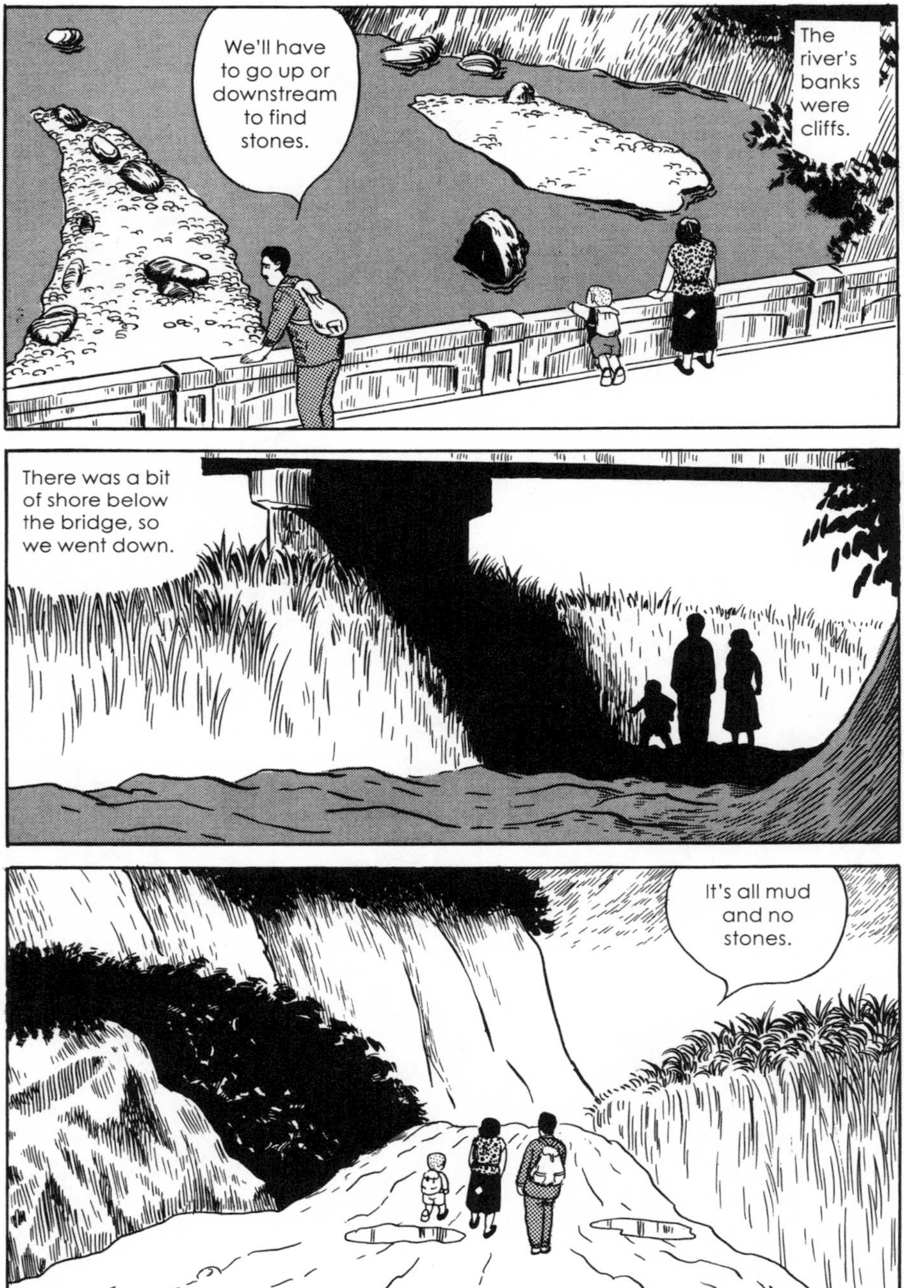
The river's banks were cliffs.
We'll have to go up or downstream to find stones.
There was a bit of shore below the bridge, so we went down.
It's all mud and no stones.

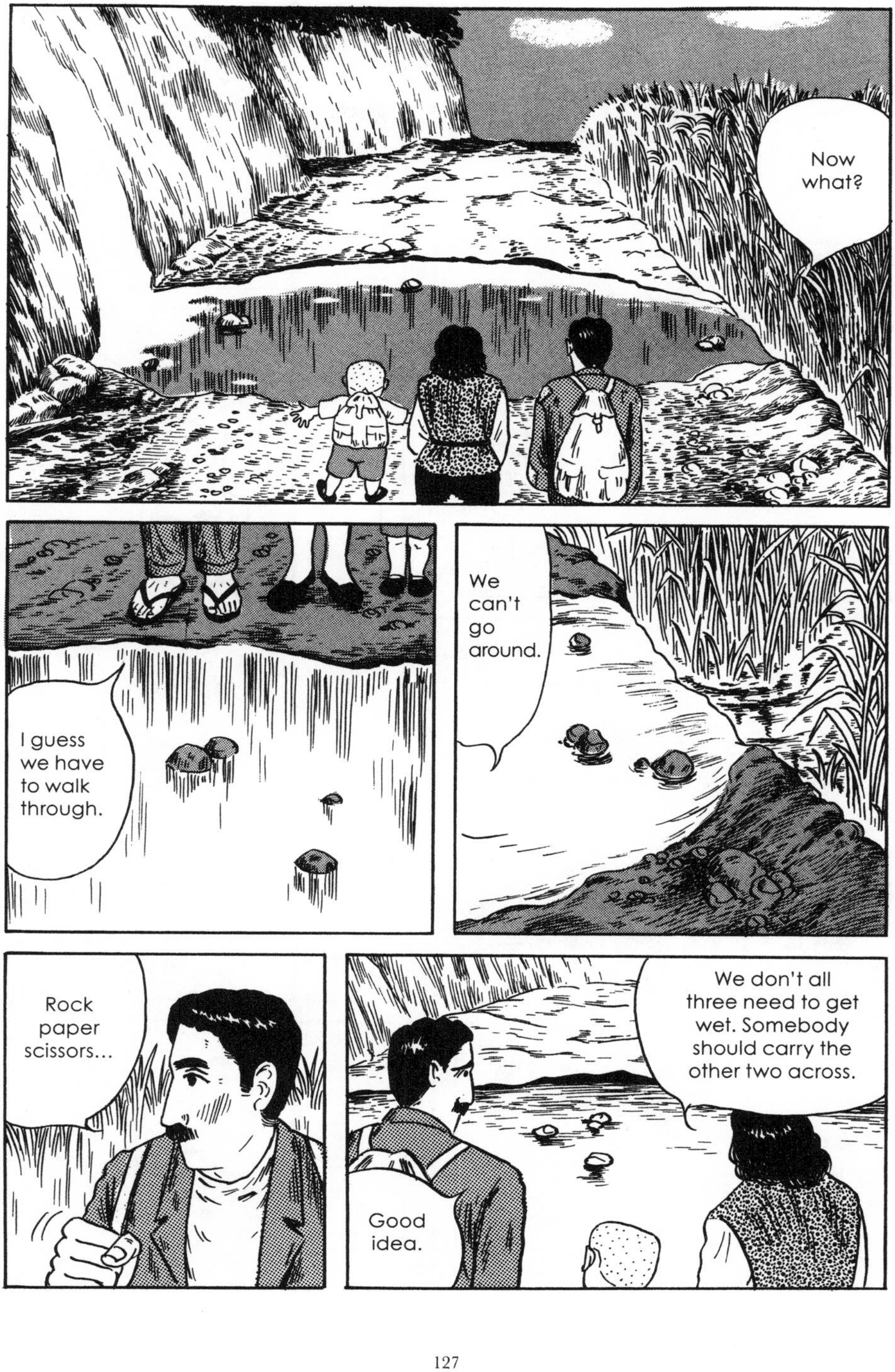
Now what?
We can't go around.
I guess we have to walk through.
We don't all three need to get wet. Somebody should carry the other two across.
Good idea.
Rock paper scissors...

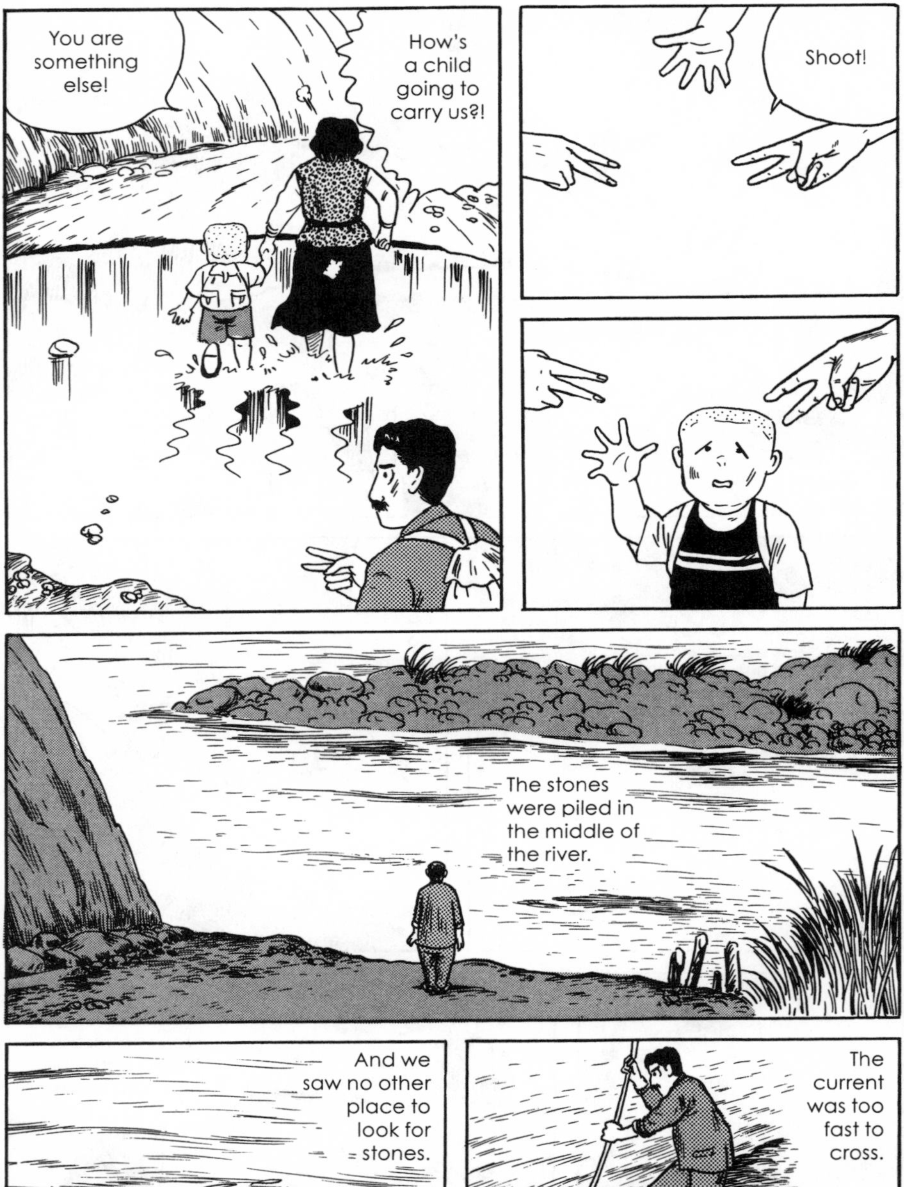
Shoot!
How's a child going to carry us?!
You are something else!
The stones were piled in the middle of the river.
The current was too fast to cross.
And we saw no other place to look for stones.

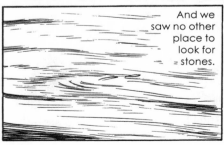

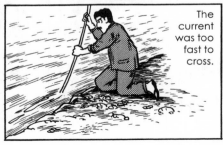

CHEEP CHEEP
Do you, like, ever...
Use your brain...?

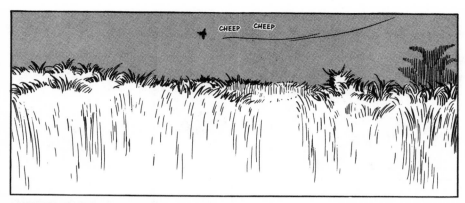

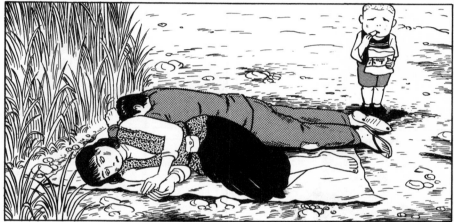

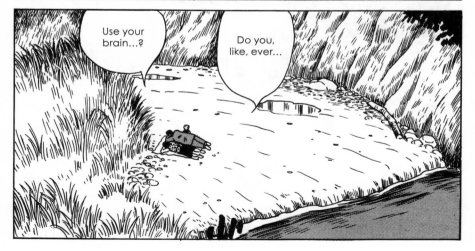

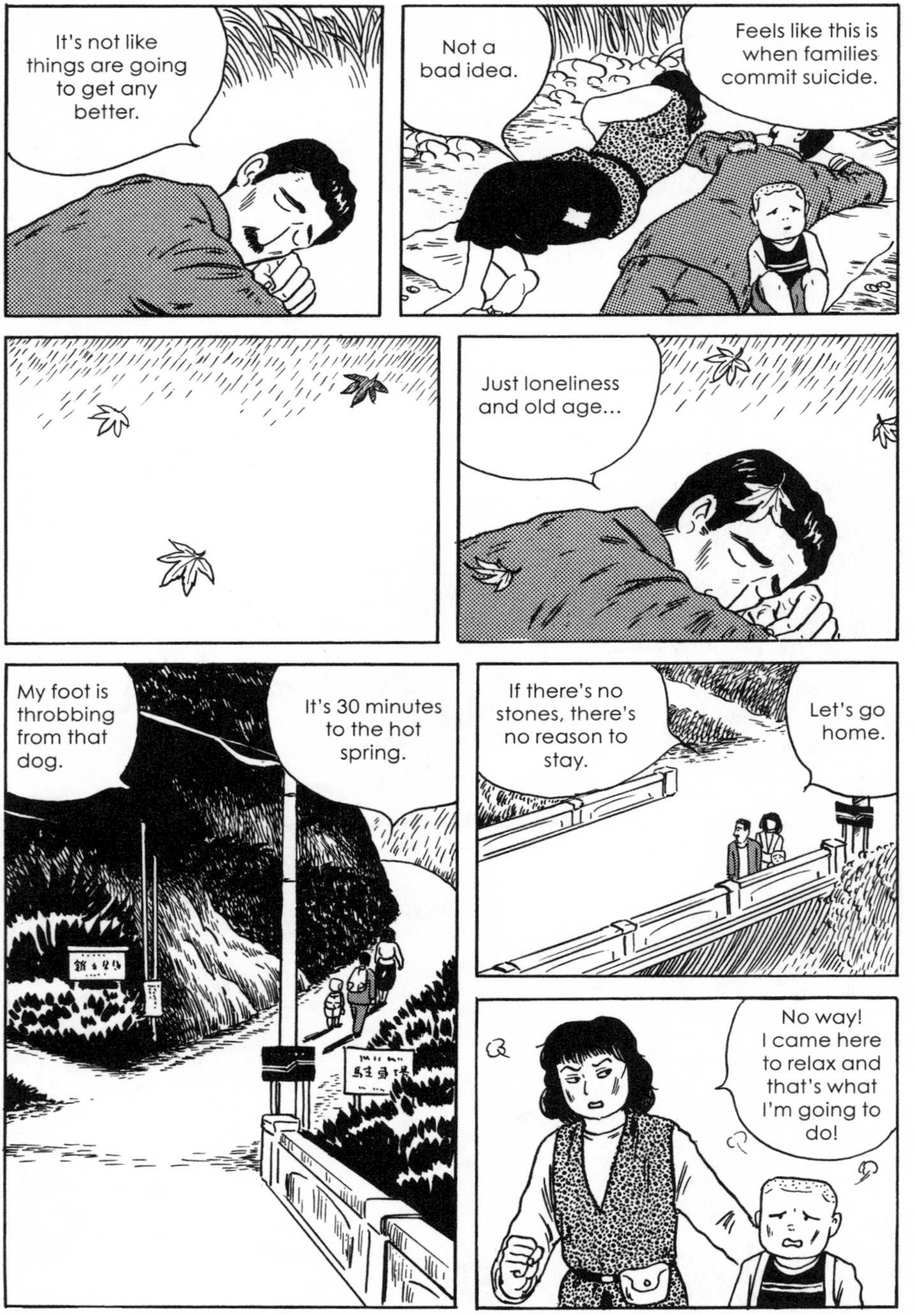
Feels like this is when families commit suicide.
Not a bad idea.
It's not like things are going to get any better.
Just loneliness and old age...
Let's go home.
If there's no stones, there's no reason to stay.
No way! I came here to relax and that's what I'm going to do!
It's 30 minutes to the hot spring.
My foot is throbbing from that dog.

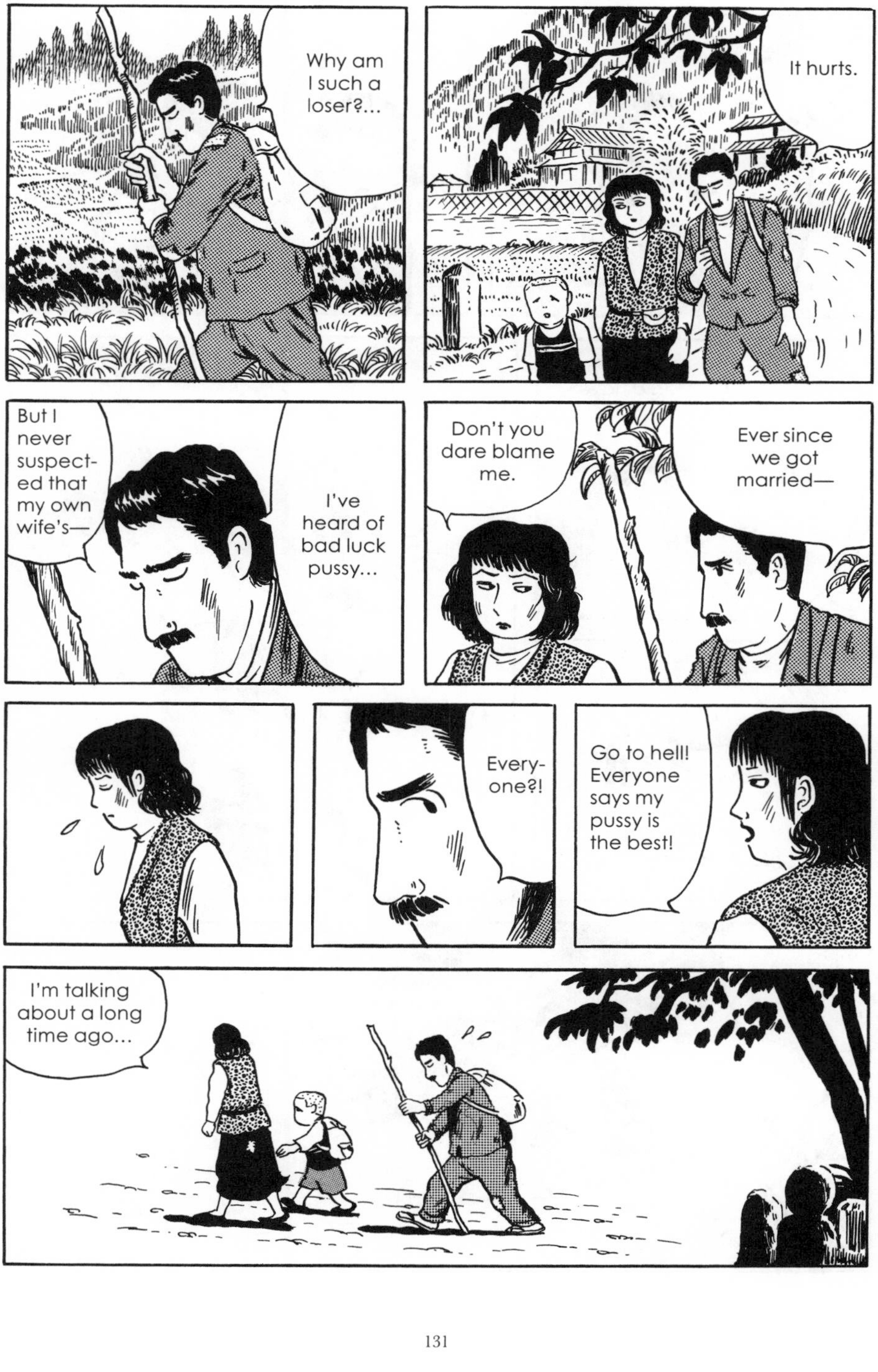
It hurts.
Why am I such a loser?…
Ever since we got married—
Don't you dare blame me.
I've heard of bad luck pussy…
But I never suspect-ed that my own wife's—
Go to hell! Everyone says my pussy is the best!
Every-one?!
I'm talking about a long time ago…

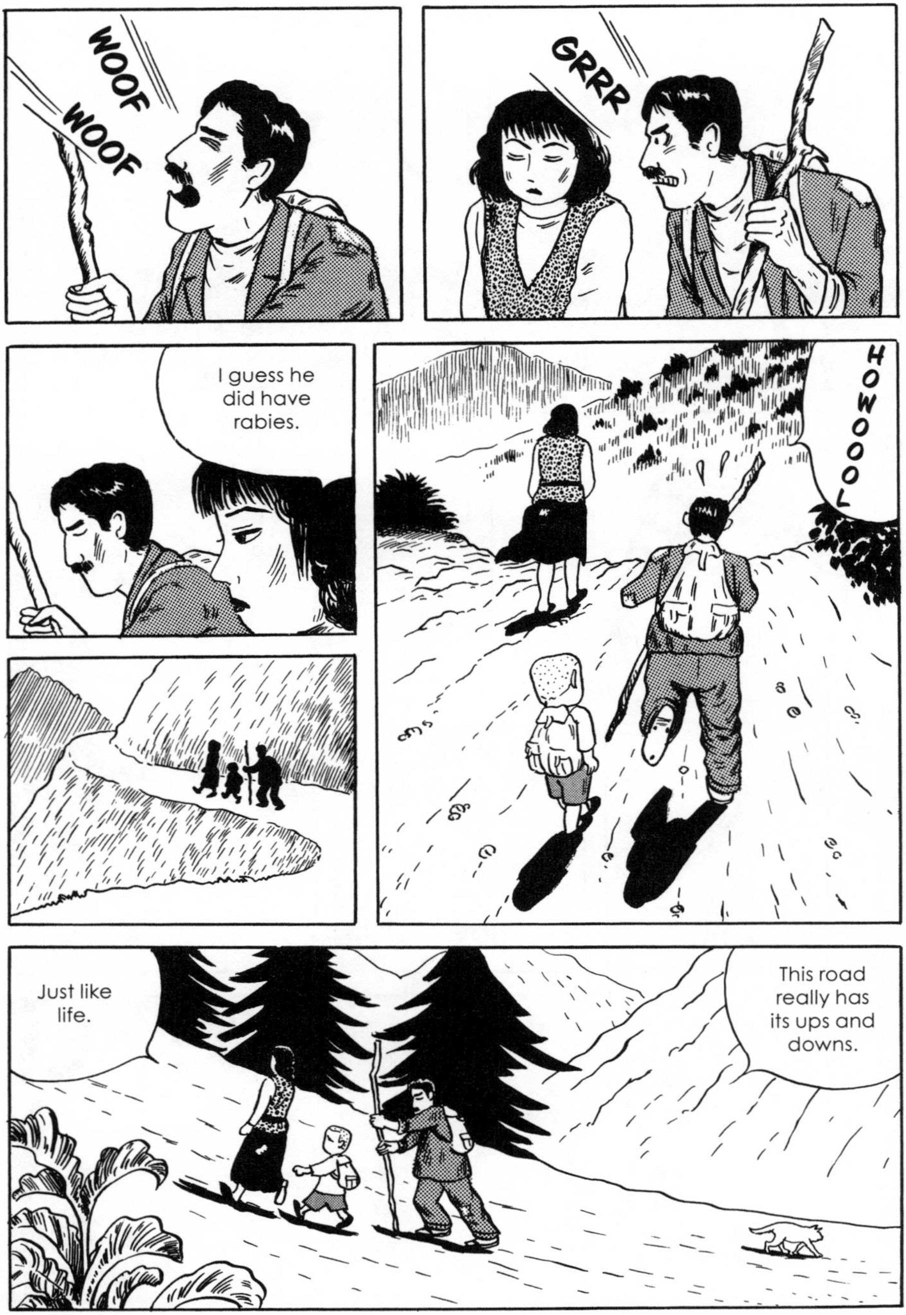
GRRR
WOOF
WOOF
HOWOOOOL
I guess he did have rabies.
This road really has its ups and downs.
Just like life.

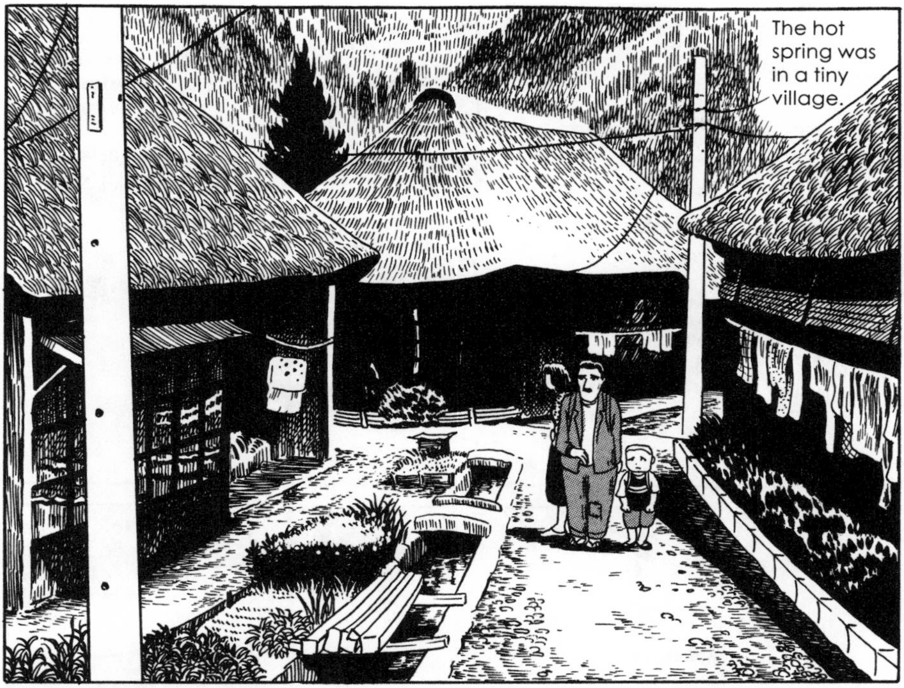
The hot spring was in a tiny village.

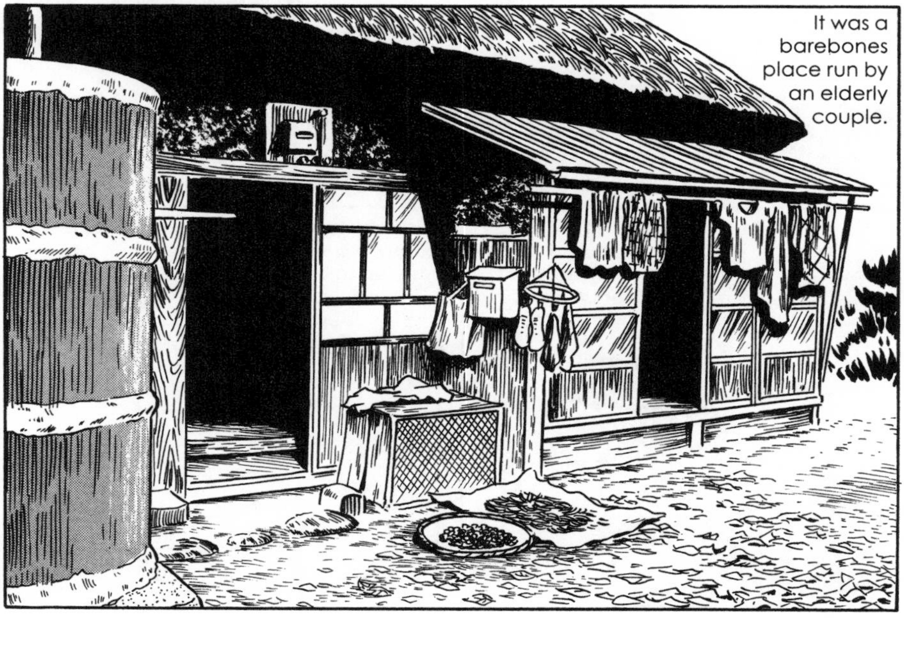
It was a barebones place run by an elderly couple.

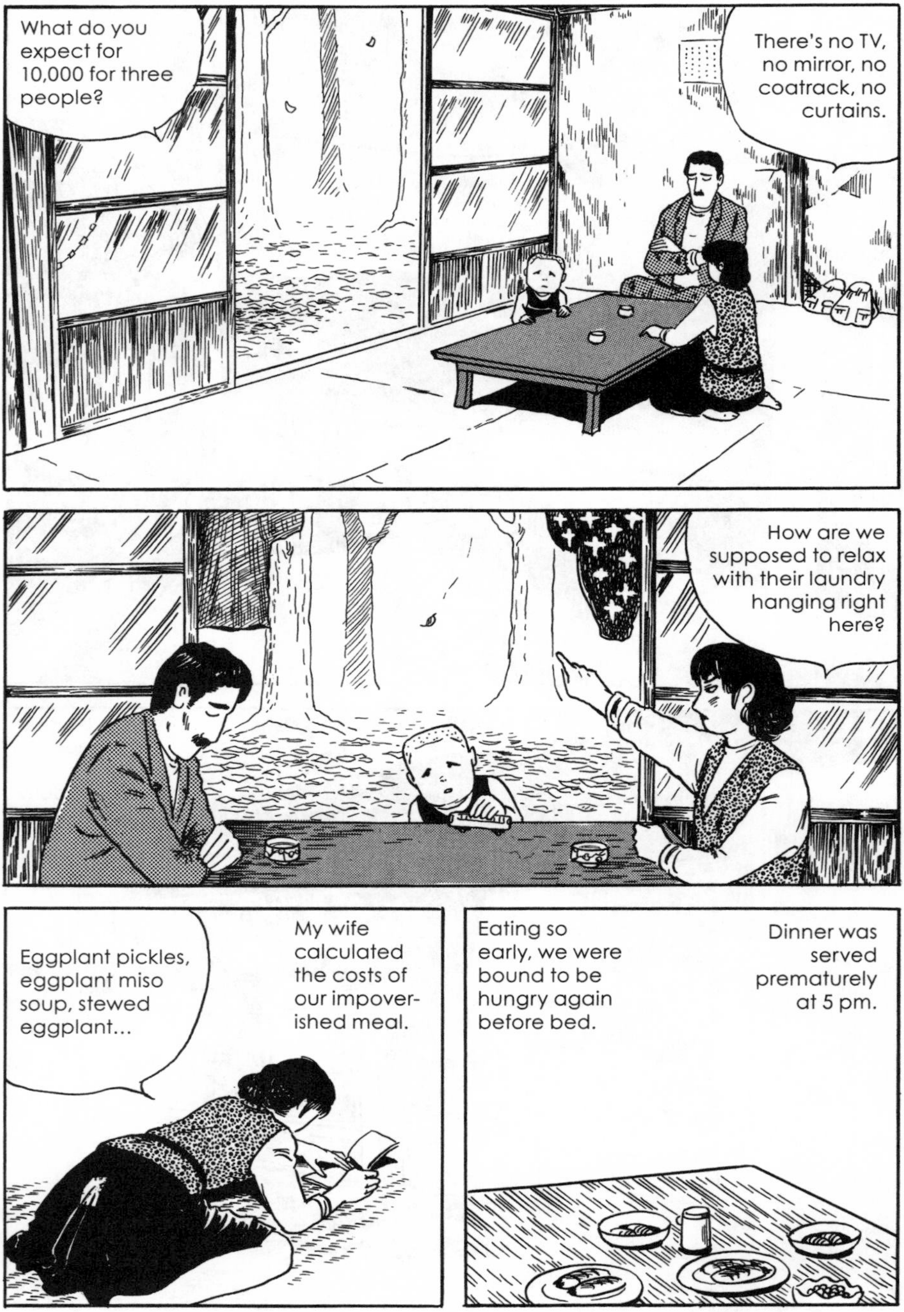
There's no TV, no mirror, no coatrack, no curtains.
What do you expect for 10,000 for three people?
How are we supposed to relax with their laundry hanging right here?
Dinner was served prematurely at 5 pm.
Eating so early, we were bound to be hungry again before bed.
My wife calculated the costs of our impover-ished meal.
Eggplant pickles, eggplant miso soup, stewed eggplant...

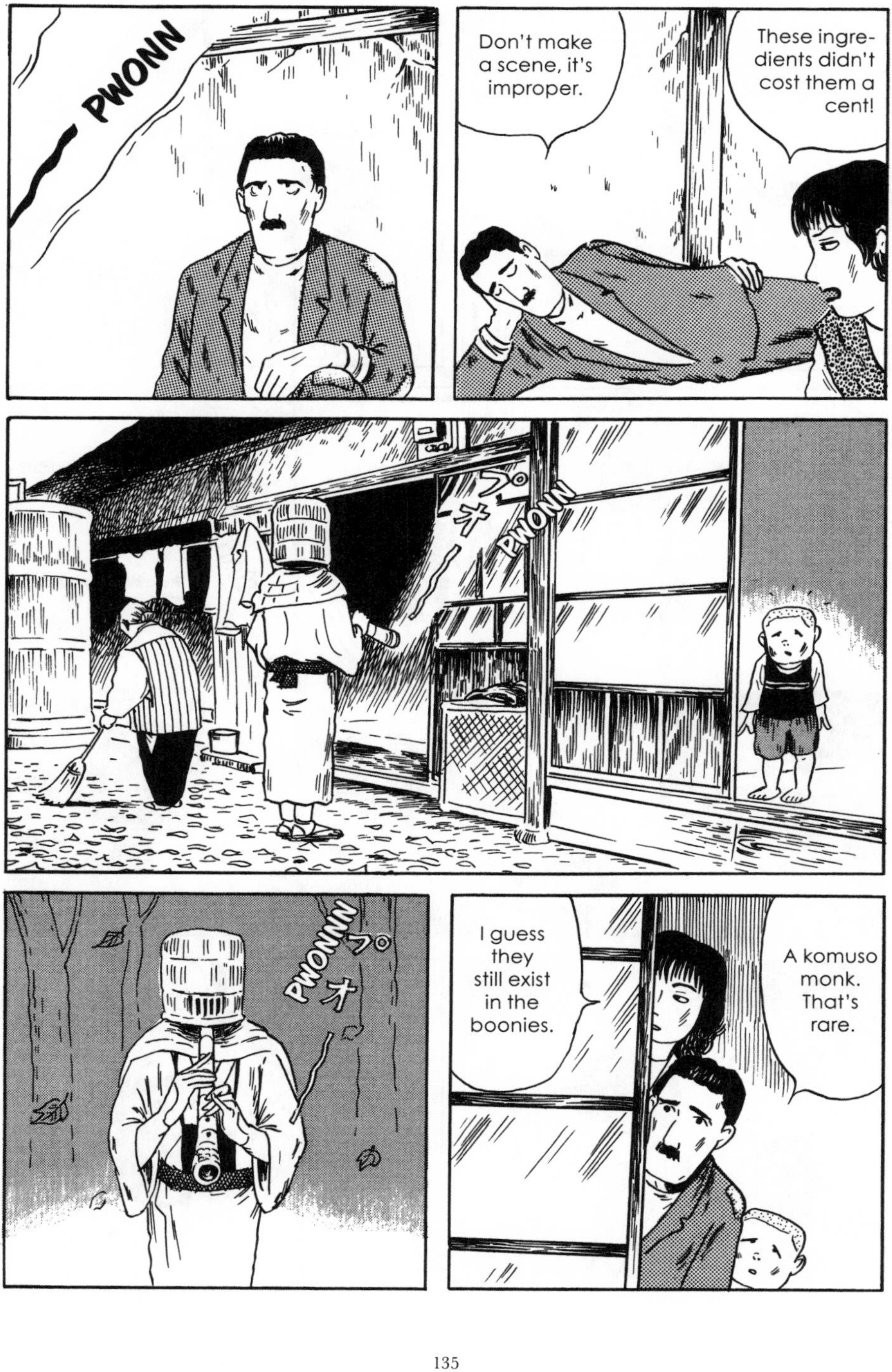
These ingre-
dients didn't
cost them a
cent!
Don't make
a scene, it's
improper.
PWONN
PWONN
プオー
A komuso
monk.
That's
rare.
I guess
they
still exist
in the
boonies.
PWONNN
プオー

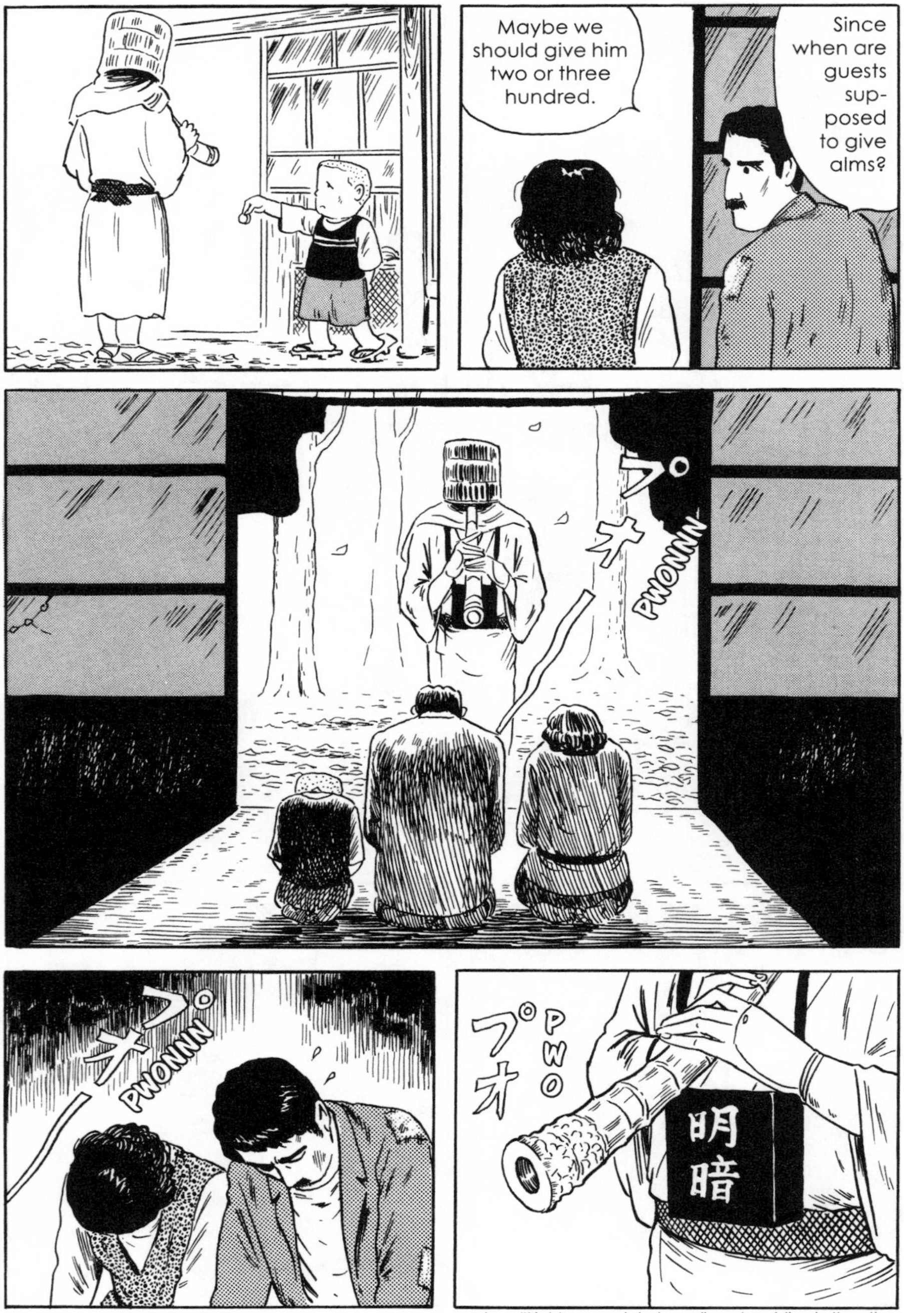
Since when are guests sup-posed to give alms?
Maybe we should give him two or three hundred.
プオ
PWONNN
プオ
PWO
明暗
プオ
PWONNN

box: "Lightness and darkness," each residing in the other

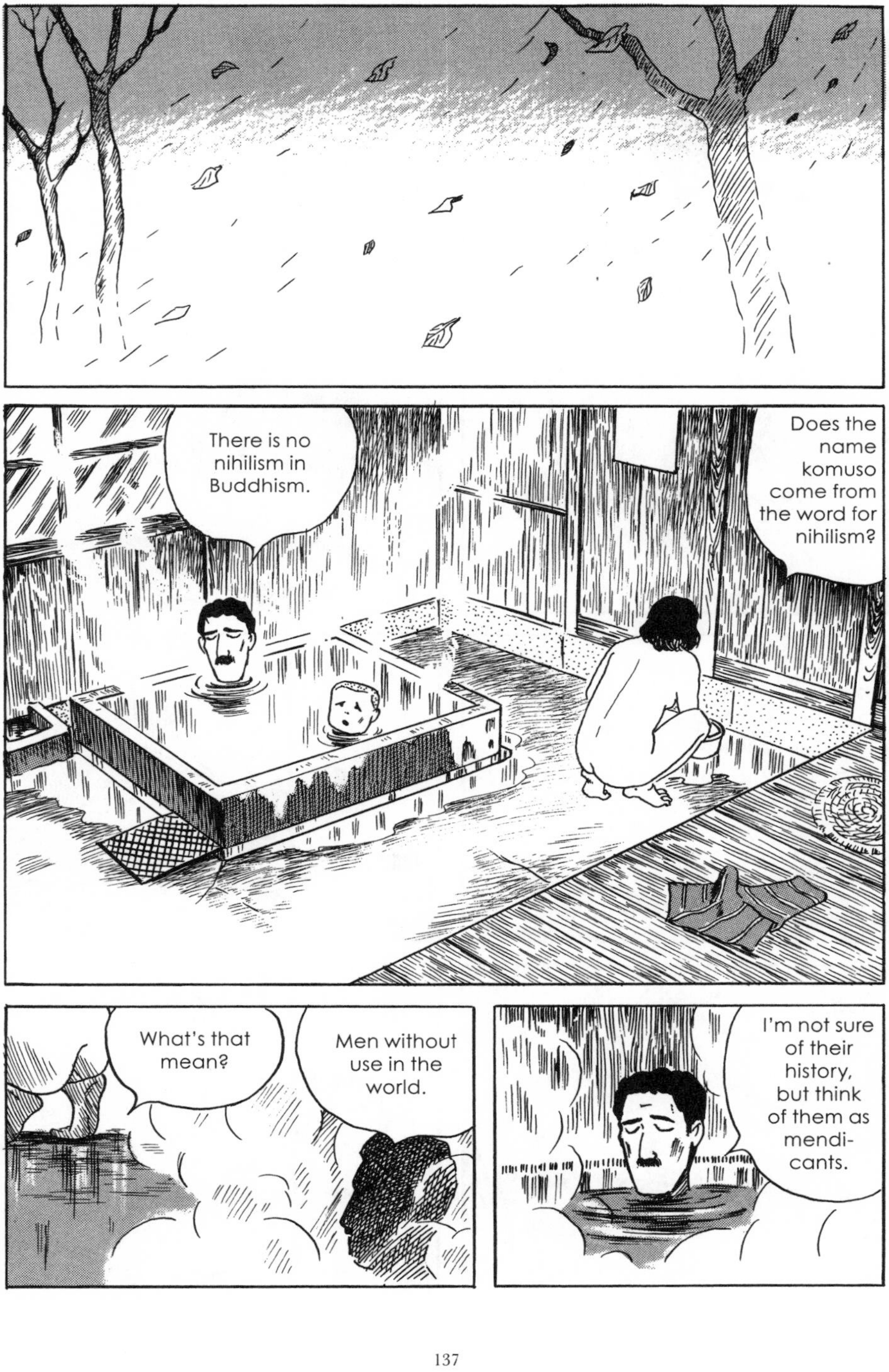
Does the name komuso come from the word for nihilism?
There is no nihilism in Buddhism.
I'm not sure of their history, but think of them as mendi-cants.
Men without use in the world.
What's that mean?

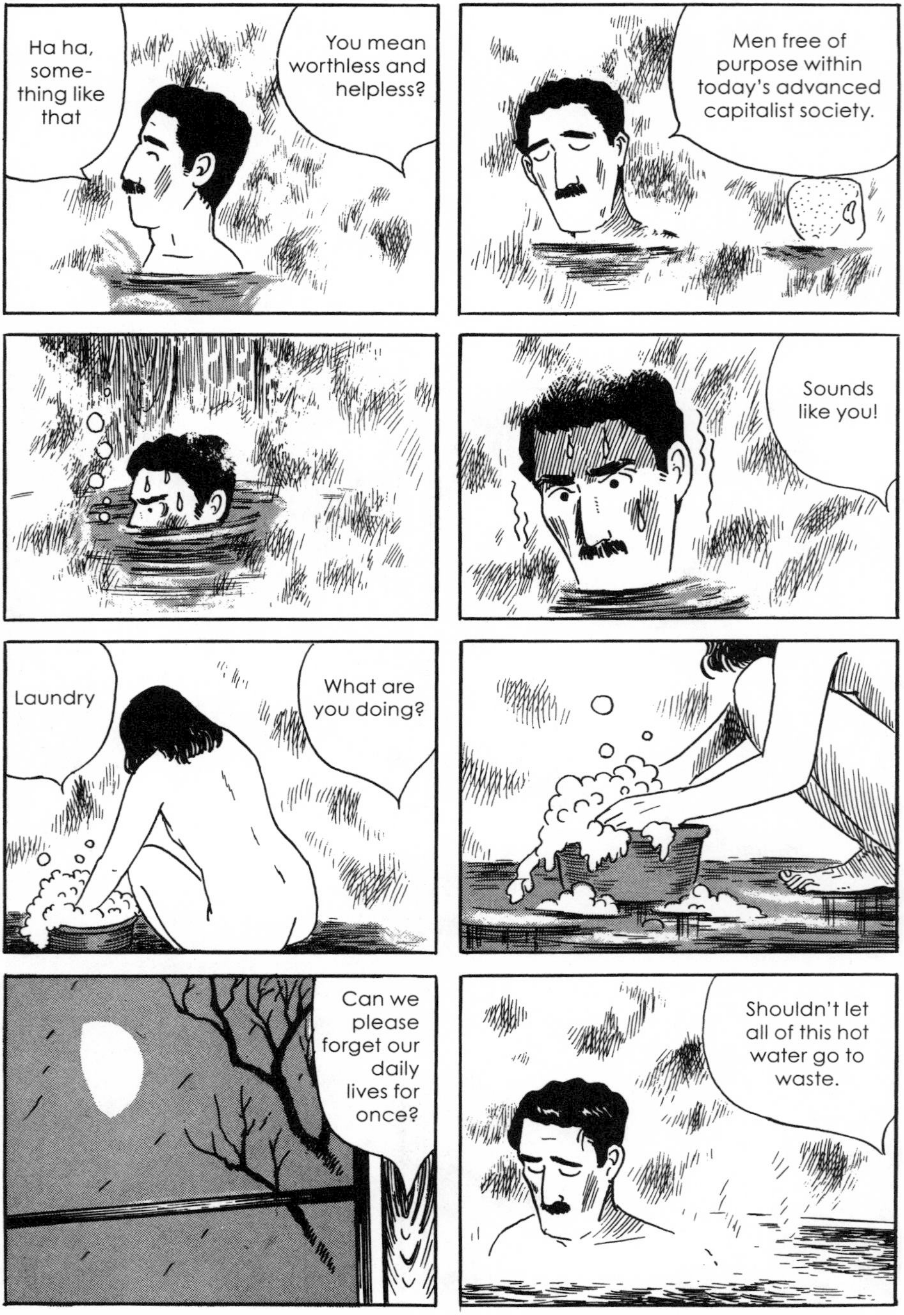
Men free of purpose within today's advanced capitalist society.
You mean worthless and helpless?
Ha ha, some-thing like that
Sounds like you!
What are you doing?
Laundry
Shouldn't let all of this hot water go to waste.
Can we please forget our daily lives for once?

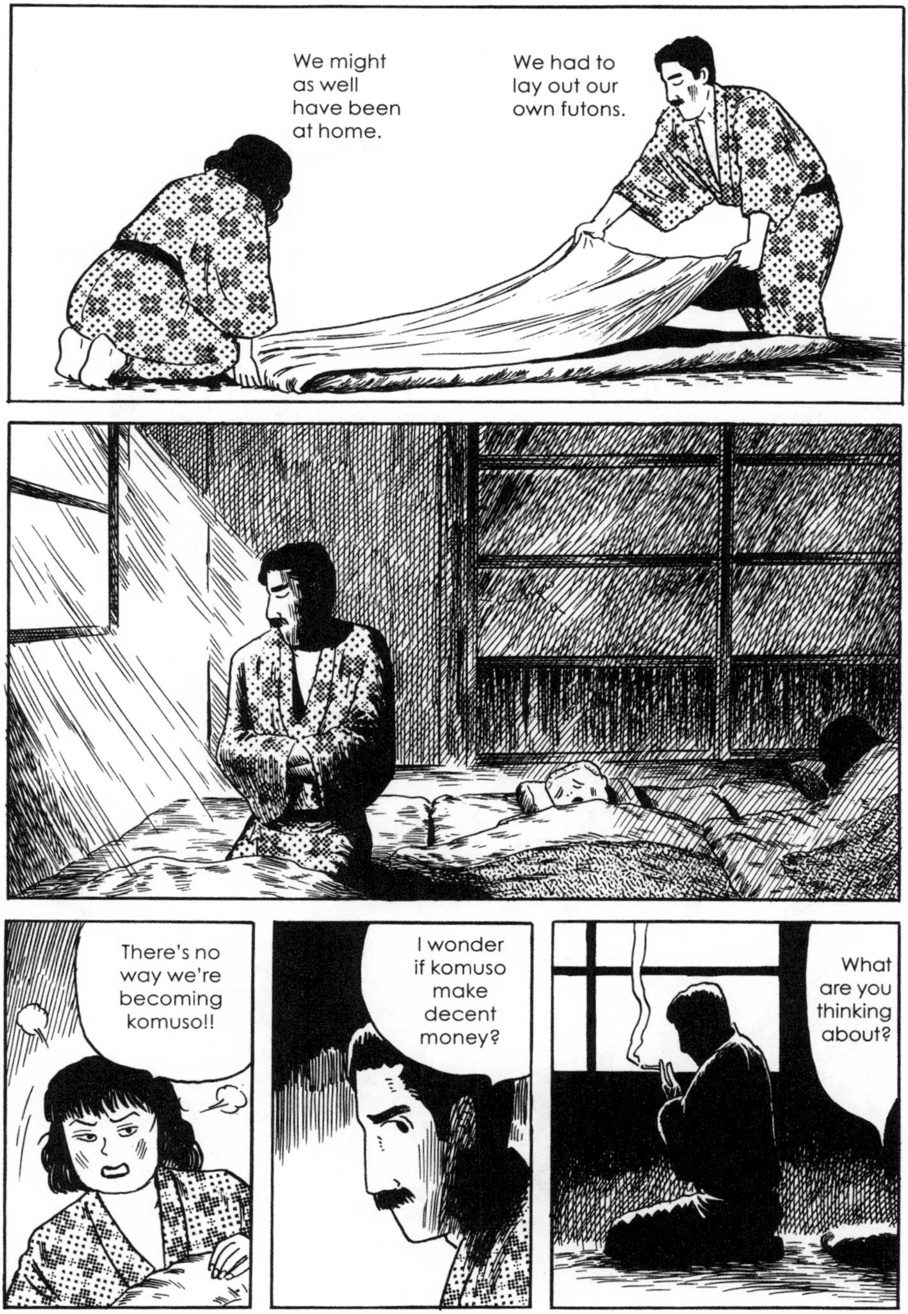
We had to lay out our own futons.
We might as well have been at home.
What are you thinking about?
I wonder if komuso make decent money?
There's no way we're becoming komuso!!

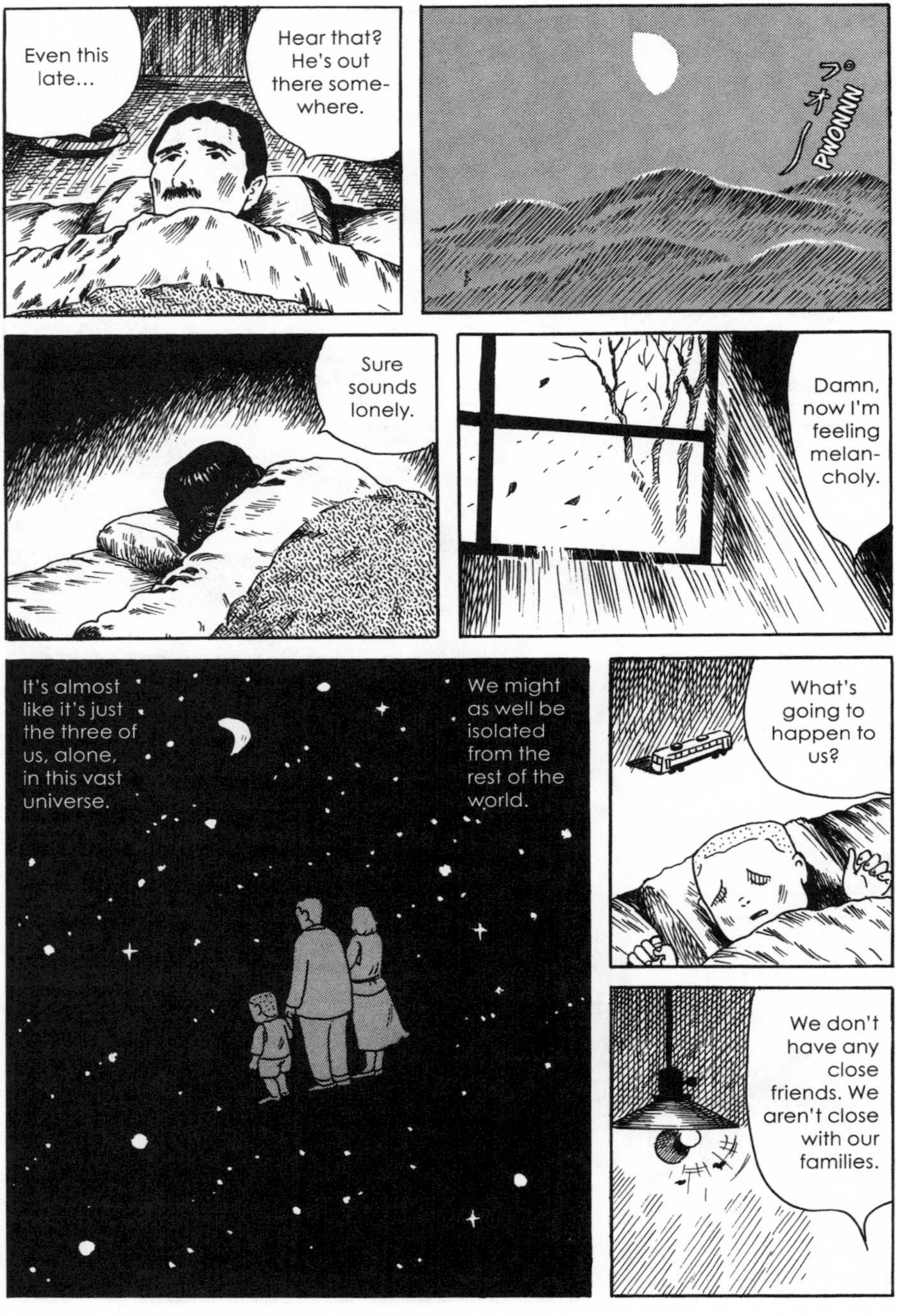
プオー
PWONNN
Hear that? He's out there some-where.
Even this late...
Damn, now I'm feeling melan-choly.
Sure sounds lonely.
What's going to happen to us?
We don't have any close friends. We aren't close with our families.
We might as well be isolated from the rest of the world.
It's almost like it's just the three of us, alone, in this vast universe.

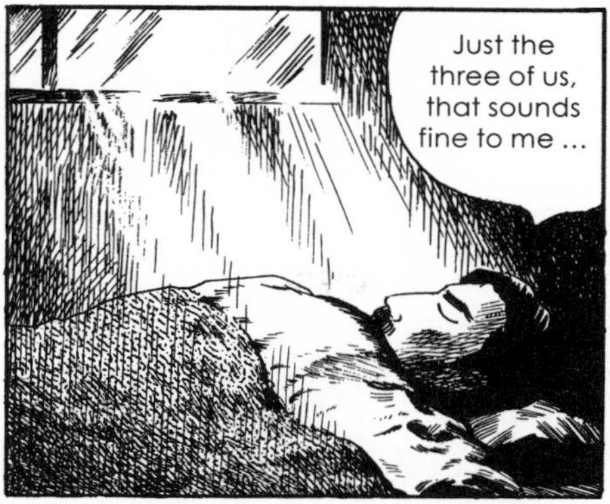
Just the three of us, that sounds fine to me ...

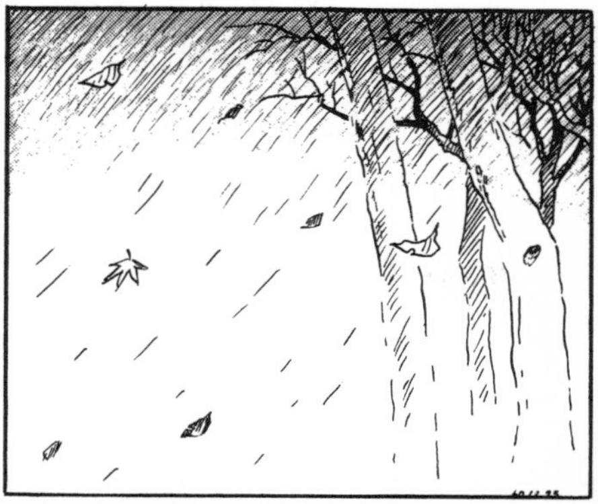

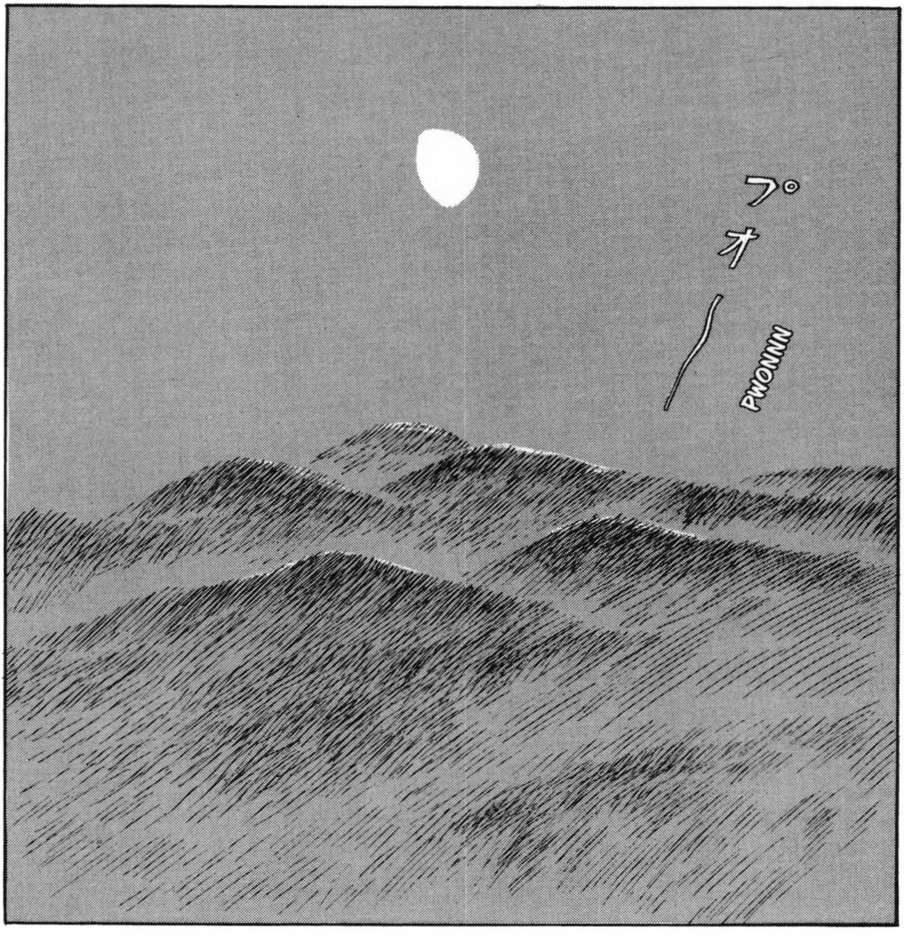
プオー
PWONNN

カメラを売る

Selling Cameras

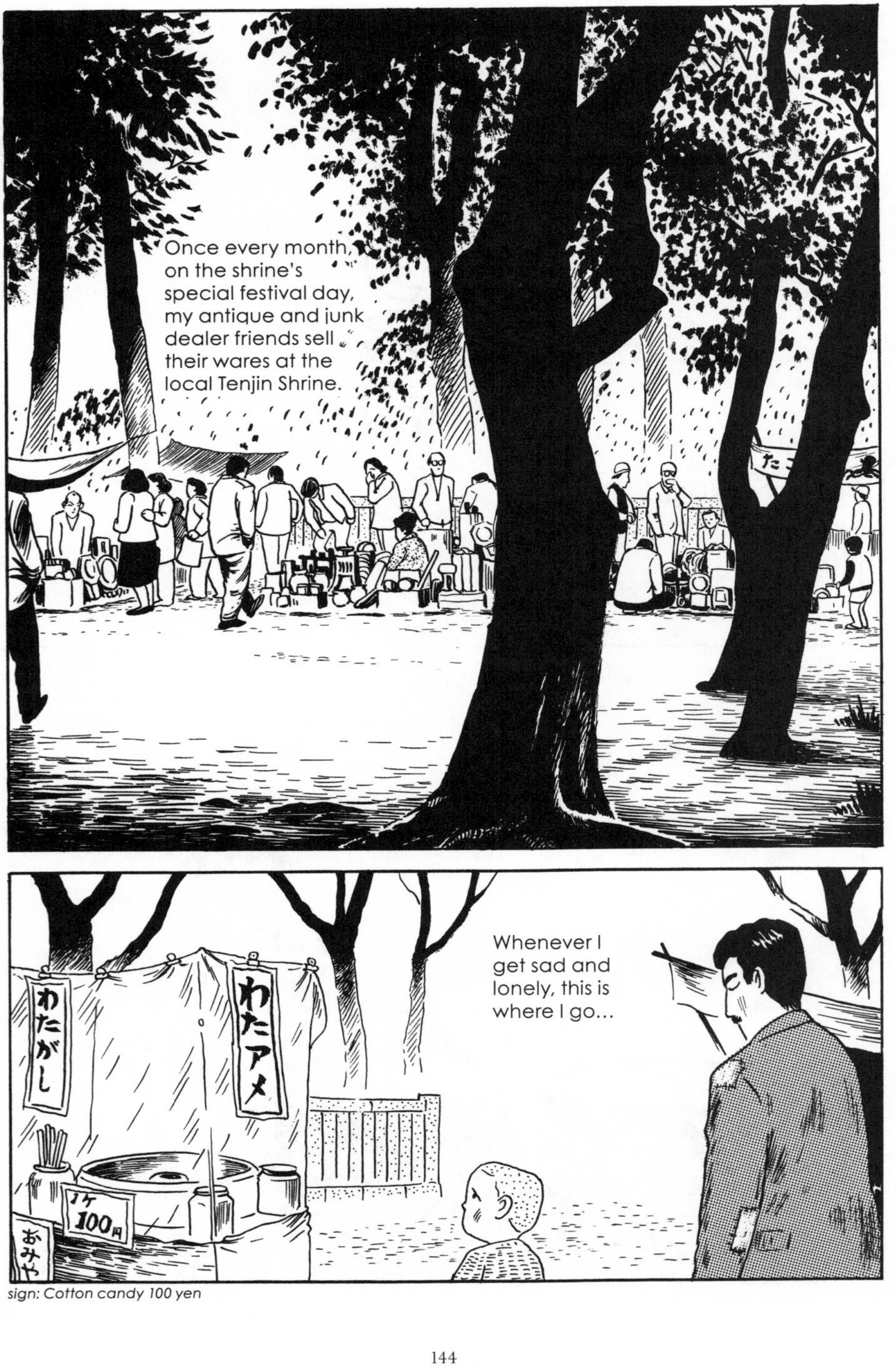
Once every month, on the shrine's special festival day, my antique and junk dealer friends sell their wares at the local Tenjin Shrine.
Whenever I get sad and lonely, this is where I go...
わたアメ
わたがし
1ケ 100円

sign: Cotton candy 100 yen

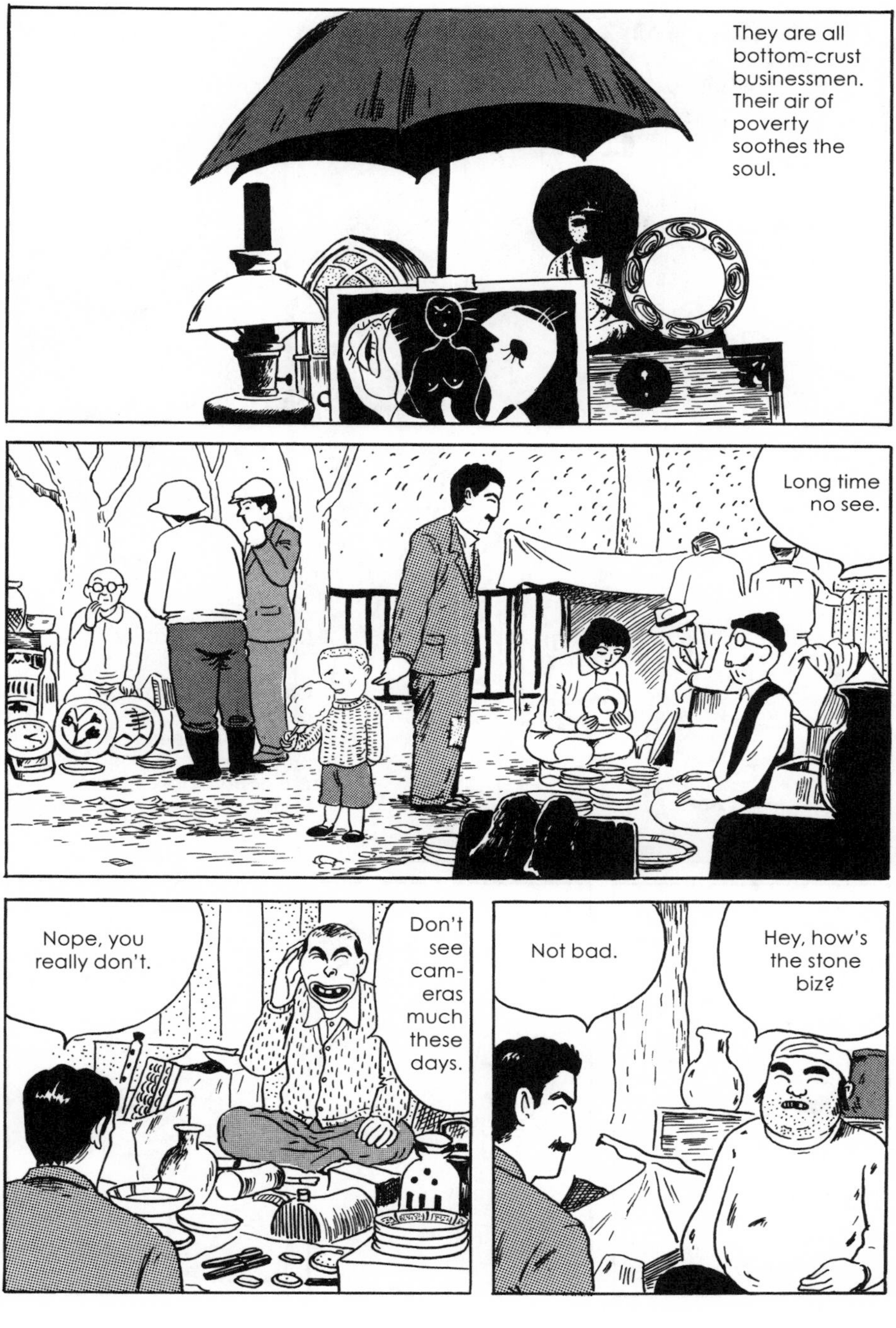
They are all bottom-crust businessmen. Their air of poverty soothes the soul.
Long time no see.
Hey, how's the stone biz?
Not bad.
Don't see cam-eras much these days.
Nope, you really don't.

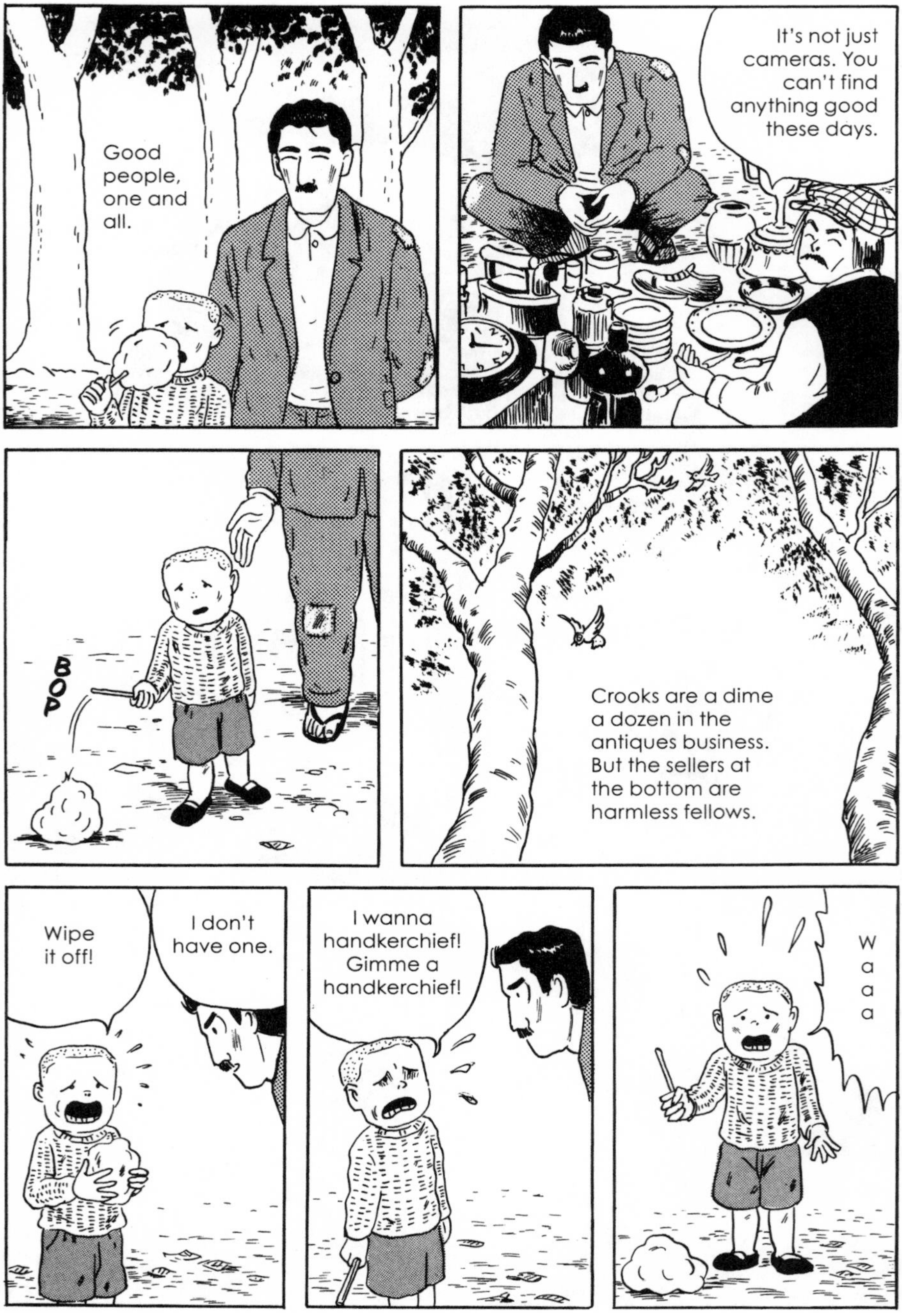
It's not just cameras. You can't find anything good these days.
Good people, one and all.
Crooks are a dime a dozen in the antiques business. But the sellers at the bottom are harmless fellows.
BOP
Waaa
I wanna handkerchief! Gimme a handkerchief!
I don't have one.
Wipe it off!

You can't wipe off cotton candy, it's sticky!
Buy me a new one!
Okay, let me take a look.
WAA
WAA
Dammit! How did so much shit get stuck in it? What am I supposed to do?
Buy me a new one!
Hey Sansuke. What's wrong buddy?
Come here. Uncle Nakata will give you some octopus dumplings.
Mr. Nakata was my teacher.
I owe a lot to him.

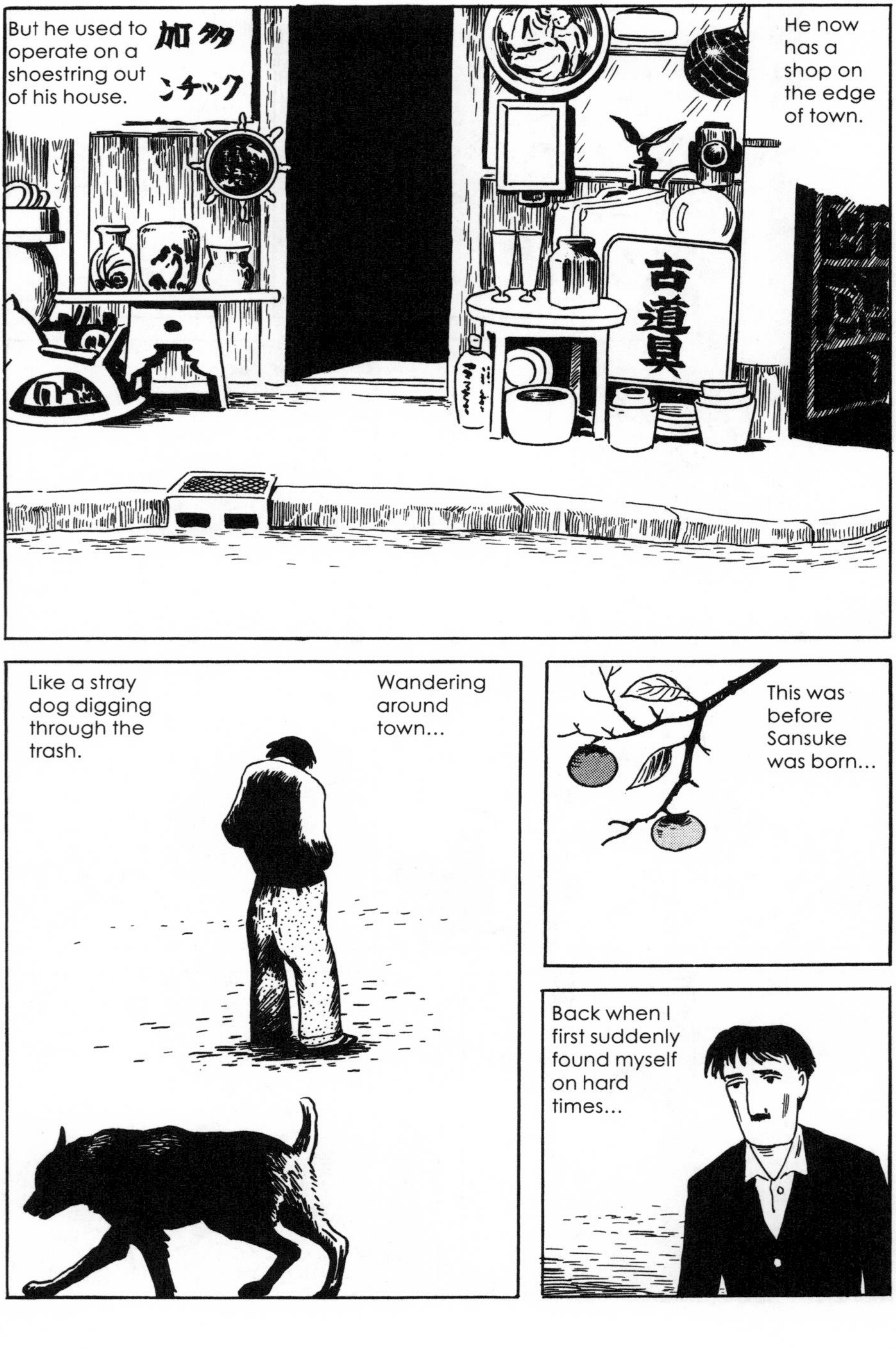
He now has a shop on the edge of town.
古道具
But he used to operate on a shoestring out of his house.
ンチック
This was before Sansuke was born…
Back when I first suddenly found myself on hard times…
Wandering around town…
Like a stray dog digging through the trash.

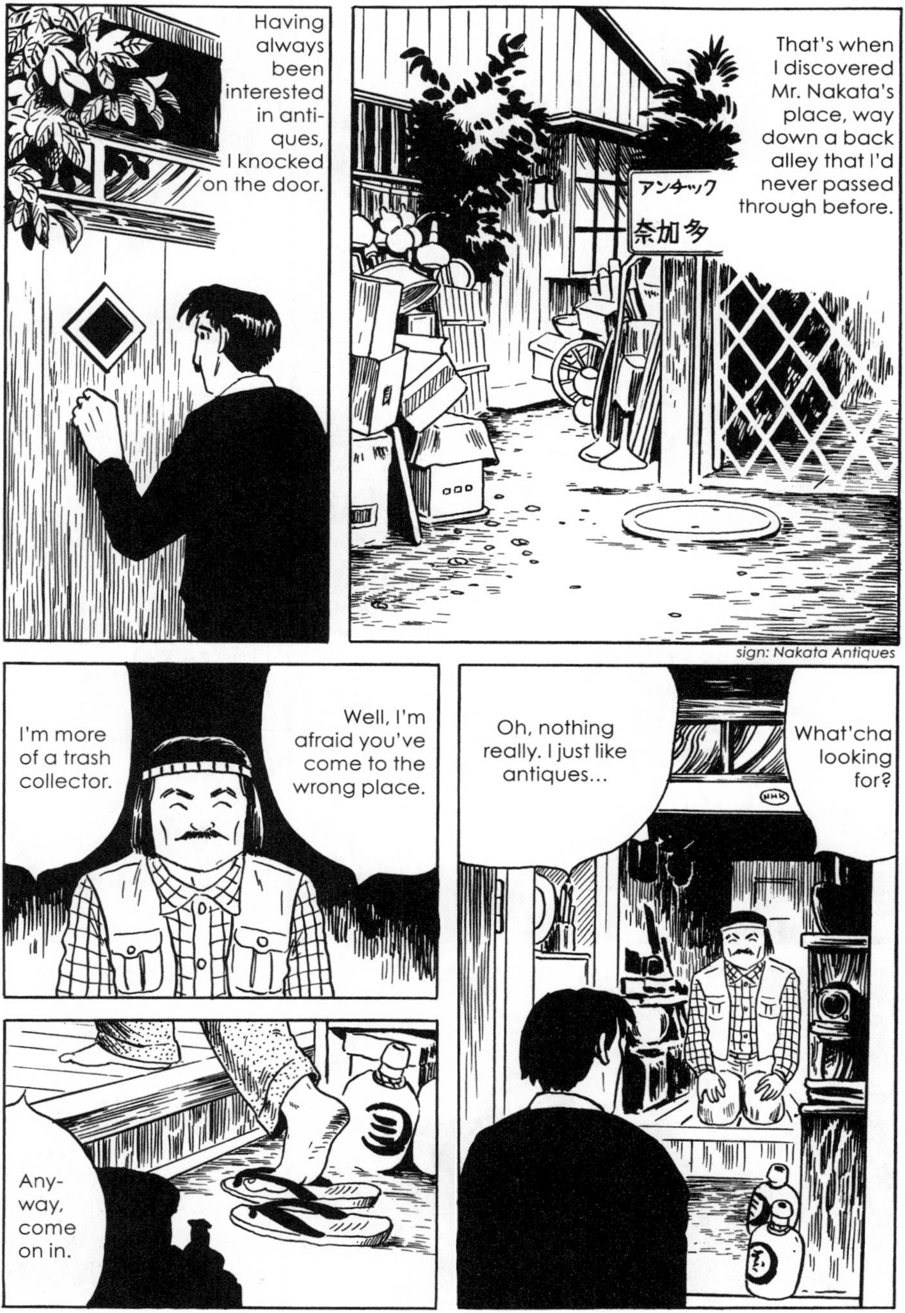
That's when I discovered Mr. Nakata's place, way down a back alley that I'd never passed through before.
アンチック
奈加多
sign: Nakata Antiques
Having always been interested in anti-ques, I knocked on the door.
What'cha looking for?
Oh, nothing really. I just like antiques...
Well, I'm afraid you've come to the wrong place.
I'm more of a trash collector.
Any-way, come on in.

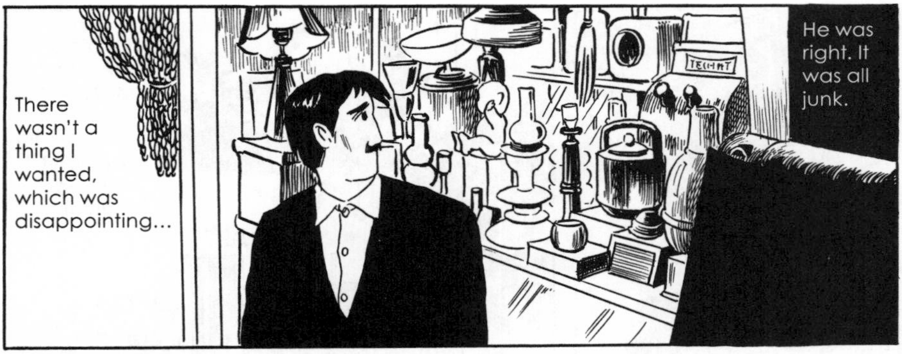
He was right. It was all junk.
There wasn't a thing I wanted, which was disappointing...

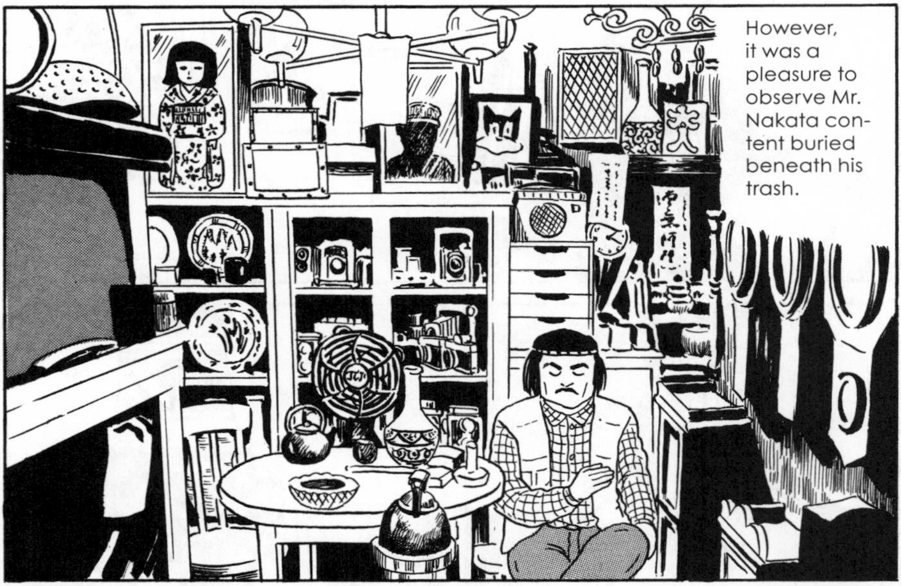
However, it was a pleasure to observe Mr. Nakata content buried beneath his trash.

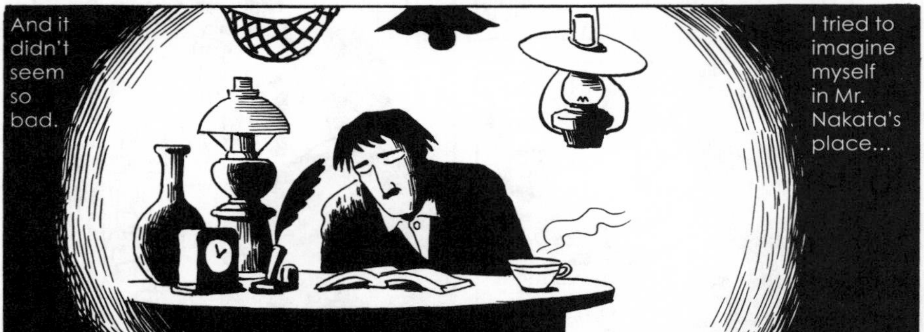
I tried to imagine myself in Mr. Nakata's place...
And it didn't seem so bad.

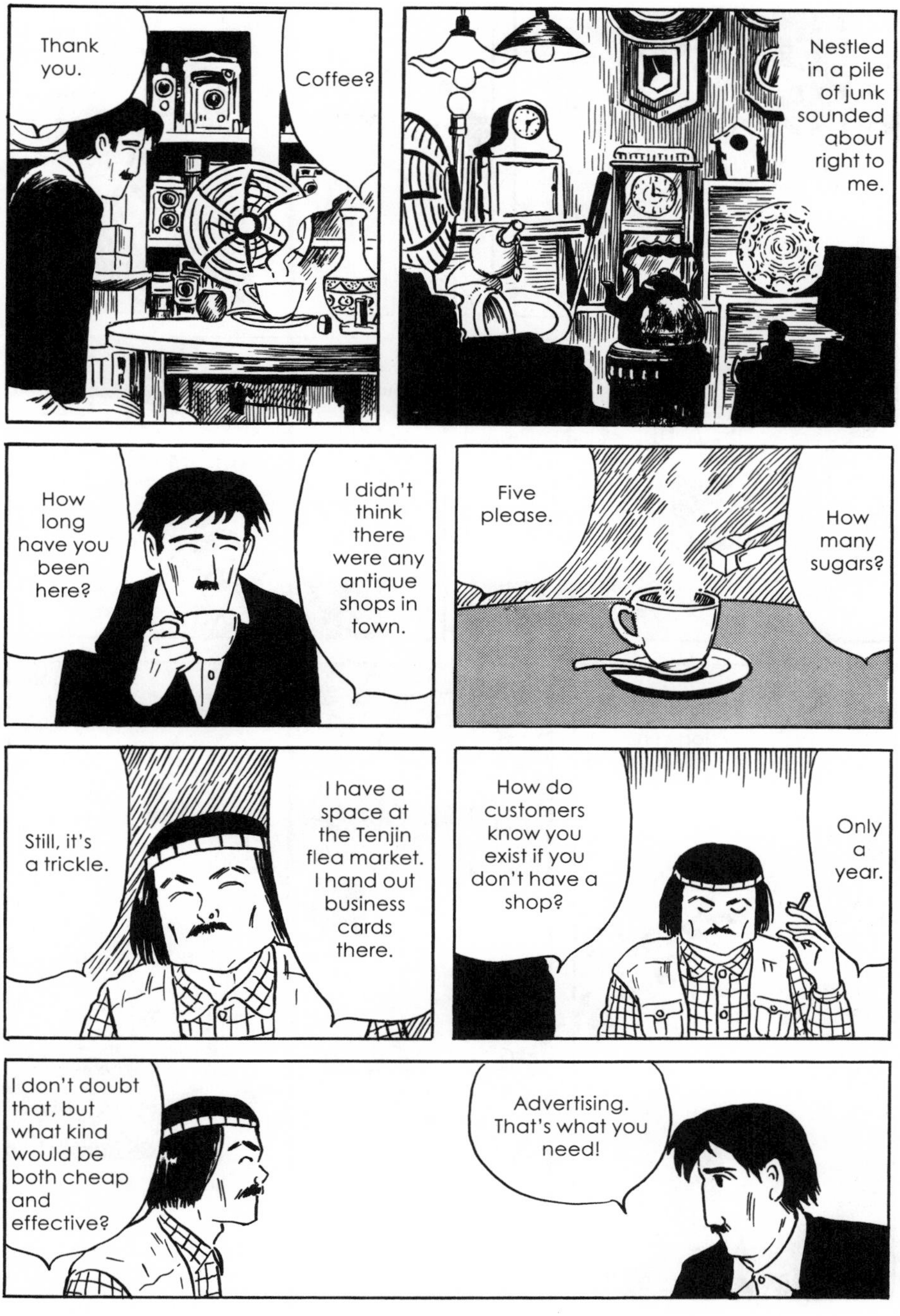
Nestled in a pile of junk sounded about right to me.
Coffee?
Thank you.
How many sugars?
Five please.
I didn't think there were any antique shops in town.
How long have you been here?
Only a year.
How do customers know you exist if you don't have a shop?
I have a space at the Tenjin flea market. I hand out business cards there.
Still, it's a trickle.
Advertising. That's what you need!
I don't doubt that, but what kind would be both cheap and effective?

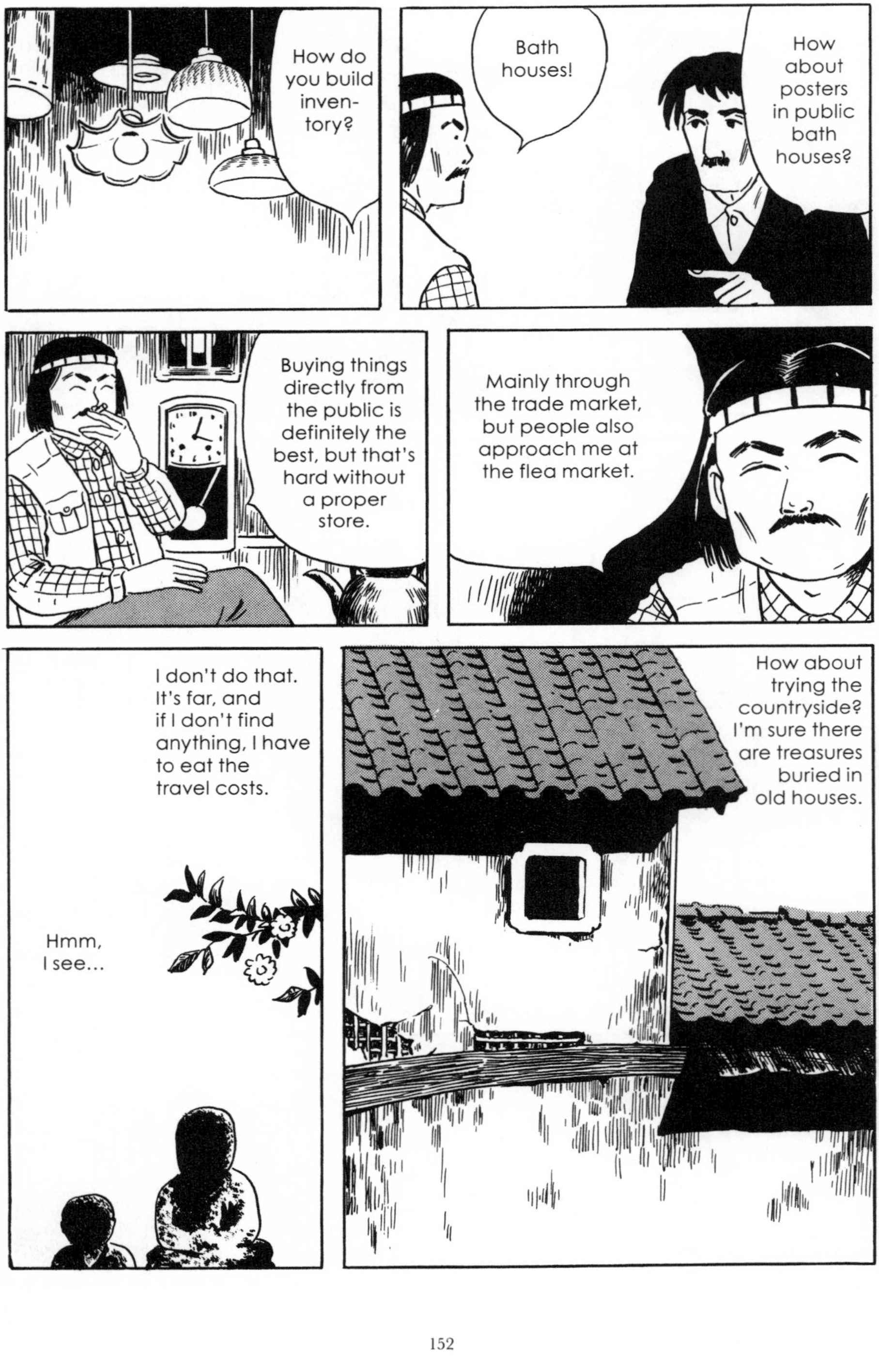
How about posters in public bath houses?
Bath houses!
How do you build inven-tory?
Mainly through the trade market, but people also approach me at the flea market.
Buying things directly from the public is definitely the best, but that's hard without a proper store.
How about trying the countryside? I'm sure there are treasures buried in old houses.
I don't do that. It's far, and if I don't find anything, I have to eat the travel costs.
Hmm, I see...

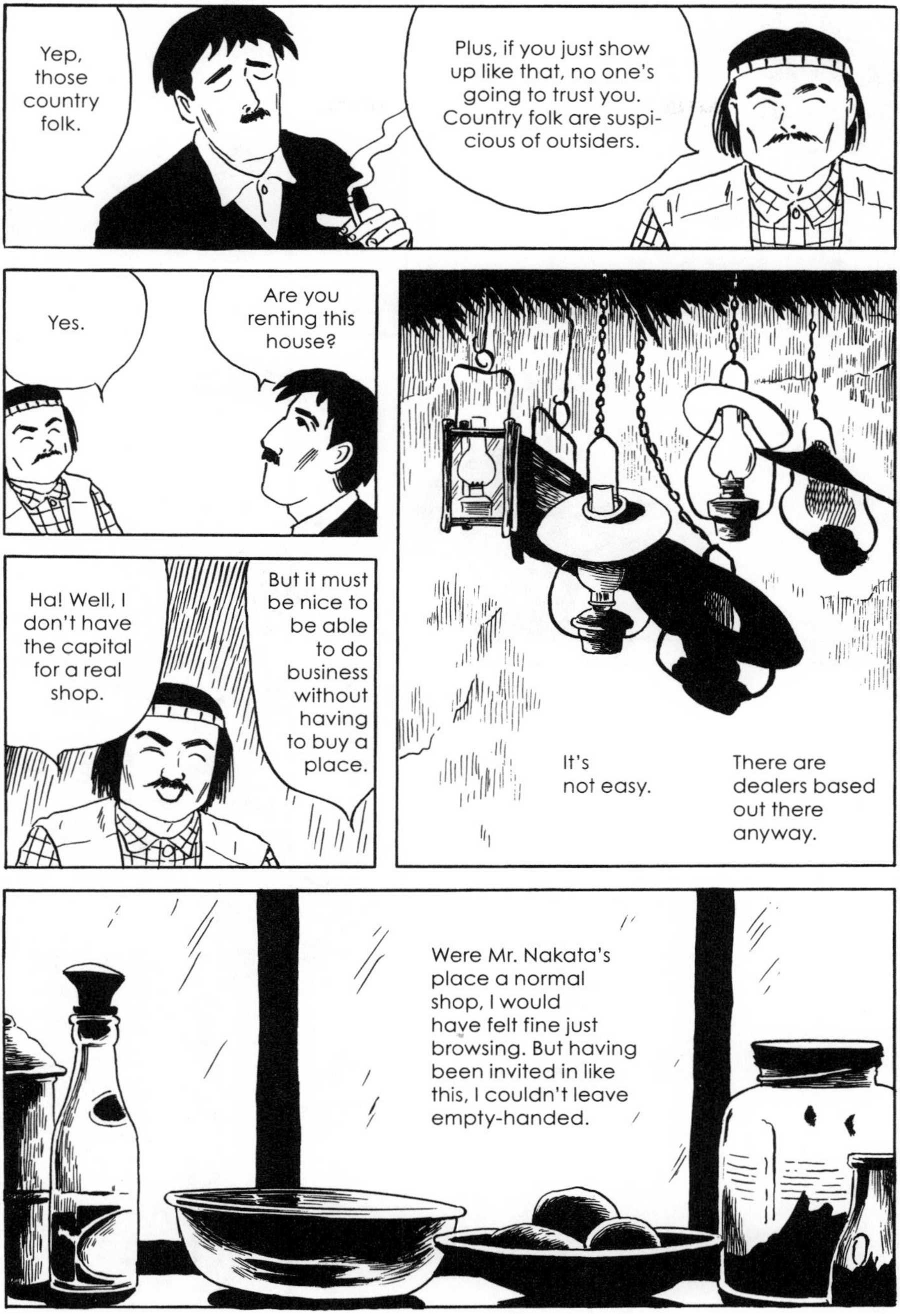
Plus, if you just show up like that, no one's going to trust you. Country folk are suspicious of outsiders.
Yep, those country folk.
There are dealers based out there anyway.
It's not easy.
Are you renting this house?
Yes.
But it must be nice to be able to do business without having to buy a place.
Ha! Well, I don't have the capital for a real shop.
Were Mr. Nakata's place a normal shop, I would have felt fine just browsing. But having been invited in like this, I couldn't leave empty-handed.

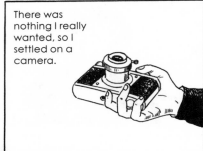

There was nothing I really wanted, so I settled on a camera.
They were strewn all over the place.
They're all broken. Take your pick, 1,000 yen.
I always thought of cameras as expensive, but I guess if they're broken they're worth practically nothing.
商店
山井書店
古書
古本

left sign: Old books *middle sign: Yamai's Vintage Books* *top sign: Shop*

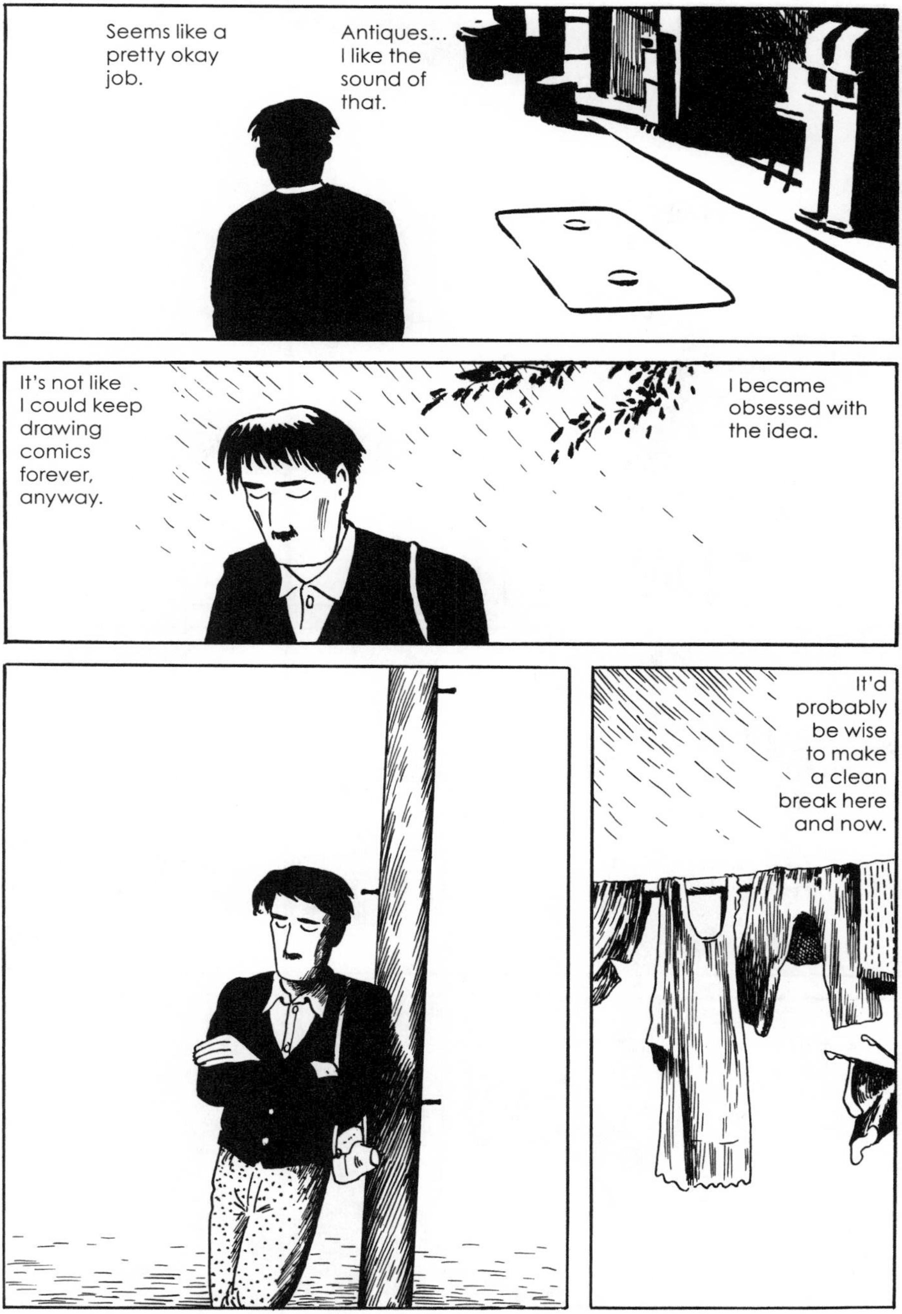
Antiques... I like the sound of that.
Seems like a pretty okay job.
I became obsessed with the idea.
It's not like I could keep drawing comics forever, anyway.
It'd probably be wise to make a clean break here and now.

Nakata's place looked something like this.
台所
4.5畳
押入
風呂
6畳
玄
He sells stuff in this 9 square meter space.
押入
6畳
玄
Two rooms and a kitchen are all I need.
But since it can't be on the second floor…
We'll have to rent a house.
A proper shop would require two different rents.
And a home business would allow me to do what I wanted with my time.

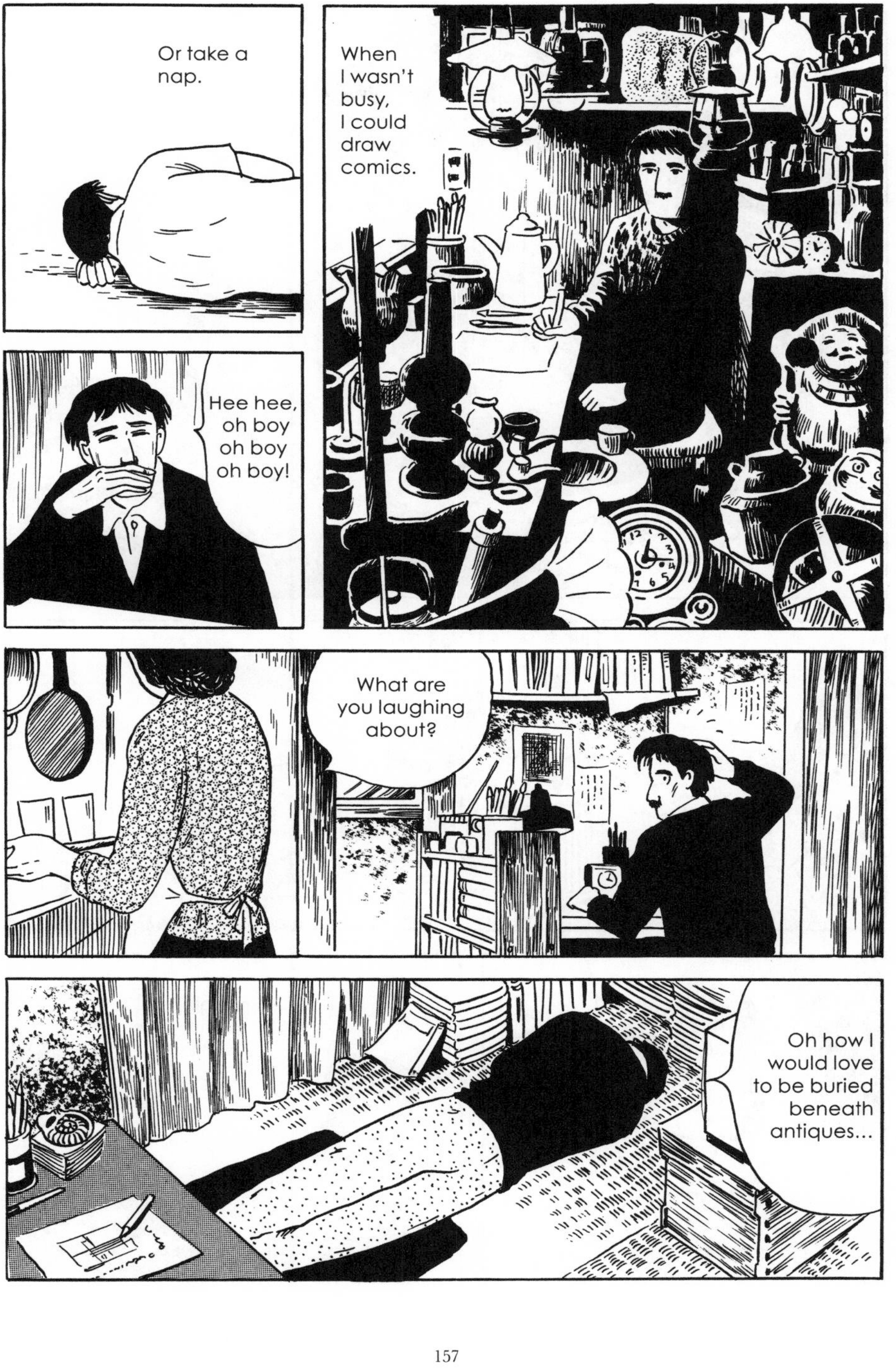
When I wasn't busy, I could draw comics.
Or take a nap.
Hee hee, oh boy oh boy oh boy!
What are you laughing about?
Oh how I would love to be buried beneath antiques...

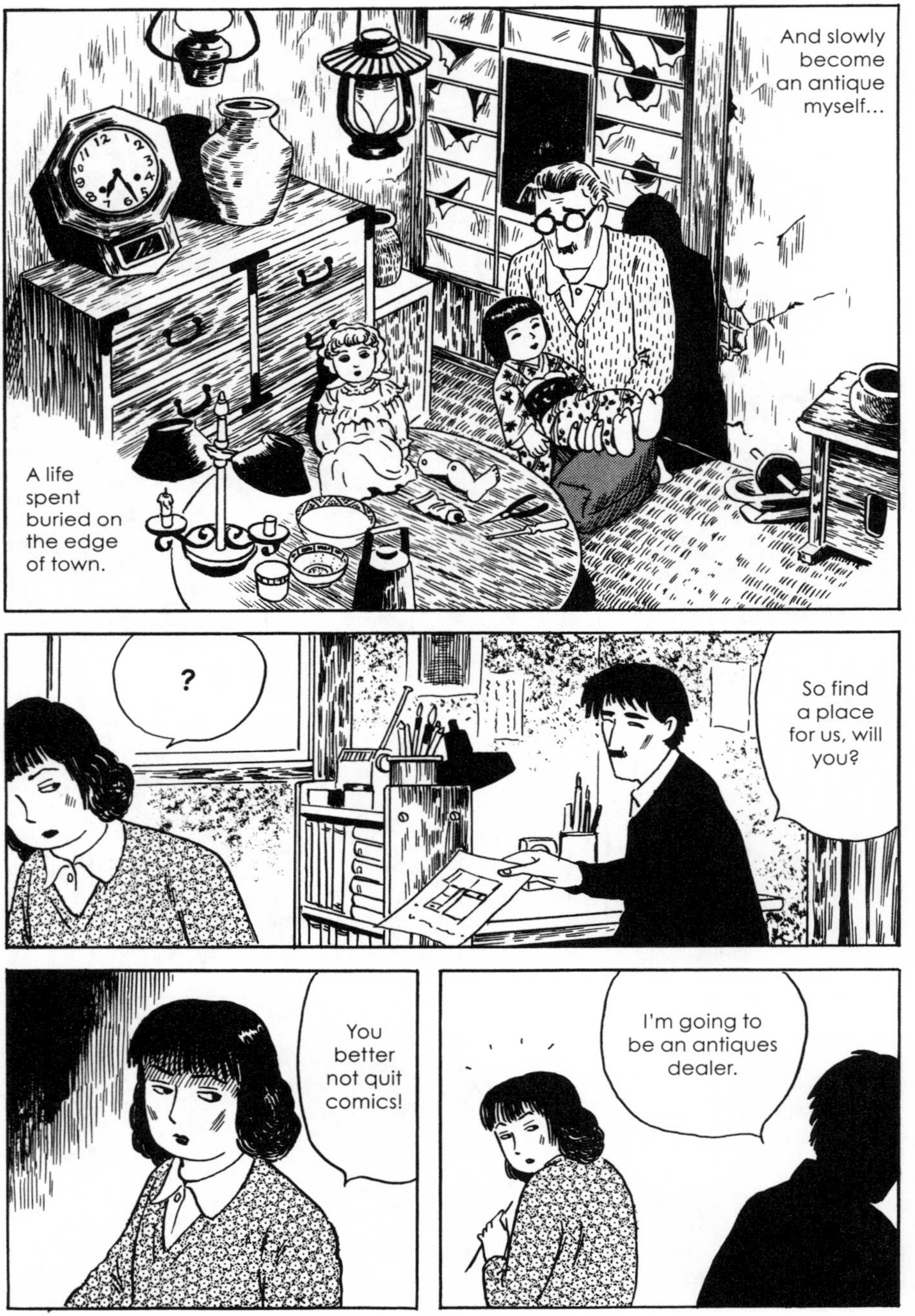
And slowly become an antique myself…
A life spent buried on the edge of town.
So find a place for us, will you?
?
I'm going to be an antiques dealer.
You better not quit comics!

As there was no harm in busting a 1,000 yen camera, I futzed around and found that fixing it was far easier than I had expected.
Okay, let's try it out.
Don't be nervous.
Oh my god. Like this?
My wife was still cute back then.

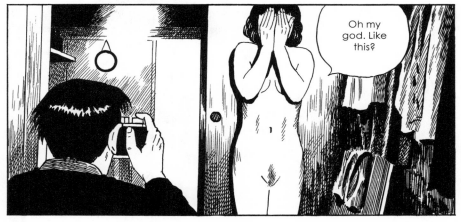

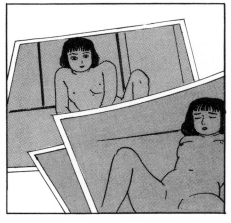

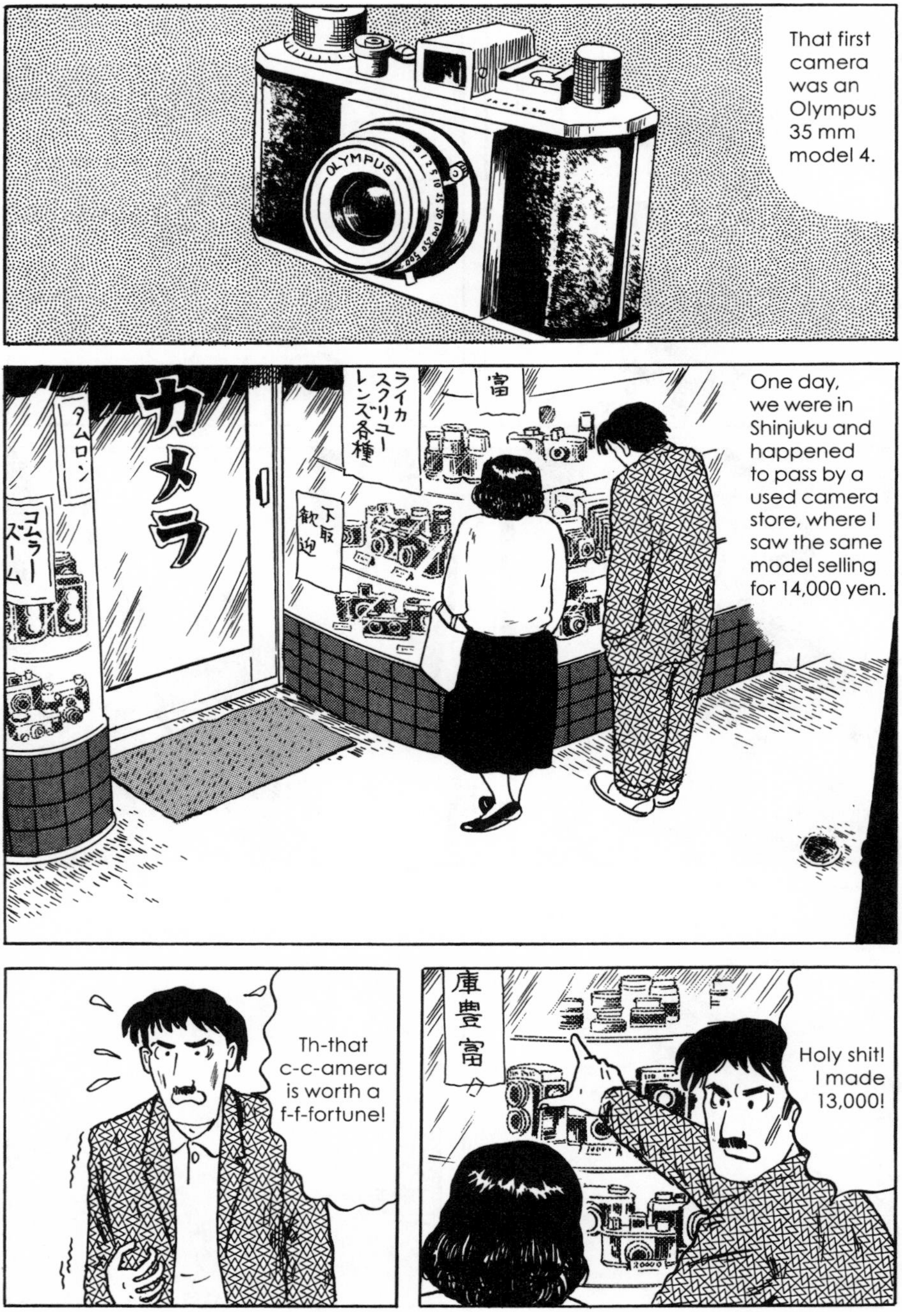
That first camera was an Olympus 35 mm model 4.
OLYMPUS
One day, we were in Shinjuku and happened to pass by a used camera store, where I saw the same model selling for 14,000 yen.
富
ライカ
スクリユー
レンズ各種
下取
歓迎
カメラ
タムロン
コムラー
ズーム
庫豊富
Holy shit! I made 13,000!
Th-that c-c-amera is worth a f-f-fortune!

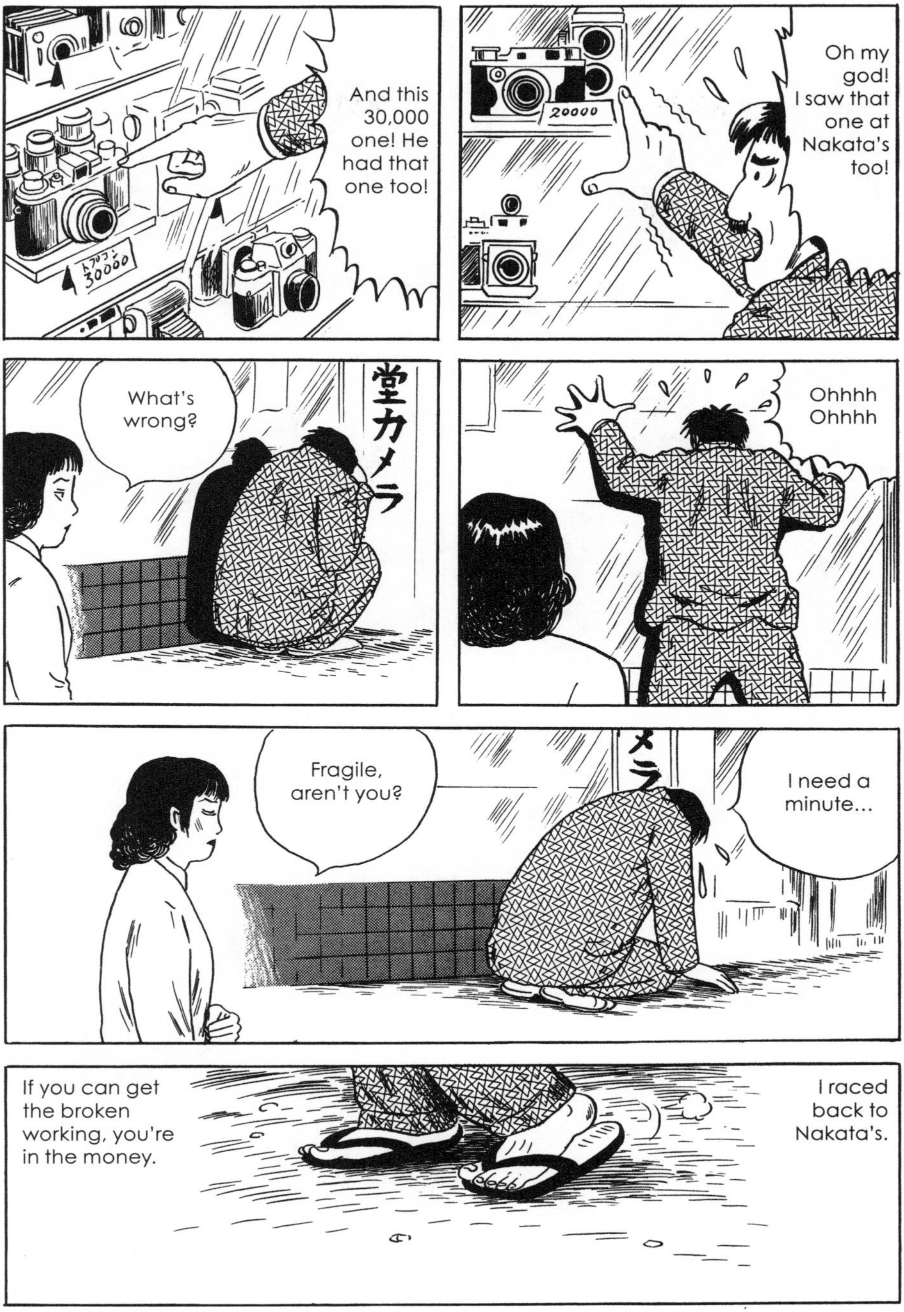
Oh my god! I saw that one at Nakata's too!
20000
And this 30,000 one! He had that one too!
30000
Ohhhh Ohhhh
堂カメラ
What's wrong?
I need a minute...
メラ
Fragile, aren't you?
I raced back to Nakata's.
If you can get the broken working, you're in the money.

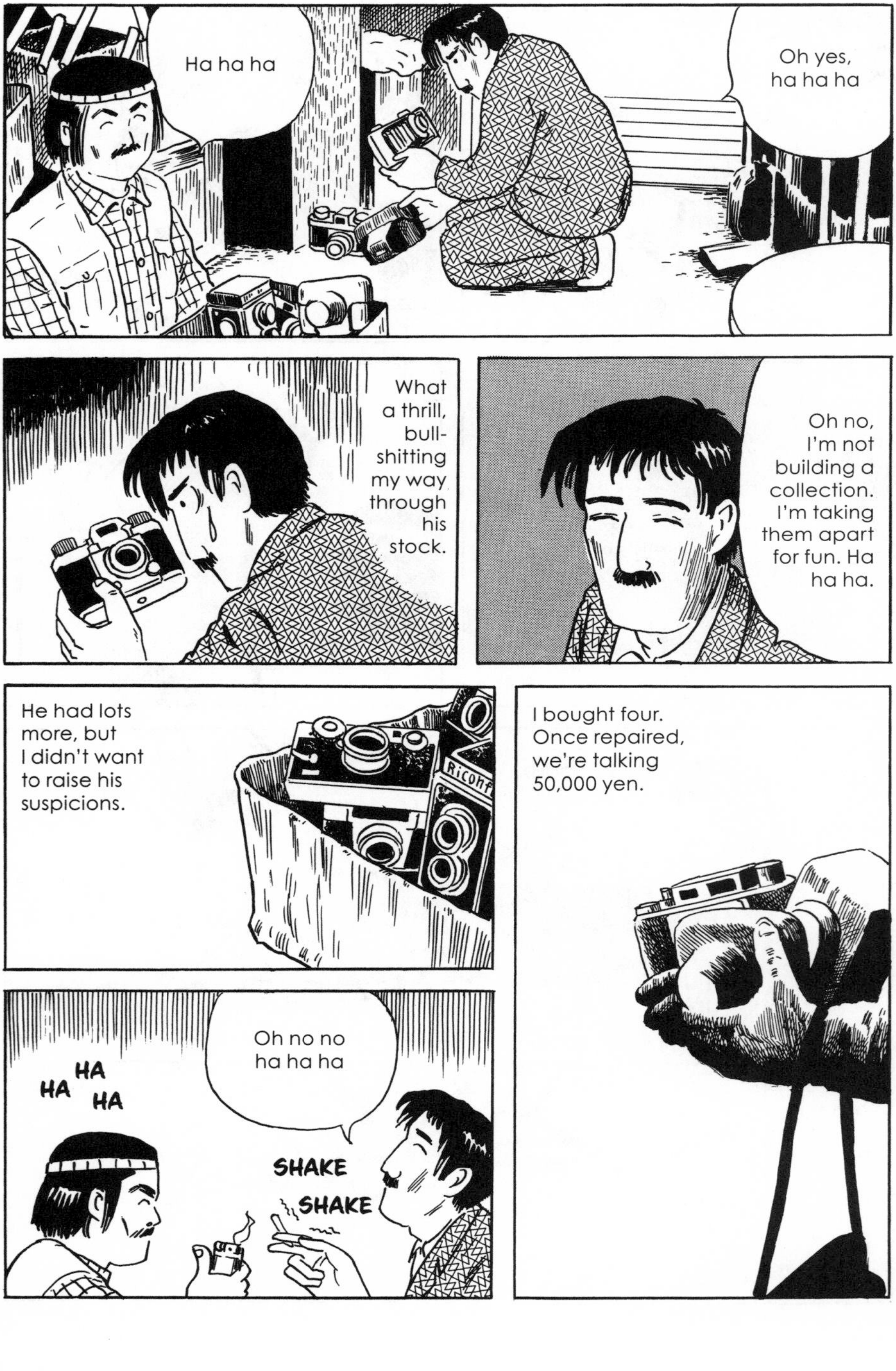
Oh yes, ha ha ha
Ha ha ha
Oh no, I'm not building a collection. I'm taking them apart for fun. Ha ha ha.
What a thrill, bull-shitting my way through his stock.
I bought four. Once repaired, we're talking 50,000 yen.
He had lots more, but I didn't want to raise his suspicions.
Oh no no ha ha ha
HA HA HA
SHAKE SHAKE

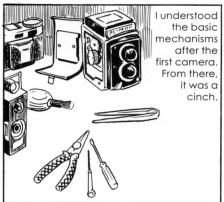

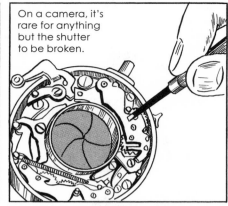

On a camera, it's rare for anything but the shutter to be broken.
I understood the basic mechanisms after the first camera. From there, it was a cinch.
下取交換セール!
From magazine ads, I learned what models were the best bang for the buck.
クラシックカメラ
カメラの歴史
From books, I crammed 2,000 different models into my brain.
books: History of Cameras, Classic Cameras
Shutter speed dial
Speed dial cam
Rear curtain control
Pallet
Sector gear
Second wheel
Escape wheel
Slow speed governor
A
B
Gear train for film
Advance lever
Ⓐ Sprocket drum clutch: this catch releases
Ⓒ finally: this catch releases
Once I get into something, my inner talents surge.
In the process of frequenting Nakata's place...

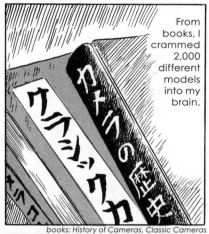

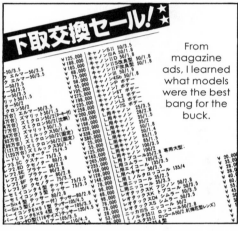

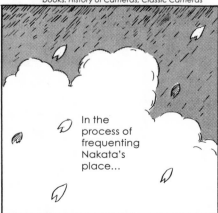

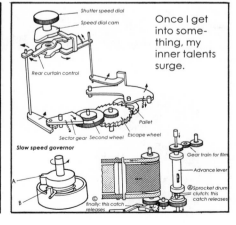

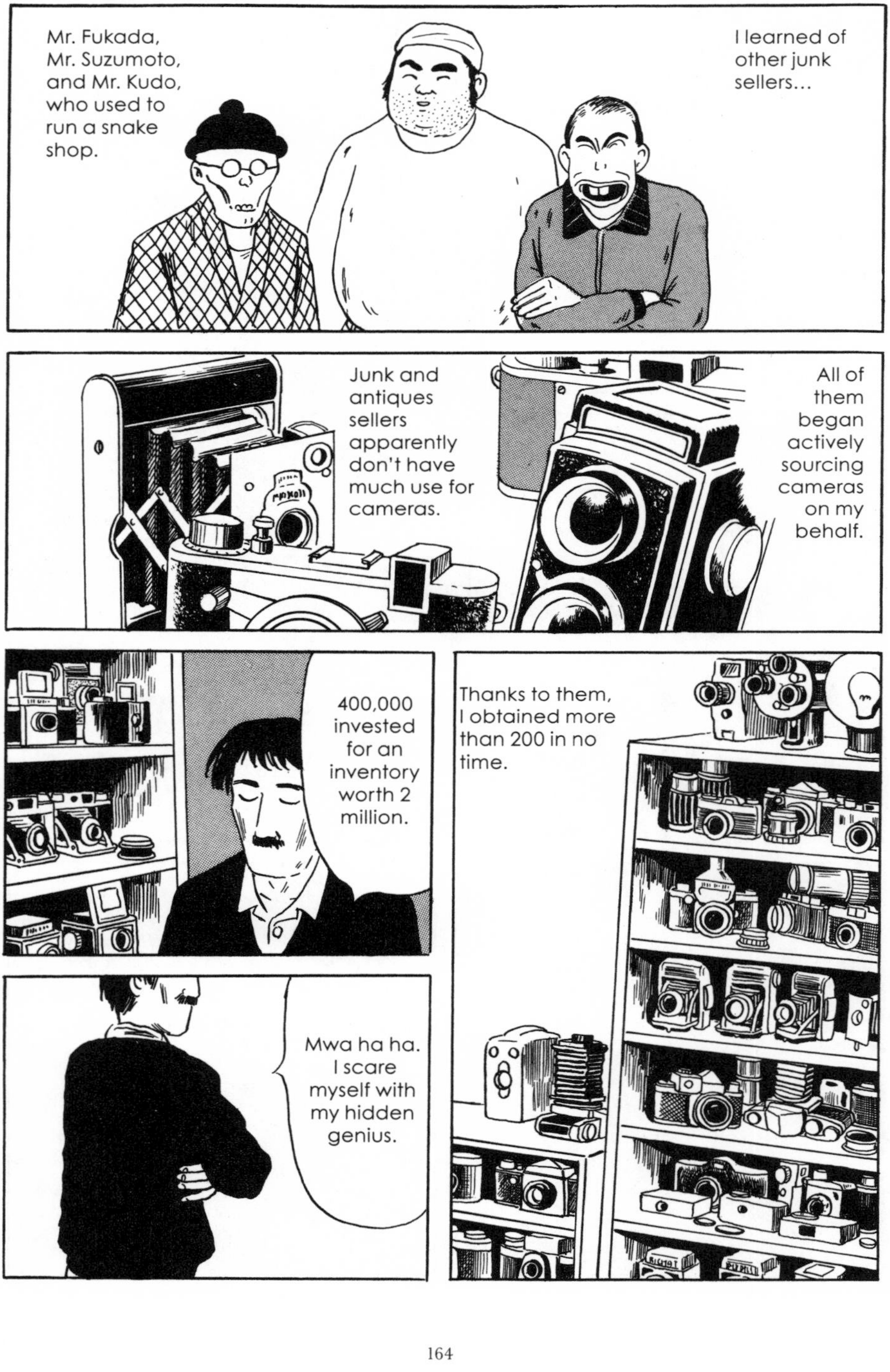
I learned of other junk sellers…
Mr. Fukada, Mr. Suzumoto, and Mr. Kudo, who used to run a snake shop.
All of them began actively sourcing cameras on my behalf.
Junk and antiques sellers apparently don't have much use for cameras.
Thanks to them, I obtained more than 200 in no time.
400,000 invested for an inventory worth 2 million.
Mwa ha ha. I scare myself with my hidden genius.

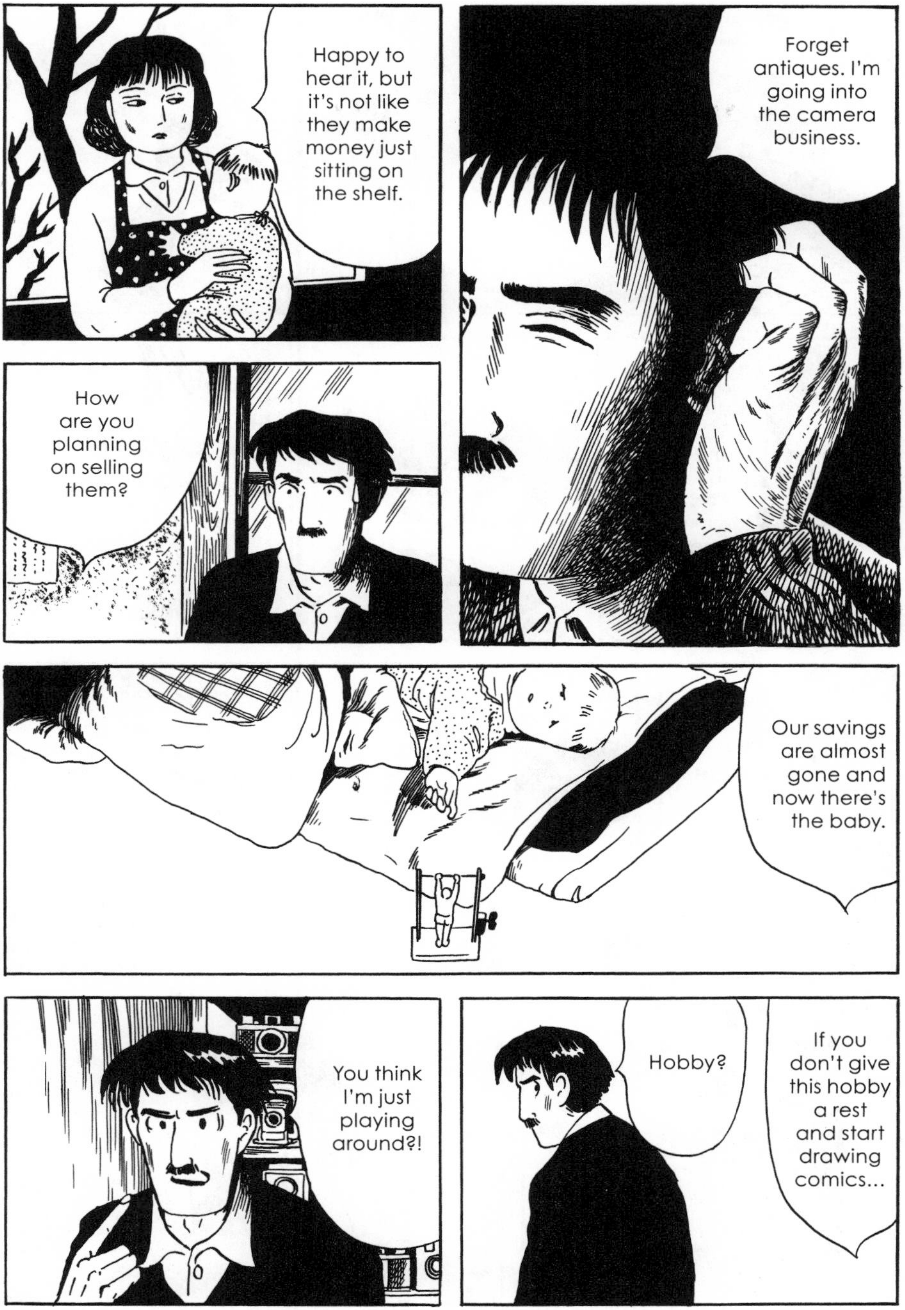
Forget antiques. I'm going into the camera business.
Happy to hear it, but it's not like they make money just sitting on the shelf.
How are you planning on selling them?
Our savings are almost gone and now there's the baby.
If you don't give this hobby a rest and start drawing comics...
Hobby?
You think I'm just playing around?!

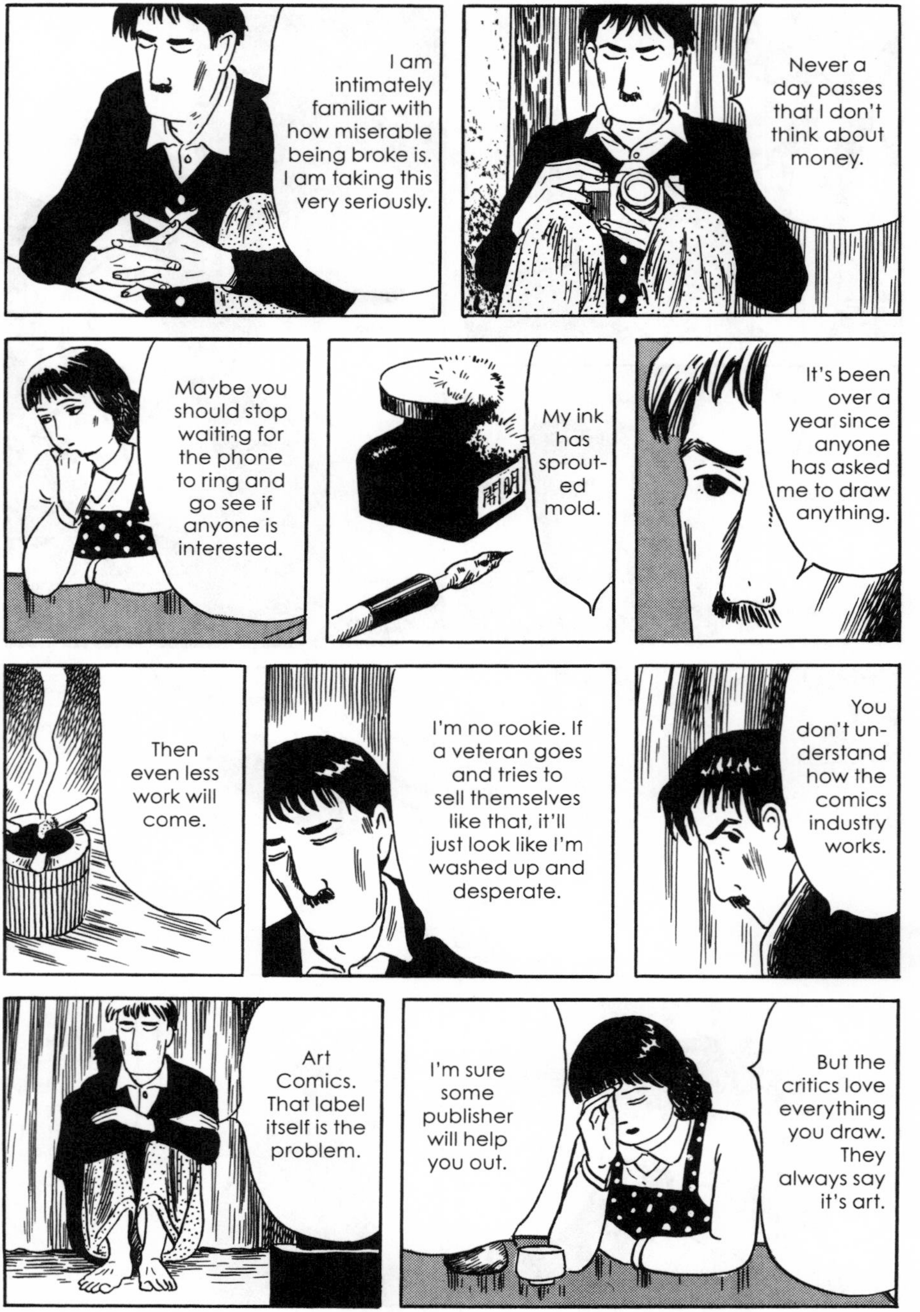
Never a day passes that I don't think about money.
I am intimately familiar with how miserable being broke is. I am taking this very seriously.
It's been over a year since anyone has asked me to draw anything.
My ink has sprout-ed mold.
開明
Maybe you should stop waiting for the phone to ring and go see if anyone is interested.
You don't un-derstand how the comics industry works.
I'm no rookie. If a veteran goes and tries to sell themselves like that, it'll just look like I'm washed up and desperate.
Then even less work will come.
But the critics love everything you draw. They always say it's art.
I'm sure some publisher will help you out.
Art Comics. That label itself is the problem.

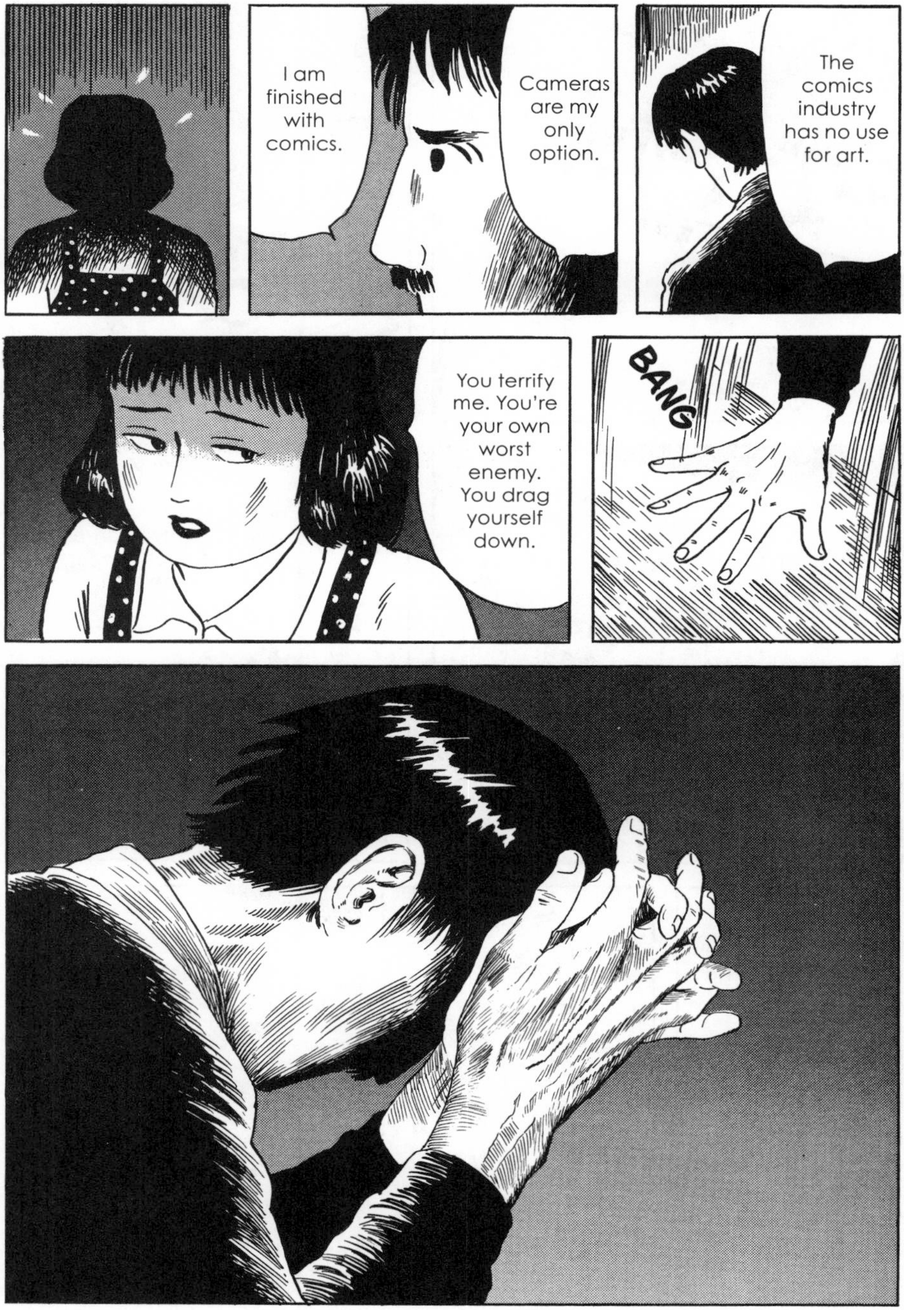

The comics industry has no use for art.
Cameras are my only option.
I am finished with comics.
BANG
You terrify me. You're your own worst enemy. You drag yourself down.

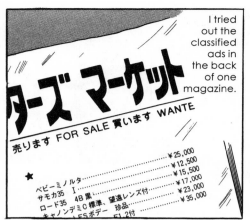

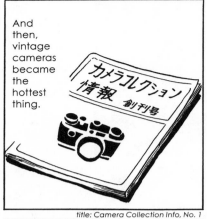

And then, vintage cameras became the hottest thing.
カメラコレクション情報
創刊号
title: Camera Collection Info, No. 1
I tried out the classified ads in the back of one magazine.
ターズ マーケット
売ります FOR SALE 買います WANTE
ベビーミノルタ ¥25,000
サモカ35 I ¥12,500
ロード35 4B黒 ¥15,500
キャノンデミC 標準、望遠レンズ付 ¥17,000
¥23,000
¥35,000
I advertised 5 or 6 cameras, and much to my surprise got 40 offers in the mail.
I saw your listing, and was interested to know if you also had...
As someone who lives in Hokkaido...
I saw your ad for the Baby Minolta...
Heh Heh Heh Heh

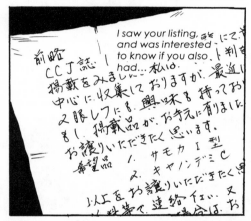

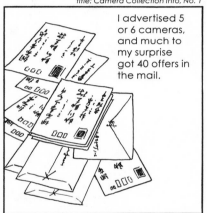

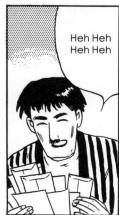

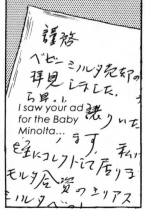

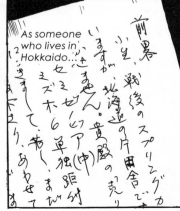

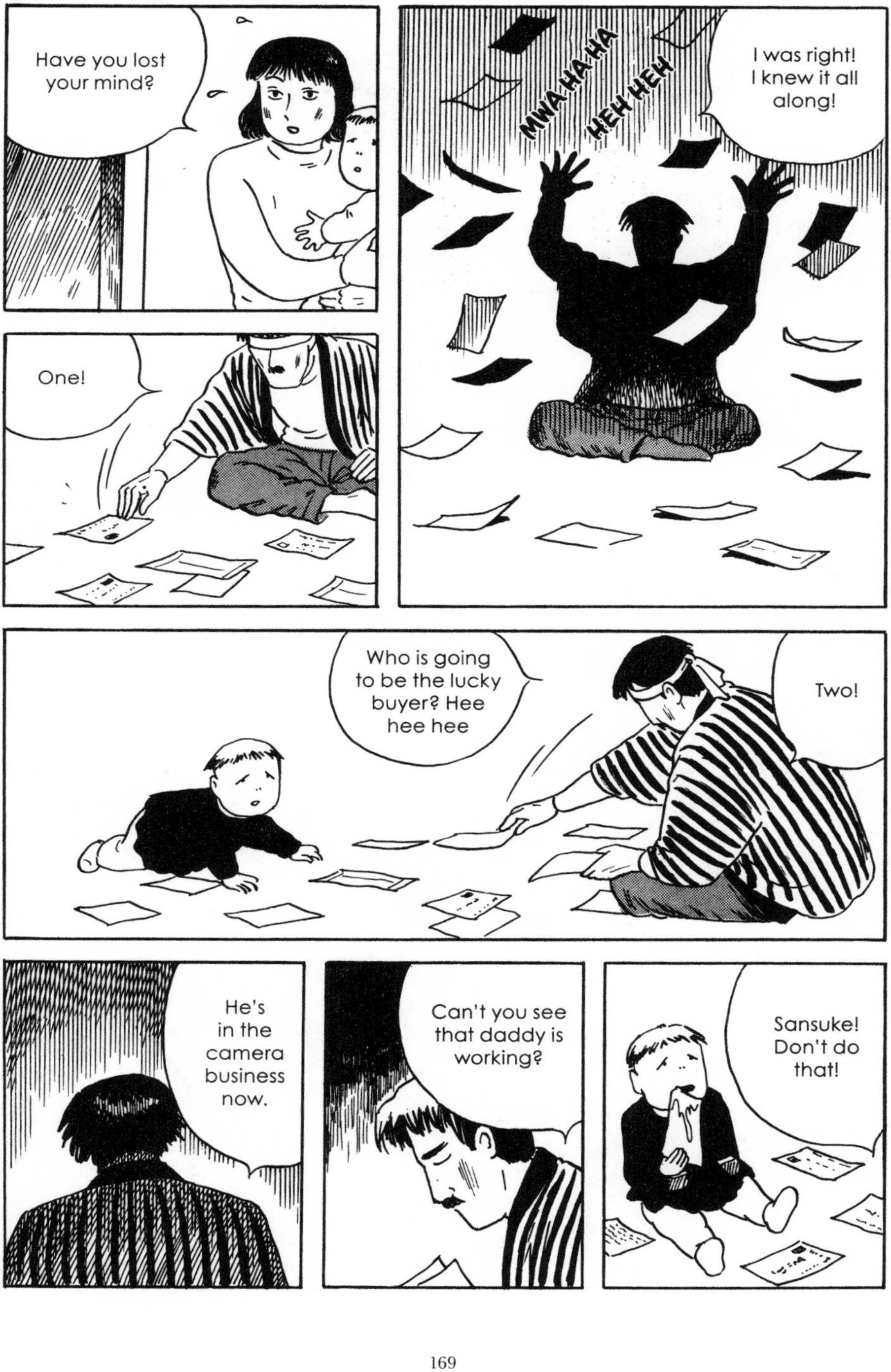
I was right! I knew it all along!
MWA HA HA
HEH HEH
Have you lost your mind?
One!
Two!
Who is going to be the lucky buyer? Hee hee hee
Sansuke! Don't do that!
Can't you see that daddy is working?
He's in the camera business now.

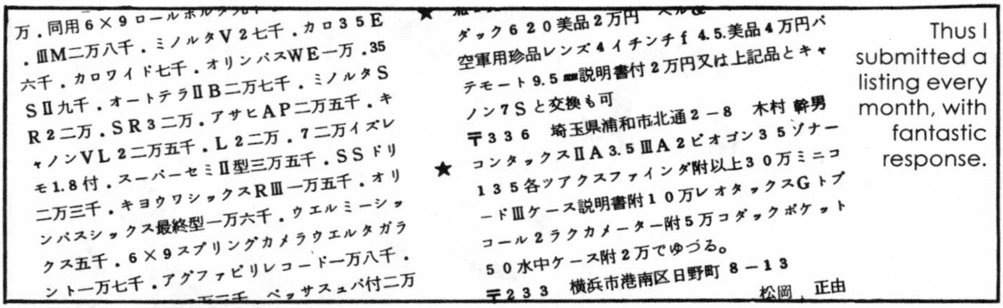
．ⅢM二万八千．ミノルタV2七千．カロ35E
六千．カロワイド七千．オリンパスWE一万．35
SⅡ九千．オートテラⅡB二万七千．ミノルタS
R2二万．SR3二万．アサヒAP二万五千．キ
ャノンVL2二万五千．L2二万．7二万イズレ
モ1.8付．スーパーセミⅡ型三万五千．SSドリ
二万三千．キヨウワシックスRⅢ一万五千．オリ
ンパスシックス最終型一万六千．ウエルミーシッ
クス五千．6×9スプリングカメラウエルタガラ
ント一万七千．アグファビリレコード一万八千．
ダック620美品2万円
空軍用珍品レンズ4インチf4.5美品4万円バ
テモート9.5㎜説明書付2万円又は上記品とキャ
ノン7Sと交換も可
〒336　埼玉県浦和市北通2－8　木村幹男
★コンタックスⅡA3.5ⅢA2ビオゴン35ゾナー
135各ツアクスファインダ附以上30万ミニコ
ードⅢケース説明書附10万レオタックスGトプ
コール2ラクカメーター附5万コダックポケット
50水中ケース附2万でゆづる。
〒233　横浜市港南区日野町8－13
松岡　正由
Thus I submitted a listing every month, with fantastic response.

text: Camera models and prices

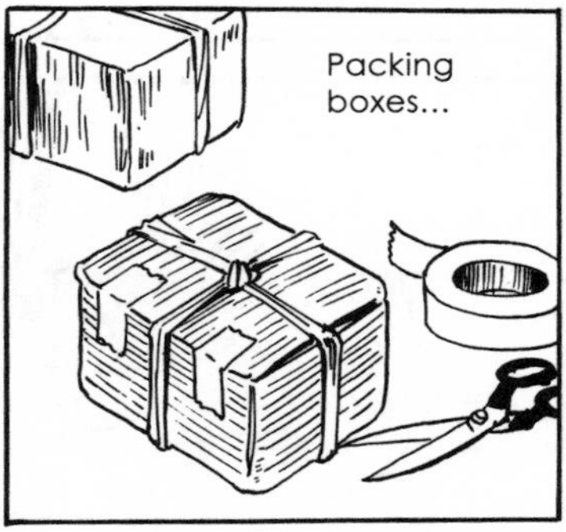
Packing boxes...

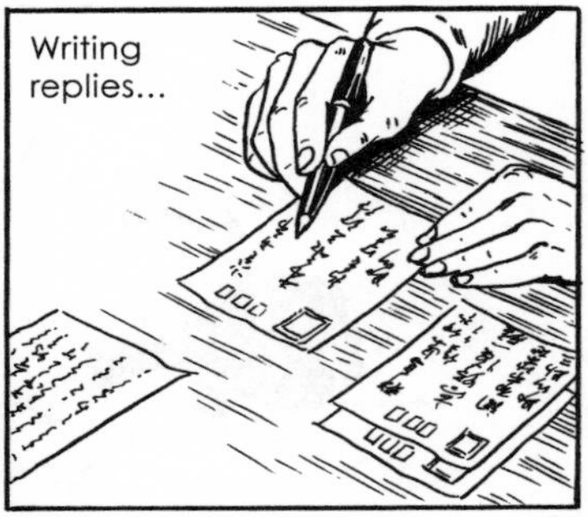
Writing replies...

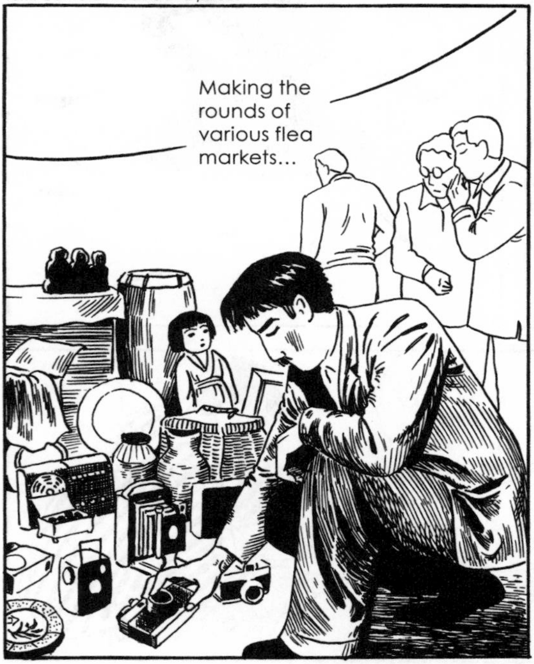
Making the rounds of various flea markets...

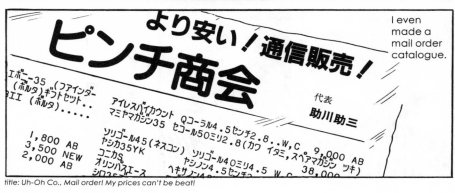

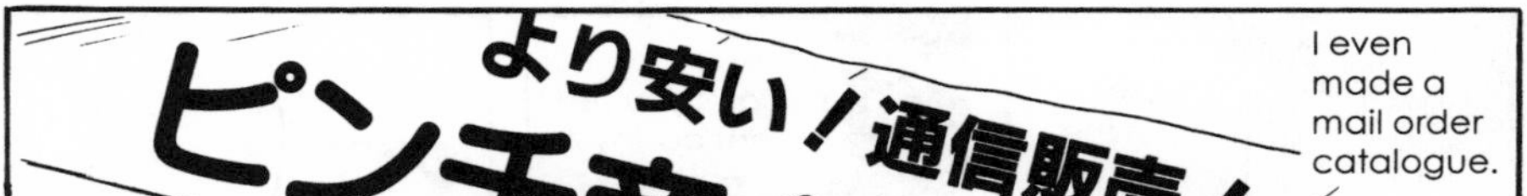
I even made a mail order catalogue.
より安い！通信販売！
ピンチ商会
代表
助川助三
アイレスバイカウント Qコーラル4.5センチ2.8..W,C 9,000 AB
マミヤマガジン35 セコール50ミリ2.8(カワ イタミ,スペアマガジン ツキ)
1,800 AB
3,500 NEW
2,000 AB
ヤシカ35YK
コニカS
オリンパスエース

title: Uh-Oh Co., Mail order! My prices can't be beat!

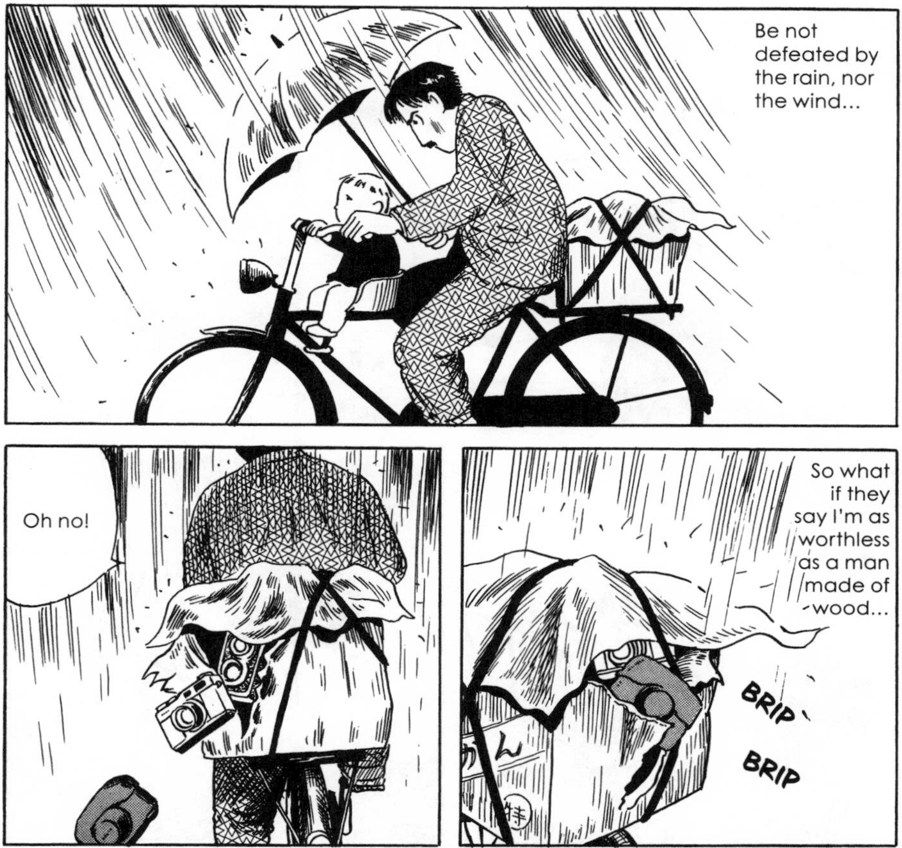
Be not defeated by the rain, nor the wind...
So what if they say I'm as worthless as a man made of wood...
BRIP
BRIP
Oh no!

note: lines from Kenji Miyazawa's famous poem, "Ame ni mo makezu"

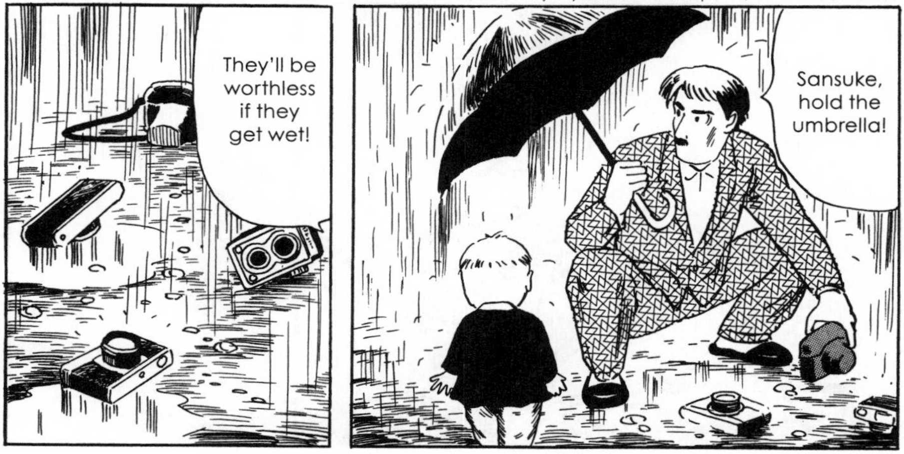
Sansuke, hold the umbrella!
They'll be worthless if they get wet!

Hold up the umbrella, dammit!
WAA WAA
We're getting soaked!
WAA WAA
Stop your wailing!
SMAK
WAA WAA

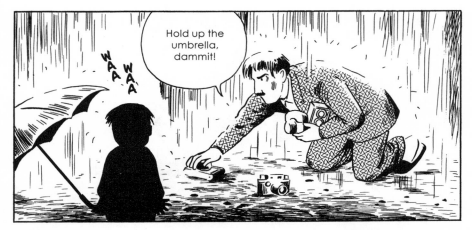

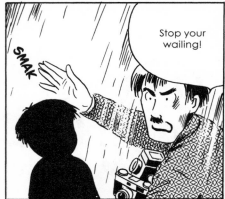

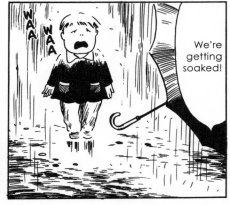

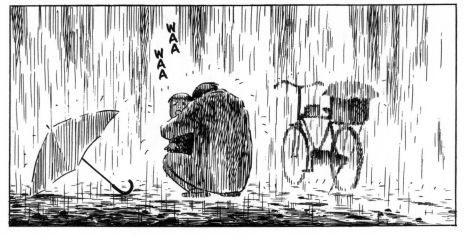

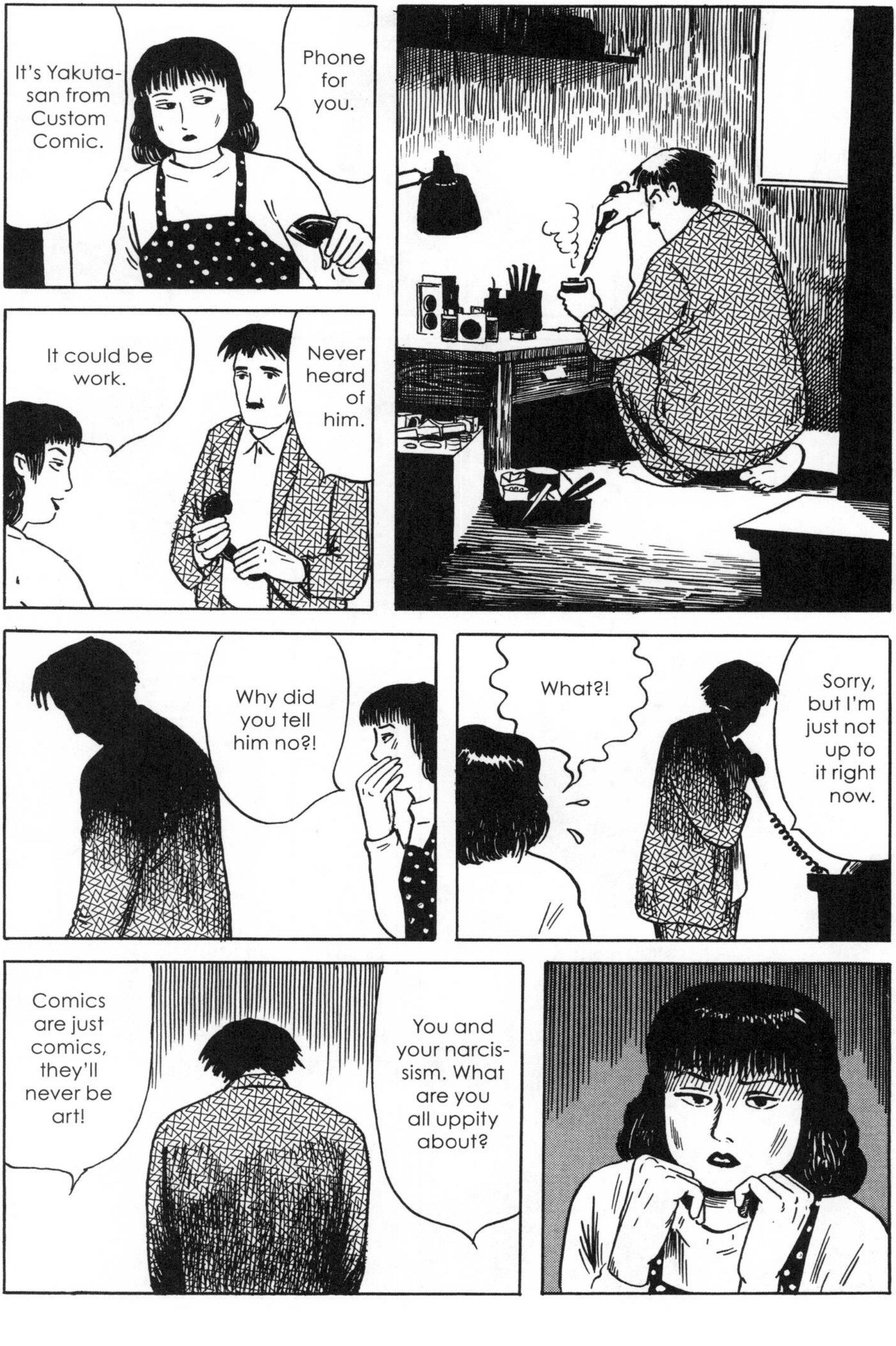
Phone for you.
It's Yakuta-san from Custom Comic.
Never heard of him.
It could be work.
Sorry, but I'm just not up to it right now.
What?!
Why did you tell him no?!
You and your narcissism. What are you all uppity about?
Comics are just comics, they'll never be art!

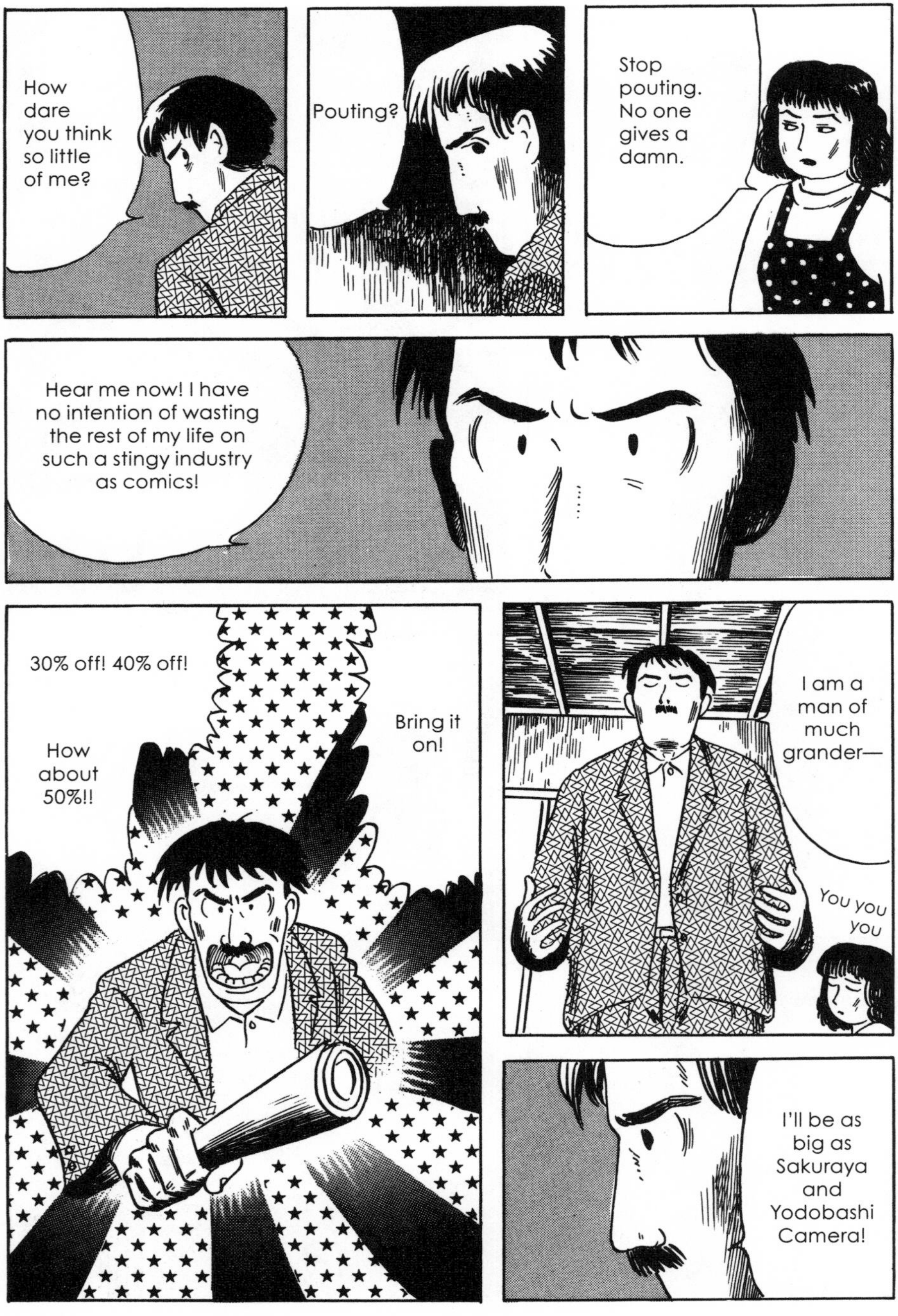
Stop pouting. No one gives a damn.
Pouting?
How dare you think so little of me?
Hear me now! I have no intention of wasting the rest of my life on such a stingy industry as comics!
I am a man of much grander—
You you you
I'll be as big as Sakuraya and Yodobashi Camera!
30% off! 40% off!
Bring it on!
How about 50%!!

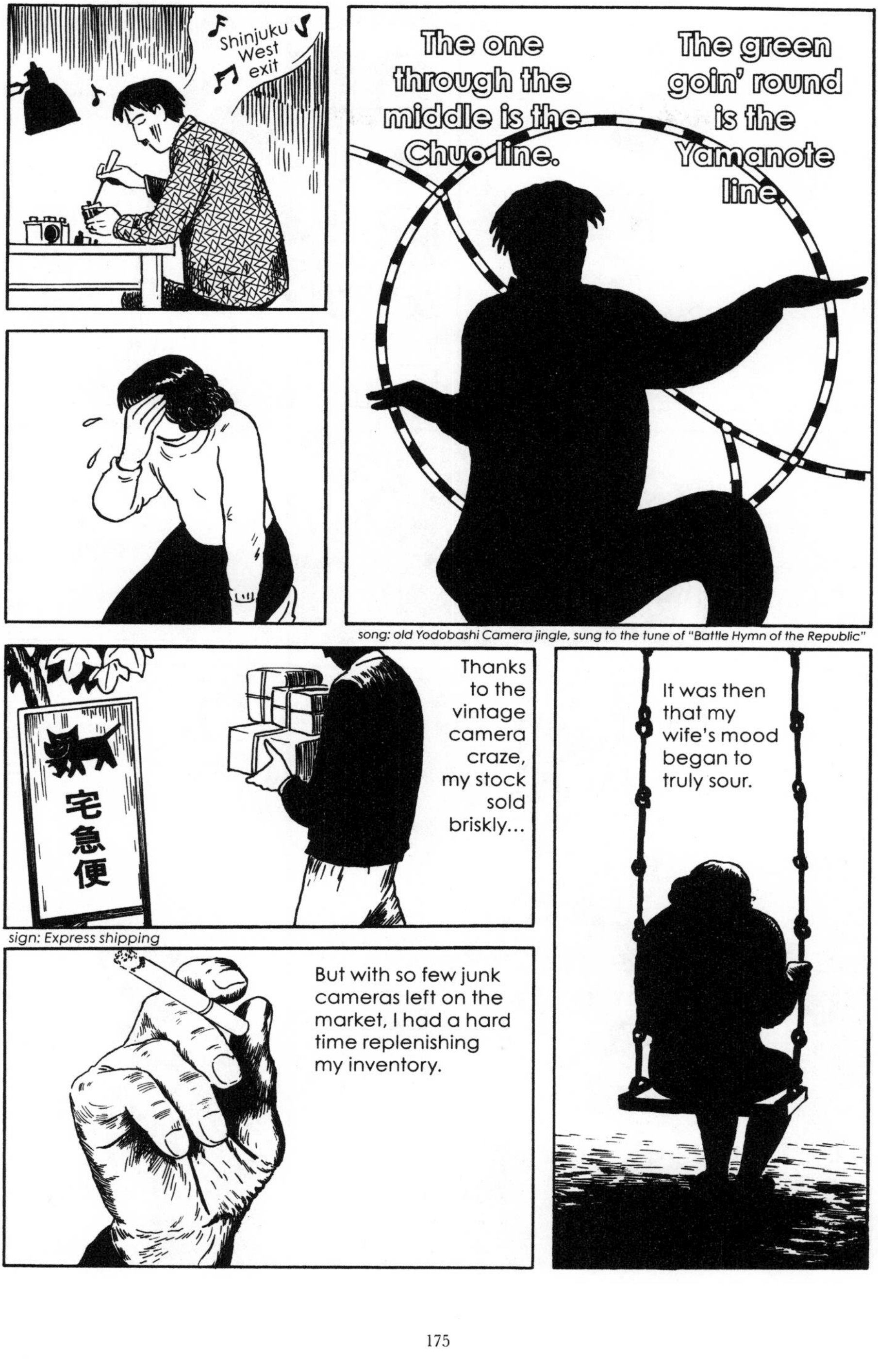
The green goin' round is the Yamanote line.
The one through the middle is the Chuo line.
Shinjuku West exit
It was then that my wife's mood began to truly sour.
Thanks to the vintage camera craze, my stock sold briskly…
宅急便
But with so few junk cameras left on the market, I had a hard time replenishing my inventory.
song: old Yodobashi Camera jingle, sung to the tune of "Battle Hymn of the Republic"

sign: Express shipping

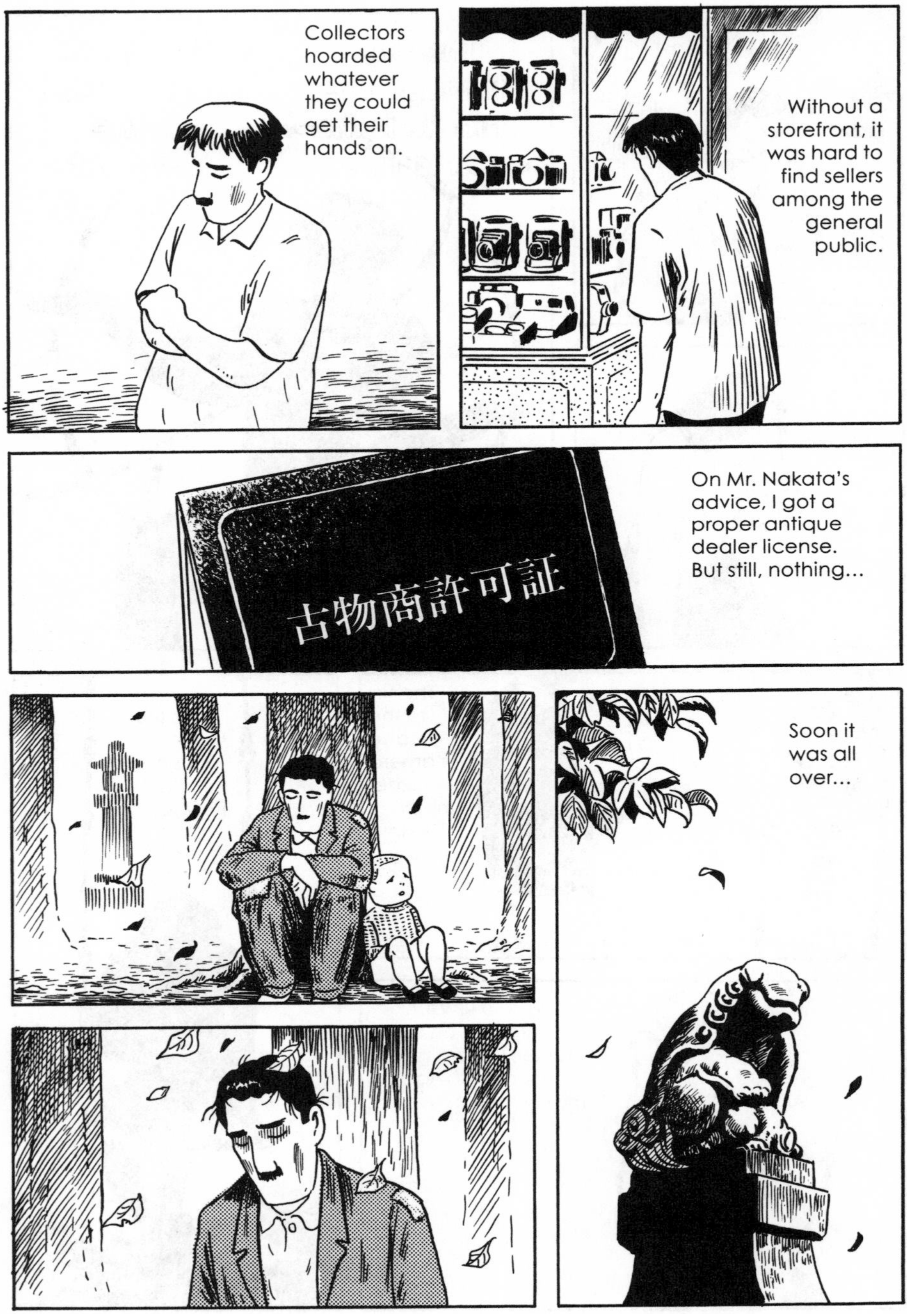
Without a storefront, it was hard to find sellers among the general public.
Collectors hoarded whatever they could get their hands on.
On Mr. Nakata's advice, I got a proper antique dealer license. But still, nothing...
古物商許可証
Soon it was all over...

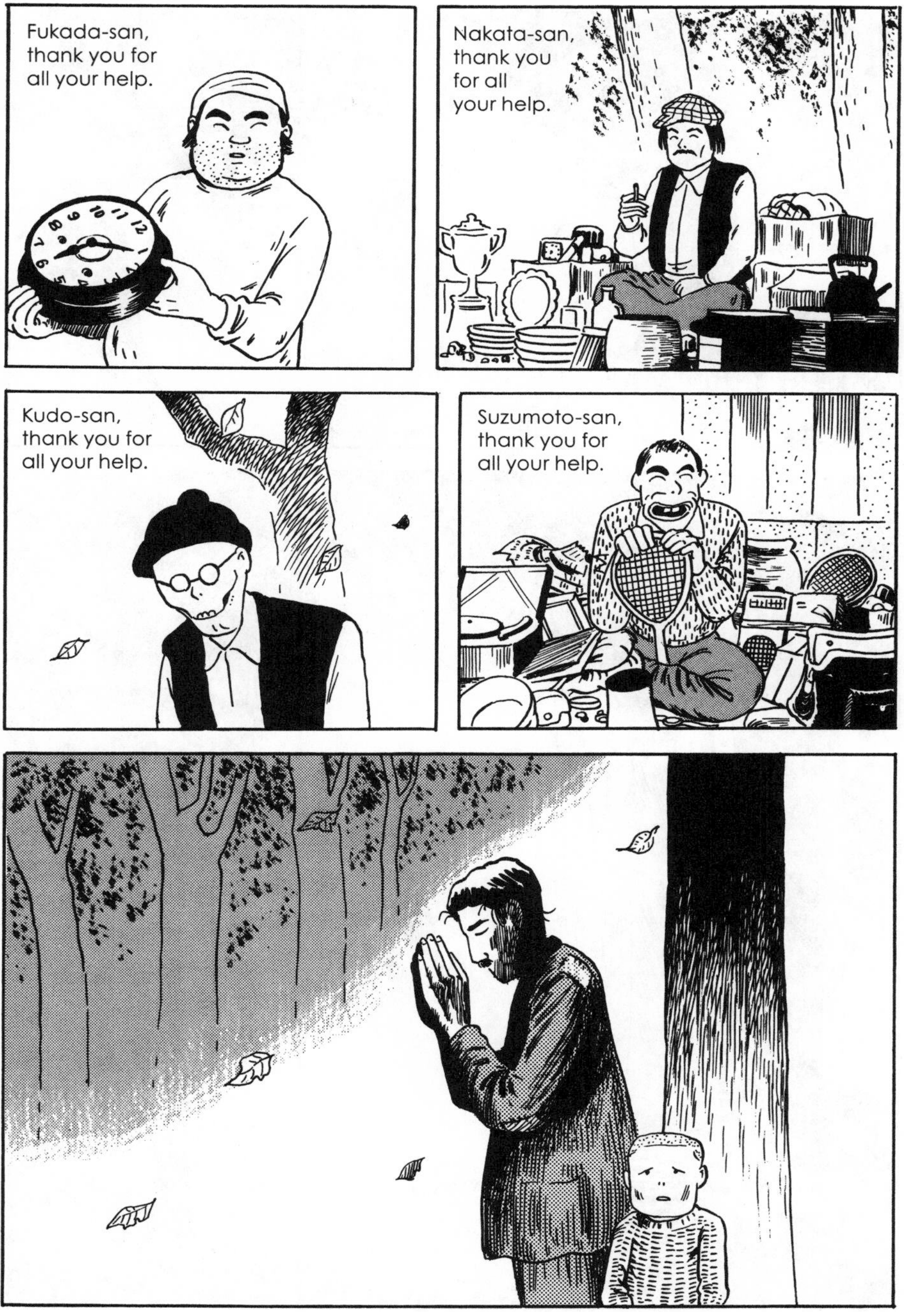
Nakata-san, thank you for all your help.
Fukada-san, thank you for all your help.
Suzumoto-san, thank you for all your help.
Kudo-san, thank you for all your help.

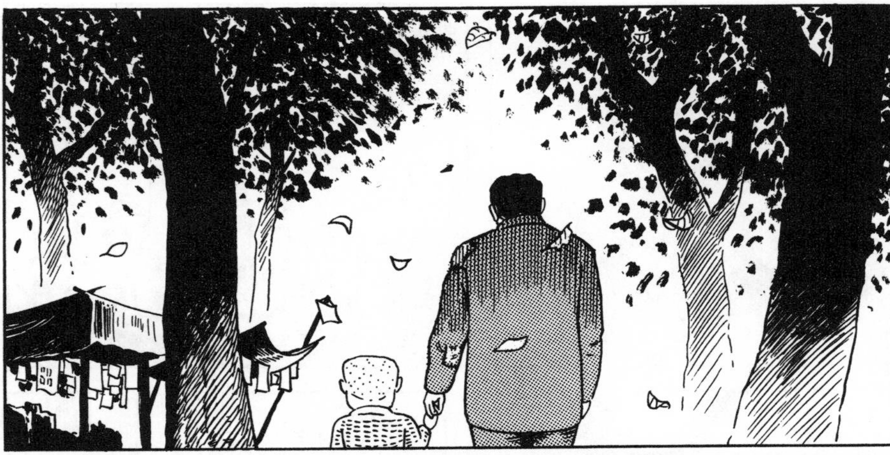
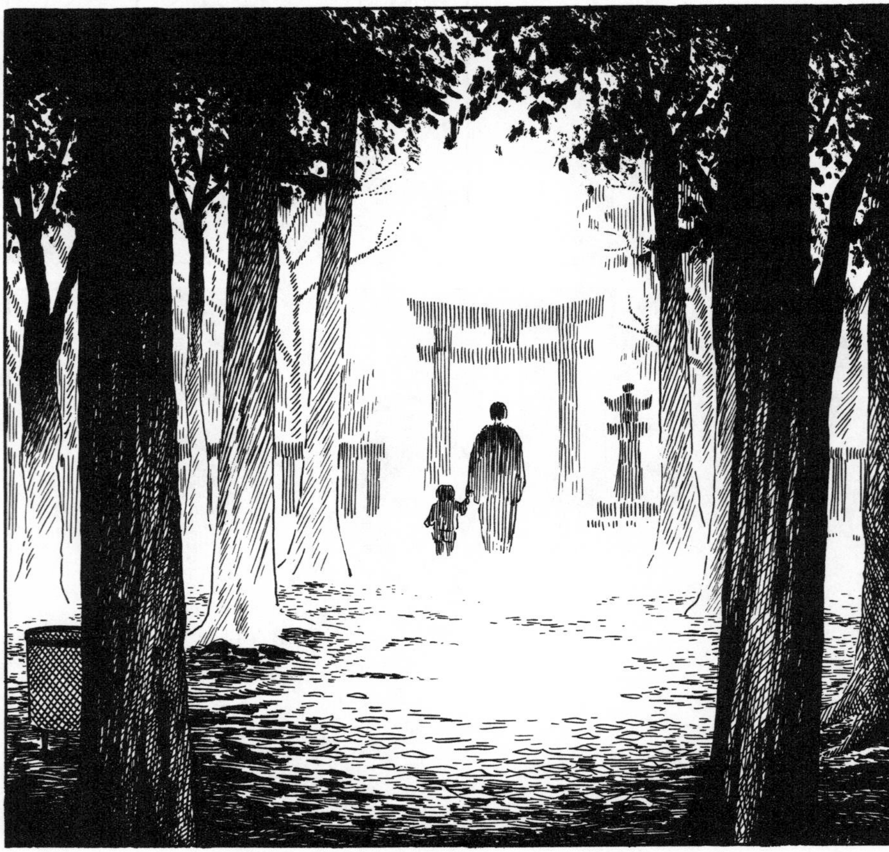

第六話
Chapter 6

蒸　発
Evaporation

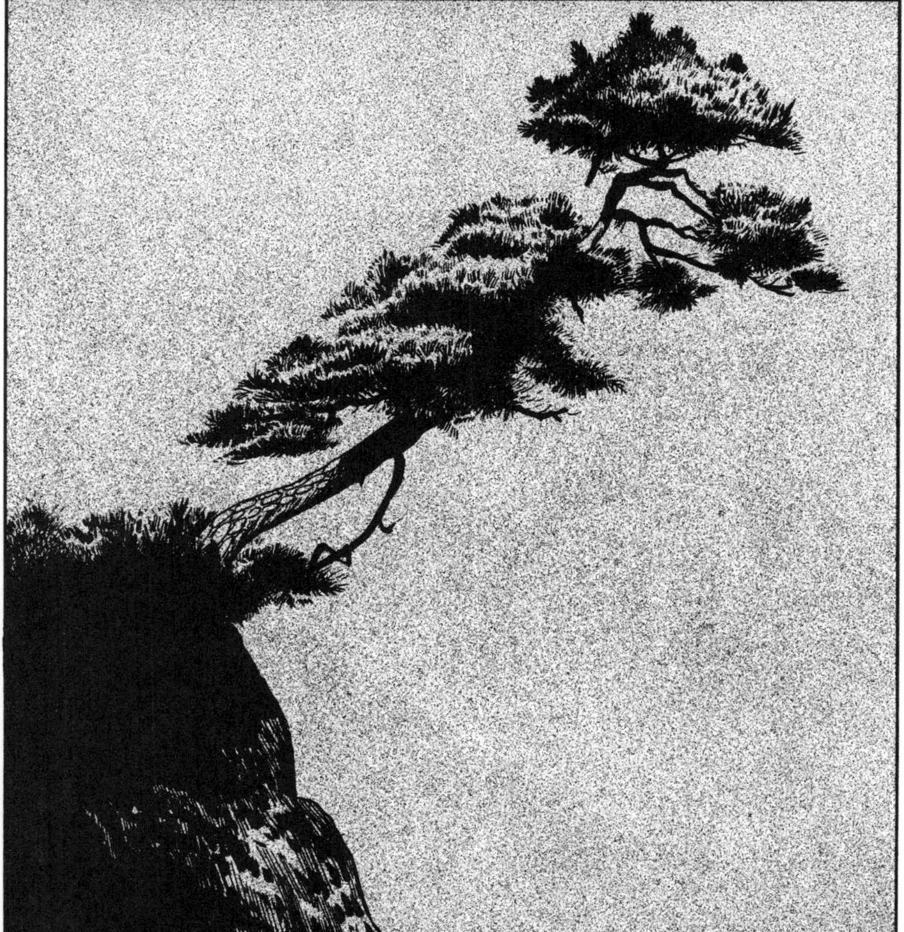

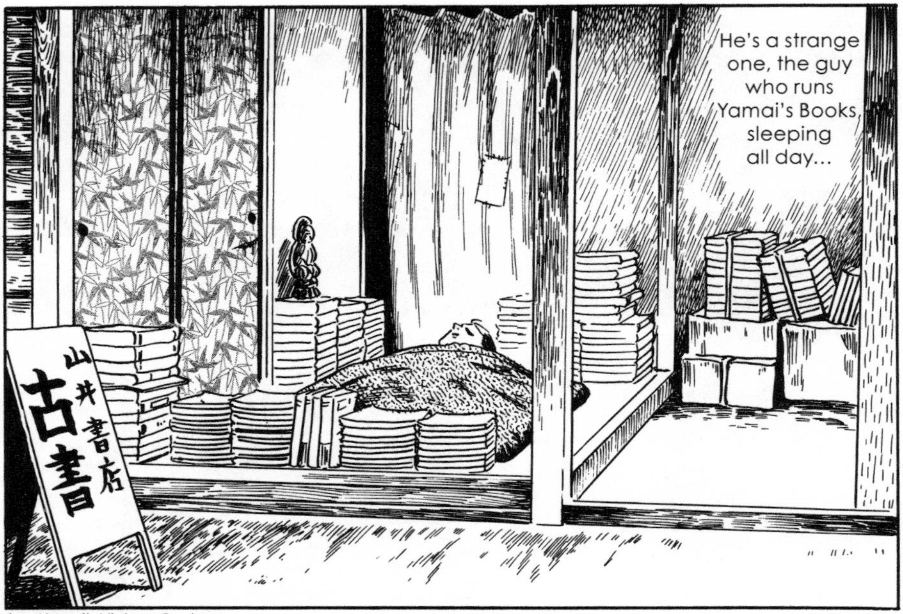
He's a strange one, the guy who runs Yamai's Books, sleeping all day...
山井書店
古書
sign: Yamai's Vintage Books

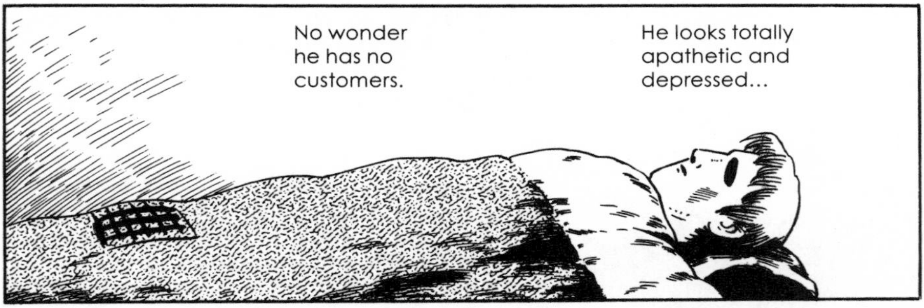
He looks totally apathetic and depressed...
No wonder he has no customers.

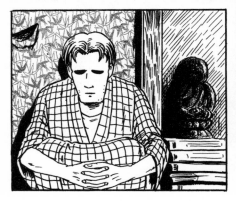

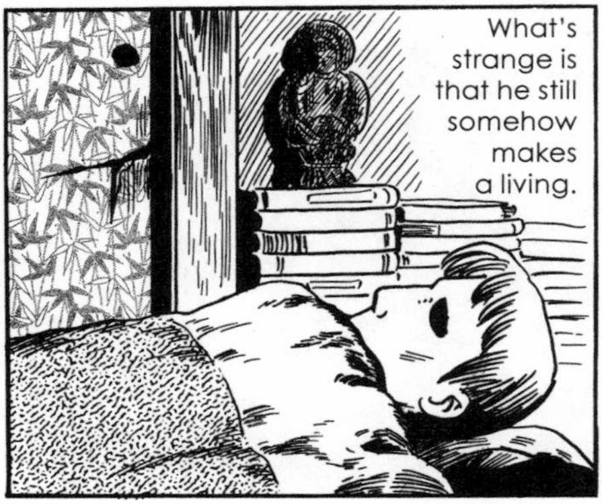
What's strange is that he still somehow makes a living.

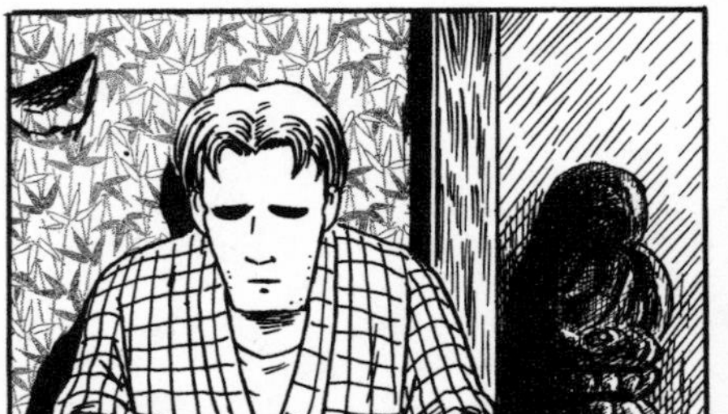

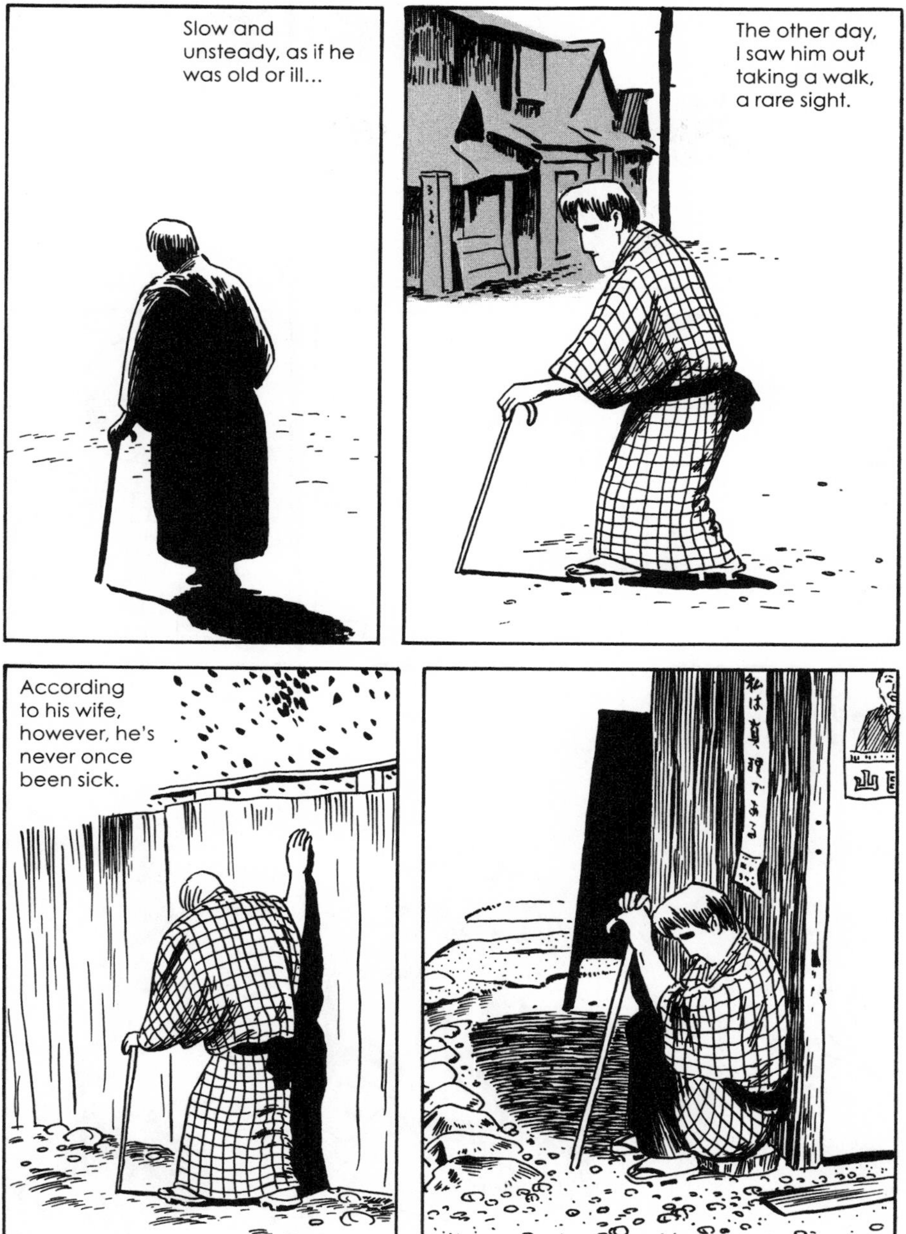
The other day, I saw him out taking a walk, a rare sight.
Slow and unsteady, as if he was old or ill...
私は真理である
According to his wife, however, he's never once been sick.

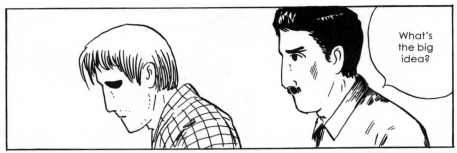

What's the big idea?
I must have gotten the idea from you.
From me?
Aren't you always lying around?
Oh, well, that's because business is slow.
水石
フェア
You can't fool me. We both know that's not a real business.

sign: Art stone fair

banner: Stones

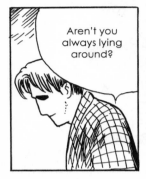

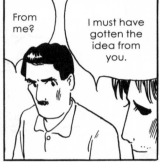

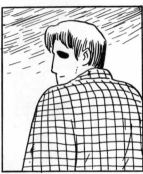

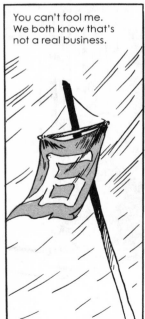

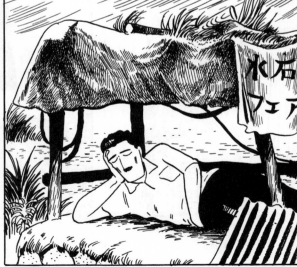

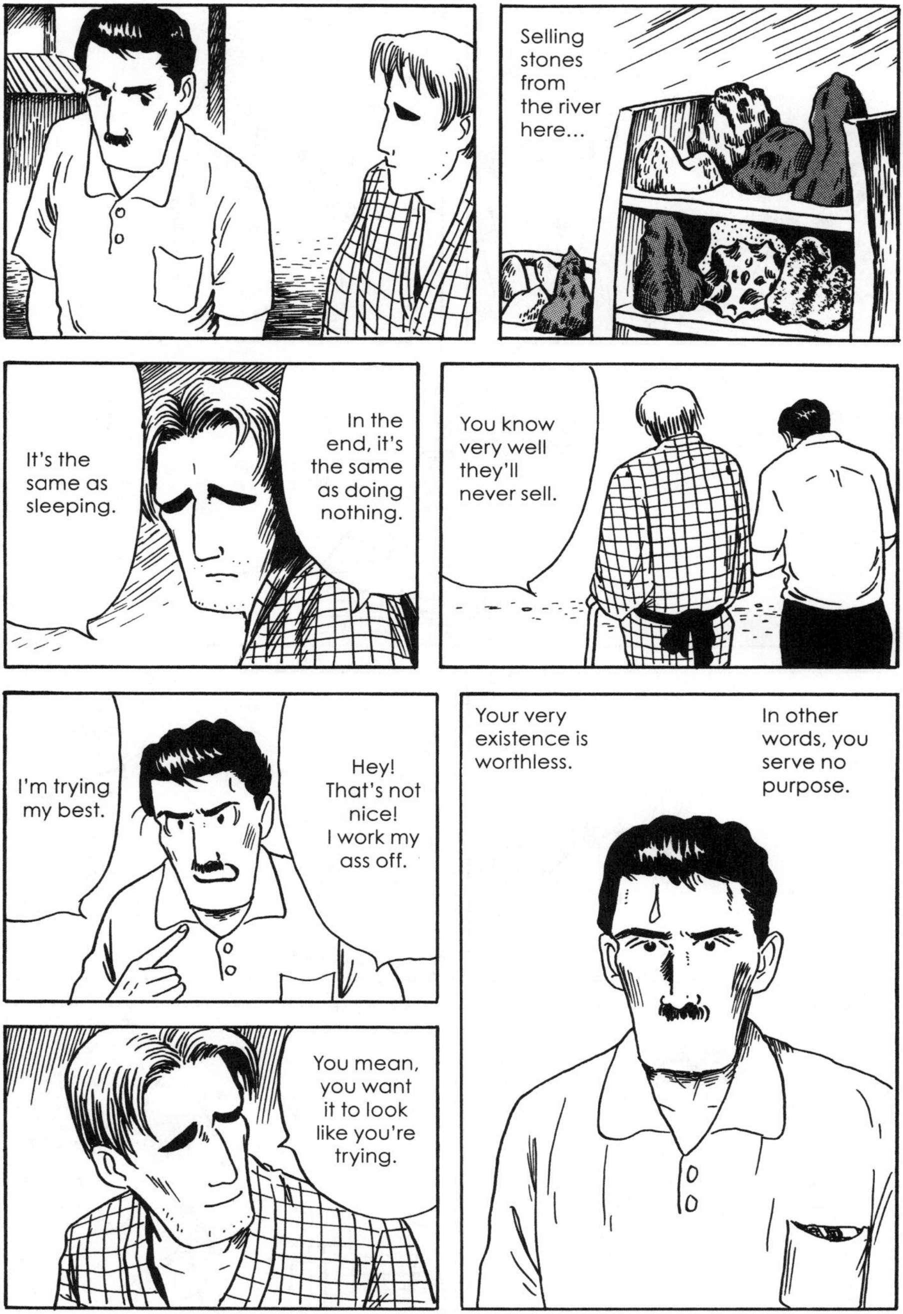
Selling stones from the river here...
You know very well they'll never sell.
In the end, it's the same as doing nothing.
It's the same as sleeping.
In other words, you serve no purpose.
Your very existence is worthless.
Hey! That's not nice! I work my ass off.
I'm trying my best.
You mean, you want it to look like you're trying.

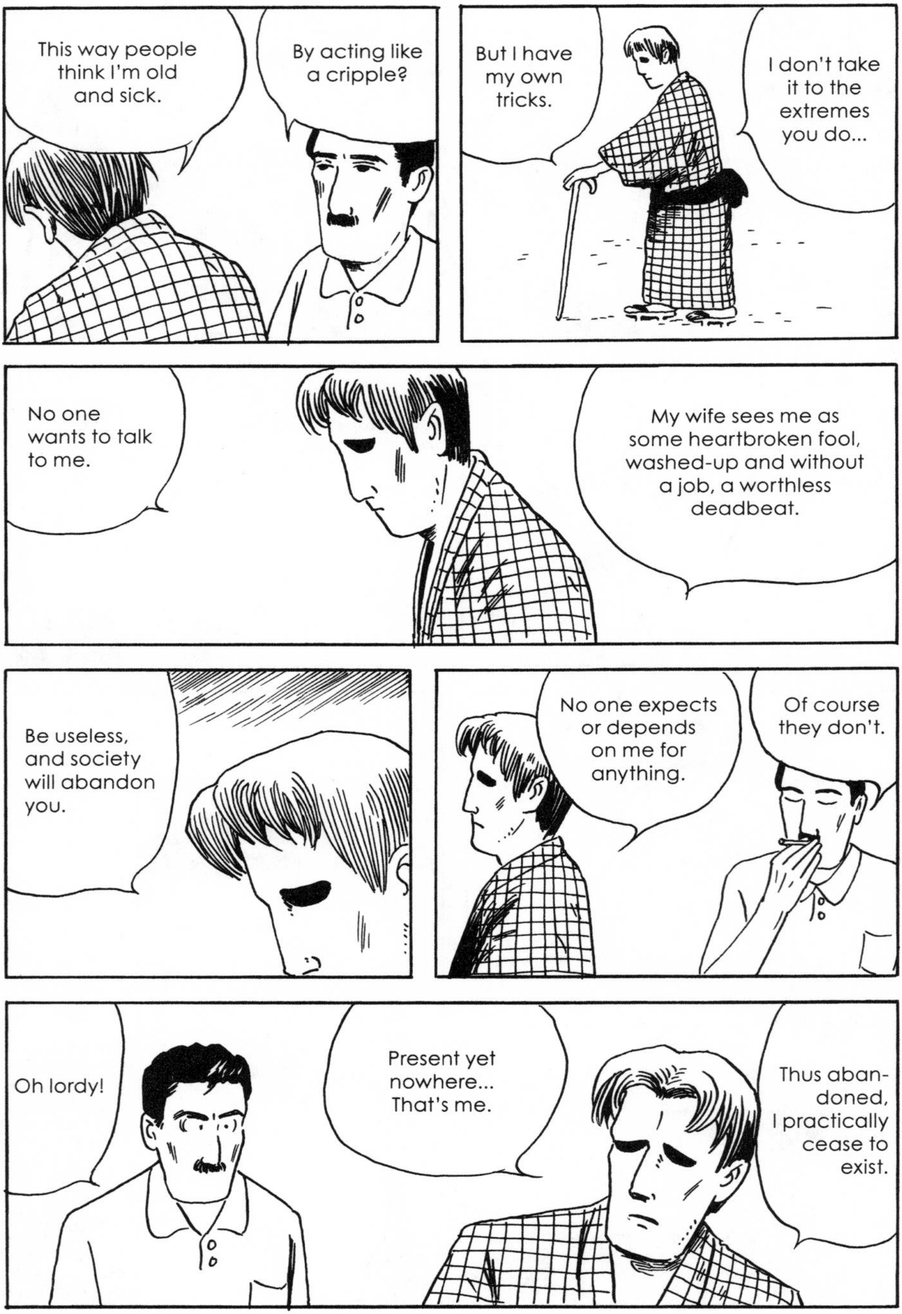
This way people think I'm old and sick.
By acting like a cripple?
But I have my own tricks.
I don't take it to the extremes you do...
No one wants to talk to me.
My wife sees me as some heartbroken fool, washed-up and without a job, a worthless deadbeat.
Be useless, and society will abandon you.
No one expects or depends on me for anything.
Of course they don't.
Oh lordy!
Present yet nowhere... That's me.
Thus aban-doned, I practically cease to exist.

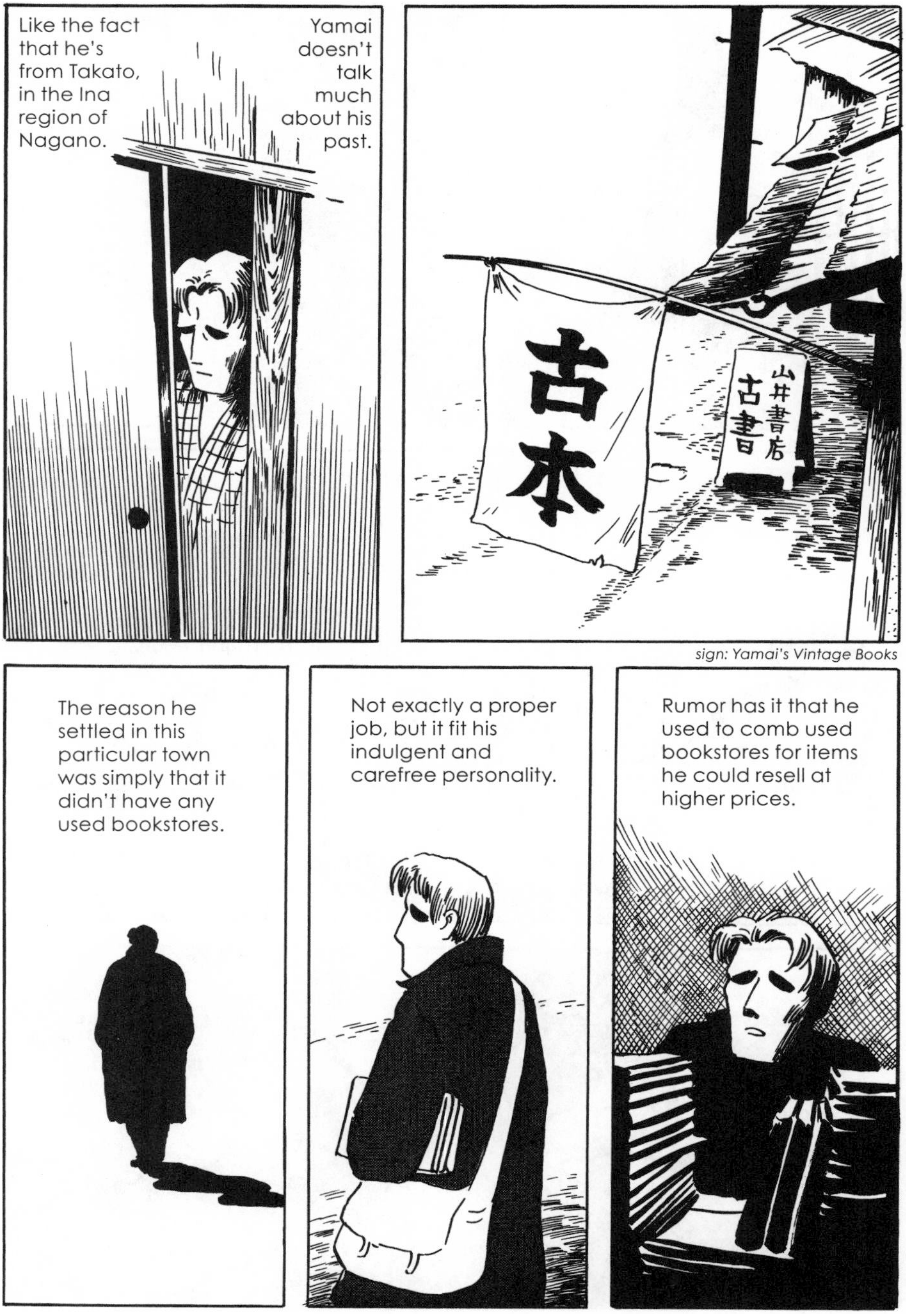
古本
山井書店
古書
sign: Yamai's Vintage Books
Yamai doesn't talk much about his past.
Like the fact that he's from Takato, in the Ina region of Nagano.
Rumor has it that he used to comb used bookstores for items he could resell at higher prices.
Not exactly a proper job, but it fit his indulgent and carefree personality.
The reason he settled in this particular town was simply that it didn't have any used bookstores.

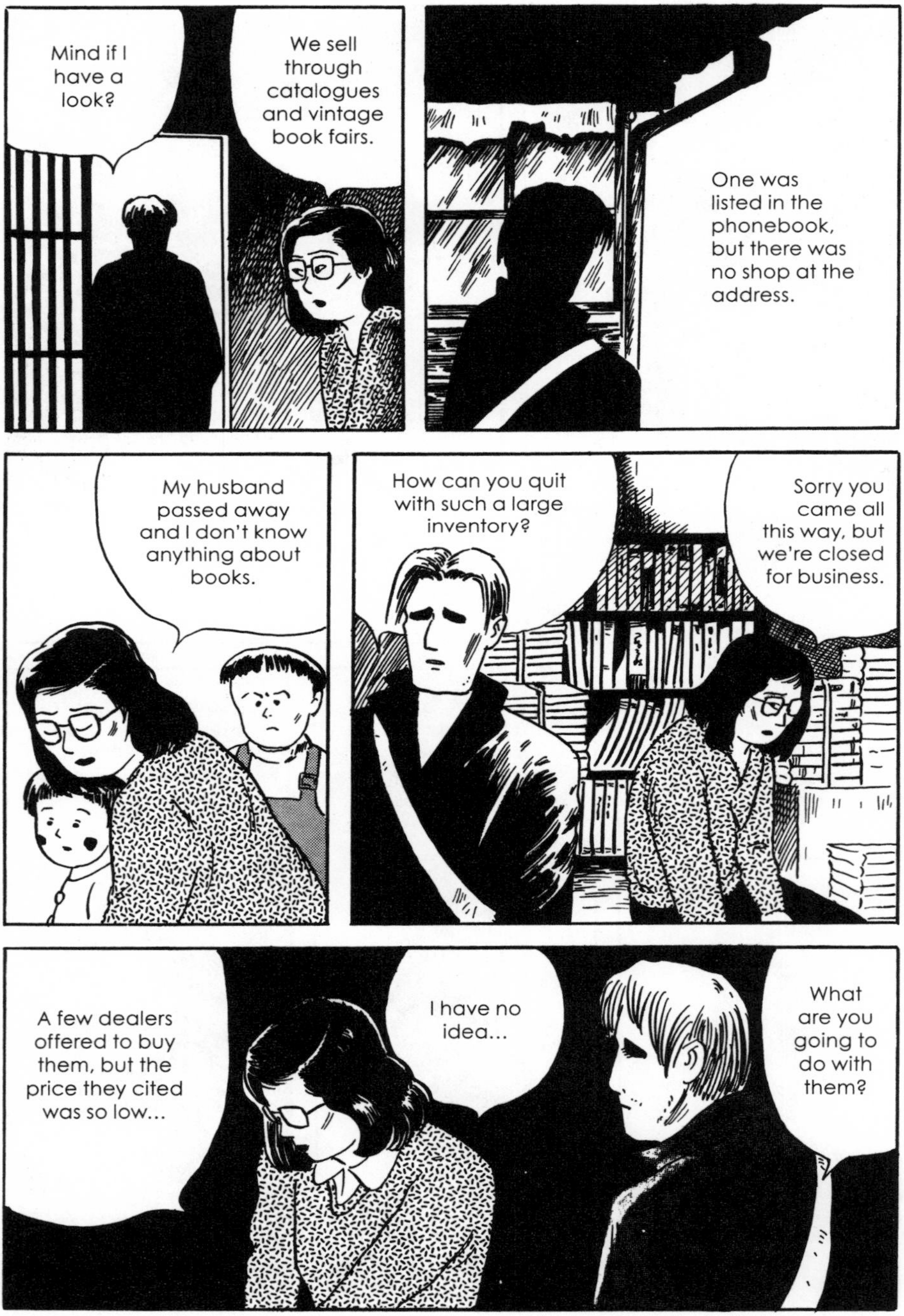
One was listed in the phonebook, but there was no shop at the address.
We sell through catalogues and vintage book fairs.
Mind if I have a look?
Sorry you came all this way, but we're closed for business.
How can you quit with such a large inventory?
My husband passed away and I don't know anything about books.
What are you going to do with them?
I have no idea...
A few dealers offered to buy them, but the price they cited was so low...

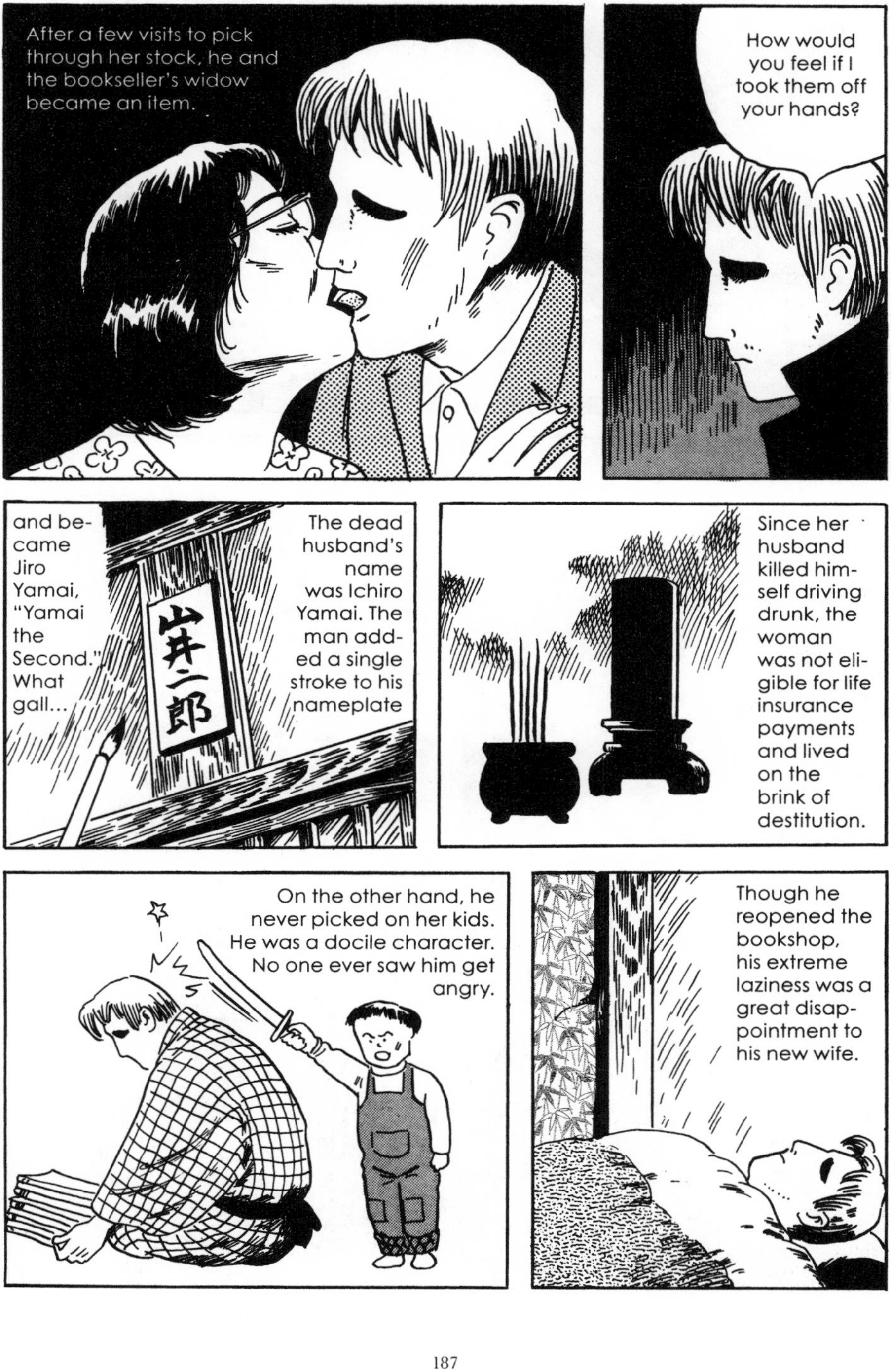
How would you feel if I took them off your hands?
After a few visits to pick through her stock, he and the bookseller's widow became an item.
Since her husband killed himself driving drunk, the woman was not eligible for life insurance payments and lived on the brink of destitution.
The dead husband's name was Ichiro Yamai. The man added a single stroke to his nameplate
and became Jiro Yamai, "Yamai the Second." What gall...
山井二郎
Though he reopened the bookshop, his extreme laziness was a great disappointment to his new wife.
On the other hand, he never picked on her kids. He was a docile character. No one ever saw him get angry.

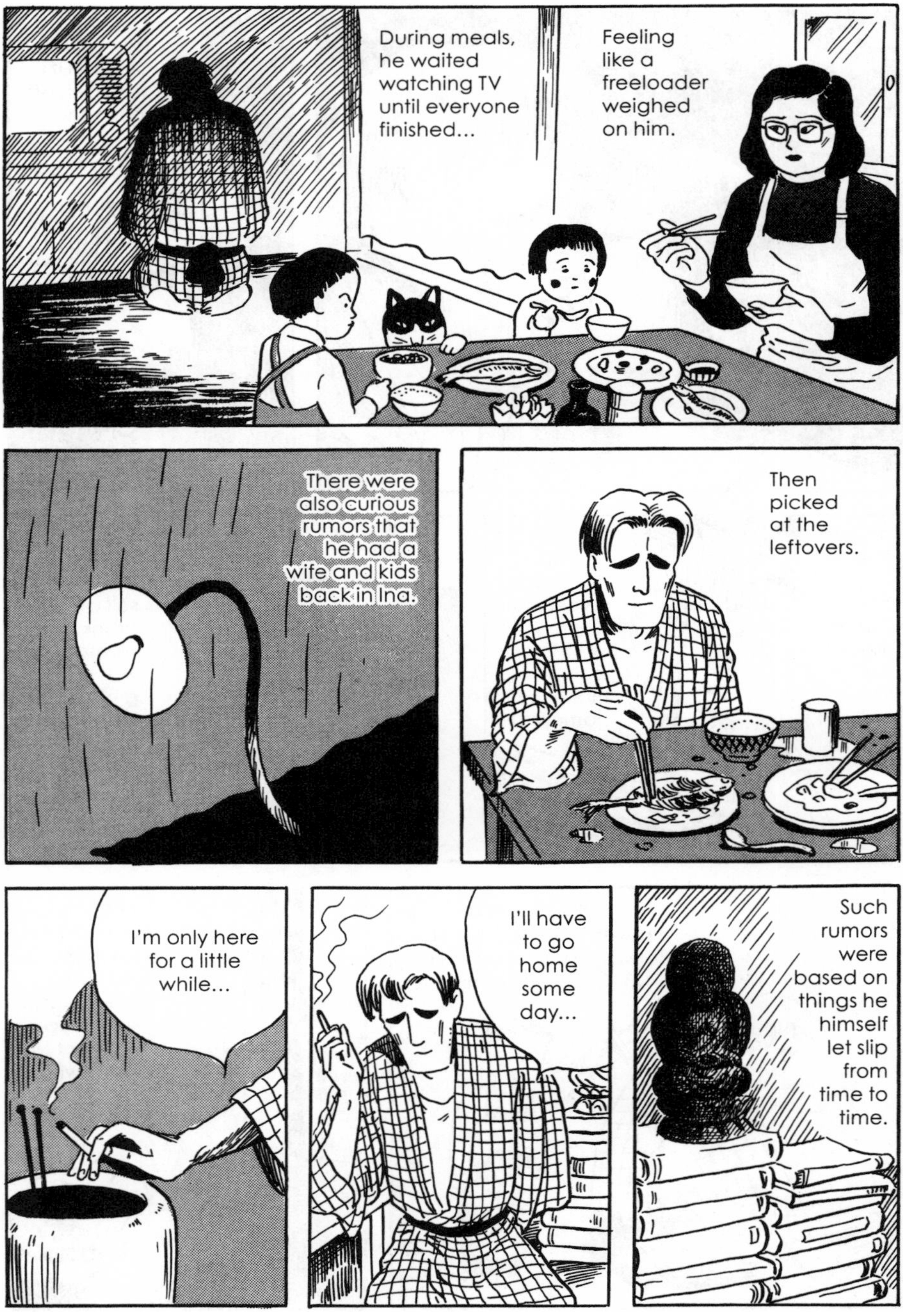
Feeling like a freeloader weighed on him.
During meals, he waited watching TV until everyone finished…
Then picked at the leftovers.
There were also curious rumors that he had a wife and kids back in Ina.
Such rumors were based on things he himself let slip from time to time.
I'll have to go home some day…
I'm only here for a little while…

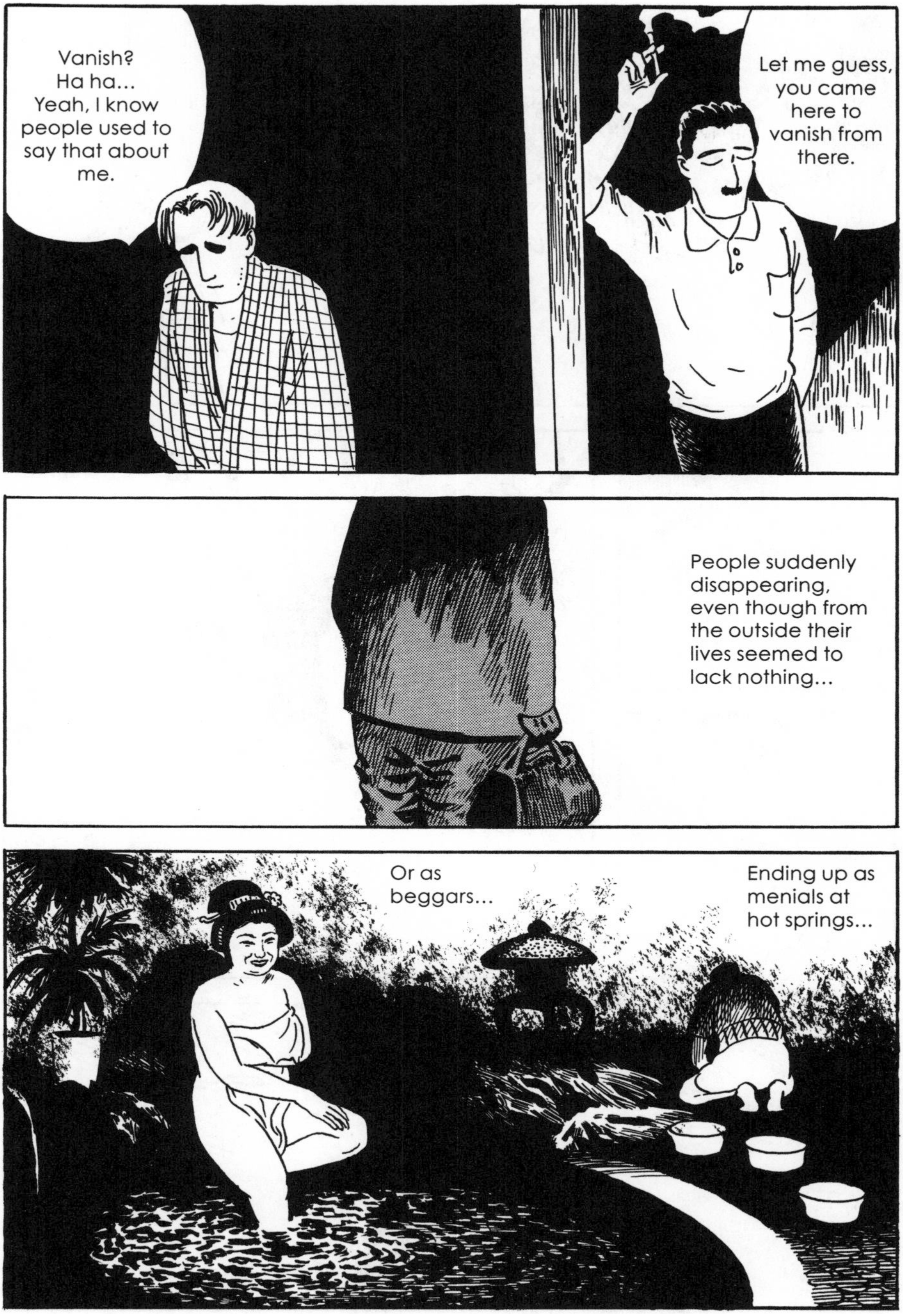
Let me guess, you came here to vanish from there.
Vanish? Ha ha… Yeah, I know people used to say that about me.
People suddenly disappearing, even though from the outside their lives seemed to lack nothing…
Ending up as menials at hot springs…
Or as beggars…

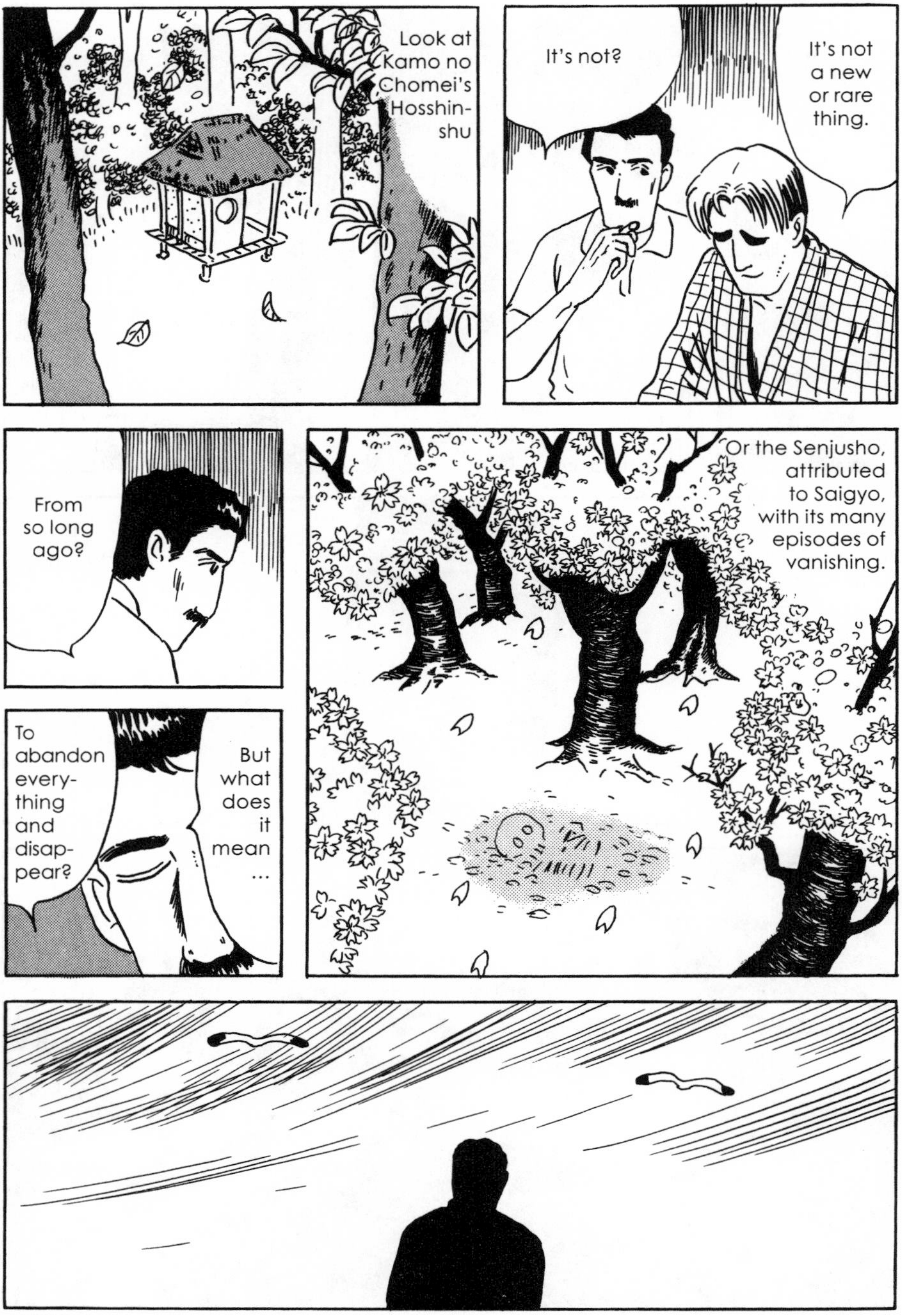
It's not a new or rare thing.
It's not?
Look at Kamo no Chomei's Hosshin-shu
Or the Senjusho, attributed to Saigyo, with its many episodes of vanishing.
From so long ago?
But what does it mean ...
To abandon every-thing and disap-pear?

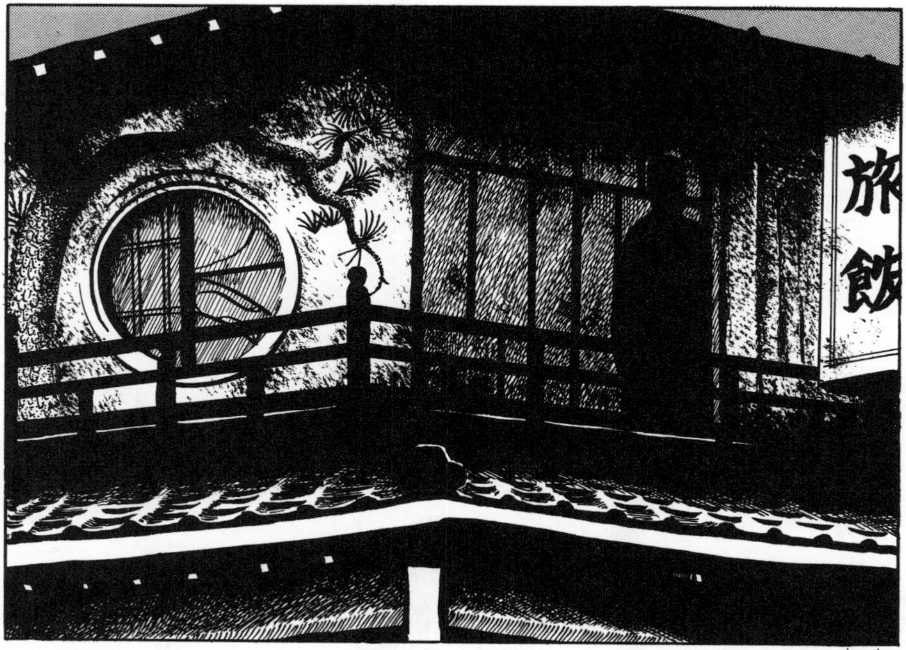
旅

sign: Inn

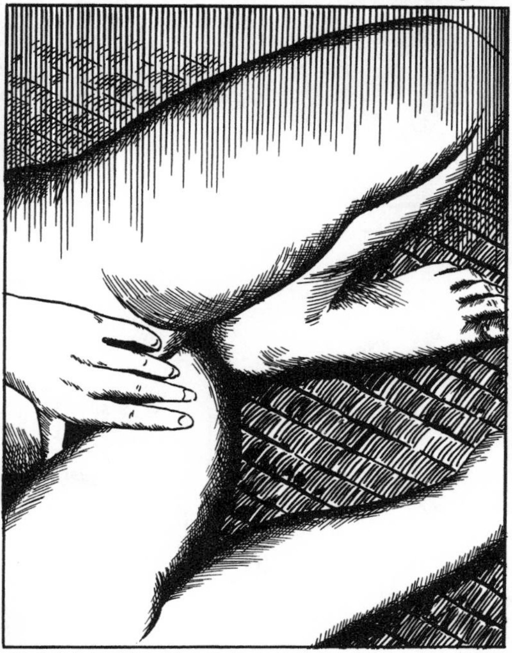

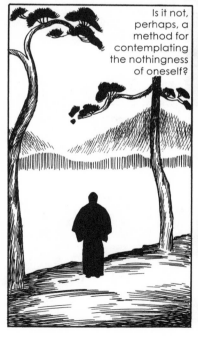

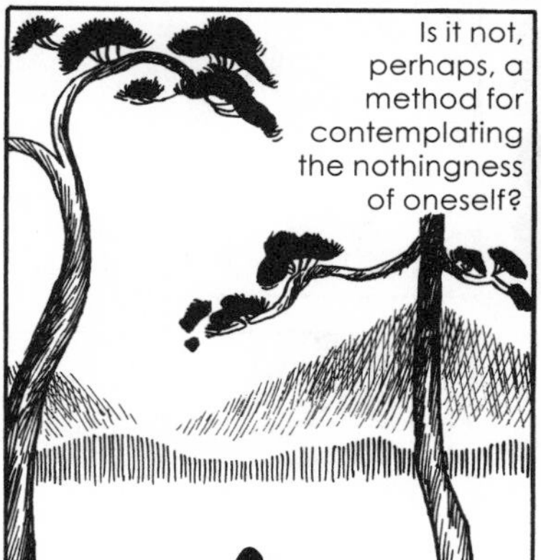
Is it not,
perhaps, a
method for
contemplating
the nothingness
of oneself?

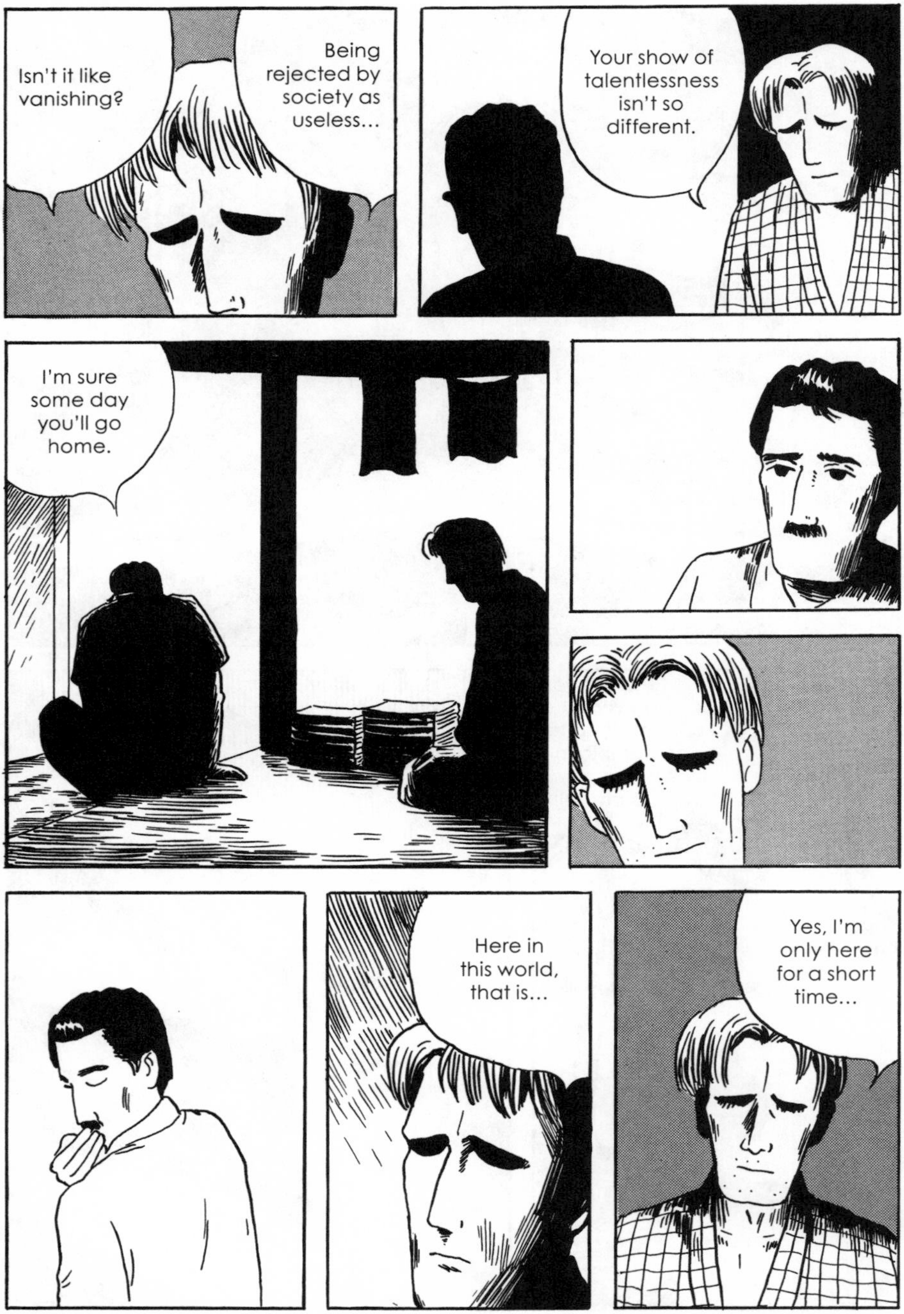
Your show of talentlessness isn't so different.
Being rejected by society as useless…
Isn't it like vanishing?
I'm sure some day you'll go home.
Yes, I'm only here for a short time…
Here in this world, that is…

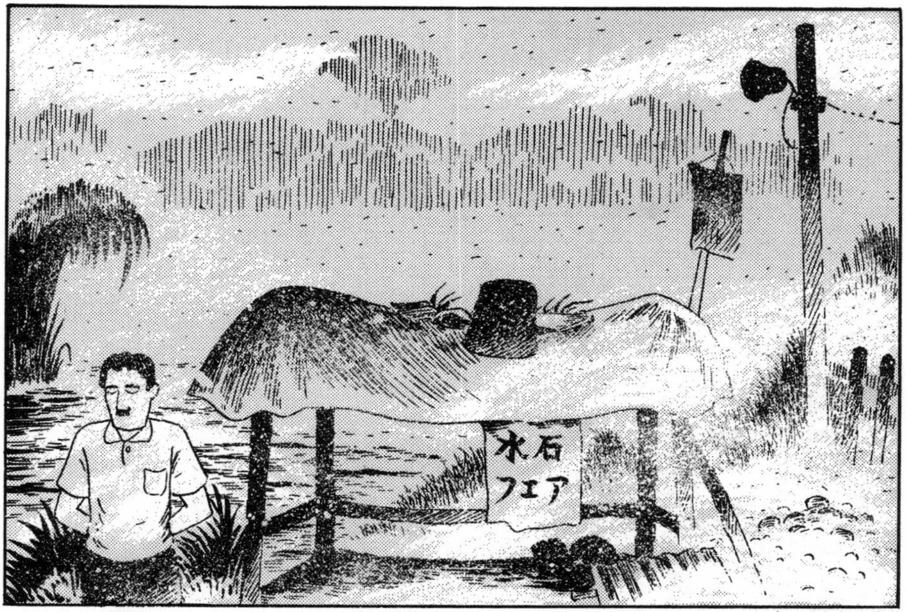
水石
フェア
sign: Art stone fair

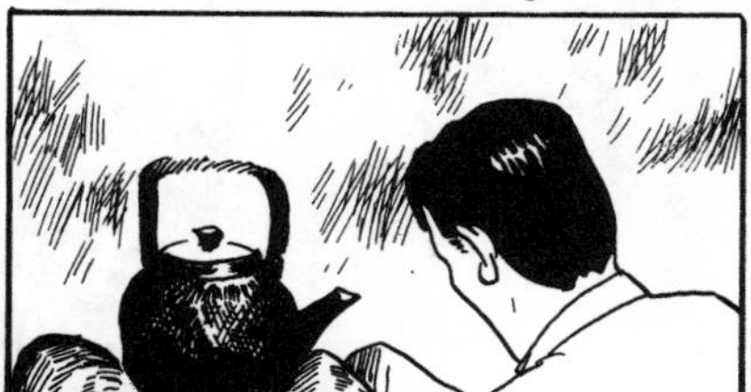

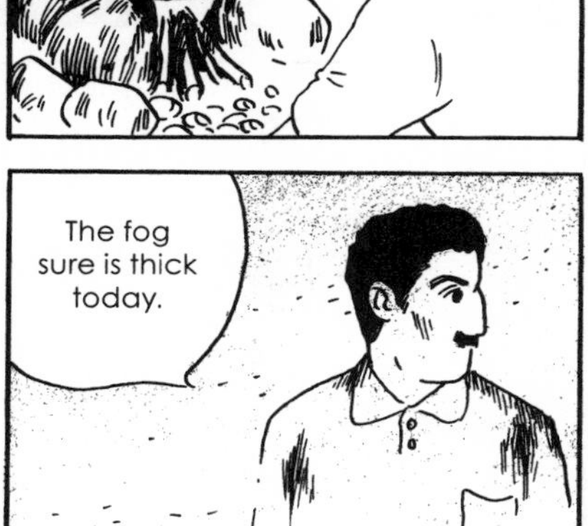
The fog sure is thick today.

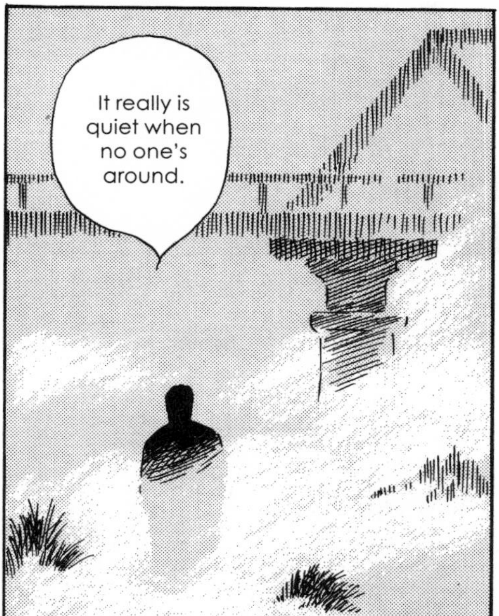
It really is quiet when no one's around.

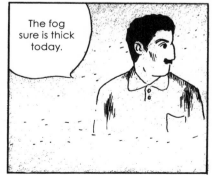

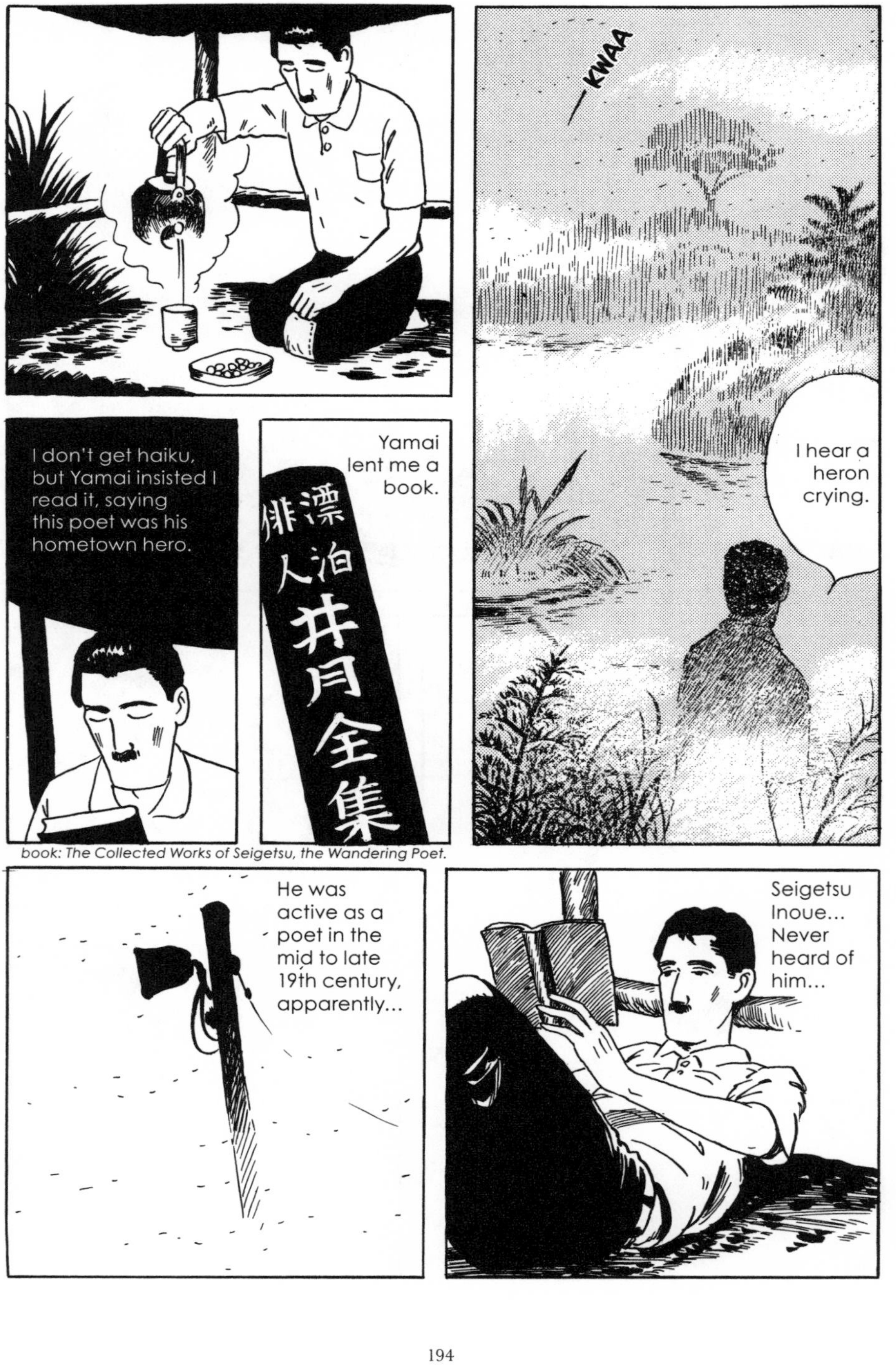
KWAA
I hear a heron crying.
Yamai lent me a book.
漂泊俳人井月全集
I don't get haiku, but Yamai insisted I read it, saying this poet was his hometown hero.
book: The Collected Works of Seigetsu, the Wandering Poet.
Seigetsu Inoue... Never heard of him...
He was active as a poet in the mid to late 19th century, apparently...

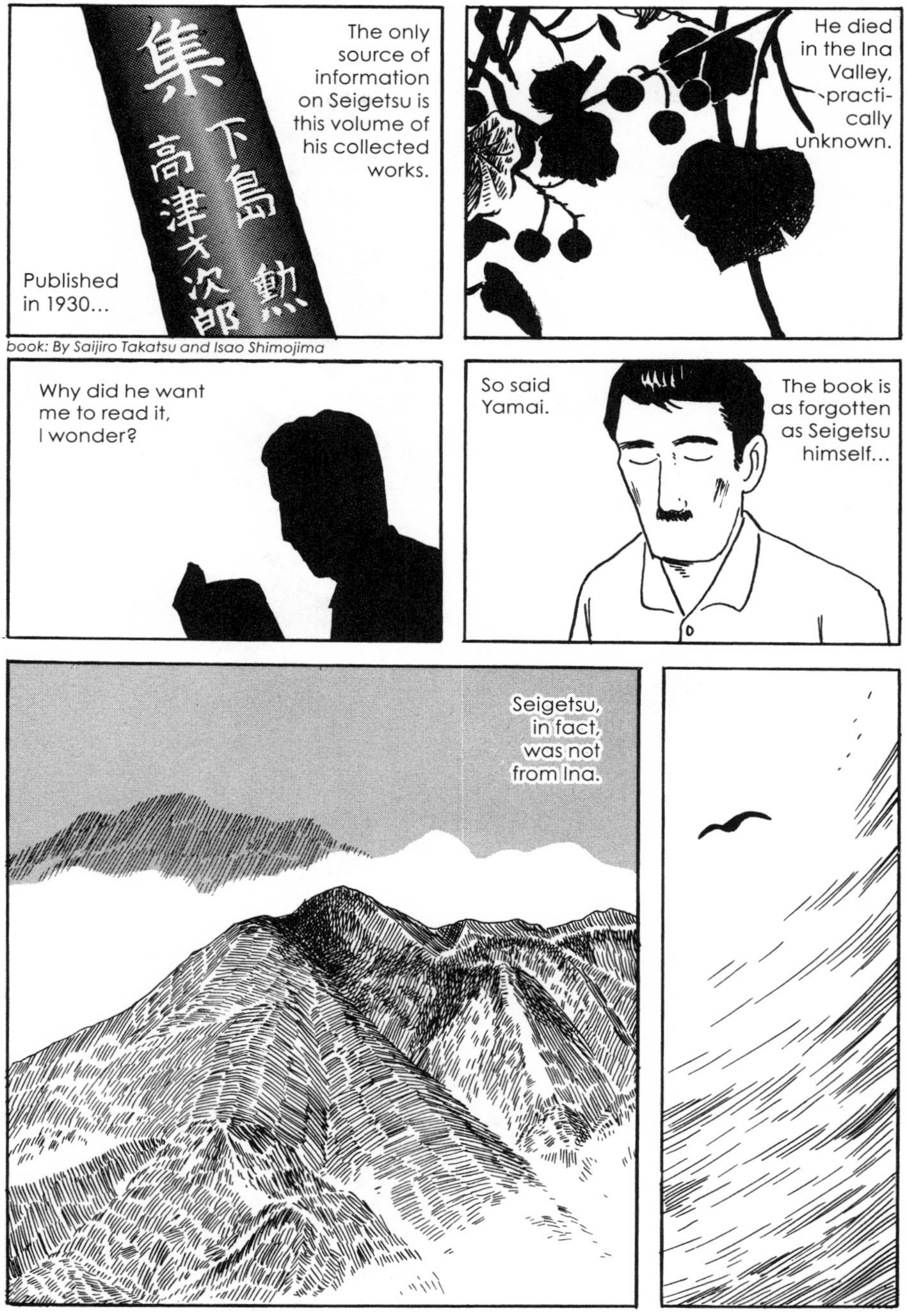
He died in the Ina Valley, practically unknown.
The only source of information on Seigetsu is this volume of his collected works.
集
下島勲
高津才次郎
Published in 1930...
book: By Saijiro Takatsu and Isao Shimojima
The book is as forgotten as Seigetsu himself...
So said Yamai.
Why did he want me to read it, I wonder?
Seigetsu, in fact, was not from Ina.

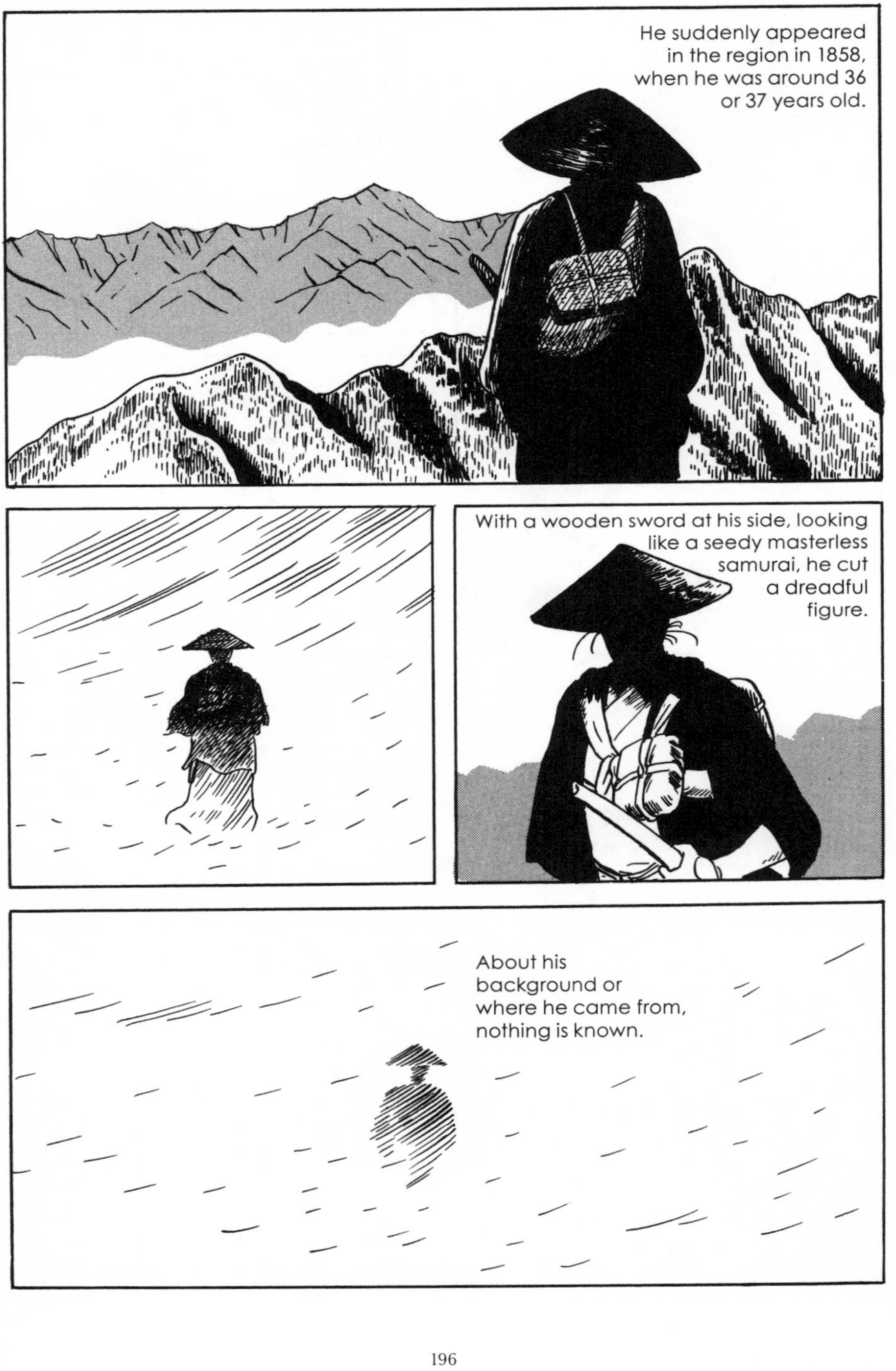
He suddenly appeared in the region in 1858, when he was around 36 or 37 years old.
With a wooden sword at his side, looking like a seedy masterless samurai, he cut a dreadful figure.
About his background or where he came from, nothing is known.

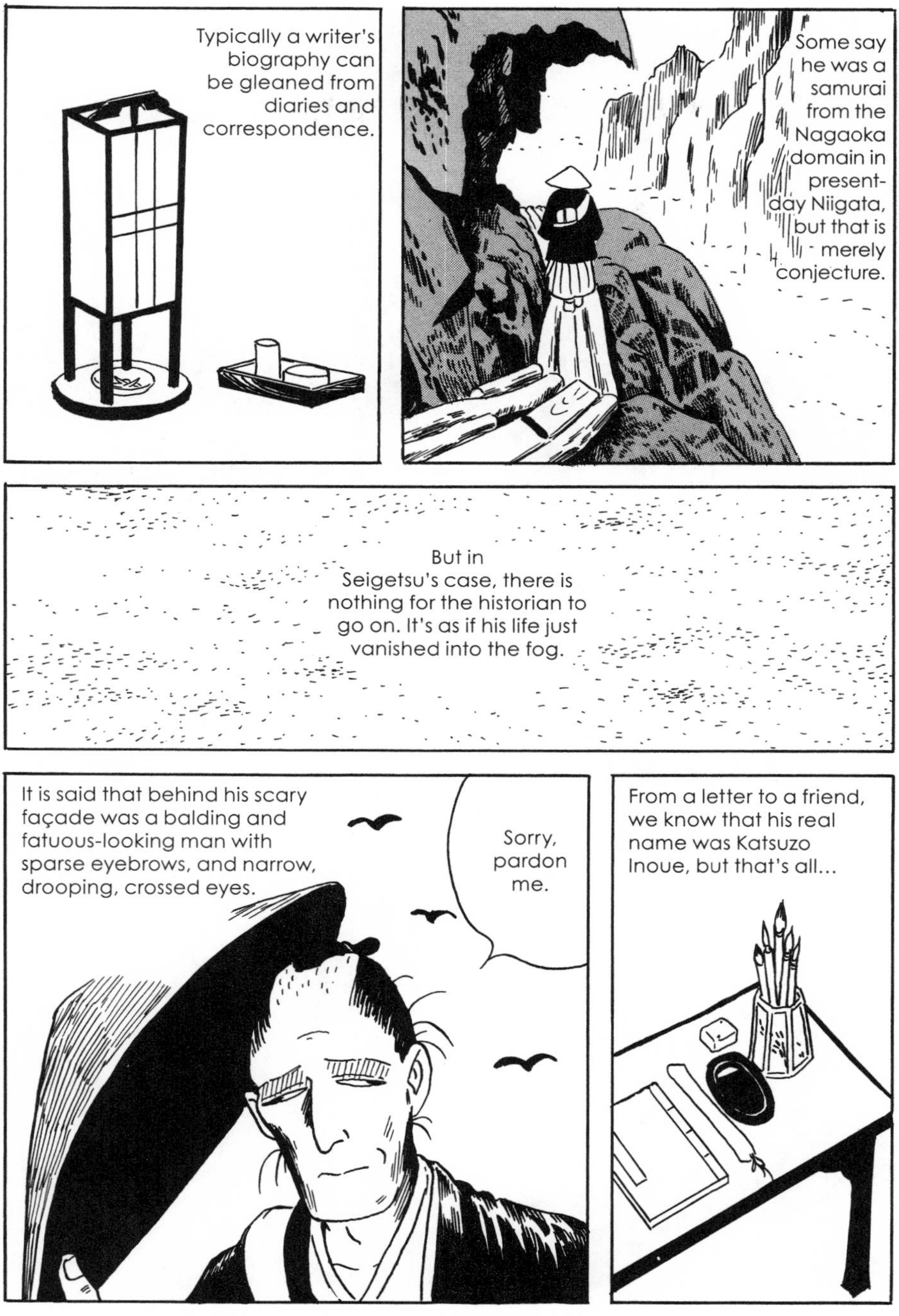
Some say he was a samurai from the Nagaoka domain in present-day Niigata, but that is merely conjecture.
Typically a writer's biography can be gleaned from diaries and correspondence.
But in Seigetsu's case, there is nothing for the historian to go on. It's as if his life just vanished into the fog.
From a letter to a friend, we know that his real name was Katsuzo Inoue, but that's all...
It is said that behind his scary façade was a balding and fatuous-looking man with sparse eyebrows, and narrow, drooping, crossed eyes.
Sorry, pardon me.

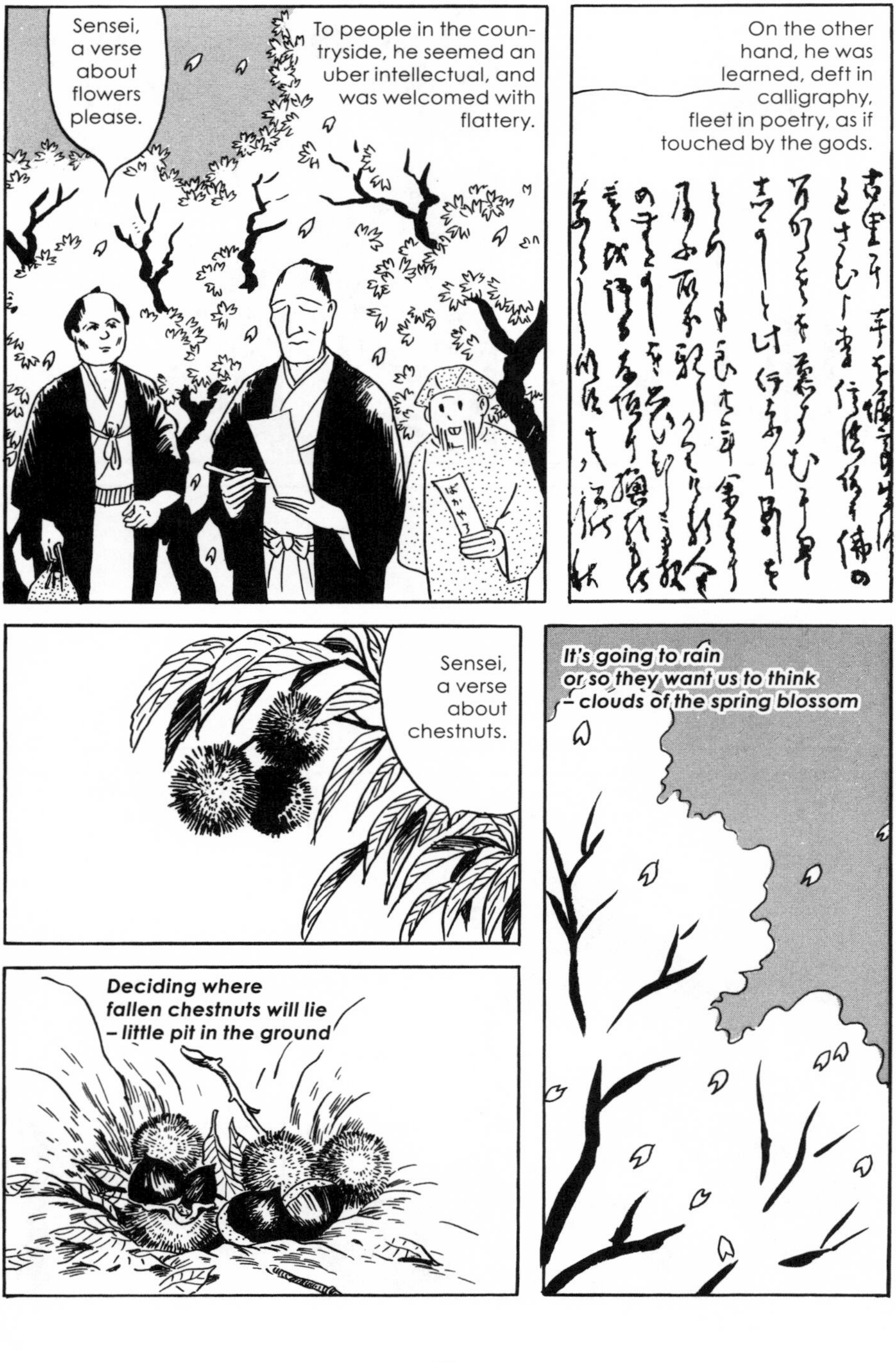
On the other hand, he was learned, deft in calligraphy, fleet in poetry, as if touched by the gods.
To people in the countryside, he seemed an uber intellectual, and was welcomed with flattery.
Sensei, a verse about flowers please.
It's going to rain
or so they want us to think
– clouds of the spring blossom
Sensei, a verse about chestnuts.
Deciding where
fallen chestnuts will lie
– little pit in the ground

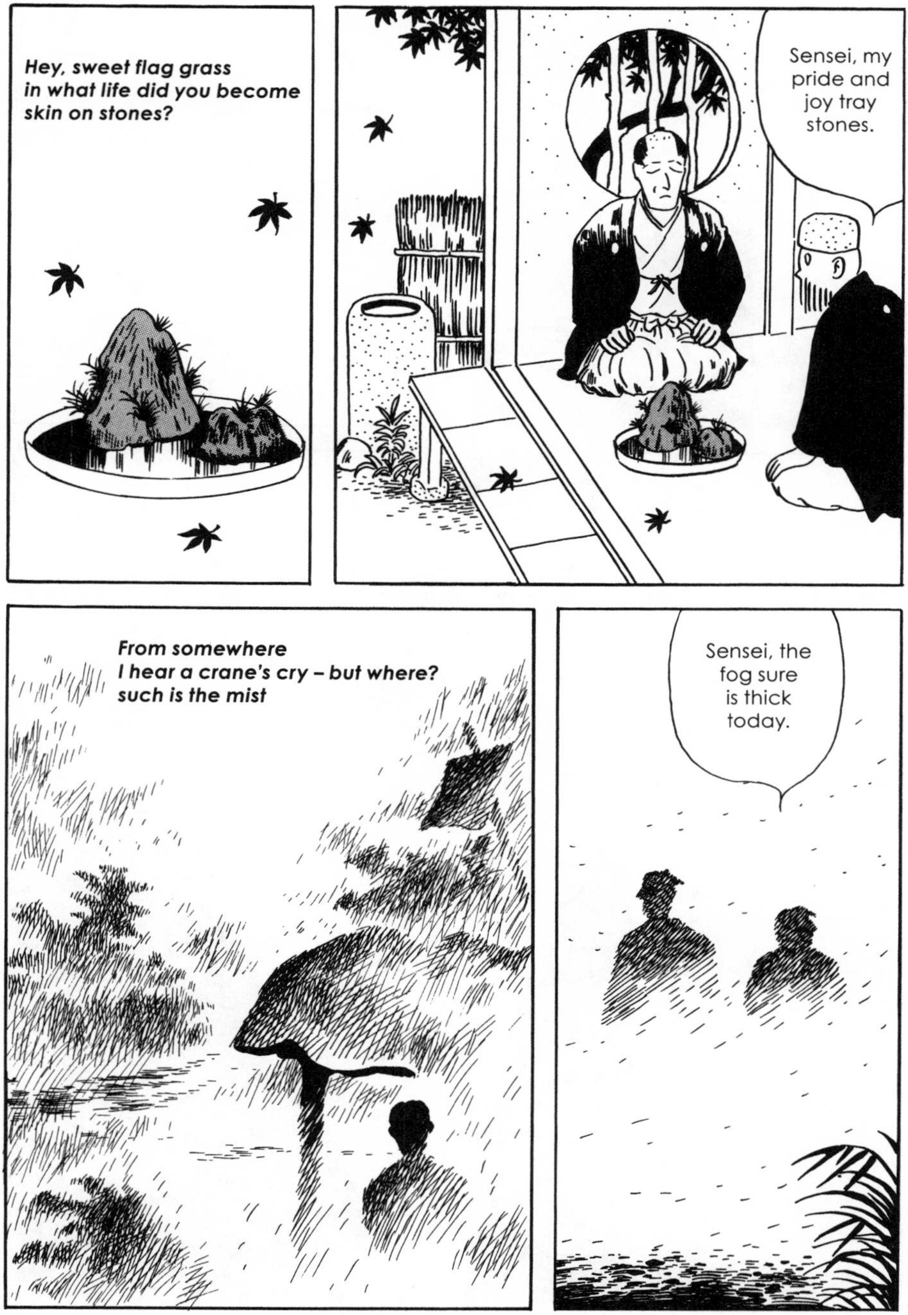
Sensei, my pride and joy tray stones.
Hey, sweet flag grass
in what life did you become
skin on stones?
Sensei, the fog sure is thick today.
From somewhere
I hear a crane's cry – but where?
such is the mist

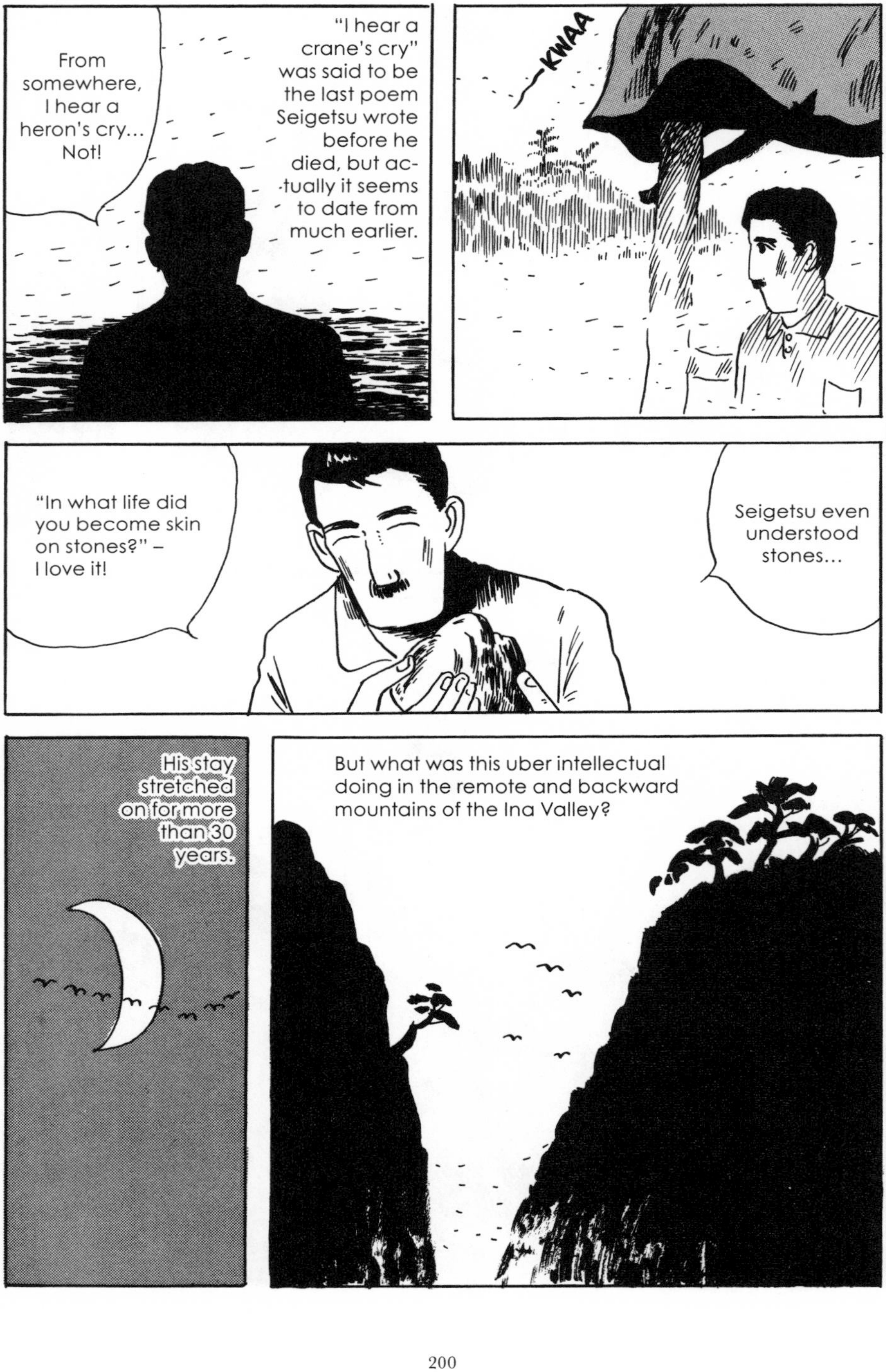
KWAA
"I hear a crane's cry" was said to be the last poem Seigetsu wrote before he died, but actually it seems to date from much earlier.
From somewhere, I hear a heron's cry... Not!
Seigetsu even understood stones...
"In what life did you become skin on stones?" – I love it!
But what was this uber intellectual doing in the remote and backward mountains of the Ina Valley?
His stay stretched on for more than 30 years.

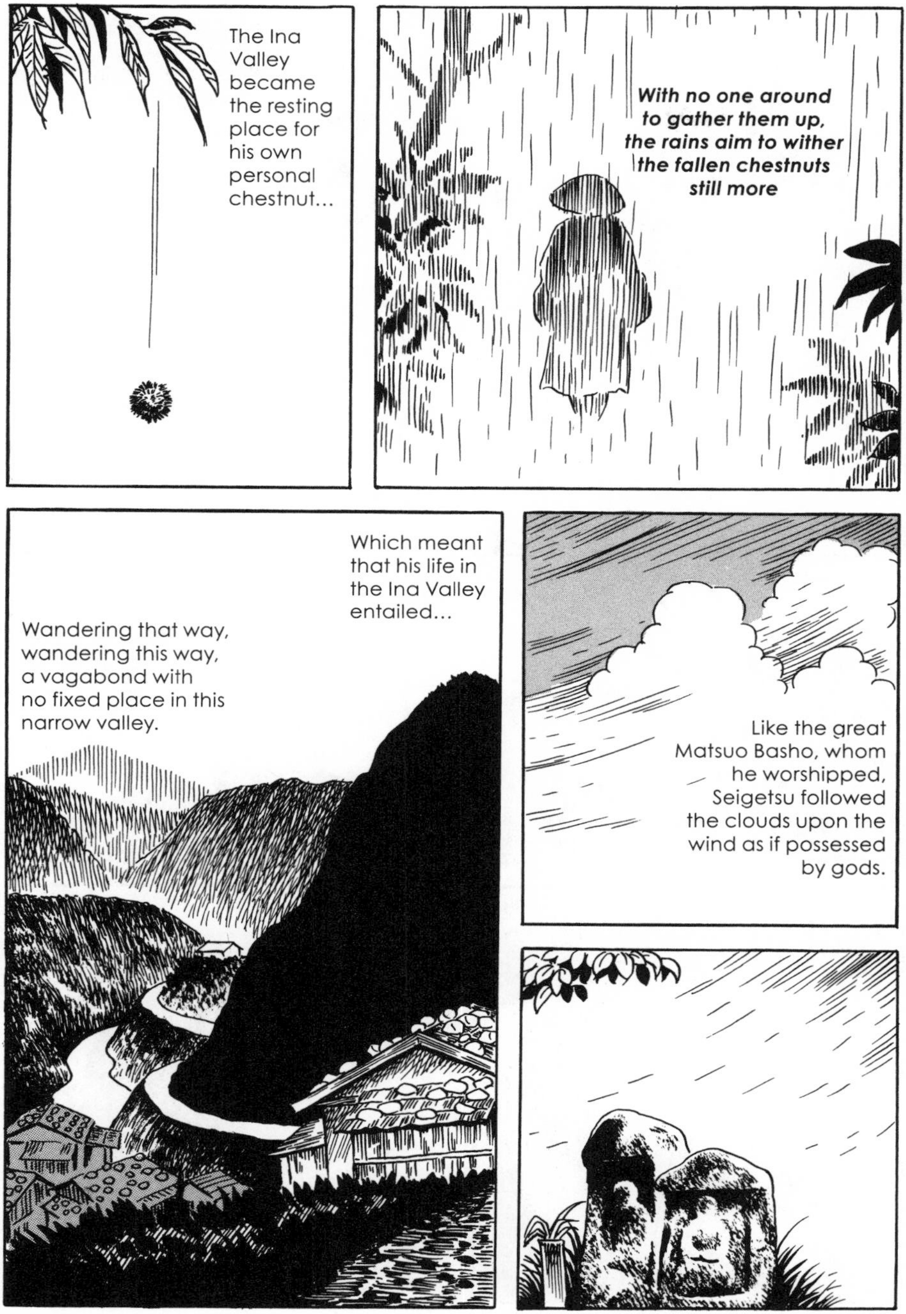

With no one around to gather them up, the rains aim to wither the fallen chestnuts still more
The Ina Valley became the resting place for his own personal chestnut...
Like the great Matsuo Basho, whom he worshipped, Seigetsu followed the clouds upon the wind as if possessed by gods.
Which meant that his life in the Ina Valley entailed...
Wandering that way, wandering this way, a vagabond with no fixed place in this narrow valley.

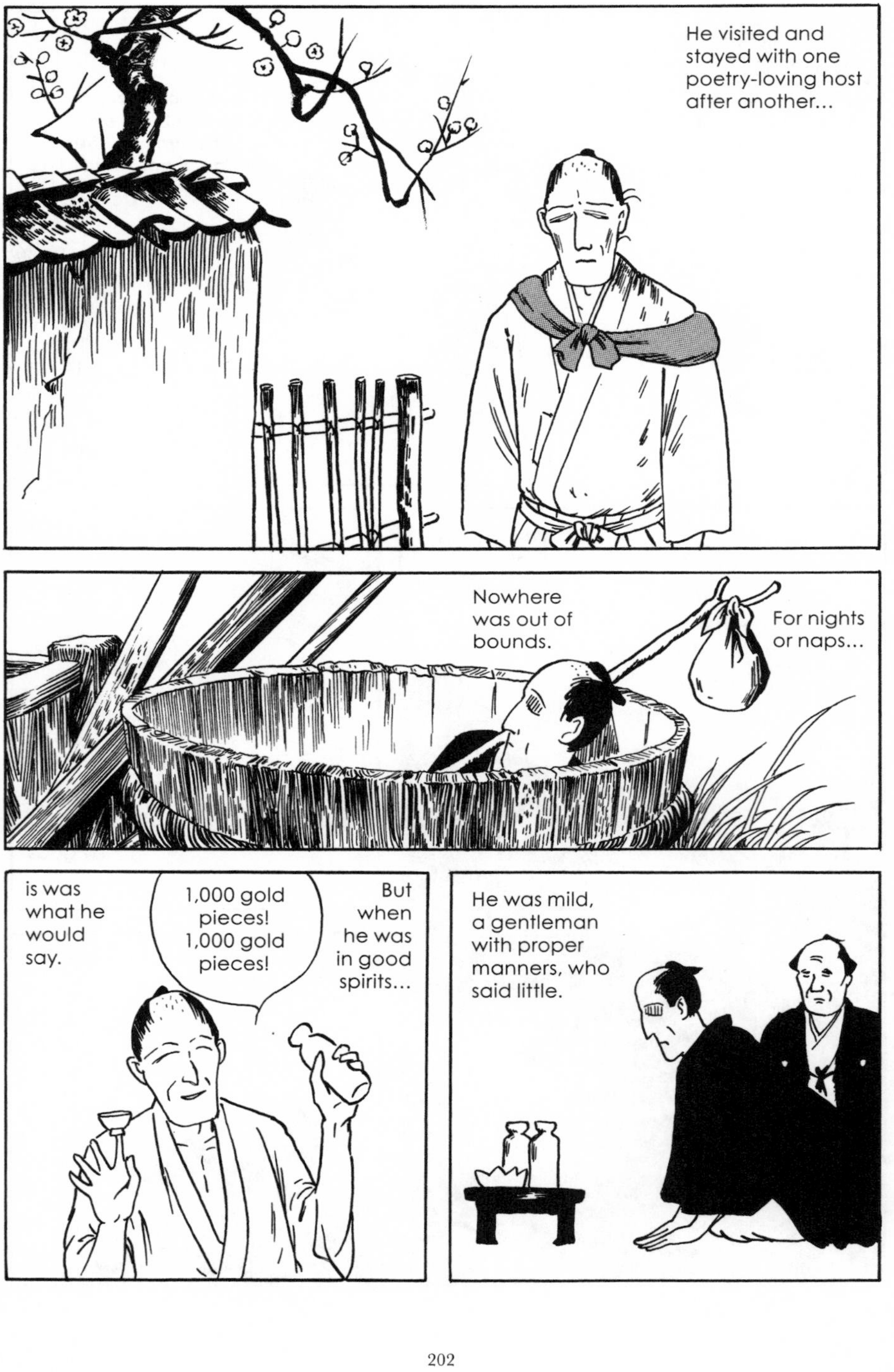
He visited and stayed with one poetry-loving host after another...
For nights or naps...
Nowhere was out of bounds.
He was mild, a gentleman with proper manners, who said little.
But when he was in good spirits...
1,000 gold pieces! 1,000 gold pieces!
is was what he would say.

He also drank without peer. Even when the sake wasn't strong, he quickly got soused.
Sometimes, he even shit and wet himself.
Before long, his body was covered in lice and scabies.
He became too much and was shunned.
Dogs chased him.
Brats harassed him.
Ew! It's Seigetsu the bum!

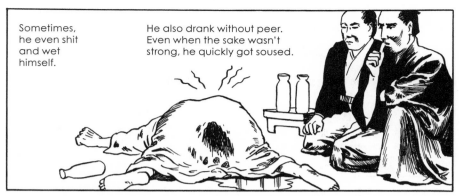

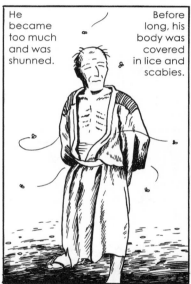

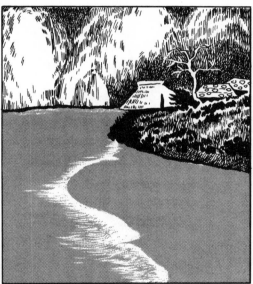

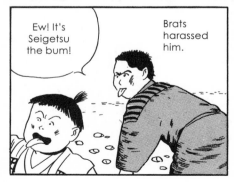

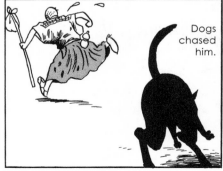

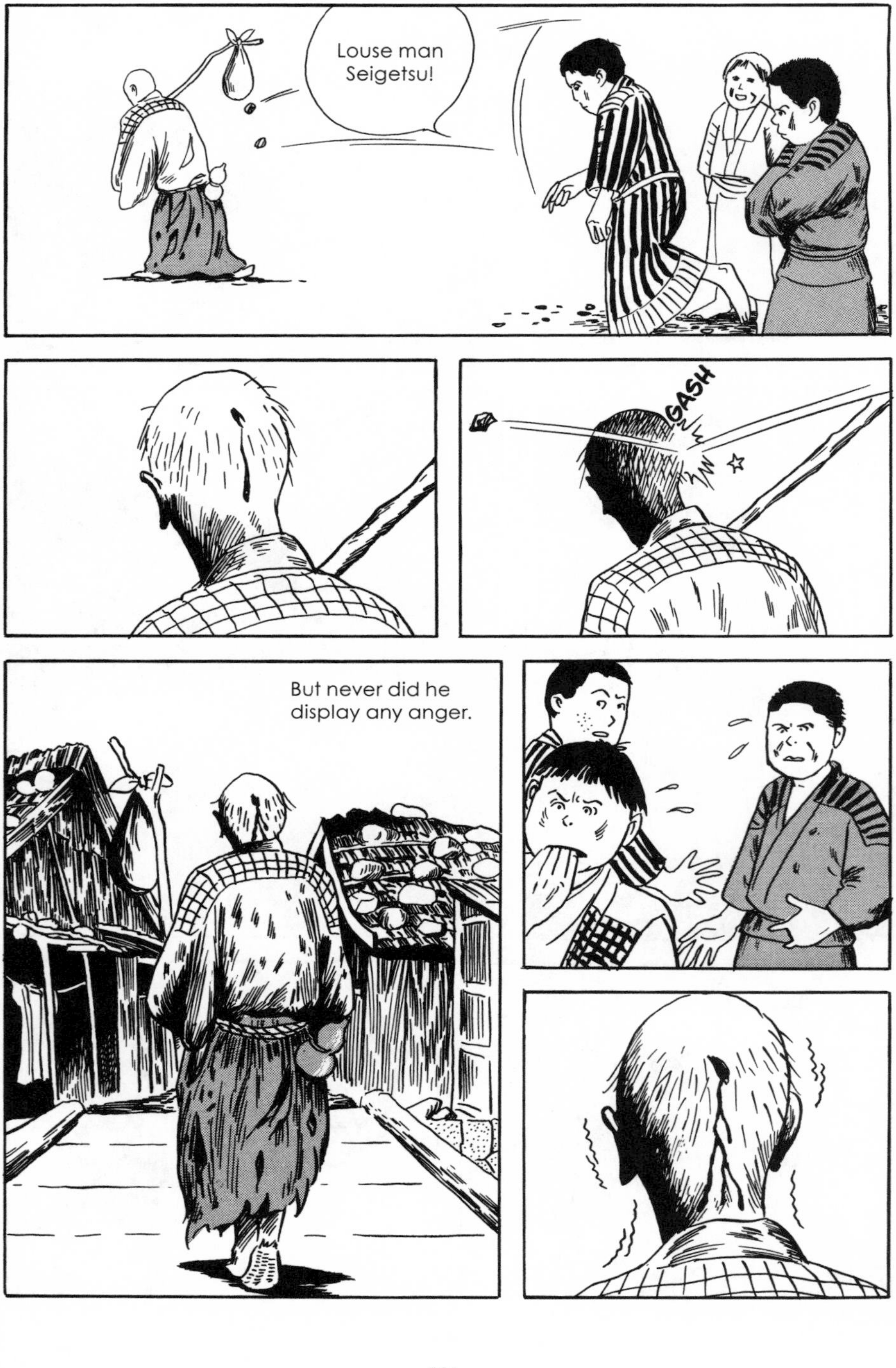
Louse man Seigetsu!
GASH
But never did he display any anger.

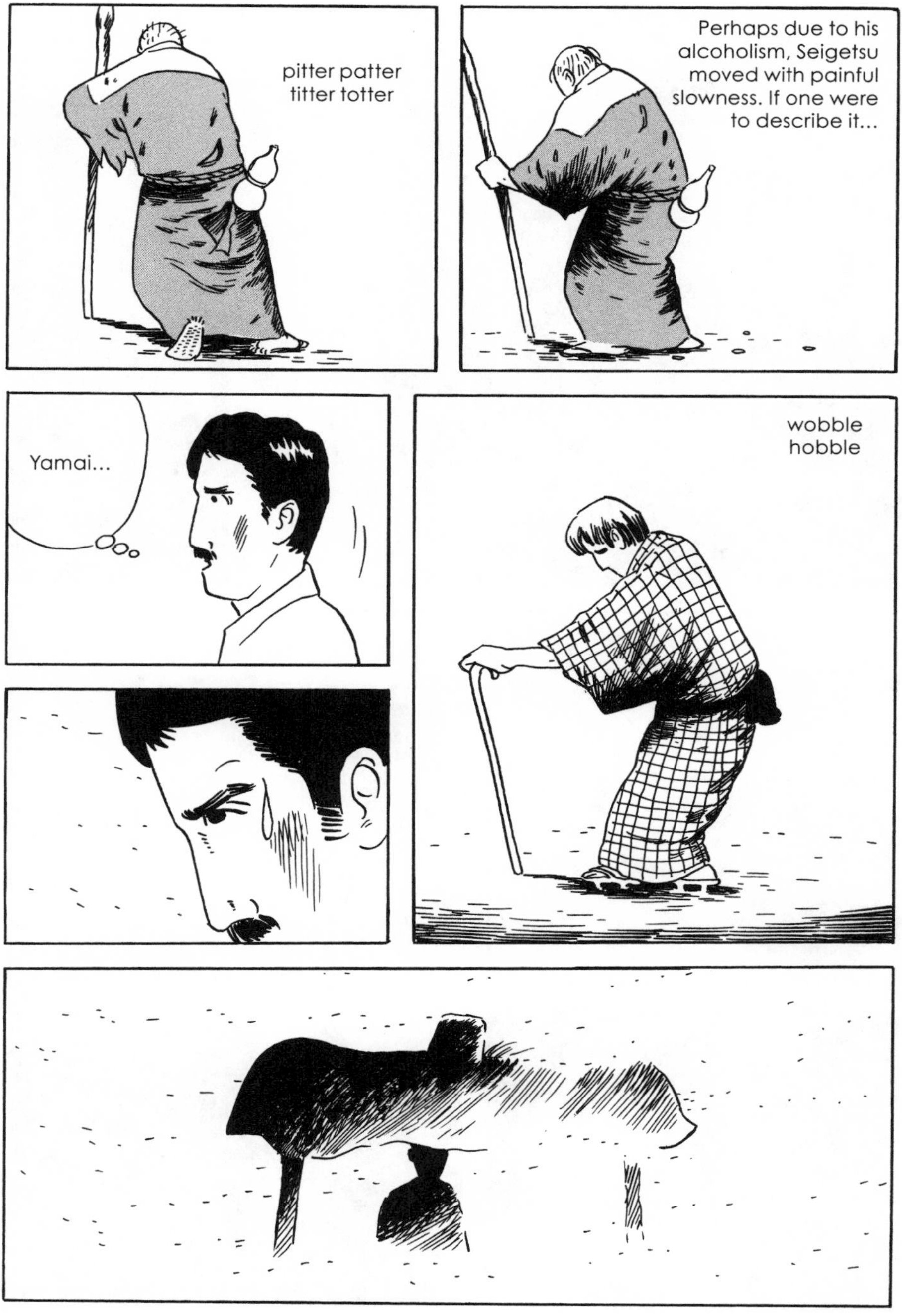
Perhaps due to his alcoholism, Seigetsu moved with painful slowness. If one were to describe it...
pitter patter titter totter
wobble hobble
Yamai...

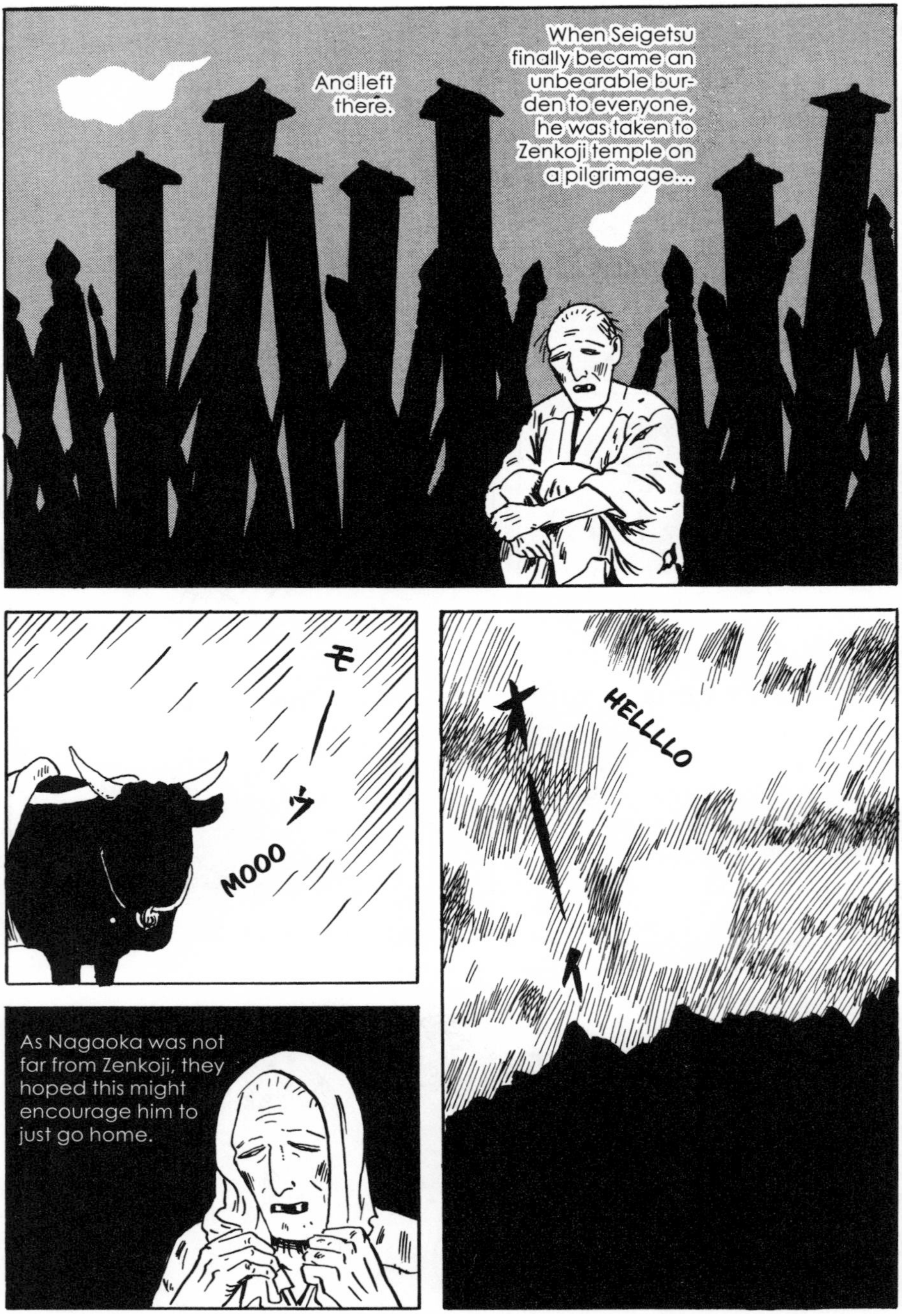
When Seigetsu finally became an unbearable burden to everyone, he was taken to Zenkoji temple on a pilgrimage...
And left there.
HELLLLO
モーッ
MOOO
As Nagaoka was not far from Zenkoji, they hoped this might encourage him to just go home.

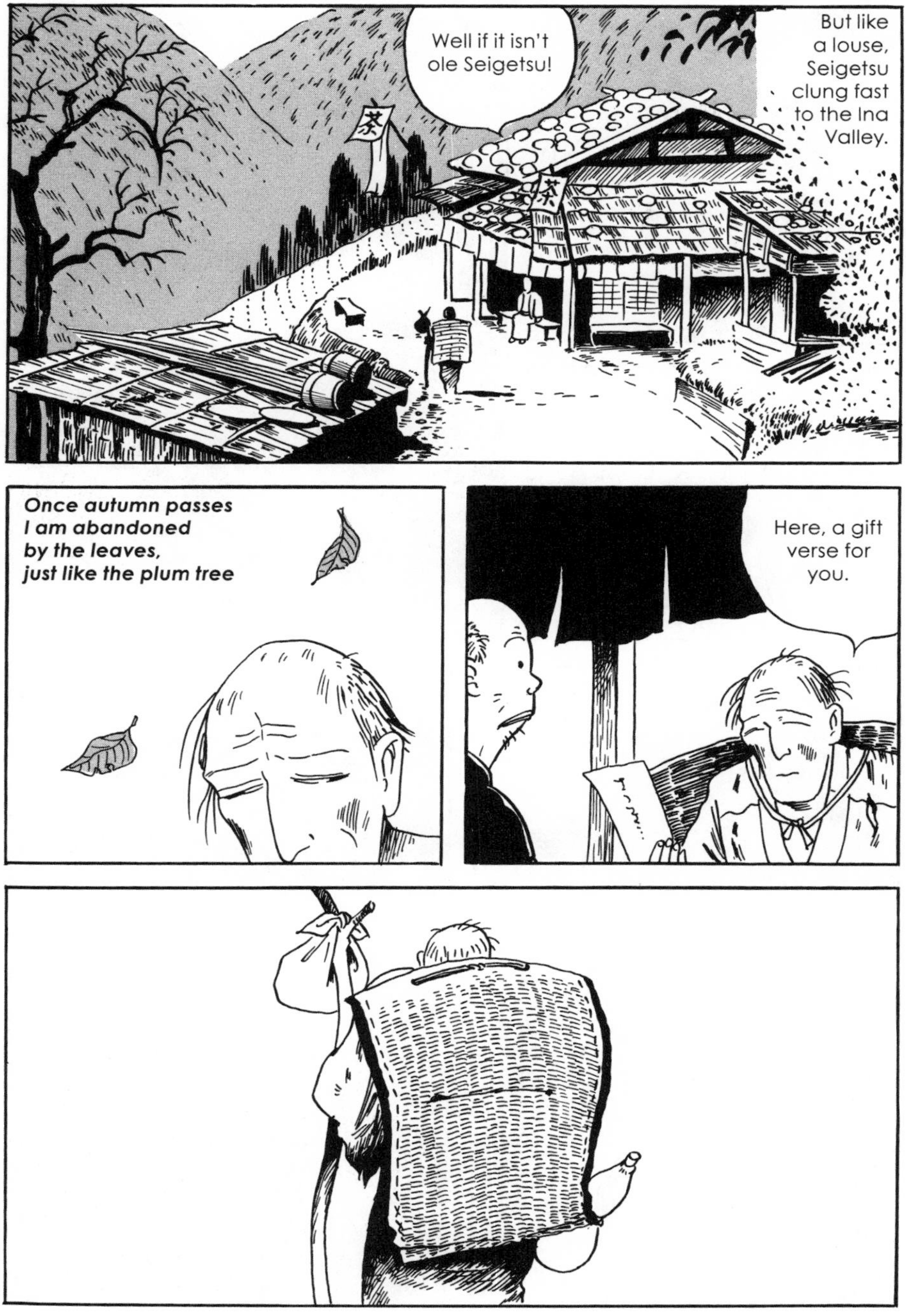
But like a louse, Seigetsu clung fast to the Ina Valley.
Well if it isn't ole Seigetsu!
茶
茶
Here, a gift verse for you.
Once autumn passes
I am abandoned
by the leaves,
just like the plum tree

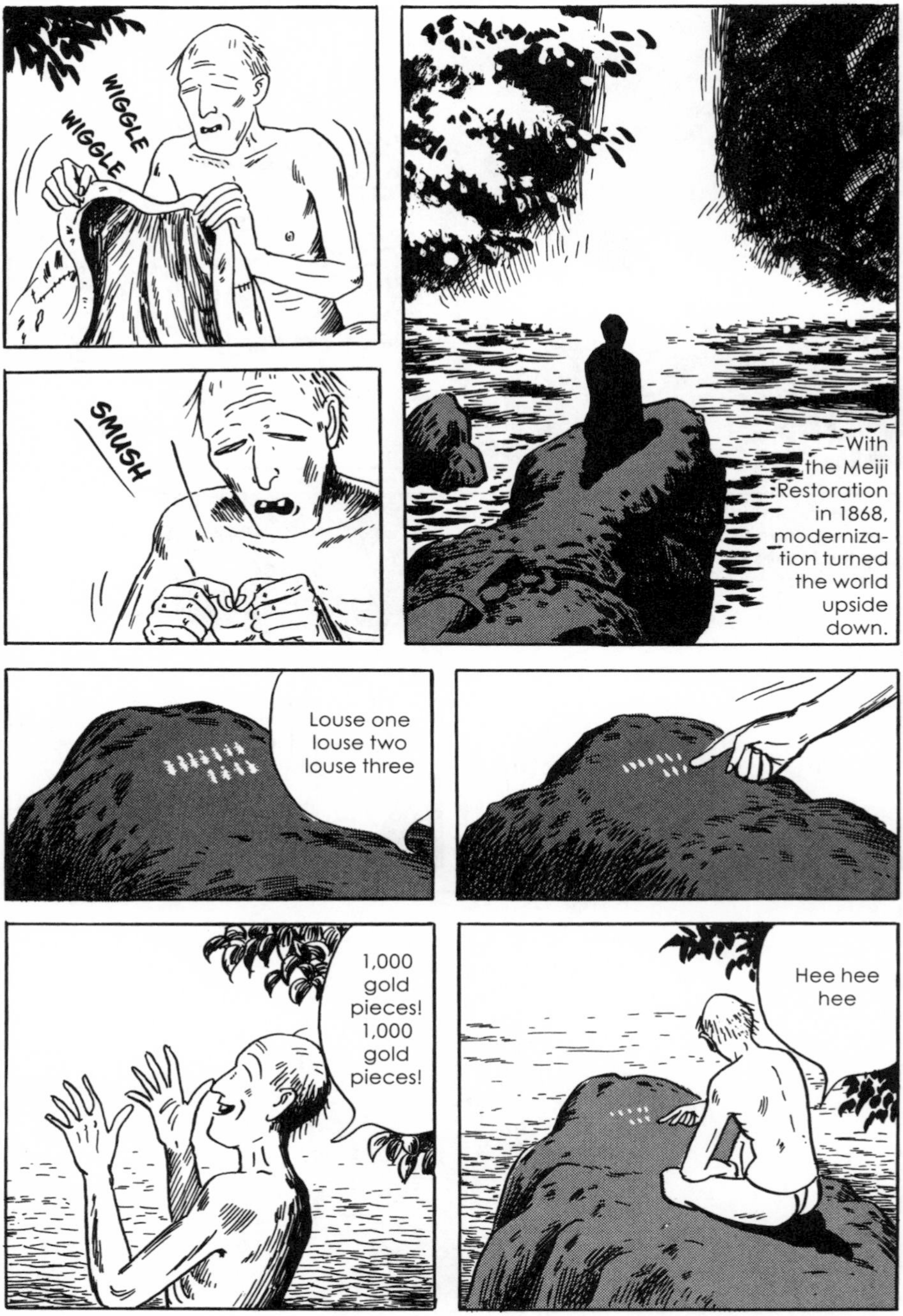
With the Meiji Restoration in 1868, modernization turned the world upside down.
WIGGLE WIGGLE
SMUSH
Louse one louse two louse three
Hee hee hee
1,000 gold pieces! 1,000 gold pieces!

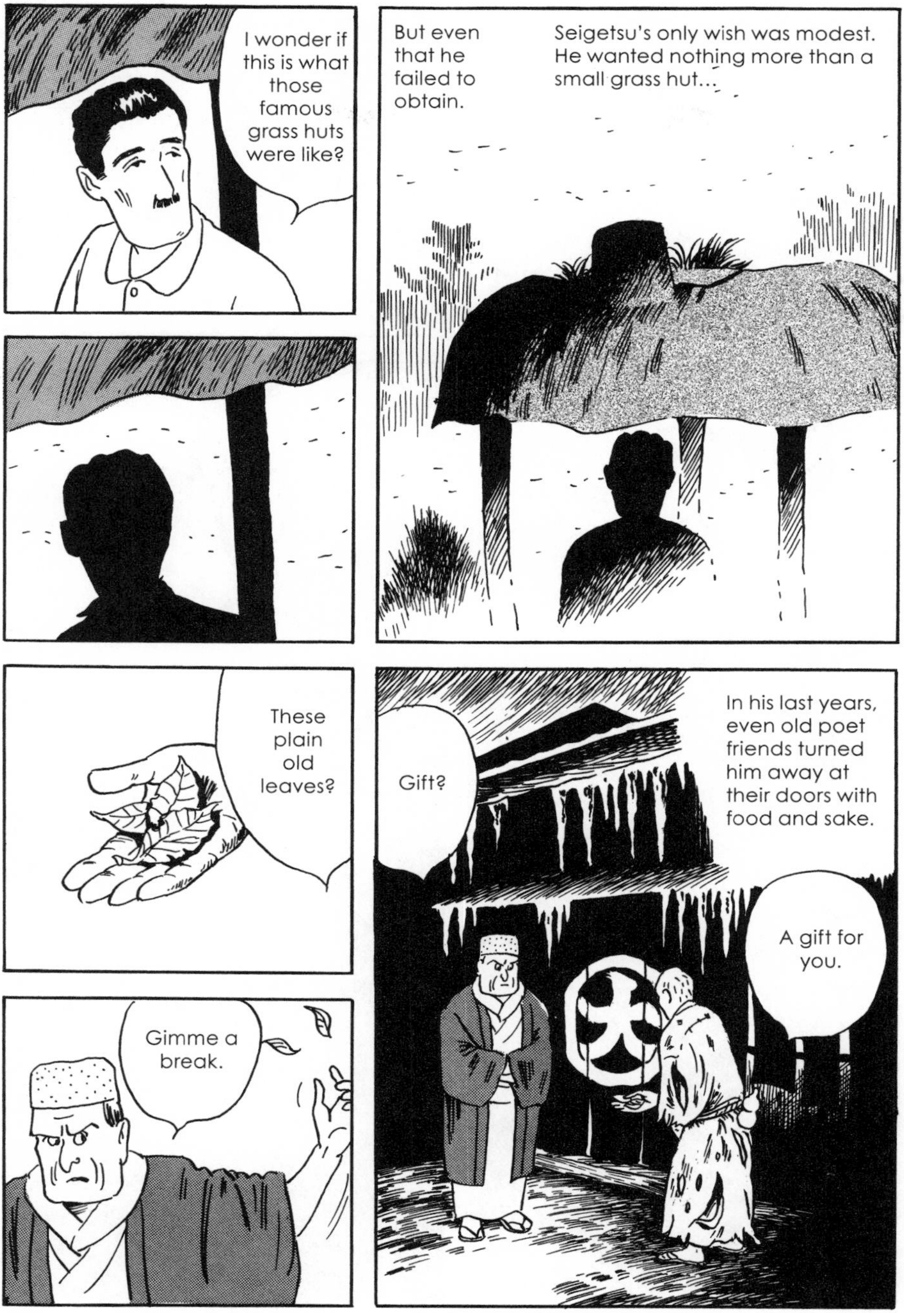
Seigetsu's only wish was modest. He wanted nothing more than a small grass hut...
But even that he failed to obtain.
I wonder if this is what those famous grass huts were like?
In his last years, even old poet friends turned him away at their doors with food and sake.
A gift for you.
Gift?
These plain old leaves?
Gimme a break.

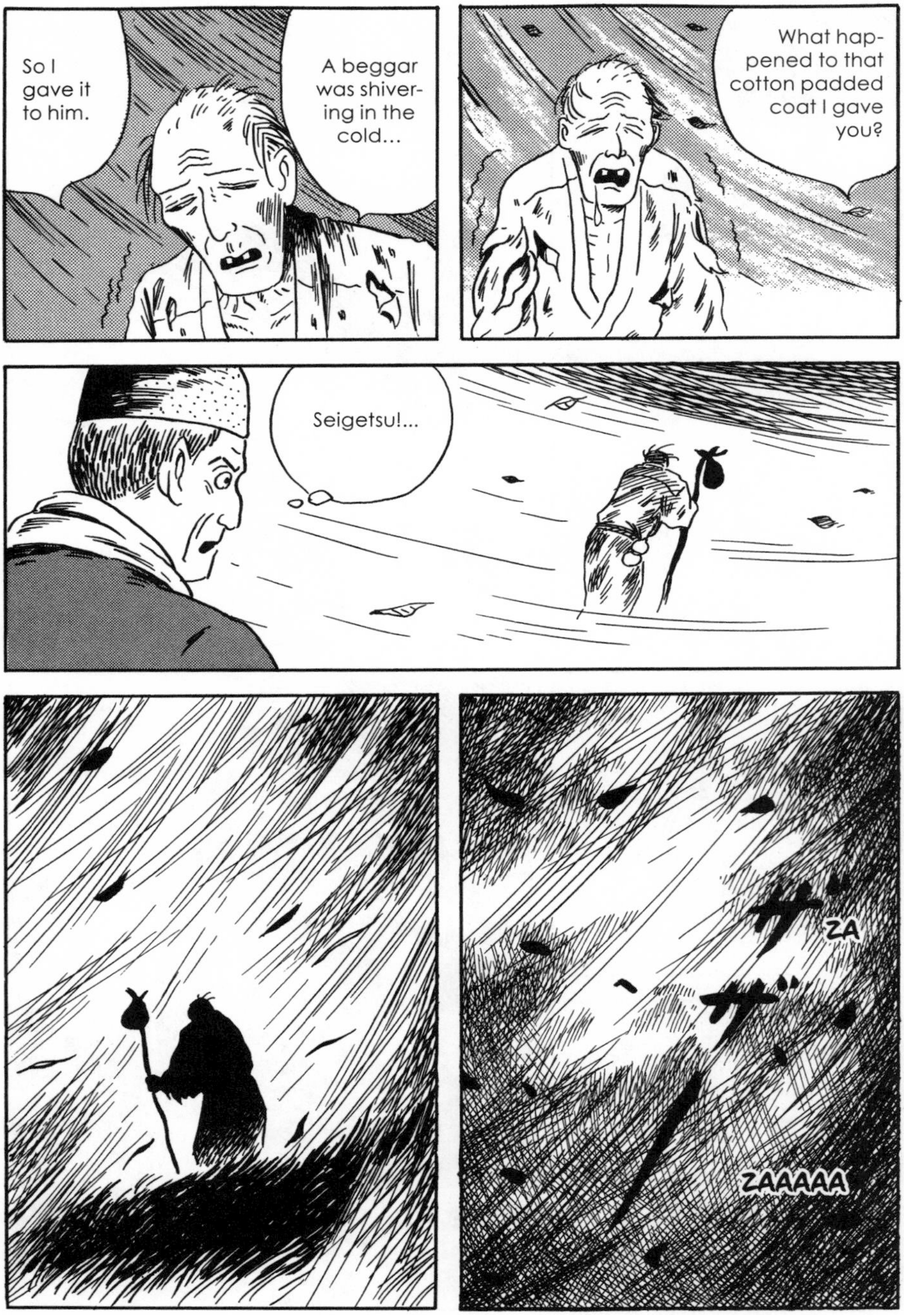
What hap-
pened to that
cotton padded
coat I gave
you?
A beggar
was shiver-
ing in the
cold...
So I
gave it
to him.
Seigetsu!...
ザ
ZA
ザ
ZAAAAA

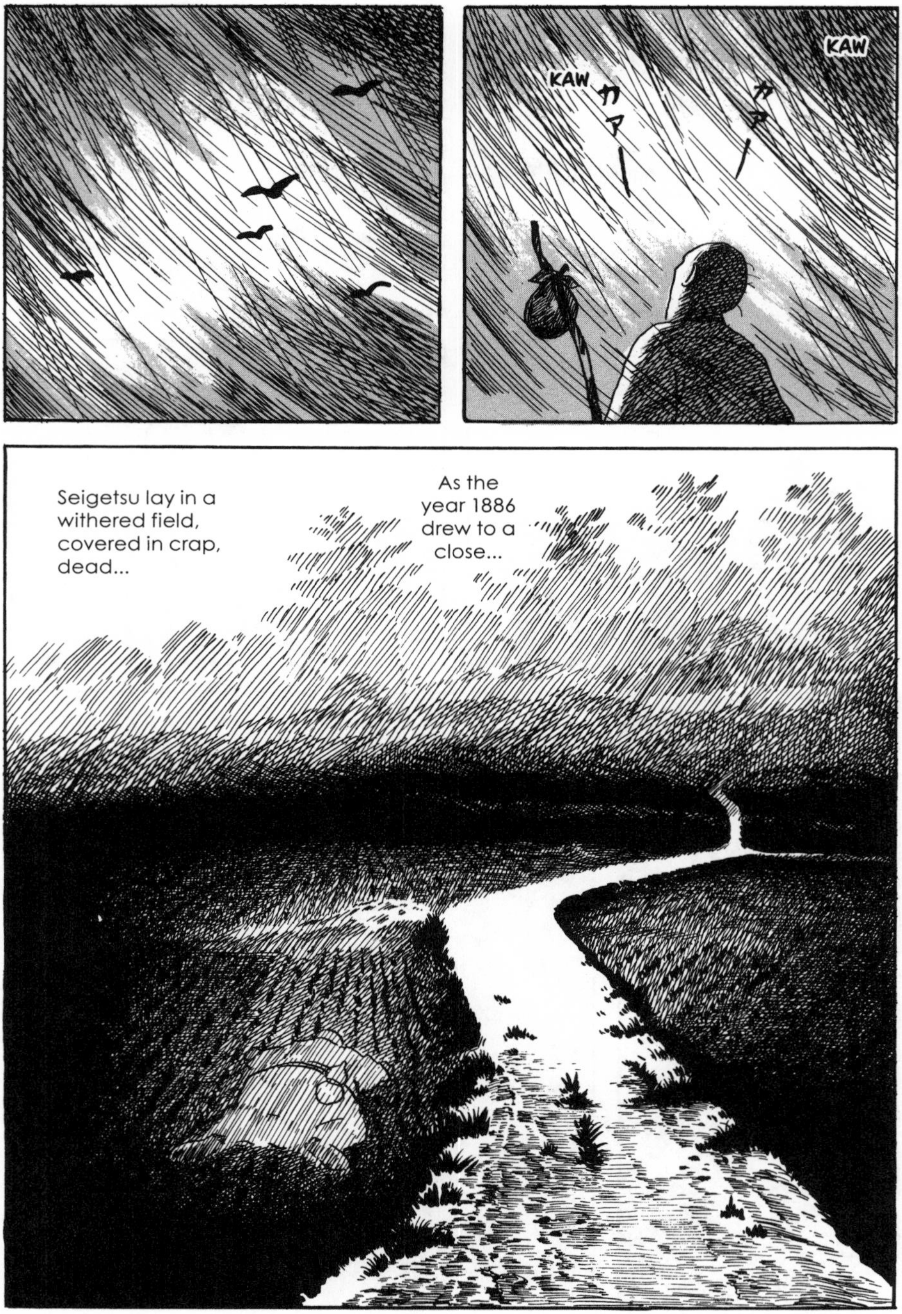
KAW
カァー
KAW
カァー
As the year 1886 drew to a close...
Seigetsu lay in a withered field, covered in crap, dead...

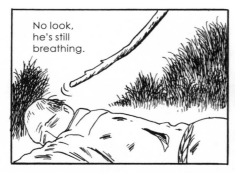

No look, he's still breathing.
I'm not touching him! He's smeared in shit!
Not sure what to do, the villagers put him on a plank…
And took him from house to house.
His closest poetry friend finally took him in.

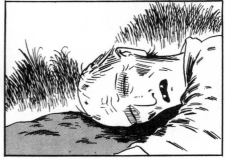

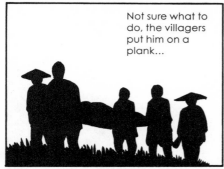

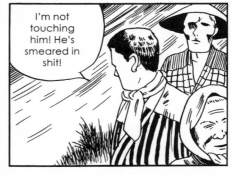

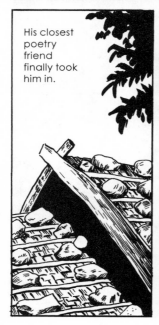

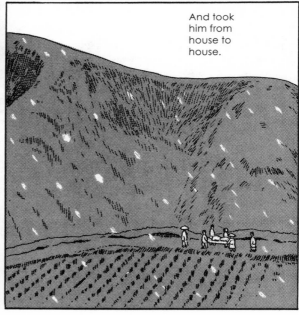

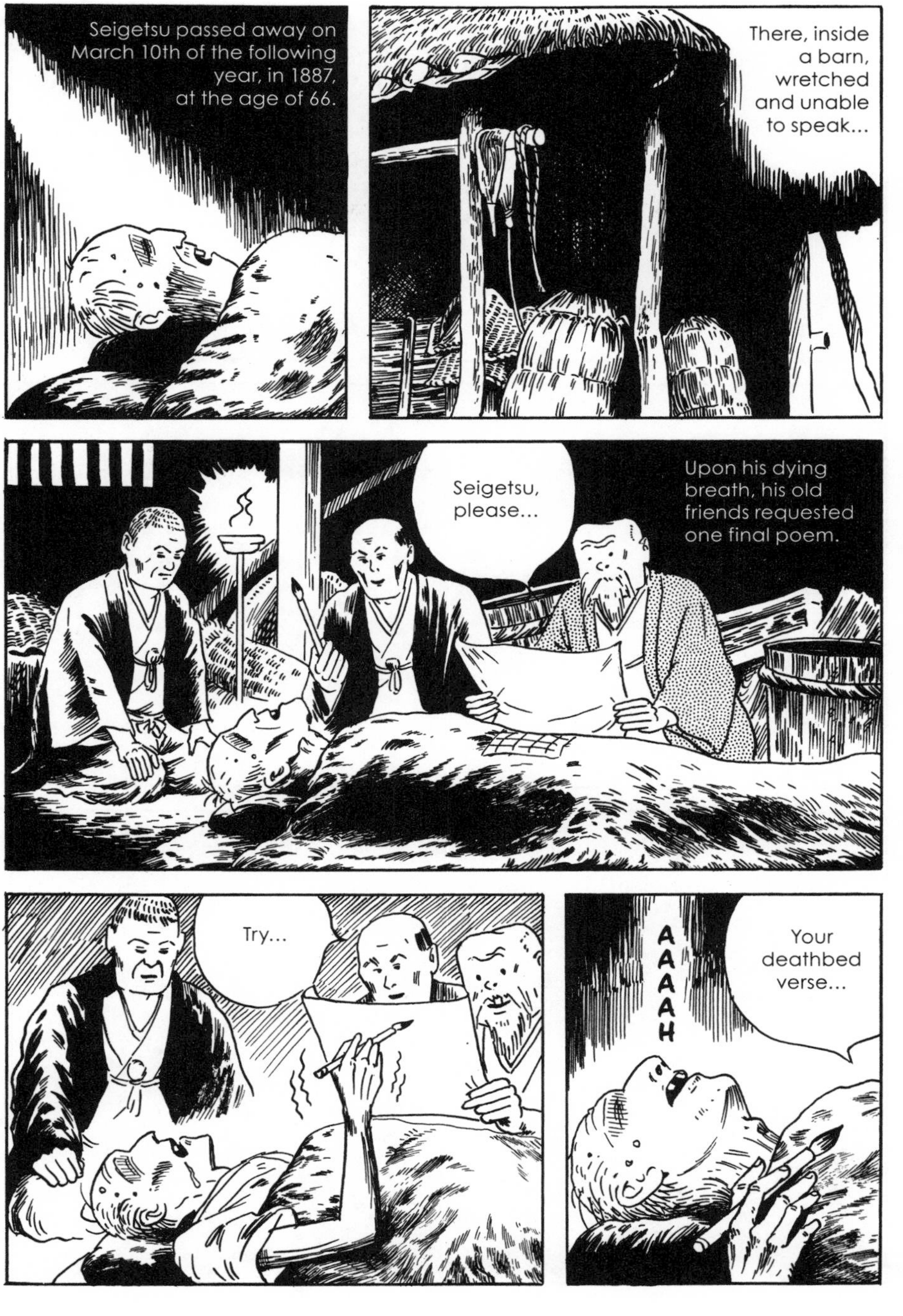
There, inside a barn, wretched and unable to speak...
Seigetsu passed away on March 10th of the following year, in 1887, at the age of 66.
Upon his dying breath, his old friends requested one final poem.
Seigetsu, please...
Your deathbed verse...
AAAAH
Try...

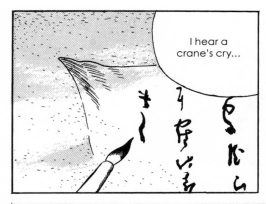

Yes… From somewhere…
I hear a crane's cry…
the mist…
the mist…

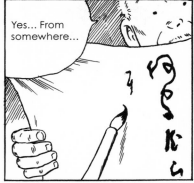

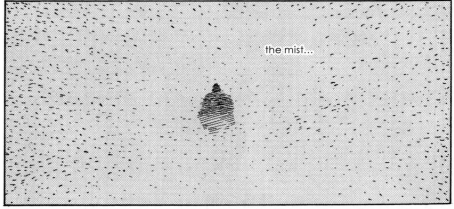

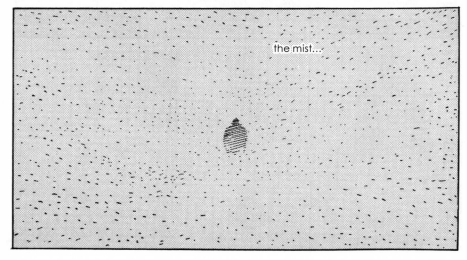

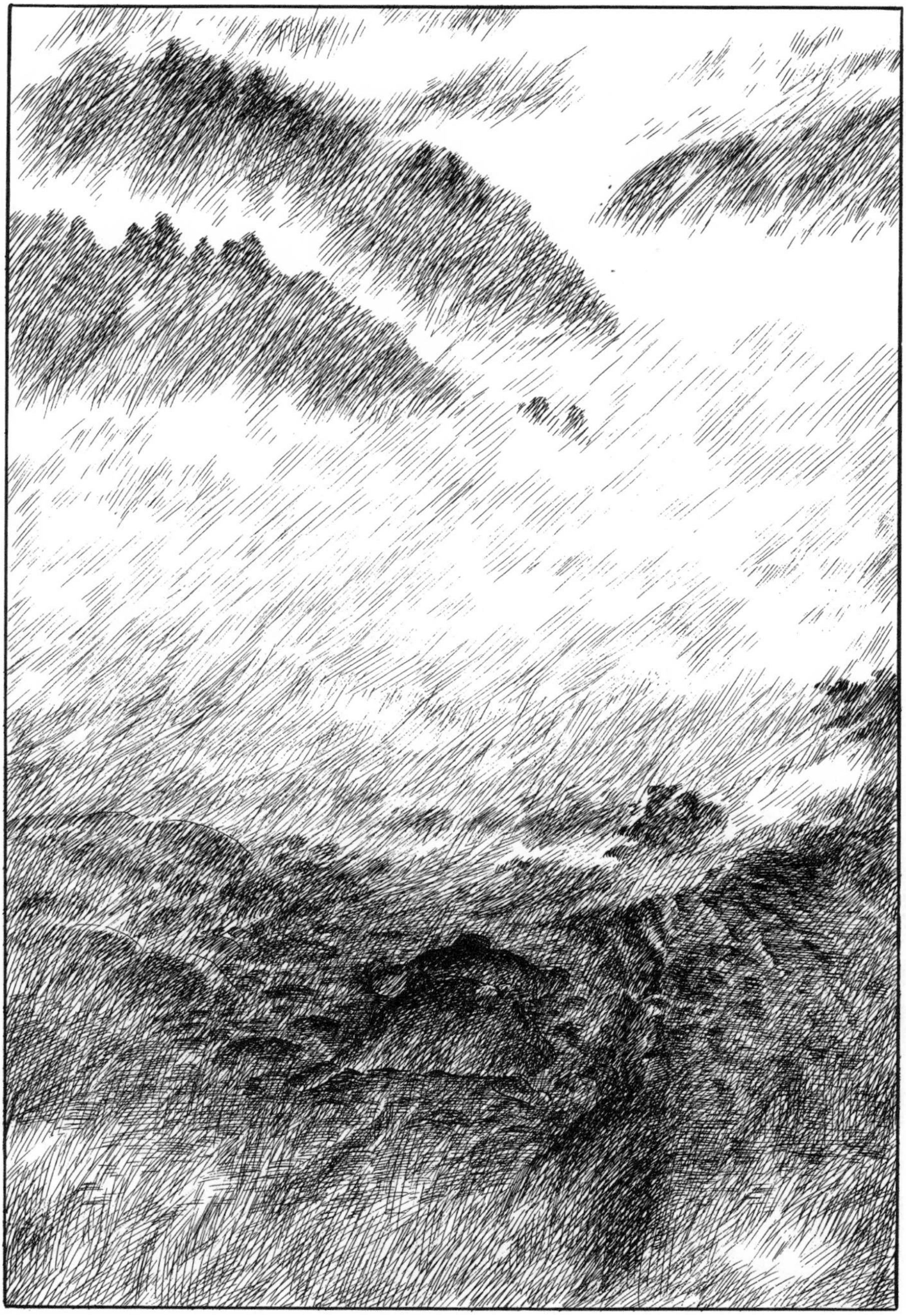

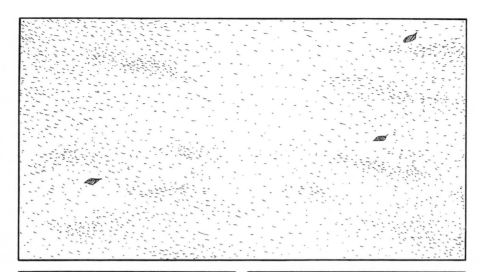

Seigetsu and Yamai, two big fat fools...

sign: Art stone fair

9   Tsuge Yoshiharu, "Atogaki," *Tsuge Yoshiharu nikki*, pp. 243–4.

10   Tsuge and Gondō, p. 40.

11   Masao Miyoshi, "Against the Native Grain: The Japanese Novel and the 'Postmodern' West," *Off Center: Power and Culture Relations between Japan and the United States* (Cambridge, MA: Harvard University Press, 1991), p. 23.

12   See, for example, the interview published in the final issue of *Comic Baku* no. 15 (Fall 1987), Tsuge Yoshiharu and Yaku Hiroshi, "Kojikiron," reprinted in Tsuge Yoshiharu, *Munō no hito* (Tokyo: Nihon bungeisha, 1988), pp. 219–34.

13   Tsuge Yoshiharu and Yamashita Yūji, interview, "Yume no riaritei o motomete," in *Tsuge Yoshiharu: Yume to tabi no sekai* (Tokyo: Shinchōsha, 2014), p. 37.

14   Tsuge Yoshiharu, "Maegaki: jisaku kaidai," *Natsu no omoide* (Tokyo: Chūō kōronsha, 1988), p. 7.

15   Tsuge Yoshiharu, "Atogaki," *Tonari no onna* (Tokyo: Nihon bungeisha, 1985), p. 182.

16   *Comic Baku* no. 8 (Winter 1986), reprinted in *Munō no hito* (1988), p. 237.

17   Yaku, p. 11.

18   Gondō Susumu [Takano Shinzō], "'Munō no hito' e no kiregire no kansō," *Tentōsha tsūshin* no. 3 (1988): 19.

19   "Maegaki," in Takenaka Naoto, ed., *"Munō no hito" no susume* (Tokyo: Seirindō, 1991), p. 11.

20   Kawamoto Saburō, "Hyōhaku no tabijin: Tsuge Yoshiharu no miryoku," *Shūkan gendai* (November 1991), p. 8. *The Peach Blossom Spring* is a fifth-century Chinese fable about a remote utopia where people live in harmony with one another and with nature, and was much romanticized by Chinese and Japanese literati over the centuries.

21   Kawamoto, "Inja ganbō: Tsuge Yoshiharu 'Munō no hito,'" *Comic Baku* no. 14 (Summer 1987), pp. 60–2.

ENDNOTES

1   Edward Fowler, *The Rhetoric of Confession: Shishōsetsu in Early Twentieth-Century Japanese Fiction* (Berkeley: University of California Press, 1988), p. xxiv. My understanding of *shishōsetsu*, and thus how to talk about Yoshiharu Tsuge's career, has been strongly shaped by Fowler's study and Tomi Suzuki's *Narrating the Self: Fictions of Japanese Modernity* (Stanford, CA: Stanford University Press, 1996).

2   Howard Hibbett, "The Portrait of the Artist in Japanese Fiction" (1955), as cited in John Whittier Treat, *The Rise and Fall of Modern Japanese Literature* (Chicago: University of Chicago Press, 2018), p. 100.

3   See, for example, Beatrice Marechal's very serviceable overview of Tsuge's career, "On Top of the Mountain: The Influential Manga of Yoshiharu Tsuge," *The Comics Journal*, special edition, vol. 5 (Seattle: Fantagraphics Books, 2005), pp. 22–8.

4   Kure Tomofusa, "Jun bungaku manga no yukue: Tsuge Yoshiharu o chūshin ni," *Yuriika* (February 1987), pp. 125–6.

5   Tsuge Yoshiharu and Gondō Susumu, *Tsuge Yoshiharu Mangajutsu*, vol. 2 (Tokyo: Waizu shuppan, 1993), p. 38.

6   See my essay "Seiichi Hayashi's Nouvelle Vague," in Seiichi Hayashi, *Red Colored Elegy*, trans. Taro Nettleton, paperback edition (Montreal: Drawn & Quarterly, 2018), pp. 237–91; and Asakawa Mitsuhiro, "The Promise and Perils of I-Comics: Shin'ichi Abe's Struggles to Draw Himself with Absolute Sincerity," in Abe Shin'ichi, *That Miyoko Asagaya Feeling*, trans. Ryan Holmberg (Tokyo: Black Hook Press, 2019). These manga fit what is known in the critical literature as the "self-destructive type" (*hametsu-gata*) of *shishōsetsu*.

7   On Yoshiharu Tsuge and *Comic Baku*, see Yaku Hiroshi, *"Comic Baku" to Tsuge Yoshiharu* (Tokyo: Fukutake shoten, 1989). Other *Baku* manga available in English include Katsumata Susumu, "Deep Sea Fish" (1984), in *Fukushima Devil Fish*, ed. Asakawa Mitsuhiro, trans. Ryan Holmberg (London: Breakdown Press, 2018); and Tsuge Tadao, *Tale of the Beast* (1987), trans. Feargal South (Tokyo: Black Hook Press, 2018).

8   Asakawa, "The Promise and Perils of I-Comics," p. x. Abe's "The Look of Vagrancy" is translated in English in this same volume, *That Miyoko Asagaya Feeling.*

wives, posits Kawamoto, represent the "real life" that reels Sukezō back in from his "pseudo-grass hut" and riverbank fantasies.[21] But son and wife are clearly more than that. The small nuclear family closed upon itself, regardless of its internal aggravations, is ultimately ballast and refuge for Tsuge. "It's almost like it's just the three of us, alone, in this vast universe," reflects Mrs. Sukegawa on page 140. "Just the three of us, that sounds fine to me..." replies Tsuge's avatar. Indeed, it was these lines, not any of Sukezō's melancholic mutterings or pontificated absurdities, that were adapted as lead copy for the manga's movie version.

Where is Yoshiharu Tsuge? People have tended to seek out his shadows upon the Tamagawa, or in the nooks of once-forlorn hot-spring towns, or lurking in his artwork's hall of mirrors. Instead, even if it contradicts the artist's aura, we might do better to look for Tsuge, as a person and persona both, in the comforts of his own home.

your skills in ways other than what society deems proper.

Alas, no one but Tsuge seems to have noticed that, especially in a profoundly patriarchal society like Japan, wives and children could suffer dearly if husbands decided to drop out. Though by no means an upholder of progressive gender values (his diary will make you flinch), Tsuge was at least attuned to the negative social ramifications of *munō* and *jōhatsu* in practice, which the contributors to *The Bible of Nowhere Man*—all but one of whom were male—were not. This was probably thanks largely to circumstance: Tsuge, who stayed home even when he was working, spent far more time parenting than most other Japanese men did.

A similar blindness obtains in the many paeans to Tsuge as a modern-day reincarnation of fabled literati ideals. Take this effusive example by critic Saburō Kawamoto for a weekly tabloid in 1991: "Yoshiharu Tsuge's appeal is clean and pure, like that of a hermit who has left the world behind. Only rarely does he produce work or appear before the mass media. As a child he suffered from acute social phobia, and still has a strong aversion to meeting people, and so he prefers hiding in his corner to being in public. He yearns to disappear and go into seclusion, and dreams of living alone in a small mountain village. Inner-city alleys, mountain mineral-spring inns, desolate seaside harbors. It is in such forgotten places that Tsuge finds his Peach Blossom Spring. One thinks of Saigyō's and Bashō's wandering travels long ago. Or the tranquility of Masuji Ibuse's stories. Wrapped up, as we typically are, in our busy daily lives, contact with Tsuge's Peach Blossom Spring provides us feelings of nostalgia and calm."[20]

How far off the mark this is! Since the mid-'70s, Tsuge's work repeatedly explored how these hoary solitary male ideals are compromised—reluctantly but typically for the better—by coupledom and family life. Sukezō's attempted recreation of a wabi-sabi hermitage on the banks of the Tamagawa River is, however heartfelt, clearly ironic. "Tsuge is torn between a desire to abandon the world and knowledge that that is impossible," wrote Kawamoto in a more balanced essay in the pages of *Baku*. "*The Man Without Talent* is a drama of the tension between those two extremes." He also thought the manga's tribute to poverty and failed effort was a "parody of *shishōsetsu*," inspired by the same national affluence many critic-fans denounced as repressive. Crying children and desperate comedy *Urusei Yatsura* (1978–1987) and the dystopian sci-fi extravaganza *Akira* (1982–1990) were priming manga and anime to become the international entertainment powerhouses that they are today. It's not hard to imagine that, for most manga readers—hooked as they were on high action spectacle, muscular trash-talking men, and sassy youths without a serious care in the world—the self-pitying, middle-aged protagonist of *The Man Without Talent* probably seemed a serious drag. So, too, its original publication venue, *Comic Baku*, sales of which hovered around five thousand copies per issue before quickly sinking to two thousand. "A commercial magazine with fanzine level sales," was how head editor Hiroshi Yaku once put it.[17] "Why are we even printing this thing?" he recalls the sales department at Nihon Bungeisha often saying. *Comic Baku*: a loser manga magazine that pinned its hopes on a loser artist who wrote about loser men.

But by the time *The Man Without Talent* was turned into a movie, fissures in Japan's real estate and stock market bubbles were the stuff of daily headlines. The bubble burst at the end of 1991, inaugurating what is known as Japan's Lost Decade. Shinzō Takano, one of Tsuge's greatest supporters as a critic and publisher since the late '60s, and one of his closest friends, set the stage in 1988 when he heralded the manga's embrace of a lower and slower standard of living as "the perfect textbook for seeing through the current conditions of advanced capitalism and middle-class society."[18] The comparatively mild editors of *The Bible of Nowhere Man*, which was published right when the bubble was finally collapsing, threw down the gauntlet thus: "'Do you fight around the clock?' 'Always aim to be one class higher'—these are the kind of slogans that assail one's ears in this information society of ours today, which is nothing but a society of *Men With Talent*. They say that loafers (*puutarō*) and freeters [who float from one part-time job to another] are increasing in numbers. But regardless of whether one is gainfully employed or not, or if one is appreciated as having skills or not, more than a few people have recently awakened to *The Man Without Talent* within themselves. A taste different from simple habitual laziness, it is about taking a vacation from reality."[19] Confident in their disenchantment, many of the volume's contributors echoed a common sentiment: that being *munō* (talentless) is not helpless and shameful, but an affirmative way of life based on using

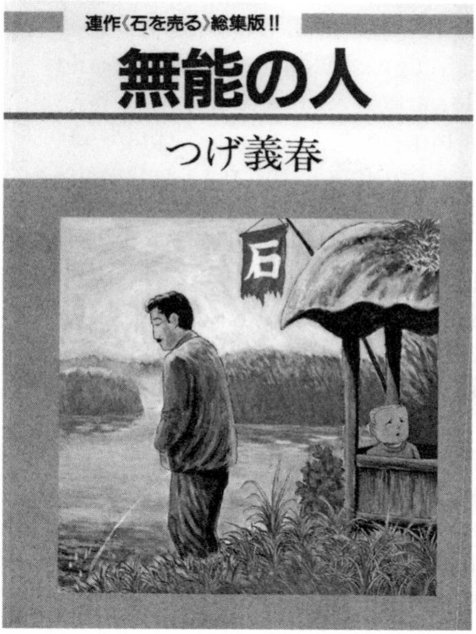
連作《石を売る》総集版!!
無能の人
つげ義春
石

The Man Without Talent, collected magazine edition (Tokyo: Nihon bungeisha, July 1987).

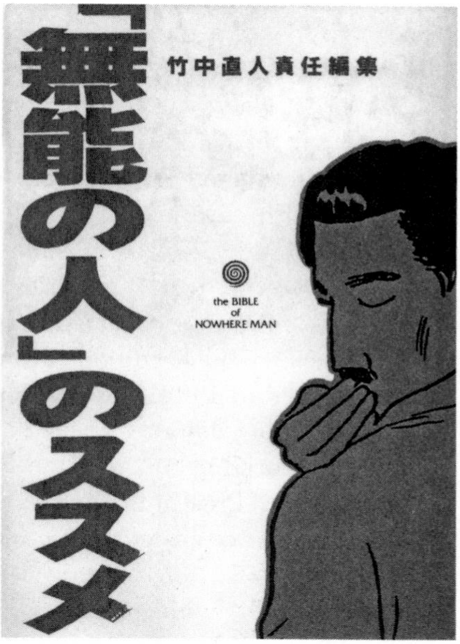
「無能の人」のススメ
竹中直人責任編集
the BIBLE of NOWHERE MAN

Advice from "The Man Without Talent," edited by Naoto Takenaka (Tokyo: Seirindō, December 1992).

This in turn led to a whole book of playful think-pieces and artistic homages officially titled *Advice from "The Man Without Talent"* (*"Munō no hito" no susume*, 1991), though I prefer the imaginative English on its cover, *The Bible of Nowhere Man*.

If you are puzzled how a deadbeat like Sukezō could be regarded a sage, consider the times. The '80s were the decade in which the Japanese economy seemed unstoppable. White-collar salarymen were compared to samurai in their self-immolating devotion. The real estate of this island nation was supposedly worth more (on paper at least) than the entire United States. Americans smashed Sonys and Toyotas in fear of a Japanese takeover. My parents cackled watching Michael Keaton trying to tame the workplace-fascist Nipponese in *Gung Ho* (1986). Meanwhile, on Tsuge's home turf of manga, on the strength of martial arts titles like *Dragon Ball* (1984–1995) and *Fist of the North Star* (1983–1988), *Weekly Shōnen Jump*—with the guiding slogan "effort, friendship, and victory"—was pushing five million copies a week. Elsewhere, hits like the teenage facedown, dead in the mud. In retrospect, the final pages of *The Man Without Talent* certainly look prophetic. Yet given Tsuge's fantastic brand of *shishōsetsu*, where fact and fiction blur and reality is plural, who is to say whether Sukezō's withdrawal was hinting at his creator's plans for imminent retirement or if Tsuge decided to follow the path originally imagined for his avatar?

Not long after Sukezō vanished into the fog, *The Man Without Talent* emerged into the light. The series was first collected into a standalone edition in 1987, as a collected magazine edition supplementing *Comic Baku*. The first book edition, a handsome hardcover with a slipcase, was published in 1988, and saw many reprintings. There have been at least three other editions since. The movie version, actor Naoto Takenaka's directorial debut, won the FIPRESCI (International Federation of Film Critics) Prize at the Venice Film Festival in 1991, instigating a slew of movies based on Tsuge's work and a new "Tsuge boom" widely covered in the press. *Garo* organized a special feature in the film's honor (November 1991), with contributions from many prominent subculturati.

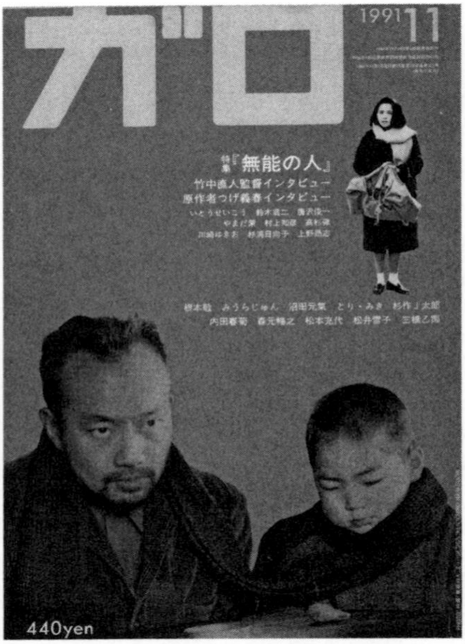
ガロ
1991 11
特集『無能の人』
竹中直人監督インタビュー
原作者つげ義春インタビュー
440yen

Garo no. 323 (November 1991), special issue on the movie *The Man Without Talent*.

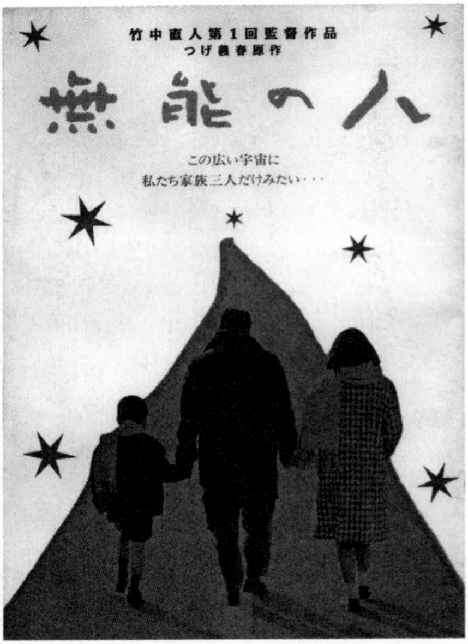
竹中直人第1回監督作品
つげ義春原作
無能の人
この広い宇宙に
私たち家族三人だけみたい・・・

Movie pamphlet for *The Man Without Talent* (November 1991), directed by Naoto Takenaka.

Comic Baku, mainstream manga publishing's attempt to revive the spirit of classic *Garo*, folded as a result, after only fifteen issues.

The end apparently did not arrive too early for Tsuge. Despair shades almost every text he wrote while drawing *The Man Without Talent*. Spring 1985, around the time of "Selling Stones": "I can't wait until I am old enough to receive social security. I'm jealous of fine artists, with their cultural honors and pensions from the art academy. The only thing an aging cartoonist can count on is social security. The sooner the better."[15] Spring 1986, upon publication of "The Stone Hunting Trip" ("Tansekikō"): "Again this time, chronic ailments assailed me while drawing. Whenever I picked up my pen, my hand trembled violently, my heart

Portrait sketch of Seigetsu from childhood memory by Isao Shimojima, from *The Collected Works of Seigetsu Inoue, the Wandering Poet* (Hakutei shobō, 1930).

raced wildly with stress, and I felt anxious that my comics were guilty of some atrocious mistake. Once that starts, I feel crippled by all variety of physical symptoms. It's been the same thing over and over since issue two. Maybe it's not manga, maybe I'm at sea from a general loss of confidence. Yet, what is to be made of the fact that the symptoms appear like an allergic reaction every time I set pen to paper?"[16]

In the years after *Comic Baku*, Tsuge continued to write occasional travel pieces and submit to interviews, though with lessening frequency. New book editions and movie adaptations of his work proliferated, providing him enough royalties to retire. But without any new manga, people began to wonder if Tsuge, master of the art of disappearance, hadn't gone the way of crazy Seigetsu, wandering the hills or lying than notoriously meandering *shishōsetsu*. Unlike the limited, everyday realism of most *shishōsetsu*, most of Tsuge's stories for *Garo* are steeped in the fantastic, the uncanny, and the grotesque. Dreams provided him material until the late '70s, and even his more ostensibly autobiographical works, like *The Man Without Talent*, flirt with magical realism. This was, after all, an artist whose first love was mystery, who immersed himself in folklore and tales of the supernatural before getting into modern literature, and who first engaged themes of travel and the artist's private life while in the employ of a cartoonist (Shigeru Mizuki) who specialized in the phantasmagoric. Especially during the years around and after *The Man Without Talent*, he frequently spoke about the wisdom of Buddhism's insistence on the insubstantial nature of perceived reality and the freedom gained by cutting connections with one's ego through mendicant practices.[12] *Shishōsetsu* critics and writers have historically privileged confessional sincerity as the standard for measuring a work's merit and its author's moral character. But for an artist like Tsuge, who believed that waking life was itself a fiction and that dreams offered their own (potentially deeper, because unmediated) reality, the realist and confessional dictates of *shishōsetsu* could only be read as an exercise in self-deception.

This was, however, precisely the genre's merit. In the fictiveness of autobiographical fiction, Tsuge found his home away from home. In the contradictions of a supposedly sincere and authentic mode of writing, he found what we might call a mode of "stationary *jōhatsu*": a way of disappearing and creating new selves without ever leaving his desk. As he explained recently, "When I write in a *shishōsetsu* style, since I say whatever I wish about myself, people often mistake it for truth. But that itself provides a kind of reality."[13] Or in 1988, speaking about when he first started drawing *shishōsetsu*-style comics in a regular and focused way in the mid-'70s, "I came to enjoy [my stories] being read as fact or close to fact, and the protagonist being imagined as the artist myself. I thought perhaps I could use the style of *shishōsetsu* to confuse fact and fiction, mislead people about what the artist is like, and thereby hide my true identity. Using self-concealment as a means of self-expression might seem twisted, but I am not particularly interested in expressing myself and have always preferred to hide. There is only one way to really do that, however, and that is to stop drawing altogether"—which is exactly what he did in 1987.[14]

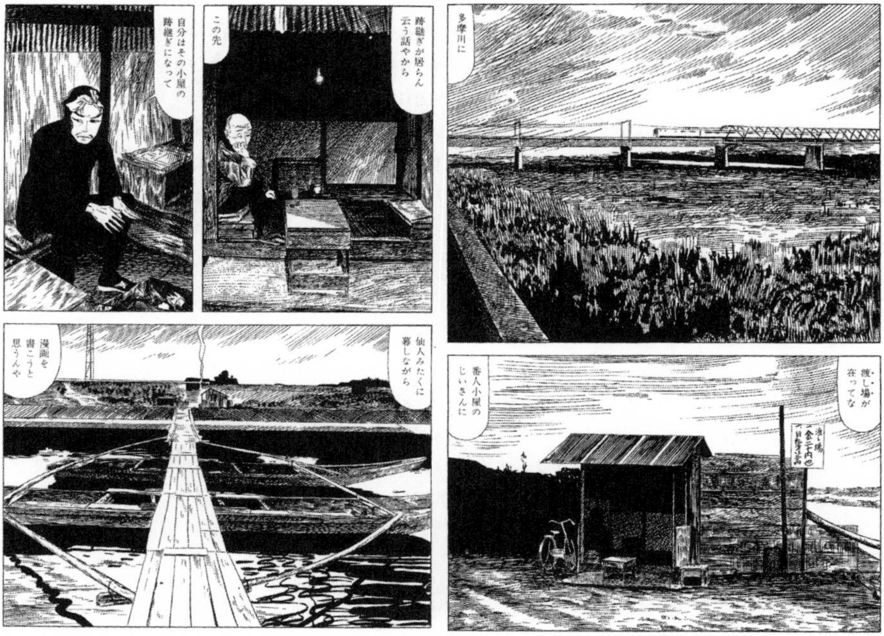

多摩川に
跡継ぎが居らん云う話やから
この先
自分はその小屋の跡継ぎになって
渡し場が在ってな
番人小屋のじいさんに
仙人みたくに暮しながら
漫画を書こうと思うんや

Shin'ichi Abe, "The Look of Vagrancy," *Garo* no. 104 (April 1972).

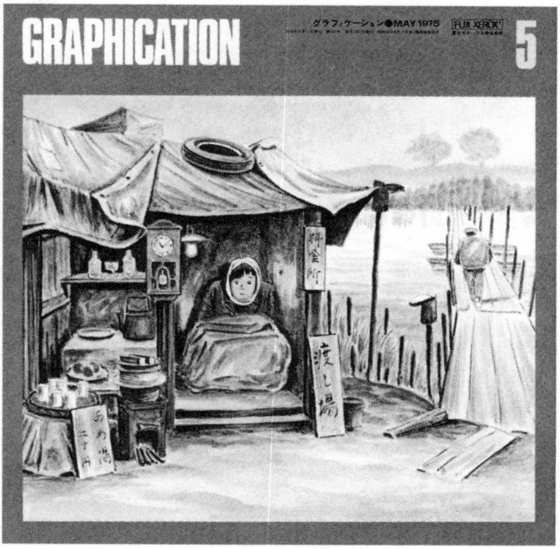

GRAPHICATION
グラフィケーション●MAY 1975
FUJI XEROX
5
料金所
渡し場

Graphication (May 1975), cover art by Yoshiharu Tsuge.

That is also why I like reading *shishōsetsu*, because *shishōsetsu* are reports of the writer's personal life (*seikatsu hōkoku*), so to speak." And the reason why he was interested in writers' personal lives, he explains, is because most of their lives were, like his own, beset by poverty, self-doubt, and neuroses, and because reading about their hardships provided him with "life examples to emulate and the encouragement to find the strength" to navigate his own.[9]

But notice the "so to speak" (*iwaba*) that caps that long quote. *Shishōsetsu* are "reports of the writer's personal life, *so to speak*." Tsuge's *shishōsetsu*-esque manga are rarely, and arguably never, straight transcriptions of his personal life. "Though I was drawing fact," he recalled in the early '90s about his breakout "I-comics" work, "Chirpy," "that differs from a diary in that one pulls together only the important parts of fact and recomposes those fragments. *Shishōsetsu* is ultimately fabrication."[10] Masking this artistry, however, was just as important in creating an effective work and drawing readers into a *shishōsetsu* state of mind. Contrary to the classic view of the genre as a sincere art of crafted autobiography, theorist Masao Miyoshi once described modern Japanese prose fiction (*shōsetsu*) in general as "an incredible fabrication that is nonetheless held up as truthful."[11] Tsuge understood this contradiction well, and consciously played with the uncanny effects it produced.

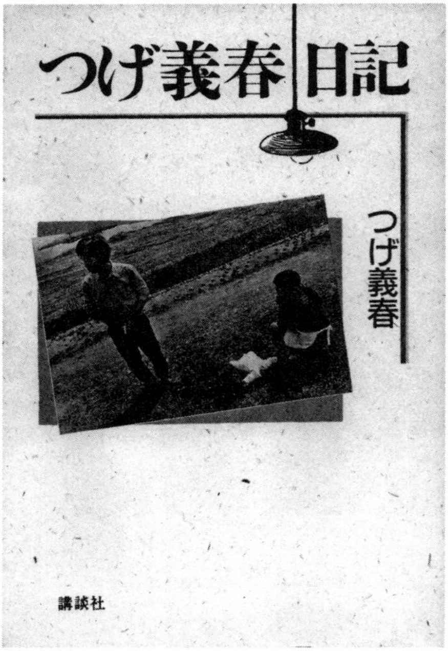
つげ義春日記
つげ義春
講談社
Yoshiharu Tsuge's Diaries (Tokyo: Kōdansha, December 1983).

Tsuge's version of *shishōsetsu* was never pure. Ever since he began drawing *shishōsetsu*-style manga in the mid-'60s, his work has rarely obeyed the formal conventions of that genre. They are, for one, far more emplotted

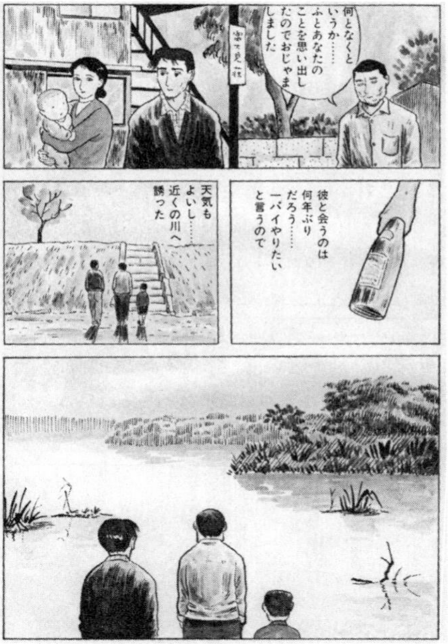
何となくというか……ふとあなたのことを思い出したのでおじゃましました
彼と会うのは何年ぶりだろう……一パイやりたいと言うので
天気もよいし……近くの川へ誘った

Yoshiharu Tsuge, "A Certain Unknown Artist," *Comic Baku* no. 2 (Summer 1984).

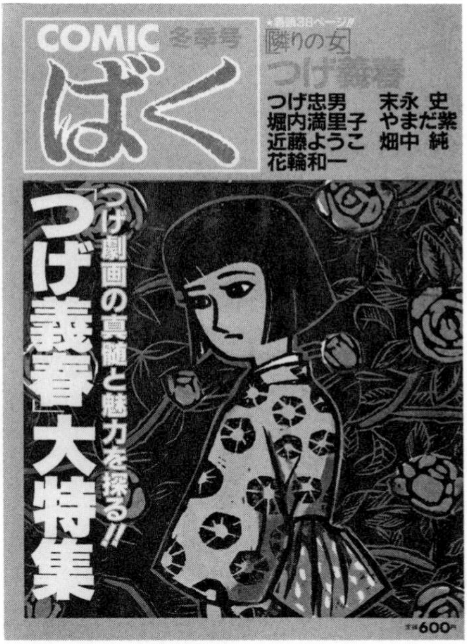
COMIC
冬季号
ばく
隣りの女
つげ義春
つげ忠男
末永 史
堀内満里子
やまだ紫
近藤ようこ
畑中 純
花輪和一
つげ劇画の真髄と魅力を探る!!
つげ義春大特集
600

Comic Baku no. 4 (Winter 1985), cover art by Jun Hatanaka based on a drawing by Yoshiharu Tsuge.

daydream of taking over the river crossing and using the kiosk as a studio, though circulating in Tsuge's work as an ideal of reclusion since the mid-'70s, was originally plucked from a story Abe published in *Garo* in 1972, "The Look of Vagrancy" ("Burai no omokage").[8] As Tsuge fleshed out Sukezō in subsequent stories of the cycle that would eventually be combined as *The Man Without Talent*, he gradually packed in more nonfiction from his personal life than in any of his previous manga.

"I'm a fan of literature and tend to read a lot, and not just works of fiction (*sakuhin*), as I also love diaries and chronologies. Sometimes that's all I read," he wrote in the afterword of the 1983 book edition of his selected diaries. "I want to know about the writer's private life and circumstances. Like what kind of illnesses afflicted them, or what kind of house they lived in, what their family structure and economic situation were like. Those are the kinds of things that really pique my interest.

ask for work at this point in his career, sheepishly presented the finished manga to his former editor at the publisher Nihon Bungeisha, instead of slotting the story into one of their existing periodicals, the publisher decided to create a new magazine, the express purpose of which (much to the introverted artist's chagrin) was to host new work by the legendary progenitor of literary/art manga. Named after a nightmare-eating animal from Chinese folklore, *Comic Baku* debuted in the spring of 1984.[7]

"Days of Walking" was followed by "A Certain Unknown Artist" ("Aru mumei no sakka," Summer 1984). Half inspired by the work of Shin'ichi Abe—who for years had been publishing far more revealing and far less embellished "I-comics" than Tsuge—the story focuses on a failed cartoonist who spends his days wandering around drunk (Tsuge was a teetotaler) with his small son, told from the perspective of a younger, healthier, decently successful friend. Three issues later brought "Selling Stones" ("Ishi o uru," Spring 1985), which essentially merged the two leads of "A Certain Unknown Artist" into a less decadent and more buffoonish single character. It, too, pays homage to Abe: Sukezō's

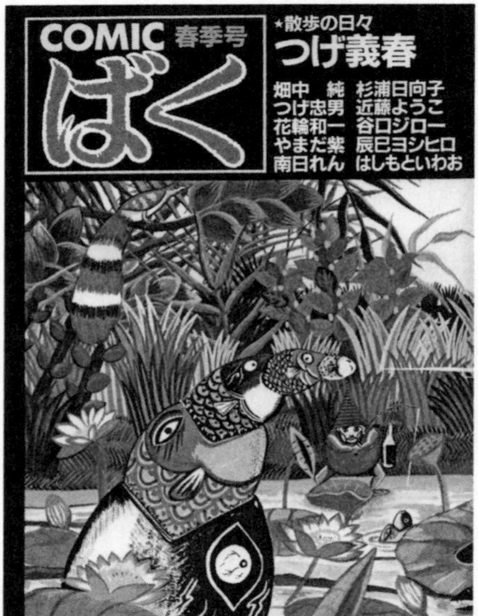
COMIC 春季号
ばく
★散歩の日々
つげ義春
畑中 純 杉浦日向子
つげ忠男 近藤ようこ
花輪和一 谷口ジロー
やまだ紫 辰巳ヨシヒロ
南日れん はしもといわお
500

Comic Baku no. 1 (Spring 1984), cover art by Jun Hatanaka.

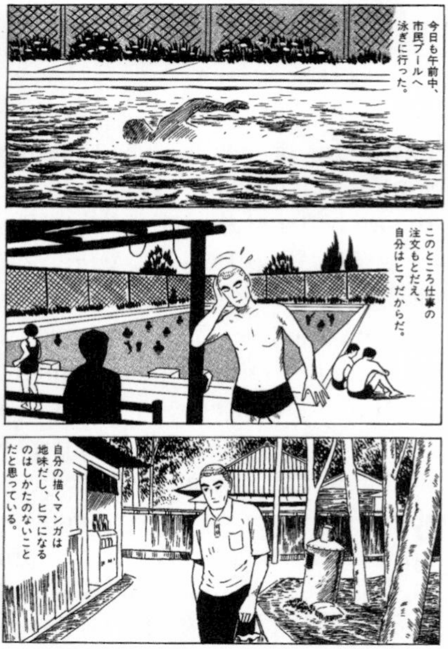
今日も午前中、市民プールへ泳ぎに行った。
このところ仕事の注文もとだえ、自分はヒマだからだ。
自分の描くマンガは地味だし、ヒマになるのはしかたのないことだと思っている。

Yoshiharu Tsuge, "Days of Walking," *Comic Baku* no. 1 (Spring 1984).

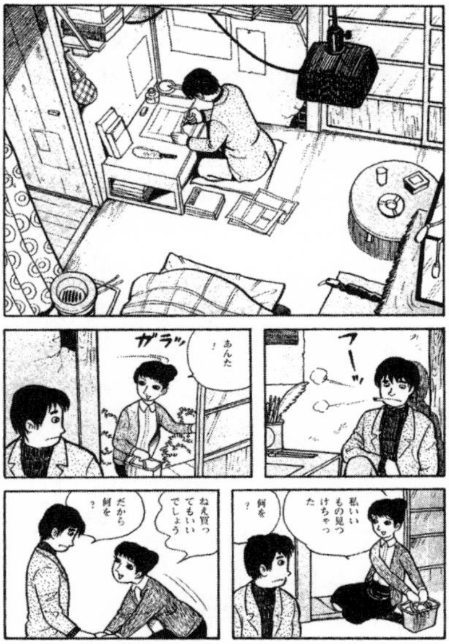
フーッ
ガラッ
あんた!
私いいもの見つけちゃった
何を?
ねえ買ってもいいでしょう
だから何を?
Yoshiharu Tsuge, "Chirpy," *Garo* no. 19 (March 1966).

classical literature of wandering and recluse monks, and ancient Japanese and Chinese supernatural tales were Tsuge's other main literary influences.

Over the course of the '70s, not only did Tsuge draw more stories based on his personal life, his protagonists also began to look more like him, versus the generic, cartoony leads of most of his *Garo* work. Many of these stories are about his and Maki's life in Chōfu, while others detail his adolescence as a teen working in factories in Tateishi (the working class neighborhood in western Tokyo where many stories by his younger brother, Tadao Tsuge, are set), and his days as a broke cartoonist in the late '50s and early '60s surrounded by scheming friends. His work in this vein helped initiate, beginning in the late '60s, a whole genre of manga focusing on young artists' personal lives. Those by male cartoonists like Seiichi Hayashi and Shin'ichi Abe are probably best known.[6] But female artists like Yōko Kondō, Murasaki Yamada, and Shungiku Uchida (one could include Maki's *My Picture Diary* here, though it's not manga) have also been moved by Tsuge's work to draw from their personal lives, branching out from the usual male themes of art, alcohol, and girlfriends to the care of thankless husbands, children, and aging parents.

After a hiatus of new manga between 1981 and 1984 (the backdrop of *The Man Without Talent*), Tsuge returned to fictionalized autobiography with "Days of Walking" ("Sanpo no hibi," Spring 1984). Drawn by an artist who had spent the summer tempering his neuroses by going on extensive walks and taking daily laps in the city pool, the story is about just that: an artist who spends his days on walks with his small son and finds solace in swimming. When Tsuge, who, like Sukezō, was not inclined to the writer/protagonists experience in their daily lives, with little attempt to flesh out other characters or relate those experiences to a wider social setting.[1] "Narcissistic, self-lacerating, nostalgic, bitter," another, though in many cases that was precisely its appeal.[2] The novels, novellas, short stories, essays, and diaristic writings grouped under *shishōsetsu* have often been assessed with reference to what is known or assumed about the writer's personal life and mental state. The writers themselves often played to those expectations, leading historians to speak of a "myth of sincerity" that has enthroned the genre in an aura of confessional authenticity. Many of its top authors, including Katai Tayama, Naoya Shiga, and Osamu Dazai, enjoyed cult followings in their lifetimes. Tsuge's favorite was Chōtarō Kawasaki, who had been active since the '20s but was not widely known until Tsuge began championing his work in the '80s. (The same fortune was bestowed upon the nineteenth-century poet Seigetsu, who was practically rescued from obscurity by the last chapter of *The Man Without Talent* and now belongs to the haiku canon.)

Though an established genre now, *shishōsetsu*-style manga were largely inconceivable until the comics medium itself gained a broad-based mature readership in the '60s, when Japanese baby boomers entered adulthood and manga authors branched out from fantasy, action, and mystery into more adult and "literary" themes. Tsuge is widely recognized as a pioneer on this front.[3] His "The Swamp" ("Numa"), published in *Garo* in 1966, an open-ended narrative centered around a lone hunter and his ambiguous sexualized encounter with a girl living deep in the hills, has been lauded as the advent of "pure literature" (*jun bungaku*) within manga.[4] He had also begun working with themes central to *shishōsetsu*. "Chirpy" ("Chiiko"), the breakthrough work in this regard, also published in *Garo* in 1966, is about a small-time artist and his live-in barmaid girlfriend, and is based on Tsuge's personal life in the early '60s. Many of his other classic works for *Garo* are narrated in the first person, and many feature another favored *shishōsetsu* theme, solitary travel. Though Tsuge claims to have neither read nor even heard of *shishōsetsu* at this point,[5] he was reading Masuji Ibuse, who, like most Japanese male fiction writers, sometimes wrote *shishōsetsu*-style stories, though he is better known for his folksy and humorous vignettes of country life. Regional history and folklore, the

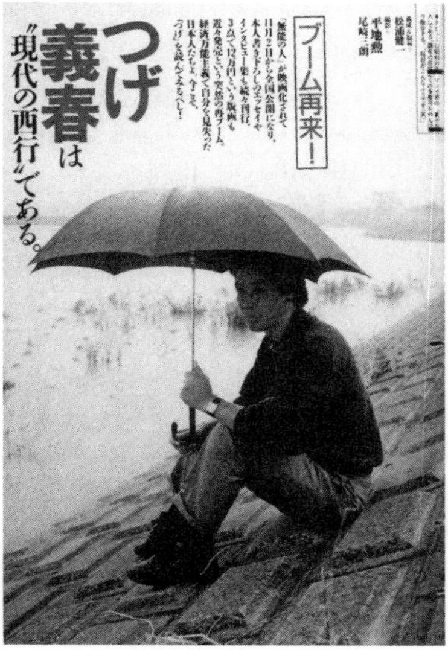
つげ義春は
"現代の西行"である。
ブーム再来!

Yoshiharu Tsuge as "the modern day Saigyō," on the banks of the Tamagawa River, in *Shūkan Gendai* (November 1991).

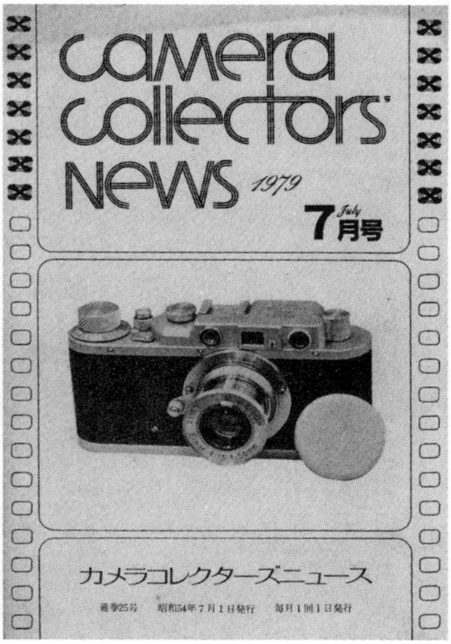
camera collectors' News 1979
July 7月号
カメラコレクターズニュース

Camera Collectors' News (July 1979), containing an early sales ad from Yoshiharu Tsuge. Image courtesy of Mitsuhiro Asakawa.

for rocks, but found none that were handsome enough to take home. Some miles downstream, in upper Kawasaki, I came across a community of bona fide "men without talent" in the form of some two dozen squatter shelters hiding in the scrub. Constructed solidly in plywood, sealed neatly with blue tarps, and in many cases equipped with solar panels, they make Sukezō's ten-foot-square hut look, well, talentless.

In sum, we fans and researchers are obsessed with looking for Tsuge in *The Man Without Talent,* and for *The Man Without Talent* in Chōfu. We are, in other words, enamored with *The Man Without Talent* as one of the premier examples of the "I-novel" (*shishōsetsu*) in comics form, referring to a genre of putatively autobiographical fiction, popular in Japan since the early twentieth century, that typically dwells on the writer/protagonist's struggles with poverty and artistic creation and their less-than-admirable interactions with the opposite sex. "A closely cropped self-portrait" is how one scholar has described the genre, referring to its narrow focus on what

River that forms the town's southern border. Over the years, many magazine profiles of Tsuge featured the artist upon the Tamagawa—walking through the high grasses on its banks, sitting meditatively under an umbrella on its concrete embankments, strolling with his family—and today numerous blogs map the sites in the area that appear in this and other Tsuge manga. Following in their tracks, I have bought one broken camera at the monthly Fuda Tenjin Shrine flea market (depicted on page 144) for three hundred yen, and gambled away a few thousand at the Keiokaku Velodrome where Tsuge's wife, Sukezō's wife, and the bird-seller Kurahara's wife worked. I approached, but did not knock on, the door of the apartment in the sprawling Tamagawa Housing Block (Tamagawa jūtaku) that appears at the beginning of chapter one, where Tsuge lived when he drew this manga. I have walked along the Tamagawa River in search of the landscape in which Sukezō whiled his days away. I have stared up at the sluice gates from which the Bird Master flew, and lunched near the spot where Sukezō's stall is depicted. I foraged

Yoshiharu Tsuge at home with his camera collection, with son Shosuke and wife Maki Fujiwara (1981), photograph by Junsuke Takimoto.

For Tsuge, *jōhatsu* is not a way to "find oneself," but rather a way to escape one's existing self and life by inducing a new self into existence. Not a truer self, but one stronger, more courageous, and freer (or so he hoped) from the severe social anxieties that have afflicted him since childhood. Many of his most famous stories, especially those for the watershed alternative manga magazine *Garo* in the late '60s, thematize this fantasy specifically, usually with strange and unsettling results. Up and disappearing, however, vanished as an option after he got married and had a son in 1975, at which point he had to find ways to evaporate that didn't require leaving home. Oddly, despite a reputation for being intensely adverse to publicity and social interaction, Tsuge chose to foreground his private life more than ever—not as an exercise to try to get over his social anxieties, but so that he might dissolve into the proliferating fictional alter egos of his work and public persona as an artist.

Initially serialized in the quarterly magazine *Comic Baku* in 1985–1986, *The Man Without Talent* (*Munō no hito*) represents the culmination of a lifetime of attempts to disappear through autobiographical fiction. As a best seller with a movie adaptation (1991), it is arguably Tsuge's most popular and accessible work. Due to the large amount of personal information available about the artist in the years in which it is set and was created (the mid-'70s to mid-'80s), *The Man Without Talent* is also the Tsuge work for which it is easiest to trace correspondences between fact and fiction. Though Tsuge never sold stones or sported a mustache, Sukezō Sukegawa's creative woes, get-rich-quick schemes, and botched family trips closely follow the artist's life, as documented in Tsuge's writing and interviews during these years. "Selling Cameras" is practically fact, but for the pseudonyms. Sukezō's neuroses and self-doubt reflect Tsuge's real-life anxieties and mental illness, which turned crippling after his wife, former avant-garde theater actress and future children's book author Maki Fujiwara (1941–1999), was diagnosed with uterine cancer in 1977 when their son was not yet two (she survived). As for Mr. and Mrs. Sukegawa's domestic tensions, compared to the standoffs and blowouts described in Tsuge's published diaries and Maki's first book, *My Picture Diary* (*Watashi no e-nikki*, 1982), they actually seem pretty tame.

If *The Man Without Talent* is primarily a portrait of a middle-aged man and his family, it is also a portrait of a place: Chōfu and the Tamagawa

WHERE IS YOSHIHARU TSUGE?

RYAN HOLMBERG

ON MOST DAYS, Yoshiharu Tsuge (born 1937) is at his home in Chōfu, a municipality fifteen kilometers west of central Tokyo. He has lived in the area almost continuously since 1966, when he took up a job as an assistant to the famous manga author Shigeru Mizuki after his own cartooning no longer sufficed to pay the bills.

But sometimes he is not at home. Of course, like most of us, Tsuge leaves his house, even if infrequently and only when necessary. Sometimes, however, he can't be found for days. He will simply disappear, which has aggravated editors for decades, and given devotees something to write about for just as long. Back in the late '60s and early '70s, he would take off for distant regions like Nagano, Kyushu, and Tohoku, hopping overnight trains, roaming from one remote and rundown hot spring to the next, calling on female fans, and entertaining thoughts of marrying and settling down with them or with local strippers without telling a soul back in Tokyo. Sometimes he would simply hide out in a Tokyo-area hotel (which is the pattern these days), so that he could be gone without really having to go anywhere. He might buy a new suit for an awards reception, then not only fail to show but also fail to return home.

For decades, Tsuge has called these disappearing acts "*jōhatsu*," literally "evaporation," which is also the title of the last chapter of this book.

THIS IS A NEW YORK REVIEW COMIC
PUBLISHED BY THE NEW YORK REVIEW OF BOOKS
435 Hudson Street, New York, NY 10014
www.nyrb.com

Muno no hito by Yoshiharu Tsuge
Copyright © Yoshiharu Tsuge 1998
Published in Japan by SHINCHOSHA Publishing Co., Ltd.
English translation rights arranged with SHINCHOSHA Publishing Co., Ltd.
through Ogihara Office Agency

Translation and essay copyright © 2019 Ryan Holmberg
All rights reserved.

Library of Congress Control Number:2019943048

ISBN 978-1-68137-443-7

Printed in the United States of America

10 9 8 7 6 5 4 3 2

WHERE IS YOSHIHARU TSUGE?

RYAN HOLMBERG